RAMA LIVE!

TALKS AND WORKSHOPS

Rama - Dr. Frederick Lenz

LIVING FLOW

Contents

Introduction 1

A Workshop With Rama 7

   Psychic Development 8

   Meditation and Kundalini 72

   Enlightenment and Self-Realization 133

Psychic Development Workshop 208

   An Introduction To Rama Seminars 209

   Selfless Giving 219

   Dharma 241

   The Caretaker Personality 263

   Psychic Self-Defense 288

   Places of Power 312

   Seeing 339

Rama Live In LA 365

   Consciousness Expansion and Desire 366

   Reincarnation and the Tibetan Rebirth Process .. 412

   Meditation 446

   Tantric Mysticism 465

   Seeing, Dreaming and Places of Power 485

   For Every Ending There's a New Beginning ... 515

   Cosmic Awareness 536

Also By the Author............................... 551

Copyright..552

INTRODUCTION

Rama Live! Talks and Workshops presents talks that Rama gave from 1982 through 1985 that were open to members of the public. Many were held at the Los Angeles Convention Center and were publicly advertised.

A Workshop with Rama consisted of 3 talks in January 1985. The *Psychic Development Workshop* was 6 talks in November and December 1985. *Rama Live in LA* was presented on 6 evenings in June and July 1983.

Advertising for the *Psychic Development Workshop* included a cassette tape, *An Introduction to Rama Seminars Psychic Development,* in which Rama described his goals and what attendees might come away with.

The talks in *A Workshop with Rama* and *Rama Live in LA* are transcripts of the live audio recordings, including Rama's question-and-answer sessions with the audience. The second evening of *A Workshop with Rama*, presented as the talk "Meditation and Kundalini", includes the first public performances by Zazen, the music group produced by Rama with three of his students who were world-class musicians.

The talks of the *Psychic Development Workshop* were separately recorded by Rama, and were available at the workshops.

Audio recordings of these talks may be heard on www.RamaMeditationSociety.org > Free Resources > Free Talks (Rama Live In LA, Psychic Development Talk Set, A Workshop With Rama). In the ebook, click on those talks on the *Resources* page.

Please listen to some of these talks if you can, in order to get a feel for what the actual experience was like for the audience!

2 RAMA LIVE!

The following typographic conventions are used in an effort to transcribe these great truths and Rama's highly spirited presentation from audio into printed form.

An ellipsis (…) is used to show that Rama makes a pause while talking, sometimes starting a new sentence.

> Well, Christ had eleven disciples. Twelve actually. And they studied with …
>
> You know he had only three years with them? And then they went off to liberate the world.

or

> Then you come up to the teacher and say, "Well, gee, Atmananda [1] … What should I do? I just, uh, I, well, gee, I … I'm not sure, I mean, should I, should I … I have this opportunity to go to college here, or I could go to college over here, what should I do?"
>
> And I'll say, "Well, how about the first school?"

While presenting the greatest truths of conscious awareness and spiritual discovery, Rama does a terrific amount of ad-libbing, inventing voices and characters, telling little side-stories, and keeping the audience in a nearly constant state of laughter.

A lot of the time, Rama's monologue and the audience laughter occur simultaneously.

The laughter on the original audio is sometimes continuous for long periods of time, interspersed with Rama's monologue. This has been edited extensively. Please consider that the printed book barely reflects the truly

---

1. In 1982, Rama still used the name Atmananda. "The Last Incarnation," in *The Last Incarnation*, 1983, describes his later name change. "Eternity has named me Rama," Atmananda said. "Rama most clearly reflects that strand of luminosity of which I am a part."

elevated spirit of the audience, as Rama continually blasted everyone with kundalini energy as he was talking and meditating.

For example,

> This is something they teach you in the spiritual teacher training academy [audience laughs] in another world.

and

> In short, if God wanted ... [laughter] ... human beings to fly through the air, walk on the water, She would have made it possible. But in her wisdom, She didn't.

Sometimes the laughter doesn't begin until a split-second after Rama finishes a thought, then the audience goes into convulsions.

> You may have found lately, perhaps not, but ... that it's more difficult to perform simple tasks. Like thinking. [audience laughs]

or

> I'm sitting up here, I should be bombarded by smile energy. And I'm feeling like ... the subtle grin [audience extended laughter].

Square brackets are used to describe something that's not spoken but is necessary to understand the context as Rama speaks.

> Let's say that you would like to become psychic. Meaning not simply that you can go down to Madam Lagoza ...
>
> [Rama mimics a theatrical fortune teller]
>
> *Who will read the leaves! I see for you, two Mercedes!*
>
> [normal voice]

or

4 RAMA LIVE!

> [Rama begins speaking in a cowboy twang]
>
>> Put up your feet and stay a spell. Ahhhh-yuh. Hang out with that kuuuuundalini. Ahhh-yuh. All them chakras a glowin'. Ah-yuh. Eternity just spinning around your fingers.
>
> [Rama resumes normal voice]

Something that Rama said to himself is shown in parentheses, which appear as a lower level "aside" on the audio recording.

> How do you do this? Well, there are different ways. You've got your (I'm sorry, I have to go through this, just bear with me) you got your Zen. Nice sounding word, isn't it? Zen. Bodhidharma started it out. We'll get him!

Indented lists and additional line breaks are used to break up a sentence into the important focal points.

So instead of this,

> Thought *is* karma. It engenders states of awareness, which engenders action, which engenders reaction, which of course is karma.

Perhaps this presents a more meditative flow, and the concepts are easier to absorb.

> Thought *is* karma.
>
> It engenders states of awareness
>
>> which engenders action
>>
>> which engenders reaction
>>
>> which of course is karma.

"Seeing", "dreaming", and "gazing" are italicized when referring to psychic perception, or inner vision. Rama explains these psychic abilities throughout the talks, and especially in *Seeing* and *Seeing, Dreaming and Places of Power.*

> That is to say, *seeing* into other planes of attention, other worlds, transacting with other beings, moving through the astral dimensions and so on. This has to do with the third eye.

Italics are applied to words that are not in our common vocabulary, the first time they appear, e.g.,

> The *shushumna* is the tube that the kundalini passes up in the subtle physical body, and one side is the little guy called the *ida,* and the other side is the *pingala.*

Italics are also used when Rama vocally emphasizes a word, e.g.,

> Thought *is* karma.

or

> This does not so much *take* you someplace or *make* you feel something, as cause you to *become* something.

A word in quotes means that in speaking, Rama put a certain emphasis on it, perhaps describing it in a new way, or to draw attention to it, e.g.,

> Now, a person isn't conscious of that, but what do we mean by "conscious"?

or

> That was an experience on their "karma card" you see?

or

> They're in fact "low vibe" as we say in the trade, which is not a judgment but an observation.

Square brackets indicate whether Rama or an audience member is speaking. The audience member's question is indented, but Rama's response is not indented. If the audience member's question could not be heard from the audio recording, it is omitted.

> [question from a woman]
>
> > These different selves that you talk about ... are they like different life beings?
>
> [Rama]
>
> Ah, very good, yes. Very often when I talk, I say, "know your selves"—with an "s"—because there are many selves within the self. And your question is, "Are these selves, selfs from different lifetimes?"

and

> [question from the audience]
>
> [Rama]
>
> Oh yeah, there's a definite battle between the Light and the Dark. The network always wins, though. We run the galaxy [audience laughter, *"whoo!"* and applause].

PART ONE

A WORKSHOP WITH RAMA

Chapter One

Psychic Development

Psychic Development.

Let's assume that you're all psychic to a certain extent. Everyone is. Some people of course are more conscious of it.

What is the psyche? What is the difference between the psychic and the occult? Or perhaps the spiritual?

I'd like to set some parameters before we start. There will be overlap, of course, there always is.

But just by way of definition … the mystical—the occult sometimes it's called—is the area of the study of self-knowledge involving the entrance into alternate planes of attention. It's the study of power essentially, mysticism.

Lower mysticism is voodoo, the occult side of it, the lower occult. Higher mysticism is something like attaining enlightenment only through power.

The psychic has to do with developing abilities to perceive beyond the physical. It's not so much a study of power—while there are some powers certainly that develop through it—but of perception.

How to become perception itself eventually.

How to become more aware of what we perceive. More aware of ourselves, of those around us, the universe, different planes of consciousness, different beings, energy, life itself.

The spiritual I would relegate to the enlightenment process more specifically. I mean everything is spiritual I suppose, but in particular the spiritual would be the entrance into samadhi. Becoming a saint. Humble, pure.

Available. [audience laughs]

So the psychic then is more the study of clairvoyance, clairaudience, seeing into the future *(yuck)*, the past.

Knowing what's going on in other people's bedrooms without having to be there and go through the experience yourself. [audience laughs]

I mean, just think of the possibilities! You could be in a hundred places at once.

The psychic is a happy study. I think a lot of people have attached a lot of strange symbolisms to it. And that really has to do with the lower occult.

But the psychic is the study of joy. It's a very positive study. It's the study of the psychic network, the networking principle of consciousness and awareness.

It's essentially the study of how to have more fun with your life and that which is beyond life and death.

Tonight we're going to be doing some exercises. We're going to be putting on sweat pants [laughter] and little leg warmers and we have a giant pyramid that we have … It's being lowered by helicopter later. We're gonna climb it. And then we're going to move it without touching it. Right.

So the psychic is a study of … It's sort of the Snoopy-consciousness in the mystical studies plane, essentially.

The heavy occult would sort of be more like Charlie Brown.

The spiritual, I suppose would be ... Oh God, nobody's spiritual anymore. It's hard. Grog [2] in *B.C.*, that's about it.

So the psychic. Well, people waste a lot of time it seems to me. I'm tempted to say, listening to me, but [audience laughs] ... you're here!

People waste a lot of time talking. You know, it's possible when I look at someone I can look inside them and it's not necessary to talk. I can. Just like reading a book. You can just go through the pages of a person. You can *see* their past lives. You can *see* selves. You can know more about a person than they know about themselves.

I would think it would be embarrassing to have somebody look at you that way if you couldn't *see* that yourself. So I think you should fight back! [thumps the armrest, great laughter from the audience]

And that's what we're going to discuss tonight. And that's how you can become your own psychic, if you will, or psychic, or aware of some other possibilities.

Things perhaps in the pathway of life that some people skip which I find rather exciting and illumining and sometimes awesome, sometimes silly.

Welcome to the twilight zone ... No, welcome to the other worlds.

How do you become psychic?

Well, you are, but the problem is, we think all the time, and as we think, our thoughts block the psyche.

---

2. *B.C.* is a syndicated comic strip since the 1960s, originally by Johnny Hart. The characters are cave people in prehistoric times who speak normal English, commenting on the foibles of life. Grog speaks in grunts, and is very happy most of the time, in a very child-like manner.

There are many levels of mind. Higher mind, lower mind, in-between mind, beyond mind. That's the best.

But, while we're in the mind there are areas of mind that very few people tap. This is no news, I understand.

The reason is because they think all the time.

In order to move into the psychic planes of attention it's really necessary to stop thought for periods of time—or just to slow thought—otherwise it's like tonight the stars are out there, but you can't see them because all the clouds are up there. But they're definitely there.

So when we stop thought—when we can push thought back—then it's very easy to be psychic.

To be psychic is not a great gift. You don't have to be exceptional. You just have to be a little bit aware.

Aware of awareness.

Let's start with an exercise if we could. This is an experiential workshop so that simply means that you'll be able to sit there and do it. You don't have to do much. You can even fake if you want to. Fake it.

We'll be doing a number of exercises tonight, usually to music.

Serious, serious group. Good.

Let's say that you would like to become psychic. Meaning not simply that you can go down to Madam Lagoza …

[Rama mimics a theatrical fortune teller]

> *Who will read the leaves! I see for you, two Mercedes!*

[normal voice]

That sort of thing. Uh uh.

But let's say that you'd like to be able to perceive the deeper truths of life or of your own being or maybe you'd like to know when someone is lying to you. That's very useful. Because people do that a lot. They do that a lot.

They not only lie to you, they lie to themselves. Those are the most convincing liars because they don't know the truth themselves, so when they say something, they really sincerely believe it themselves, and it's very hard to tell because they don't know themselves, you see.

So, let's say you'd like to know that the peanut butter is going to be good before you pick it off the shelf. How do you do that?

How do you become aware of eternity, of God, of immortality? I ask a lot of questions.

If you'll close your eyes please.

Now I'd like you to relax.

We're going to do some very simple meditative techniques. It's not really necessary for you to do them phenomenally well tonight, rather this is just a run-through so you can practice them at home.

You'll find that these methods of expanding awareness are extremely powerful, and if you practice them, oh, even once in awhile, let alone once a day, you'll see that you will become extremely sensitive and suddenly you will start to *see* inside people, inside yourself, you'll just come to know things … having to do with all of life.

Yet they're so simple you can be fooled by them, they're so simple.

What I'd like you to do to start with, is to focus on what the mystics call the third eye.

The third eye is an energy center. There are seven principle energy centers—also known as chakras—that are contained, not in the physical body but in what we call the etheric or subtle physical body, which is body of light or energy that surrounds our physical body.

What I'd like you to do is to focus your attention on what they call in Sanskrit the Agni Chakra, which is the psychic energy center of vision.

It is located between the eyebrows and about half an inch above.

If for a moment, you would take one of your hands, and touch a finger to that spot. Everybody just take their hand up there for a second like I am, and put a finger right there, very, very gently.

Now what you're really doing is not focusing on the body, but let's say you want to focus in that area. It doesn't have to be a pinpoint but just that general area. Very good, you can put your hand down.

What I'd like you to do is to close your eyes, focus your attention on that spot. Relax.

And see what you *see*.

Now this is not hypnosis. It's meditation.

And what you're trying to do—eventually—is to stop all thought, but that takes quite a while, unless you've been doing this for sometime, or you're just gifted.

So what I'd like you to do, is to focus your attention on the spot—and it might help you, this is up to you, this is the optional part—to picture ... light ... sort of a turning light, going in a clockwise direction, going round and round. You see?

Right there. Focus your attention there and relax for a minute.

Now naturally when we do these exercises together, I go into a psychic state of consciousness, of course, and increase the energy to make it a little bit easier for you.

We'll be listening to a little bit of music while we do this—just to even things out a little bit, all the different energies—and then we'll talk about the psychic network, the network of light that all people who are engaged in the psychic studies are part of.

Not just in this world but in many other worlds.

So if you'd close your eyes, focus on that spot and just for about three or four minutes I'd just like you to relax. This is just to get you to relax so we can have a good evening here. Good.

We live in a dark world. It's a beautiful world, God knows.

But it's a very dark place where people suppress each other, they fight each other, they destroy each other, they destroy their environment. You could get a very negative attitude after awhile if you'd studied history or just watched television.

[coughing in audience]

God, disease is rampant. I know it's terrible isn't it? There's lot's of flu around and stuff, and I'm sure you'll have it by the end of the night. [audience laughs]

But if we make the psychic energy high enough, everyone will walk out ... cured.

I don't know, but anyway ... You almost went for it!

So you could start to get a really—yeah, you could get kind of a negative attitude towards life if you just, if you just, if you just ... right?

It's true. I skip every other sentence since you're psychic. This is how you work up to paragraphs.

So ... right? Yeah, you see it works ... yeah ... good!

Oh well.

There's a psychic energy network. This is one small planet in one small dimension in one small corner of a very large eternity.

And there are many other worlds with highly developed beings that do not necessarily muck around so much with each other and try and destroy each other.

They've sort of doped out certain principles. I say greetings in 64 languages. Right?

And they're part of what we call the psychic network.

There's a networking of higher beings throughout the universe. It's a networking of goodwill, of higher energy, of hope, of light, of knowledge.

And as you develop in your lifetime or through your series of lifetimes, gradually you become aware of the network.

The network works for you all of the time.

When you're ready at a certain stage in your evolution the network actually makes its presence known to you. Certain events in your life will work out a certain way, so that very positive things will happen to you, that lead you to self-awareness and self-knowledge.

The psychic network, of course, exists not just throughout the universe, but in our own planet naturally.

While there are 4 billion soon to be 8, soon they say 16 billion people on the planet Earth by the year 2015.

Some of those individuals are aware, very aware and there's a network between those individuals which you can join and be part of, and you don't have to pay any dues, and you don't have to get a card to carry.

It's the psychic network.

Let's assume for a moment that you're here because there's something special about you. Now of course there's something special about everyone, but the thing that's special about you is your awareness.

Just your interest in the psychic suggests that you're fairly evolved, that you've had a great many lifetimes, from the point of view of reincarnation. Otherwise, the rain would have deterred you, or something else or someone else would have tonight.

And so instead you've come to explore awareness. This says something very good about you. Sincerely.

And as you continue your journey of self-discovery you'll begin to feel the presence of the psychic network.

This is 1985 and it's the beginning of a cycle of time.

A very dark cycle of time I suppose you might say.

The next 30 years are going to be a very difficult period for humanity and humanity may not—even as we all know—survive the next 30 years.

A lot depends upon a few people.

People get a negative attitude about life. They feel that, "What difference can you make? What difference can an individual make?"

You see? And that's just not true at all.

Individuals make all the difference in the world, because you have to understand personal power—psychic power—and how it works.

You see, one person can live—a Buddha, a Christ, a Krishna—and they can change a whole world.

You might say, "Well, there's still a lot of terrible things in the world, all kinds of problems and darkness."

Do you know how much worse it would have been, had they not been there?

You could say, "Well, look at what people have done, to what they said. They took it and corrupted it or used it to advance themselves," but still do you know how much darker the world would be?

If it was not for the psychic network, if it was not for people like yourself who have an interest in higher attention, the world would be a very, very dark place.

Darker than most people can imagine because it's not just numbers … in the psychic realm we deal with power.

Power is measured in evolution. The average soul goes through 84,000 incarnations, approximately, give or take whatever. That's a lot of lifetimes.

Now the thing is, most of the souls in this particular world are not that old, but some are and those few that are, of course, they're interested in the psychic and spiritual and so on—you know that stuff.

Those individuals have had a lot more lifetimes, and therefore, have a lot of personal power.

And when you use that power, one person—who has a good intention, a good thought, who delves into the psyche, who looks inside themselves—can offset the negativity of thousands and thousands of individuals.

We'll talk about psychic development, of course, tonight. We'll do lots of exercises, answer your questions.

But I'd just like to set a tone that is perhaps a little more positive than we hear sometimes … because we are entering into a dark time.

You see periodically there are dark ages in the world. It's not horrible. You might say it's meant to be. It's part of the cycle of life. It's a purgation.

But what makes a Dark Age?

Oh, I'm sure we could trace socio-political causes, perhaps. What causes those things to be?

There are currents in the universe. Energy currents in what we call the subtle physical or astral realm.

These energy currents affect all of us all the time. Most people are unaware of these currents but that doesn't mean that they aren't affected.

You may not be aware that someone is doing something good for you and helping you avoid problems if they don't make themselves known to you. But you still reap the benefit of the effect.

So in the same sense there are currents through the universe.

Everything is made up of energy. All of life. Matter itself is made up of energy.

We are energy. Our awareness is energy. Our bodies are energy. All of life is energy.

And there are both physical—what we would call physical—and non-physical energies.

Our physical body of course is affected by the physical energies and our non-physical body—the subtle physical body—is affected by the subtle or non-physical energies.

These energy currents are vortexes and they sweep across the cosmos and they follow a pattern very much like our universe does. There's an order there, of a sort.

Right now we're entering into a dark time. Actually we've been in it for about 10,000 years.

It's getting darker.

This is a very important time for people who are psychically developed.

This year 1985 is a turning point in the vibratory patterns of our world, and what that means is there's a great deal of lower astral energy that is coming into the consciousness.

You may have found lately, perhaps not, but … that it's more difficult to perform simple tasks. Like thinking. [audience laughs]

No, if you're sensitive psychically, you're picking up on what's going on. Things that would have seemed very easy—concentration and so on and so forth.

Very basic things are a little more difficult.

It's because the energy is changing. Now, most human beings of course have no consonance with their environment.

That is to say, they don't remember what it was like yesterday. In other words, you're depressed for an hour, you may have been happy for ten years and now it's going to be like you've always been depressed. Your whole life has been awful. It's always been bad. You see?

That's the New York City consciousness. [audience laughs]

But it's not true. Of course your life was great up until, you know, you went to New York [more laughter].

Until that hour.

So what am I trying to say? Well, what I'm trying to say is that we should do another exercise.

The second exercise has to do with perception. And what I'd like you to do is to do this exercise with the eyes closed and with the eyes open.

To begin with, we're going to start—in a moment—with the eyes closed, and what I'd like you to do is focus on the center of the chest.

There are seven principle chakras or energy centers.

There's one at the crown of the head, the third eye which we focused on a moment ago, there's one around the base of the throat.

These are called *nadi*.

There's one around the center of the chest—the solar plexus area, the base of the spine, and halfway in-between the solar plexus and the base of the spine.

There are also nadis or psychic energy centers in the hands, feet, different parts of the body. Again, they're not exactly in the skin but they're in the subtle physical, etheric body.

Now, what we're going to do is focus first of all on the central axis, we call it the heart center although it's not really associated with the physical heart. It's right in the center of the chest.

This is the psychic energy center of love, and also for developing the psychic senses.

The psychic senses primarily develop through focus on two psychic centers. The third eye, and what we call the heart center.

And if you divide your time between these two centers, as a focus during your meditation, you will find that you will very quickly develop all the psychic sensitivities. Very quickly.

The lower centers, the three lower centers, have more to do with the mystical—which I spoke about before—which is the study of power.

And the highest center has to do with spiritual enlightenment and illumination.

The throat center really has to do with creativity, with the arts, with the … that sort of thing.

They have other associated functions.

But for our purposes the two that are interesting—as far as developing the psyche and your psychic senses, the ability to see on other planes of consciousness, just to "know"—are the third eye and the heart center, and those are the two we're principally working with tonight.

I'd like you to focus, here, right in the center of the chest.

For a moment let's do this little finger thing again. Take one of your fingers and place it right here in the center of the chest. Just touch there for a second and close your eyes and feel that area.

Now this is an area within your being of perfect light, perfect luminosity.

The psychic planes are very luminous planes of attention. They're filled with all these beautiful lights, and when you clear your mind of thought and settle down and relax a little bit and you focus on this point, you will *see* and experience other dimensions of light.

The experiences that you have while focusing on this psychic center will be very, very different than the experiences with the third eye.

The experiences that you have while focusing on the heart center will have more to do with understanding, with intuition, with feeling.

You're going to re-sensitize your being to all sides of life so that you will be able to perceive things without having to think about them, without having to go to a place or a location. Things like that.

It's more of the feeling side of the psyche.

The third eye, on the other hand, is the visionary side of the psyche.

That is to say, *seeing* into other planes of attention, other worlds, transacting with other beings, moving through the astral dimensions and so on. This has to do with the third eye.

Think of that as, the third eye is the eye—which *sees* all of life—particularly life outside of the physical realms and mental realms.

Whereas the heart center has more to do with feeling, understanding, love, knowledge, things like that. There's a certain amount of overlap, of course.

So now for a moment let's focus on the heart center. And this time, rather than try and *see,* our interest is to feel, to experience.

And why don't we start with something very basic, like the energy of everyone here.

We have a lot of sentient beings, a lot of living beings in the room here with us, and I'm sure there are some non-physical beings that probably slipped in with a few of you.

Brought some of your friends, eh? Oh well. They don't have to pay admission.

So what I'd like you to do is to close your eyes—to focus on the heart center—meaning just put a little bit of your attention there.

You don't necessarily have to imagine or visualize anything, or if you'd like to, you can just imagine a glowing light there. 'Cause there is.

It's a very bright light actually.

And I'd like you to just feel very, very sensitive and then just perceive the energy shifts that are taking place in the room.

There are a lot of very powerful people here tonight. Everyone here is interested in the psyche so those are all highly advanced people. They may not look it, but they are!

That is my experience and that is what I *see*.

So if you would focus your attention there, and let's just try feeling. It's a very simple exercise.

Try not to think too much, or if you think a lot, ignore your thoughts and have nothing to do with them.

Listen to the music if you like, a little bit—if that will get you out of your thoughts—and just feel, how you feel.

I'm sitting up here, I should be bombarded by smile energy. And I'm feeling like ... the subtle grin. [audience laughs extensively] It's like somebody with a [facial] tic.

Now, this is important. OK, now you may think this is silly and you're darn right, it's silly. More things should be.

You're dealing with the psyche. And in order to deal with the realms of knowledge and power that you enter into in the psychic fields, you have to be able to be very light.

Because otherwise—as you start to go through the interdimensional vortexes—you'll have real problems.

You have to be very light.

It's like ... Psychic development is like ballet. It's like dance. You have to be completely fluid and be able to sometimes shift through hundreds of levels of attention, hundreds of dimensions within moments.

It's very quick.

So you need to be very light.

So part of the reason we focus on the heart center is, this develops a lightness in one's being, a sense of love, of awe at the magic of life and existence.

And smiling is a big part of it. Now, you don't have to smile at other people. That's up to you.

OK, but it's good to smile by yourself sometimes, because it's a sign that you love yourself, and that you love life.

And the psyche is engaged fully in love all of the time.

Now it may seem strange, you say, "Well what does that have to do with being able to know what someone is thinking?"

The reason you don't know what someone is thinking—the reason that you don't *see* into other dimensions—is because you're too heavy.

The balloon, you want the balloon to go up in the air. And so you fill it with helium or whatever. But if you have all these sandbags attached to it, it can't go up.

Well, the sandbags are the attachments that we have inside ourselves.

And there are many selves inside the self.

You see, you're not just composed of one self, but there're literally dozens or hundreds of selves, under the surface.

And in psychic development what we do is, we learn about each of our inner selves.

There are different voices inside the psyche.

We're not just one individual. ... We're all schizophrenic. [audience laughter] I thought that was good, but ...

So, in order to deal with the many sides of our being ... in other words there may be someone inside you

[Rama switches to a comically mean voice]

> who's real nasty, hateful, Ooh, I hate everybody! You next to me, and you! Owww!

[normal voice]

You know what I mean? No, there could be a self in there like that. Way down underneath somewhere.

You see?

Then there's the self that's sitting there. You know,

[Rama comical happy voice]

> "blah de blah de blah de blah."

[normal voice]

That self, right? But inside there could be this other one, [Rama snarly voice] arrgh!

See, and in psychic development you have to go through yourself and confront all of your different selves.

They all have lunch [audience laughter].

They get together. It's nice. And you can put it on your IRS form and everything. It's a business lunch if you're in psychic development. You took yourselves out [audience extended laughter].

Right? Why not? So …

You've got to start digging inside.

Now, in order to do this, it's important to be able to smile.

I know it sounds ridiculous and it is. That's why it's good. There should be more ridiculous things in life.

Right. OK, so we're going to try this again, if you will.

The first part of the exercise, I'd like you to sit there and not smile [audience laughter].

I know, you're thinking to yourself—I can read your mind—"I spent seven dollars for this?"

Yes you did! [Rama and audience laugh] We all make mistakes. So …

See, now had you been psychic, but … [audience extended laughter]. You're not supposed to smile in the first part. No matter what!

Then, a smallness … a little tiny grin will begin to appear. Not much. Don't go … a little foreplay here, OK?

Then gradually the smile will get bigger and bigger and bigger.

Then you can stop with the smiling, we're done with it [snaps fingers], we let go.

We never feel love or any other emotion. It doesn't matter. We detach from it [snaps fingers] thoroughly.

You have to be able to let go of all emotion for the next step.

What we want to do is ride emotion as high as we can, to the highest level of emotion.

Then we drop it. Because emotion is a stratified plane of awareness, and you want to be able to leap beyond it.

There are things beyond emotion, or we could say they're "psychic emotions," but they're not the ones we usually perceive in our waking states of consciousness.

So what we're doing is using emotion, it's sort of like a ski lift. We're going to get on the ski lift of emotion and we're going to ride it up to the top.

But then there's another lift from there, which has nothing to do with emotion.

So first you need to be able to make yourself kind of happy, be silly, smile a little bit. And then we'll ride that up for a minute, and then we'll stop, and then we're going to do something a little bit more intense. OK? Good.

Just relax.

Try to feel the stillness of eternity.

Eternity is very active. Life is real busy all around us.

But just beyond in the next dimension there's absolute perfect peace and stillness.

And there are doorways to go into that stillness.

And beyond that stillness there's much more, the whole universe, endless universes.

But the door is the psychic gateway.

And it's right in the center of the chest or the third eye.

So focus on the center of the chest, and now try smiling a little bit just to yourself, a happy little smile. And then we'll do something else in just a moment. Just do that for a minute or so.

[silent meditation]

Energy is very subtle when you first start the study.

In the beginning, sometimes it's hard to know if you're experiencing anything or if anything is changing.

So it's a good idea—if you're interested in psychic development—to set up a little schedule for yourself, of practice.

Some of you are naturally gifted. You have a certain amount of vision. Perhaps you developed it in another lifetime. Perhaps it came by chance. Who knows?

But if you'd like to develop your vision further—your sensitivity, your energy level, your awareness, your use of your total mind—it's necessary to practice. The practice is fun. It's hopeful and it brings tremendous, tremendous personal power to you.

But this is the issue that I'm concerned with.

What are you going to do with all this power when you get it?

It's been my experience, as a teacher, that many people who develop power don't use it very well. By power I mean power of the psyche.

Now I'm not a terrible moralist particularly. I think you should have whatever you want in life. As long as you don't infringe upon the rights of others. That's fine.

But we're unleashing here a very powerful thing. The human psyche. It's endless because it's networked with all of eternity.

We discuss what we call the second attention.

The first attention is the waking consciousness.

The second attention is a step above the waking consciousness.

All of us have a series of levels of mind. Not mind in the physical sense of the brain but of awareness, and let's say that these different levels of mind—for most people—are separated.

You know the cheese with the paper between the slices? Right. Exactly. You're psychic, you understood.

So in the same sense, mind is separated and the question is, "Are those little cheeses aware of each other?"

If you're very psychic you'll know, but the levels of your mind are not necessarily aware of each other.

So for example, you are—right now—operating on certain higher astral planes. Parts of your being are.

But your lower mind, not that it's particularly low but what we call the lower mind, the thinking mind.

[Rama makes a slight gagging sound] That one.

Yeah, that mind! That mind is not necessarily aware of what the other levels of mind are doing.

Psychic awareness or psychic development is not so much a development in terms of developing …

We think of developing as a cause and effect process. OK, I'm going to develop a picture; there was nothing there, and I put it in the developer and that sort of stuff, and I come up and there it is. If I'm going to develop muscles, I'll go down and I'll lift weights.

Psychic development—it's almost a misnomer because there isn't really anything we really develop. Rather what we do is, we "envelop".

We simply dissolve the layers—this is the paper between the slices—and the mind becomes unified.

We make the mind aware of itself, and the aspects integrate in new ways.

This is psychic development.

And there are very specific age-old practices for doing this. A few of which I'm teaching you this evening.

Now, as you do this, you become very, very powerful.

More so than you might realize.

And the question that comes up—it's part of the study naturally—is, what to do with that power?

This may not sound like much to you right now.

You're saying …

[Rama adopts a snarly voice]

> "Well, ha ha, power, what are you talking about? I come here, a couple of dollars to watch his hands move and there's nothing! I don't feel nothing! [audience laughs] Nothin'!"

[normal voice]

Oh yeah? Wait until you get home. See how you feel then. Heh. I'll show you. But anyway.

So the question is ...

If you practice these exercises and you engage in psychic development—which some of you already do—what are you going to do with the tremendous power that you unleash?

And that in fact you do.

Well, it's my suggestion—and that's why I brought up the psychic network earlier—that you join the psychic network.

No forms to fill out.

If you become aware that there's a networking of energies of all people who are engaged in the *higher* aspect of the psychic study—and beings in other levels and other dimensions—then you might say a protection comes with that.

A knowledge comes with that.

If you're seeking power not just for it's own sake, which is interesting, but also because you'd like to do happy things for others.

Then, if you join the network, any power you develop will increase hundreds of times—but in the correct way.

If you don't join the network, you're on your own. You're an individual perceiver out there. A little band of molecular perception bouncing around in the cosmos.

And then you're more subject to certain karmas that can come up from abusing the powers.

Now again, I don't believe in commandments necessarily, or anything like that.

Except that one does not interfere with the processes of life. That's really the only psychic commandment.

Naturally, to understand that commandment, you have to understand the processes of life. Which is what the psychic study is for. To delve into that. To plumb the depths of the universe.

How do you develop psychic power?

To begin with, it's necessary I would say—at least once a day or every other day—to sit down for a period of time and practice.

And if you would practice focusing either on the third eye or the heart center—for perhaps 5 minutes, 15 minutes, a half an hour, whatever you're comfortable with—you will find that within a month's time, your entire awareness field will change.

And as one month leads to another, your psychic development will unfold.

During an individual session when you're sitting to practice, it's good to sit up straight, normally.

You can practice lying down, but it will not be as powerful, because the kundalini doesn't flow quite as well as when the spine is very straight.

You can lean, you can be in a chair or sit on the floor, whatever you like.

During an individual session you can, if you will, switch! You could focus for awhile on the heart center, focus for awhile on the third eye whatever you will.

Stay with one center. Or what I suggest is begin with one center.

Let's say you were going to sit down and it's late afternoon. You came back from work or something and you're sitting down.

And focus on your third eye, let's say to start, or the heart. Either one. And stay with it for about 5 minutes.

For about 5 minutes focus, and after awhile you'll begin to feel a lightness as if you're floating. That's one of the first sensations that you're going outside of the body awareness. You may see dazzling displays of color.

You may see nothing and feel nothing at all initially. That doesn't mean that something isn't happening.

All week long you work. You don't necessarily get money every day. Suddenly a check comes in. But it was accruing.

So during an individual session, you should not necessarily expect to feel too much. But about 10 or 15 minutes after the session is complete, you will notice that you will go through a tremendous awareness change.

And the more intensity you put into the session, the greater that change will be.

So normally it's good to sit down, and let's say for the first 5 minutes, focus.

Then after that you don't have to focus if you don't want to. You can just let go, and try and relax, and just let the feelings flood through you. As you move into the psyche.

If you find you become a little earthbound—in other words, if you start to think a lot ...

If suddenly you're not feeling too much—you sat down for 5 minutes, you were very focused, everything felt wonderful for 15 minutes—then you're getting caught up in the maya again.

At that point, if you go back to the focus for a few minutes, it'll clear you again.

What kind of experiences can you expect?

Well, in the beginning as I said, the experiences will be a little bit subtle. To start out with initially, you'll just feel better! You'll have more energy because that's what you're tapping into, is cosmic energy.

You'll have a more positive attitude, but then … something else will begin to happen.

You'll begin to *see* inside people.

Now it's very important to respect the privacy of others. True it's wonderful to develop these psychic gifts and it's great to be able to look inside the person next to you.

> ॐ But there's a code, an unwritten code that is part of the psychic network, and that is to never interfere with the privacy of another's thoughts, unless they wish you to.

And you will be sensitive enough—as you clear the psyche—to know that.

Now, of course, there's unintentional *seeing*. It happens all the time. As you become more and more psychic you're just going to look at people. You'll walk into a room and you can look at fifty people and understand each one completely. In an instant.

Because we step out of time in the psyche, you see.

We move into a timeless dimension where we can accomplish many, many things simultaneously, a thousand things can happen—outside of time—in what we would say is a second.

It's like a fantastic computer, the psyche. It processes tremendous bits of information all at once.

What's the purpose? What's the purpose of all this?

Fun, a cheap date. Does he or doesn't he? You'll know for sure.

What's the purpose of this?

PSYCHIC DEVELOPMENT

Well, if I can get historical just for about 5 seconds.

They used to burn witches. You know who the witches were? Most of them? They were ordinary people who weren't ordinary.

In other words, they were individuals who were highly evolved, who had psychic gifts. Now of course I'm dealing with an accepted knowledge of reincarnation.

But even if you don't believe in reincarnation, and you only believe in the psychic abilities, it will work out the same way.

Throughout history, people with psychic gifts have been persecuted. Burned at the stake, french-fried, mashed. They've done some pretty horrible things.

And as a matter of fact, the psychic network has sent a number of emissaries, from other worlds to this world, and I'm not talking flying saucers.

You're going to say, [Brooklyn accent] "Flying saucers, he's nuts." [normal voice]

I'm talking, flying spoons. [prolonged laughter] You always knew, didn't you?

[Rama affects an eager voice]

> "Oh, yes, Rama I always knew it was spoons. I always knew!"

[normal voice]

No.

Through the process of incarnation—OK, we're all involved in this great cosmological process—our souls are eternal with thousands of lifetimes.

And the soul in its evolution goes through different worlds and different incarnations.

The psychic network sometimes sends advanced souls to worlds that are not that advanced, to bring light, to bring knowledge.

And of course, the reaction of this particular world has not always been too thrilling to the emissaries. That's why that movie is so fascinating, *Starman*.

Because even in popular fiction, they very well catch the idea of what would happen, of course, if—in this case—an alien from another planet, sort of comes down basically to the Earth.

And what would happen to somebody with all these psychic abilities. Well, it doesn't have to be science fiction.

I mean, higher beings have evolved and come into this world and been born into this world many times, and they usually have a terrible time. Many of them, terribly killed.

One can't "kill". The soul is eternal, but it can certainly interfere with your style a little bit.

Now why does this happen? Why does humanity …

Every time the net sends somebody down, the being—unless they're extremely inaccessible—is destroyed. Why is this? What is this thing in human consciousness?

I mean, even if it's not a fully enlightened being. If it's just someone with a lot of light. A Martin Luther King, a John Kennedy, a Gandhi. Why do we have to kill them always?

It's easy to understand.

Within the psyche there is a battle. Now I'm not speaking psychic but psyche.

If you look at the broad range of evolution, you'll see that there are polarizing forces.

Sometimes we call them *yin* and *yang*, dark and light, whatever you want. Make up words. Fwaz and Znoid. Right.

There are polarizing forces in existence, and there's an interplay between them.

Now, certain forces or energies resist light. That's their nature.

> Someone is in a dark room. They can't see. We shut out all the lights. They hear another voice in the dark room that they can't see.
>
> And that voice says that if the lights come on everything will be awful. It will be horrible. Everyone will be blinded.
>
> Everything that you've done wrong will be exposed.
>
> Terrible things will happen to you.

One believes the voice, because there's no other voice, in the world of darkness.

So, in human consciousness, when people feel or are in the presence of intense light—highly evolved beings—they freak out.

They either run to them, to worship and adore them—which is ridiculous—as opposed to just sittin' and have a good time with them.

Or they run away, or they seek to destroy them.

Because if you allow that being of light to live, that means that you have to accept that they are that, because obviously you recognize them. That's why you want to destroy them. Some force within the self.

And that means that individual will have to go through a change and some self-examination.

In other words, it's easier to shoot the person who's telling you the truth, sometimes, than deal with it. That's the mentality very often in this particular world.

Now, that hasn't stopped the network from sending higher beings in.

Because those higher beings have done a tremendous amount of good, and they make you aware of your own infinite possibilities.

It's just someone who has progressed a little further than you, who says "There's so much you can do with life. There are so many incredible possibilities. Life is endless."

What human beings experience down here, you know, this is …

Did you ever have to go to detention hall in high school? Yeah? Yeah? Aw, come on. You did. Yeah.

That's what the Earth is like. The Earth is like the detention hall of the universe. [audience laughter] Not jail. Detention hall. Different. It's where you have to spend the extra hour.

This is the planet you have to keep coming back to, until you get it right. I know. It's a nice planet though.

Another exercise.

I'd like you to close your eyes.

And imagine that a small frog is sitting on your nose. Nooooooo! [audience laughter] Strange thoughts you have.

OK, I'm going to teach you how to read somebody's mind, but you'll have to promise, you know … See? You got it, right? See, you're learning.

PSYCHIC DEVELOPMENT 39

It's really much easier, because you can just save a lot of phone bills, and things, and ... No, it's nice, you just know. You know.

OK, how can you become clairvoyant?

OK. This is very, very simple.

What I would like you to do ... is to—in a moment—to clear your mind.

And I'd like you to imagine a glass sphere. A big ball of glass, or a glass-like substance, and it's in the air. Now you don't have to get a mental picture of this. This doesn't have to be 3D.

But I just would like to introduce the concept to you of a sphere. Kind of like a basketball, only clear.

Yet not so clear that you can't tell that it's a sphere in the air. That's why it's like glass. You can see a little something.

Now inside this glass ... There's everything inside this sphere, everything.

All knowledge.

Again, you don't have to imagine this, but it is there. It's in the universe. There's a place like this. And we're going to tap into it.

Now let's say that you would like to know something.

That knowledge already exists.

Anything that you could possibly want to know already exists, in this sphere. This sphere is surcharged with light and energy.

And all you have to do is meld with it. OK, we're going to do a little Spock stuff here.

What I'd like you to do is to become aware that this sphere exists in another world, in another dimension.

And simply thinking of it will put you in touch with it.

Now when you want to find something out, when you want to develop your clairvoyant senses …

During the exercise, you don't think about what you want to know.

Because if you think about what you want to know—you won't find out what you want to know—because you'll be too busy thinking about what you want to know.

So that's why we introduce a medium in-between ourselves, and that which we want to know.

It's a kind of a distraction but it also leads us someplace, in this case.

So what I'd like you to do, is to imagine this sphere of light. It can be any size you want. It can be thousands of meters across. It can be a few feet, a few inches. Size is not important.

And you don't have to ask yourself a question. You can practice that at home, or you can if you want to.

But let's say you would like to know something.

Meaning you would like to know what someone thinks about you really. You would like to know, would it really be beneficial to purchase this particular car? Would it really be beneficial to ask this person to marry you? Would it really be beneficial to … ?

Or it could have to do with other things. You might like to *see* into a particular plane of attention. You might like to understand something that happened to you in your past, so you can overcome some of your conditioning.

- ॐ Whatever it is, you would think of it, first. Then forget about it.
- ॐ Don't ponder it over and over, because that will interfere with the *seeing* process. In *seeing* we must become absolutely precise and clear.
- ॐ And then simply imagine. Again you don't have to see a picture. The sphere I have described, it's like a glass sphere, a sphere of light. It's filled with light.
- ॐ The light changes constantly within it. You don't have to picture it. But just know that it's there.
- ॐ And then I want you to meld your mind with that sphere.
- ॐ Simply, feel that your mind and that sphere are coming closer and closer together.
- ॐ And that your mind is entering the sphere or vice versa until your mind actually becomes that sphere.
- ॐ And then just dwell in that place for a couple of minutes. And after that you will know whatever it was you sought to know, with clarity.

Your mind may doubt it. Now again you may get this information and afterwards you'll say, well that couldn't be or that's not …

Those are your doubts, and you can listen to them if you choose.

Naturally you should experiment a little bit with this before basing any great decisions upon it, only because it takes a while to learn how to clear yourself properly.

Once you clear yourself properly, it's very easy to do.

To know whatever you need to know in life.

Naturally if you have conflicting desires …

> You want to buy the new Ferrari. You know you can't afford it. You meditate on this sphere. Should I buy the Ferrari? The obvious answer is, "No. Way. Harry."

And you know that, and you get mad, and you say, "Well that can't be the right answer," because it's conflicting with your desire. You see? Well, what did you expect? Why ask?

You already know what you want to hear.

But if you reach the point where you are open to other possibilities ...

Like the truth? Then this works ...

It's "dandy". (That's a good word.)

OK, let's try it. Let's not—but this time, let's not think of anything that you want to know. Let's just practice focusing on this sphere.

- ॐ Close your eyes please. Just think of the sphere.
- ॐ Imagine a huge field of light, an ocean of light, an eternity of light.
- ॐ And there's this sphere in it, which has compacted light in it, which shifts constantly.
- ॐ It's clear, yet it is luminous, and what you want to do is feel gradually.
- ॐ There's no special technique for doing it, except wanting it.
- ॐ You must feel gradually that your mind is melding with the sphere, and this sphere with your mind, until there's no difference.
- ॐ And then just abide in that state for just a couple of minutes.

PSYCHIC DEVELOPMENT 43

- ॐ When thoughts come in and out of your mind, ignore them.
- ॐ Feel that these are the thoughts of your surface mind. They have nothing to do with the sphere.
- ॐ This sphere will not give you thoughts as such.
- ॐ It'll rather just be feelings. Don't try and understand them. Just let them enter you as you enter it.
- ॐ Until a kind of completion takes place and then you will disengage automatically at the right time just after a couple of minutes.

We'll play a little music while we do this. Yes? Good. Visualize the sphere. Just think of it. You don't have to see it. It's there, in another dimension. Good.

I'd like to answer a few questions, and get into some areas that you might be interested in.

The psychic is such a vast area to explore. There's so many things, so many avenues to pursue, and I'm sure you have particular interests.

So what I'd like you to do is, if you have a question, to raise your hand.

And I'll do the best I can to answer—perhaps not only the question you're asking—but another one that I might *see* that another part of you is asking.

Which is, of course, how one does it in the psychic world. Yes?

[question from the audience]

> "What if you meet somebody and you're being psychic or aware and they have bad energy. How can you protect yourself?"

[Rama]

Well, obviously the first protection, if you meet somebody and you're psychic and they have what we would call bad energy. They're in fact "low vibe" as we say in the trade, which is not a judgment but an observation.

What can you do to protect yourself?

Well, the first thing obviously is being able to *see* it. If you don't *see* it, then you won't know it, but they will still affect you.

So your *seeing* is very, very important.

It's very unfortunate when you can't *see* it because if you can't see it naturally … You know it's like a … You sit down next to someone and they have some disease and you can't see it but it communicates to you and you get sick. See if you knew you could have avoided the situation.

So the real way to avoid the situation is not simply to see it when you see them physically but to *see* it when you got up that day and avoid the encounter.

That's the very best if it's going to be a serious problem.

So for example you're about to get on the 405 freeway. But if you're psychic you can *see* that there's going to be a problem down on the freeway, so you take another route. That's one possibility, but there are times when that can't happen or something else is supposed to happen.

So, for example, I *saw* that it was going to rain tonight, months ago, when we booked this workshop. And I told many of the people I work with that, don't be disappointed if it rains and so on and so forth, because you know it's inevitable.

Now, one could say, "Well great Rama, big deal. So you could *see*. So you could *see* it was going to rain. It didn't do you any good, did it?"

And I would say, Right! Except that I also *saw* that the night to have the first in a series of three workshops was on the 7th of January, 1985. And that that was much more important than the rain, which would offset or make more difficult attendance for some people.

Because I could *see* that on the 7th, the energies would be in a certain state, to provide the kind of workshop that we were supposed to do.

Or, you could say that I just *saw* that that's when it was going to happen because that was the future.

So it really didn't matter a damn what I wanted. Because that was destiny.

Or you could say that there are multiple destinies and you can pick and choose different ones, but picking the right destiny does not always mean picking the most pleasant, but picking the one that's the most truthful, and on and on and on. It just depends on what level of perception you're looking at.

So coming back to your question. What can you do when you run into somebody who has bad energy?

The best thing to do is to go quickly in the other direction.

If you can't do that … If you need to be near them, try and put physical distance between yourself and that individual. It's like a radio transmitter. If you're close to the transmitter it's more intense. Fifty miles away you may not even hear the station. Twenty-five it will be very loud.

So the human aura has a radiation factor. There's an energy factor, and distance makes a terrific difference.

Particularly, within about a four-foot or three-foot radius, a person's aura is the strongest.

You'll notice sometimes, when you run into somebody who wants to give you a hard time.

[Rama mimics a snarling voice]

> They walk right up to you and put their face in yours, you know. They're just gonna let all that hate and anger …

[normal voice]

… or whatever it is they're doing just zoom into your psyche.

So if you just step back a foot or two, it makes a tremendous difference. Also by creating a little bit of physical distance, you're creating also a "psychic cut" between yourself and that individual.

The people who affect you the most are the ones you love.

This is the rule of the psychic study.

The people you have to be most careful of are not strangers. They affect you the least.

In order for a person to have a very powerful effect upon you psychically, you have to be emotionally open to that individual.

So someone you trust, someone you're concerned with, someone you love. These are the individuals who can affect you the most.

That's why in families there are so many problematic situations from the psychic point of view. Or in love relationships, or things like that.

Because we open ourselves up to a person, because there's one side of them that we love, but then there may be another side or a subconscious self or another self that is antagonistic, or has problems or whatever. So we take in both energies.

So if it's a stranger, it's not too much of a problem. You just have to feel relatively detached, and it'll bounce off. You'll survive. You'll go home, meditate, take a shower. You'll feel better.

Water is very important. Water neutralizes psychic energy. If you have a bad encounter ...

If you went to a power place and let's say that things didn't go well there. You went out to the desert or something.

Or if you're in a job where you deal with the public a lot. If you're a physician you deal with people physically, if you touch them a lot. You're in proximity.

It's a good idea to take a lot of showers. Because it cuts, it neutralizes negative psychic energy.

Living by water is always a very good idea, if possible.

Things like that.

But water is also a reflector of psychic energy too, which is why many power places are near water.

So I would only be concerned about ...

Avoid the situation if you can. If you can't avoid the situation, just go with it, and just try and be polite.

Read Dale Carnegie's *How to Win Friends and Influence People*. He gives lots of useful strategies for dealing with difficult people in situations. And that will probably take care of it.

If it's someone you are close to emotionally and they're not in a good phase, then the situation is a little bit more complex, and what's necessary is to become very detached.

Which doesn't mean that you don't love someone. It just means that at this time, their behavior is not acceptable to you. Their inner behavior.

So what you do is, you just shut off a little switch for a while, and you put a little wall up which says,

> "I'm on the other side of this wall. I love you very much but it's not going to help me or help you to allow you to hurt me. As a matter of fact, you'll just engender a lot of bad karma for yourself.
>
> "So I'm just going to withdraw for awhile, and hang out, and then when you're in a better mood we'll try again and if you're not, we won't." You see?
>
> "I love you but I don't think that what you're doing is right." You see? "It's not with light, or just doesn't agree with me."

So the first thing is, if you're psychic enough, try and avoid the situation.

If you're not, but you can *see* it, you're still in pretty good shape, because you know what's going on.

And put some distance between yourself even on a physical level between yourself and the individual.

Try not to get emotionally involved. As soon as you open your emotions, then you're a target. You're easy to take out completely, no problem, psychically.

Naturally some people are more powerful than others and they have a greater effect. Some people have more personal power and they can use it for good or ill. So you have to try and assess that.

Also it's a very good idea when you first meet people, to really "scan them" very thoroughly, so you won't be surprised later.

That doesn't mean that someone won't be your friend. It just means that you see that your friend has various sides. Like all of us, they have their strong points and their weak points.

And that way you don't get surprised if the bill shows up in the mail and it's larger than you thought.

So all human relationships are basically contractual battles of power.

It's supremacy. Everyone's trying to beat everybody else. To be more powerful, to be in charge of the relationship. There's this constant tug of war on an occult level between people.

There's another way to go about it.

You can network psychically on a higher level, but most people of course don't tend to do that, so if that's what you do, but you're dealing in a world of people who don't do that, it's a very good idea to present an image of yourself—that is fairly strong.

See, if people pick up on the fact that you're psychic … You see, a lot of psychic people tend to be kind of … too nice.

And therefore they get pushed around, because they think that's part of being psychic or being spiritual. It has nothing to do with it whatsoever.

One can be nice but not be gullible, or allow oneself to be injured by others.

So it's necessary then to assume—to a certain degree—a stance of power. Now this may or may not suit you. But this is what I recommend to my students, and this has a lot to do with the way you dress, the way you speak.

In other words you need to paint a picture for the world—for a world of people who are not necessarily psychically attuned—that is acceptable in their genre of categories, of images from the collective unconscious. And if you do that, they won't give you a hard time.

In other words, if somebody sees you're a pushover, they're going to push. Again there's that propensity in human nature—we see it again and again in the world—to destroy the innocent.

Remember, it's not this way in all planes and all worlds! This world is not a good representative sample of existence. [audience laughter, then applause]

So be hopeful. That's important to realize. Like I said, it's detention hall. What do you expect? Now, you're in here for some reason! [audience laughter]

[Rama takes a question from the audience and responds]

My friend here said that she sometimes *sees* the future. Maybe when someone is going to die or something like that. Just death?

And uh ... Work on the stock market! [audience laughter]

You can do wonders at Las Vegas you know if you... But anyway, so ...

What's happening is you have evolution from another lifetime, and it's coming back. And you probably didn't do a lot in this life to develop it, right? It's just sort of happening? Right.

That's really exciting, because that means that there's a lot more to come, but it's a very good idea not talk to too many people about it, because they'll probably ... burn you. [laughter]

People don't tend to understand. They never have. You're just a little ahead of everyone else—and that can be problem—so it's a good idea to confine your remarks to individuals who understand.

I know some good psychiatrists. Noooo! [laughter] Just teasing.

It's a good idea to confine your remarks to people who understand.

The question here, though, it's like you're coming into an inheritance. You didn't earn the money, or maybe you did in another life, who knows. But in this case you're inheriting. It's coming in. It's a surprise, [wondrous voice] "Aaaah!"

PSYCHIC DEVELOPMENT 51

You can run through it real fast and have nothing but trendy clothes left to show for it. Right?

Or you can use it for other purposes. Put some of it back into the network. Help others. Get things for yourself. Make more. There are different possibilities.

You have a gift but you need to develop the gift.

Also, sometimes, this may not be your experience, but for a lot of people it's frightening!

It's really a strange thing, because you begin ... not only are you having these visions, but there's a sense that you're changing, and you don't understand how or why, and you realize that there's—gradually—a distance between yourself and other people.

In other words, you can *see* things other people don't. And after awhile it just becomes a common everyday occurrence, but you can feel alienated that you're sort of out there on your own by yourself, you see?

So that's why it's very important to network with people who are like yourself.

You don't want to exclude other people. Your friends are your friends but it's a good idea to make some new friends. To meet some individuals who are perhaps like yourself or maybe even a little further along.

And then the other possibility, of course, is pursuing the study. And if you pursue the study you can develop your gift.

You see, what's happening to you is happening by itself.

But let's say that the psychic stuff that's coming back to you, your ability to *see* the future, to perceive things, to deal ...

Maybe that's only a portion of it and that part is coming back easily, but the rest may not come back unless you develop it consciously.

So you're a natural, to a certain extent. But some people are very upset by that.

Or, let's say that there's a time in your life—maybe some of you have experienced this—there's a time in your life when you were very psychic, when these visions come, and then if you don't do anything with it, after awhile it stops.

Now, some people are happy about that. They were very disturbed by it. They're leading a typical bourgeois middle class existence, and suddenly they start to have prophetic visions. It doesn't fit into the framework, you know. There's not place in the Cuisinart for it.

So, for such a person, it really freaks them out, and you know they just want "Mork and Mindy" forever. So they're happy when it goes away.

But other people aren't necessarily so happy when these abilities go away. So when they're happening is the time to develop them and to channel them properly. And that's why I make you aware of the psychic network.

There's a psychic network, and you can tap into it at any time. 24 hours a day. It's there.

It's a network of light and energy, of people who are like yourself on this planet—or further along and in other worlds—who are very, very advanced. Who can aid you in your journey.

Some day you may meet a teacher—a physical teacher—to work with, or you may just tap into the psychic network. Whatever's supposed to happen will happen.

But you shouldn't feel alienated and alone. This is a normal part of the growth cycle, of a being.

And everyone—at one point or another—will go through this experience, and you have many ahead of you that are actually much more wonderful. You're just beginning your journey.

[question from the audience]

[Rama repeats the question]

You're hearing high-pitched tones.

[audience member replies]

"Yes."

[Rama]

OK. What that means is one of two things.

You're either going deaf [audience laughs] or—in your case—what's happening, is you're changing planes of consciousness.

And when you change planes of consciousness, there's a tone. There's almost a sound that you hear. Very high pitched.

[audience member continues very briefly]

[Rama]

Yeah. That's it. You're changing planes of awareness. You're shifting from one awareness level into another and during the moment of shifting you hear that sound.

[audience member]

"It happens mostly like in the morning or late at night."

[Rama]

In the morning or late at night there's more psychic energy.

You see, from 9 to 5 the psychic net is sort of down a little bit. [audience laughter]

Because everybody's out there and they're all ...

[Rama mimics snarling]

"Arrgh, arrgh!"

[normal voice]

But late at night particularly, from about midnight till five, the psychic net swings. That's when it really ... It cooks. So you'll find normally your experiences will be in that range.

One of the biggest mistakes that we see people make in the psychic field, or in self-discovery in general, be it mysticism, psychic development or spiritual development—you see it in the enlightenment process, too—is what we call an over-focus on the second attention.

By that I mean, you spend so much time spacing out, that you lose touch with life. And it's very, very important not to do that.

You have to correlate your development—in other spheres of attention—with making your mind stronger and stronger, making your life more together, cleaning out your closets, getting your tax forms filed on time, keeping your checkbook balanced, keeping your life in order.

Everything in your life, the further out you go, the tighter your life has to be.

And when you do that you avoid a lot of problems.

But sometimes you see people, you give a psychic workshop, and you see a few people who walk in, and they're kind of like ... looking at the walls. These are probably very nice people. Maybe they're architects. [audience laughter] Oh well.

These are probably very nice people.

What happened was, they've just gone out there a little too far. Space brothers, you know. They're just out there a little too far, and they see and perceive a lot of different things, you see. But their problem is that they can't quite relate at all, to the world that we live in.

In the psychic, we don't want to get stuck in one world or the other. The point is to be able to slide between worlds 'cause there're thousands and thousands of worlds. So you want to be fluid and not get hung up in any one level of attention.

That's what I was talking about before. It's like a graceful ballet in the more advanced stages of the study, where you can snap [Rama snaps his fingers] and roll through thousands of levels of attention. They're endless. And not get hung up in any one place. Right? Right.

[comment from the audience]

"I'd like to call an etheric doctor to help a friend."

[Rama]

An exercise to call an etheric doctor to help a friend. Listen, the doctors I've seen lately you wouldn't want to know.

[audience member continues briefly]

[Rama]

No. Psychic healing is a whole 'nother subject.

And it's my feeling that the person who needs healing should do the invoking themselves.

In other words, if someone is ill ... We all get sick from time to time. And one day we die.

If that individual feels the need to bring in what we would call "Help from another plane of attention," they will feel that themselves and they will go after it themselves.

For us to interfere with their destiny—unless it's a very young child—is not necessarily a good idea.

Because what you may do is, channel a force that will aid that person, but perhaps they needed to go through that disease. That was an experience on their "karma card" you see?

So it's a good idea not to interfere. Let them do it themselves. That's really the best, in my opinion. It's hard when you love somebody. It's hard.

[Rama calls on someone] Yes.

[question from the audience]

> "More details on contacting the psychic network."

[Rama]

Box 404 ... [audience huge laughter] Well, it's really not so hard to do. Just click your heels three times! [huge laughter]

How do you do it? All you have to do is ... meditate, focus, think about the network.

It's there. It's something that you'll discover.

But there is no formal process that you have to go through. In other words, if you practice one of these exercises that we showed you—for tapping in—tonight.

We've done three primary exercises, and we focused on the third eye, the heart chakra—the two primary psychic centers—and of course, then we did the exercise with the sphere for clearing oneself.

After doing any of those exercises, if you will just feel the network of energy, the psychic network. Just open yourself to it.

That's a start. During the day, you can think of the network. Think of that energy. Think of those higher beings.

Now the "law of supply and demand" with the network.

If you join the network, there's one thing you're supposed to do.

ॐ And that's give more than you take.

So the way the network works is very simple.

All day long you're going in different stages of awareness. You're thinking different types of thoughts. Happy thoughts, sad thoughts, you're frustrated, you're in love, whatever it may be.

Once you patch into the network, whatever you think and feel goes into the network, and affects everyone on the network.

So the law of the network is—the rule of thumb is—always put in more than you take out.

When you patch into the network you will feel light, energy, consciousness coming to you.

You don't have to understand from where it comes. It's a gift.

There may be some beings who are aware of you—whom you are not aware of—who are aiding you. You don't need to be aware of them. If you need to be aware of them they'll make themselves known. Sometimes it's better not to know. It just comes and that's enough, and it will get you through.

But your part in the network is simply—when you could get depressed and feel crummy—not to. And say, "No, because I'm patched into the network and I want to put in something positive."

And instead of just letting yourself go down, think something positive. Be creative. Be excited about your life.

So the rule of the network is, to put in more energy than you take out. That's what makes the network strong.

Is that when we could just give up for ourselves, or be frustrated, or say "what the hell," we don't—because we're affecting somebody else.

And in this way, the network brings out higher love inside you, and as that higher love evolves, you'll find yourself patching into the network more and more and more.

You will find then, as you begin to consciously think of the network and feel it—it's a psychic thing, you'll feel it—that you will begin to meet people who are involved with the network in one way or another. You'll just start to run into them. You'll be drawn to them. It'll happen. Let's say the network arranges everything.

It's all taken care of.

But the beauty of the system is that you don't have to go to anyone to do it.

It's all done, wherever you are, at anytime. It's always there. The networking of higher energies throughout the entire universe is always present.

And there's news on the net. If you're into the tech of the net. There's a lot going on. I mean there's all kinds of transactions taking place on the net. Messages, information. It's not just waves of good energy. I mean there's billions and zillions of pieces of information being processed.

And as you become more sensitive through your psychic development, through your meditation—through, you know, eating at the right restaurants and stuff—gradually you will find that you will become more cognizant of what's passing on the net.

But just always try and put in more than you take out, and that makes the net stronger for everybody.

[question from the audience]

> "Does the network naturally advance your karma, your soul?"

[Rama]

Yes. Absolutely. Sure, the network advances your karma and your soul. Yeah. Any, any higher actions, any higher thoughts that you have create good karma.

Thought *is* karma.

It engenders states of awareness

>which engenders action

>which engenders reaction

>which of course is karma.

So, of course!

See, what you're doing is—look, on your own you're out there, an individual perceiver. It's tough out there. You know what I mean? Life is like a big Brillo Pad some days. The return of household products. And so what's a mother to do, right? It's tough.

So when you plug into the network, of course, you're joining something that actually is a flow with yourself. It's a higher aspect of life. Just most people on this planet are not too aware of it.

But in other spheres, there are universes where everybody meditates, where there's no war, there's none of this nonsense at all. And for them it's just everyday, the network is life.

Psychically attuned people—meaning people with higher evolution and higher development—are having a tough time, because we're entering a very dark cycle and it's been getting drastically worse for the last six months. Honestly.

And it's a wonderful time to help people and to aspire. I don't mean to couch it in negative terms. It's not bad. It's just the thing that's happening in life. It's a stage of life. But it's something that has to be dealt with.

And people who are not well grounded are going to have a terrible time.

In other words, people who are innately psychic and spiritually developed, you know, like my friend over here. Maybe they have a gift, they don't understand it.

It's going to be very, very confusing. They're so sensitive, and as these energies are shifting and polarizing in the coming times. Particularly in the next thirty years.

There's a cycle from around 1985 to around 2015.

It's going to be very difficult for these people if they don't have a solid practice, you know, meditation every day, whatever it is. People who they share those experiences with.

Unless they're just very strong perceivers. Because what was easy before and apparent and clear, has become very confused.

It's not the individual's fault. It's the time.

It's something that's just happening right now, in our world.

That's why more prophecies have been made about the next thirty years, than any other period in history.

They've been making them for thousands of years about this little thirty or forty year time period, because those prophets obviously were psychic, and they could *see* a tremendous energy shift taking place.

And so they would then try and interpret that energy shift. Well, they *see* global this, or you know, that or the other thing.

But what they were feeling was an energy shift, which is now taking place. We're in it now. It's begun.

And it's an exciting time. It's as easy to attain enlightenment now as it ever was, but if you're not very well grounded, it's confusing.

So the first step—I'm giving you a practical suggestion here. I'm just going my usual long way around.

The first step is to realize that what's happening is not your fault.

In other words, if you're sitting there blaming yourself, because you are not used to these states of confusion and suddenly they're occurring—OK—the normal thing to do is just to get down on yourself and get very heavy with yourself and say, "Oh it's me, I'm bad, I'm wrong."

You'll just begin to have more negative thoughts and negative impressions. They're just more available at the moment.

So you need to discriminate. You need to separate yourself and say, "No this isn't me. This is the condition." That, in itself will begin to clear things for you.

If you don't understand who's shooting at you, you're in big trouble. When you understand, you can kind of duck and get out of the way, and then eventually, you know, leave the scene.

So what's happening is, a lot of people are very confused right now. You're going to be seeing it more and more in the coming times.

And not just psychic people. It applies to everyone, but for them it's the most painful, because they're aware and they're losing their awareness.

It's a very strange thing that's happening, but if you plug yourself more into your practice, basic disciplines, meditation, working on your daily life, plugging into the network. You know things like that.

You'll find it will really offset it, and what could be a difficult time could be a very exciting and wonderful time.

Most of self-discovery is extremely private—in my opinion—and you don't have to start a fellowship or do this or that. Maybe it's just information that's applicable.

We're only here for a little while on this Earth. You're just here for a few more years and what's between now and then, is personal.

It's your experience, and for each person it's different.

Maybe for one person, it's just to be still and to *see* more of eternity. Maybe it's to love their family more. Maybe for someone else, it's to go on a spiritual quest. Maybe for someone, it's to make a lot of money, to have experiences.

It's different for everybody. There's no singular answer.

Self-discovery is highly personal. So as you become more aware, that awareness will show you always what is the right thing to do—if you trust it.

If you don't trust it—of course, then you don't—you don't use it.

[question from the audience]

[Rama]

Oh yeah, there's a definite battle between the Light and the Dark. The network always wins, though. We run the galaxy [audience laughter, *"whoo!"* and applause].

[woman in the audience]

"I don't believe that."

[Rama]

You don't believe that? Well that's too bad. So which side are you on? [laughter, clapping] But anyway, I don't want to get into politics.

But I'd like to do another exercise if I may.

I'd like you to focus this time on the very top of the head. This area right here. [Rama gestures]

This is the crown center, and this is the center of spiritual energy.

This provides a very different type of experience than focusing. The others are gateways. They are journeying places.

This does not so much *take* you someplace or *make* you feel something, as cause you to *become* something.

You might say it gives a knowledge of the soul, knowledge of light, whatever you prefer. But we move into the spiritual realm.

As we explore the psychic realm, it leads us inevitably to the spiritual realm, because all realms are connected.

It also leads us to the mystical realm, because all are parts of eternity. And as we go into one part we *see* all other parts—all of life—as a web that's connected.

So the spiritual exploration of life is something that some people—of course, who are involved in the psychic study—move onto. It's sort of the graduate school.

And that's the enlightenment process.

So just to get a sampling of that, what I'd like to do is have you focus your attention, just … you're focusing—kind of—just above the head.

That area. There's a band of energy there. You might say it's another gateway, of a certain type of force or energy.

Now these gateways are just things that you walk through. They're in the astral body.

But we don't stay with them, we move onto something else. Into other dimensional planes, or beyond dimensions to nirvana.

So I'd like you to focus there, and I'd like you to—actually this time—to visualize something a little bit, with your eyes closed.

And that's … I'd like you to feel that there's gold—but not a dull gold but a very bright, like shimmery gold light, all around the top of your head—and what it's doing is, it's like a rain.

It's coming down through the top of your head and soaking through your whole body.

And this is the kundalini. And we're going to bring the kundalini down, instead of up.

And as you do this, you'll feel it saturating through your whole body, and it'll just make your body feel really wonderful. And it cleanses the psyche and the spirit.

And it works very effectively, particularly of course—as all these exercises do—with repeated practice.

So if you close your eyes, focus your attention on the top of the head just for a couple of minutes. Relax a little bit.

We've had a lot of exciting, interesting discussion here, and now let's take all that energy and use it, to go a step further. Into the beyond.

And so if you focus right at the top of the head.

And just visualize a kind of rain of golden light, shimmery light. It's the light of eternity, the light of God or immortality just passing through you.

We are that light. It's our essence. It's our substance. It's beyond words and definition. It is.

[silent meditation for a few minutes]

Before we end our evening, I'd like to give you some thoughts on things you can do to increase your psychic awareness, other than practices like the ones we've engaged in.

There are many, many things you can do.

Some simple ones, of course, include nature.

It's a very good idea to spend some time in nature—or let's say not around other people—to clear your energy field. A lot of time is not necessary, but some time.

Just even an occasional day—where you go for a hike in the desert or by the beach or some place when it's not crowded—allows you to feel your own psyche.

You see, one of the things that you have to do, is figure out which are your thoughts and which are the thoughts of others—that other people are thinking—that you're just picking up.

Because as psychically attuned people, you pick up a tremendous, tremendous amount of thought from others.

And most people grow up psychic—and they don't realize that they're psychic—and they think or assume that the thoughts in their minds are their own thoughts!

Because no one ever walks up to you and says,

> "Hi, I don't know if you realize this, but you're just a little bit more sensitive than most people.
>
> "And you should be aware of that."

And also, of course—the society, the world, whatever—we want to conform so badly. A part of us wants to be like every body else.

Not recognizing, of course, that we should just be ourselves, whatever that is. That's the best. That's our own natural, evolutionary pattern.

So, spending some time alone is very good.

Trying to spend time with other people, of course, with high psychic energy.

Practicing compassion for others.

Which doesn't mean doing something for everybody, or thinking that we're a savior, or that—you know—the world smiles on us to help everybody.

But rather ...

Just sending out—in other words—an understanding, non-judgmental energy to others, can make a terrific difference. Not only for others, but for your own level of attention.

A certain amount of time each day to just reflect.

It might just be lying down before you go to bed. It might be practicing an exercise. It might be taking a walk.

But reserving a time each day to cleanse your psyche and to renew it.

You may engage in—of course—the practice of meditation or something like that, which of course leads to higher development.

Or you may just be innately psychic—a little bit—and just find quiet moments. It depends on what you want, how far you want to go with it.

But the thing that you need to watch most carefully, are your interactions with others. Because people—who are psychic, as I suggested—tend to pick up more energy and impressions from others, than they realize.

And those who affect you the most, are the ones you're emotionally close to. And you need not be physically close to people you're emotionally close to.

In other words, if someone you love or someone you just are open to—maybe they were a friend twenty years ago—but you've maintained an open dialog inwardly with that person.

But maybe they're not the person they were maybe twenty years ago. Susie or Bob was really nice—but maybe their life has led them in another direction—but you're still open and still picking up that energy.

So it's a good idea sometimes to just take out a piece of paper, and write down everybody in your life who you felt really close to.

There won't be that many people.

And then evaluate that. Feel that out and see how that feels. Is that still viable? Do you still want to feel that open to that individual?

I'm not suggesting that you shouldn't feel close to people, but just that you need to be …

You have to recognize your sensitivity.

It's very important, because if you don't recognize your sensitivity, it gets trashed.

You have to recognize that you are sensitive, that you are a bit psychic.

Everyone is.

But just for you that evolution is coming out now. That development is happening now, and to pretend it's not there, you'll find you'll get sick more physically because you'll pick up impressions of others.

You'll just have a lot more confusion. Things like that.

This happens to a lot of really nice people who are just too sensitive and too open, and they didn't learn that they have to just lead a slightly more secluded life.

As I suggested before—you know I was kidding around about it—but it's very serious.

People with psychic gifts—and just these natural abilities—have been persecuted in this world for a long time. And it's good to be not too loud about your sensitivity unless that's your calling.

Some people, they do that. Some people, that is right for them. They just go out into the public view and say, "Yes I am this and that's how it is."

And that hopefully gives strength to other people who are the same way, but that's not for everyone to do. You have to gauge what's right for yourself.

But it's a good idea to practice inaccessibility, in my opinion.

Because otherwise, you open yourself up to ridicule, which isn't necessary and won't help that individual or won't help you.

It's funny. Psychic people are so trusting, so many of them.

And I think it's a good thing to be trusting. I'd rather be trusting than not.

But I think one can be trusting and a little realistic at the same time. They tend to look at just the good side of people and that's a wonderful thing to do and you shouldn't stop doing that.

But you should also take a detailed inventory of the other side of the individual. Just so you'll know. That's more honest actually and then you can actually be a better friend to someone.

And also the other thing to do, is to constantly work on the physical.

Again, the tendency is to spend too much time in the second attention, to resist wanting to deal with the work world, with the reality of life in the physical. But the physical is God, too.

And if you put some time and energy into that, it grounds you. And you'll find that you can traverse higher and higher spheres of attention without getting spaced out, without not fitting into the world.

You can do both. You should be able to—very articulately—if in fact, you are psychic.

And I would suggest that all of you have that propensity, because otherwise power wouldn't have brought you here tonight.

Just some thoughts on the way.

I'd like to thank you for coming this evening. We've all joined our energies and created something good. How good? You'll find out when you get home! [audience laughs]

But I think that you'll be pleasantly surprised.

You may find yourself in kind of a nice state of attention tomorrow.

You may just meditate a little bit and *see* that there was a lot of light here from a lot of different people and that, you know, it was networked. This is how networking is done. It happens a lot.

A lot of networking happens in sleep, the dream planes.

Which of course, we didn't even begin to discuss, you know. One can go on and on with this material.

But in *dreaming,* a lot of people network with the higher beings, and move into other currents, astral currents, different worlds.

Some dreaming is just of course the subconscious just playing with images, but sometimes it's journeys into higher reality.

Particularly in the very early morning hours.

Not always, but that's just the psychic time. One, two, three, four in the morning, when the world is asleep. Just the frequencies are more clear. It's easier for certain signals to be received, you might say.

But then a lot of people then will have dreams, later in the morning of course, that are more earthbound.

And you tend not to remember, you know, the earlier are more psychic ones.

But certainly any endeavor you make to expand your awareness will just give you a much better life.

Certainly it's painful to be aware. Of course! Hell yes! it's painful to be aware.

But it's also tremendously beautiful, and the two have a funny way—sometimes but not always—of going together.

But there's much, much more beauty than pain.

But somehow it enlarges us as beings—to experience a little bit of pain—so we understand the pain of others.

We get outside of our own cocoon and *see* what's out there.

And of course the beauty is so incredible. If we just become sensitive to it.

So recognize you're in special position, and if you feel that and use that ... Not as I see it but as you see it. I'm just here to encourage it.

Each person has their viewpoint, their mythology, their way of seeing things. I don't mean to contradict any of them.

I'd just like to join my energy with yours and say it's nice to be here.

Good night.

[long applause]

CHAPTER TWO

MEDITATION AND KUNDALINI

Tonight is not the end of the world. This is our hot tip of the evening.

[audience laughs, then Rama laughs with them]

Oh well. Tonight we're going to be talking about trigonometric ratios. [audience laughs, sound of opening zippered cassette case]

And kundalini, and meditation, and music.

We're going to be doing three meditations tonight. You'll be learning three meditation techniques to use the kundalini.

And essentially what I'm going to be doing with those techniques is using the kundalini, moving it through your subtle physical bodies—to raise you into altered states of attention—while showing you how you can do that yourself.

Tonight, three of my friends and three of my students—they're one and the same—are going to be performing some live music. As you see we have amplifiers, we have speakers, we have headphones, we have all kinds of things.

And tonight we're going to have some live music for the meditations. We'll be doing three meditations of approximately 10 minutes to an hour each. [audience laughs]

About 10 minutes to 15 minutes each, throughout the evening, and so we'll have some music to meditate to.

I like to use music in group meditations because it's harder to hear the megaphones and … [audience laughs]

This is something they teach you in the spiritual teacher training academy [audience laughs] in another world.

And so we'll have lots of music tonight. Lots of sound.

The kundalini is music. It's energy, it's excitement, it's power.

And in the back, someone heard that word, and they said …

[Rama mimics a loud, greedy voice]

"Power!"

[normal voice]

No, not that kind of power.

Power. Pure unadulterated power. Limitless. Mindless. [Rama laughs]

Whoa! No. [audience laughs]

Power. That's the kundalini. The kundalini is the life force, it is the essential energy of existence. It's the hidden ingredient in life.

[Someone sneezes, Rama says "Bless you."]

It is … what makes it all work.

So tonight we're going to be talking about meditation and kundalini.

How many of you, if any, are new to meditation? Could you raise your hand, please?

A few, a few. Great. Good. Alright, well, then let's begin at the beginning. That's usually a good place.

Meditation.

Why do you meditate? I suppose it's different for everybody.

Some people meditate because they need more energy, and when you meditate, of course, you get a lot of energy. A tremendous amount of energy.

Some people meditate because they are sick and tired of their lives, of the world, of the way people abuse each other in this world, and abrogate each other's freedoms.

And essentially they want out. Sort of, "Stop the universe, I want to get off." They just feel that there's more.

The life that we see on our small planet is not necessarily a great reflection of the entire universe.

The planet is beautiful. The animals are beautiful. The people are beautiful.

But they tend to destroy one another. And that's not necessarily an operative principle in all dimensions.

So some people meditate because they want to get the larger picture on life, because it could get kind of discouraging if this was all there was.

There are thousands of worlds. Thousands of dimensional planes. Billions. Endless. Life is endless.

MEDITATION AND KUNDALINI 75

It's discouraging. [audience chuckles] It goes on forever. I mean that's a long time. And you're eternal which means that you have a great deal of time on your hands.

So tonight I'd like to use a little bit of that time, and discuss just about anything that seems … irrelevant … and by discussing all things that are irrelevant we'll find that what is left over is relevant.

And what is relevant? That which you can't discuss, which is why we meditate, because when we meditate we enter into silence, stillness.

Meditation essentially means having a great time.

Some people, they've applied a sense or a feeling to the meditative experience such that—I like that phrase "such that" [audience laughs], yeah, just trying to loosen everybody up a little bit—such that meditation has become a quantifiable religious experience.

Which means that it's not any fun. [audience chuckles]

In other words, meditation has been turned into a tool …

[Rama mimics a revolutionary]

    of the bourgeoisie! [audience laughs]

[normal voice]

No, I'm sorry [audience laughs], wrong incarnation. [audience laughs]

I get … You know, I'm in different ones at different times, and I [Rama snaps his fingers] got to bring it around, and get it straight. Sorry, this is the … this is the … Right! America!

Meditation …

[Rama mimics a friendly New York voice]

... is wonderful! It's just terrific. It's so wonderful, I don't know why don't you do it more? [audience laughs]

It's just ... It's the best!

I mean, you know ... It's the best thing since sliced kundalini, right?

You know, it's terrific! How do you meditate? You should never ask.

[normal voice]

It's easy. All you have to do is stop all your thought and you're ... that's it! [audience laughs]

See, now you know!

Admission, 7 dollars. Meditation, taught. Mission, accomplished. [audience laughs]

That is the secret!

Now, you might—of course—ask, "Well, how *do* you stop all your thought, Rama?"

[Rama, quietly] And I would say "Well, that's the art isn't it?"

[audience pauses, then laughs]

Tonight, we're going to have three very talented musicians playing, and I assure you that the first time they sat down and played, they never thought they would end up where they are [audience laughs].

Tonight I'm going to fry them with the kundalini. They're going to be within the 12-foot range, that's the kill range on the kundalini level [audience roars].

These guys have never been on stage with me. They have no idea what

MEDITATION AND KUNDALINI

they're in for. But we'll all be very chic and casual and hip about it, you know, and just ... [audience laughs].

I like it.

So, anyway, you're trying to meditate. How do you do it? Boy, we're gonna learn!

[Rama mimics comical intensity]

We're gonna learn how to do this meditation thing. When you leave here tonight ... you won't. [audience laughs]

How do you meditate?

Well, you have to learn to be very, very gentle to start with—with yourself—essentially.

Because meditation is not something that you force, you see? It's something that happens to you because—I don't know—life gives you a gift.

There are billions of people out there walking around ... And they wear a lot of shoes. [audience laughs]

Have you ever thought about that? [audience laughs] But anyway.

There are billions of people out there walking around and ... they don't meditate! You can tell. They're not having a good time with their lives.

It's bad out there, friends! You know, it's just ... people are not happy! It's just not working. You know?

One nation trying to destroy another. One race trying to destroy another. One religion trying to destroy another. It's the same old story, over and over again. It's because they don't meditate.

Now, I'm not suggesting everyone should meditate. Far from it. Meditation is for very few individuals.

When I speak of meditation, of course, I'm speaking of something that's a powerful experience.

Some people speak of meditation as kind of relaxation. [Rama mimics snoring]

And you do the mantra. [Rama snores, audience laughs]

That's—nah—that's not, that's not what I'm talking about. Nah.

Meditation is the entrance into alternate planes of consciousness. [Rama makes a chanting sound like, "Dzoouu"]

Yeah. It's fun. So, the way, the way you do it, is by not trying to be too good at it, too quickly.

This is essential. Because otherwise, you won't have fun with it.

If you expect anything in particular to happen—the stars to spin in the sky, light to flood your being, the kundalini to surge through you—uh, give it a month [audience laughs]. Don't expect that to start out with.

Because you'll be very discouraged, because it probably won't happen.

At best, at the beginning you'll just kind of, be kind of confused. And you're not sure what you're supposed to do—and you're trying to do the stuff that they say—and you don't even know why you're doing it.

And I don't know why you're doing it either. [audience laughs]

But I do know that if you do that for a long period of time, you will change in ways that ... I can't understand. But that's neither here nor there.

So how do you meditate? Well, the way you meditate is, well, there's not just one way. There's a lot of ways. That's why it's difficult to talk about because

MEDITATION AND KUNDALINI 79

there's so many ways to meditate.

A good way to start is with love.

Love is perhaps the strongest force in the universe.

When you meditate with love, what you do is you feel love, and love is like a bird, you kind of ride it. You get on it's back and you ride it up very very high, above the thought level.

You're trying to stop thought, but all your life you've been thinking. You've been "taught to *thought*", to analyze, to look at things.

[Rama mimics Sgt. Friday from the 1960s television series *Dragnet.*] "Facts, gotta have the facts, ma'am."

Remember Friday, on *Dragnet?* [audience chuckles] Yeah. So you've gotta have the facts, right.

But here we're gonna do something about the word "facts". Who could … ? I could care less.

What facts? You call those facts? Wh- where? I don't see a fact. You see any facts? [audience chuckles]   I'm looking for a fact. [Rama gestures as if looking under things]

This is called "fact finding?" Ohhhhh. [audience laughs] Bad. Bad. I know.

So, I don't know anything about facts, but I do know how to meditate. And all you have to do is stop your thought. And if you stop your thought for a sustained period of time, you'll enter into other states of attention.

But fortunately, the good news …

I know this is ridiculous, but bear with me. I'll get through this phase.

The good news … is that you don't have to stop thought completely, to be able to meditate well.

Isn't that good? Whew! Because it takes a long time to be able to stop thought impeccably.

What you need to do … is to detach yourself from thought.

The serious part of the talk.

There are essentially three stages in learning how to meditate.

In the beginning, you're simply sitting and trying to practice without any concern of what is happening, what is not happening, whether you're gaining benefit from it, and so on. You're just trying to do it.

And this is the stage of ignoring thought.

In the second part of the practice, we stop thought for limited periods of time. And we don't stop thought, what we're doing is learning to think specific types of thoughts.

In other words—thought control.

[Rama mimics a mad professor] *Mind control!*

So. Thought control. Sorry, slipped again. [audience chuckles]

The third stage is no thought.

Now "no thought" is not the end of meditation. That's the beginning of higher meditation. That means that you are about to experience the other aspects of your being.

You are an endless conglomeration of awarenesses. You're not one singular self. You're a corporation. Inside you is eternity. Everything's there.

A human being is not so simple. You know, we're told that we're Ted or Sally or Willie or whatever.

And that we grow up and have experiences and we die. Or maybe we go to heaven—I don't know—but I do know that has nothing to do with what life is.

You're eternity.

You have thousands of selves inside you.

And meditation is a process of peeling back the layers of the self.

We start with peeling back the personality form from this lifetime, your current one. The mental conditioning, the things that they told you.

[Rama mimics a silly kid voice] "Girls wear pink."

You know, that sort of thing.

Because these are ridiculous ideas that human beings have come up with. And in every culture they're different. I mean, there's no arbitrary standard of truth.

And what they do is block you from being the totality of yourself.

Meditation is not for everybody! I'll grant you that. That's for sure.

Because when you meditate, you're going to become conscious. And most people don't want to be too conscious, because they're afraid!

They're afraid of awareness, they're afraid of life, they're afraid of being happy.

Now that may sound ridiculous, and I would have thought so a long time ago. But having been around the world a little bit, I've seen that it's not ridiculous. People really don't want to be happy. They go out of their way to be miserable.

So if you want to be that way, I can't do a thing for you. Nobody can. Because you've already set the program and it's running. You debugged it. Misery!

[Rama mimics sobbing] "Nothing's going to work out. Everybody's against me. Life has no meaning." [back to normal voice]

You're right there. But … [audience laughs]

Well, it doesn't need a meaning. I mean a meaning is an arbitrary thought formulation that we affix to it, because we're in the mood.

Life is its own meaning. It's its own raison d'être. It's exciting.

The kundalini is the energy. The energy. [audience laughs] Of existence.

Kundalini is the life force. It's given different names. Sometimes they call it *prana*. Sometimes they divide it into different segments, in Sanskrit the *apana* and the *samana*, and all that sort of fancy terminology.

Sometimes it's called *shakti*. Nice names, I like the sound of them.

All it is, is energy. It's the life force. The more life force you have, the more you can do. The more alive you are.

The kundalini is said to reside in the base of the spine.

Now it's a bit of a misnomer, because the kundalini really is not so much in the physical body, as in what we call the subtle physical body, or body of energy. Also known by some as the astral body—that surrounds the physical body—the etheric body.

When you *see* someone's aura, that's just the outer reflection of the subtle physical body.

MEDITATION AND KUNDALINI

The subtle physical body is about the same shape as the physical body, although it can change shapes. It can become thousands of different things.

But it does have a basic structure.

And the way it works is—of course, as you all know—there are seven primary chakras or energy centers that run along, theoretically, along the spinal column.

And the root chakra—at the very base of the spine—is where the kundalini is said to reside.

The kundalini is thought of as a serpent, as a snake, it's something that's coiled. It means coiled. It's gonna spring out!

Kkhhuu! [Rama mimics the sound of a snake striking]

It isn't really like that. But it sounds good. It's much more intense than that. It's much more complete.

The kundalini is not some little snap thing that goes *whip!* OK?

The kundalini is the totality of the universe. All of the life energy of existence is going to flow through you. You will be in thousands of planes of consciousness at once or beyond all in nirvana, absorbed.

Or maybe having a sandwich with a friend. Confronting an olive. [audience chuckles]

And you can *see* the life in that olive. You can know what it is to be an olive. [audience chuckles]

You can! Because you can detach your attention from yourself and go anywhere. You can wander the universe. Big deal. So!

So to meditate then, what you need to do, is to be able to free yourself from your ideas and your thoughts. Which are probably wonderful—

[Rama suddenly mimics a shouting accusation] *Liar!*

[audience laughs] No, they're probably wonderful!

Wonderful thoughts and ideas you have. Great.

But sometimes there's something more, and that's beyond thought.

Because all of the higher dimensional planes, the higher realities—the infinite cosmos itself—is beyond thought.

It's certainly something that you can experience and be. As are the other aspects of yourself.

Why are people unhappy? People are unhappy because they don't understand life. They're unhappy because, I mean, it's obvious why they're unhappy.

Maybe it's better to look at what makes someone happy. By happy I don't just mean "hummm", but … complete, aware, conscious, poignant, caring, loving, unaffected, cosmic, simplistic, humble, excited, passive. Everything!

You're everything.

We're a stage. And there are players. And they come and they speak the speech. The loves, the experiences, the cares, the sorrows, it all passes through us. We're the audience. We're watching. We're the participant. We're the reviewer.

We're everything.

To know that, to know that truth. To know that awareness and still not get too stuck on yourself? You know, so you're like, not …

[Rama mimics an arrogant deep voice] "God's gift to the world." To avoid that. Yuck.

MEDITATION AND KUNDALINI 85

To be conscious of life, to love! To be free.

And yet to be able to deal with the world effectively. To be able to handle that freeway traffic. To be able to deal with pain.

And love. And ecstasy. Ecstasy can be painful when it's intense enough. When the kundalini surges enough, the ecstasy is so complete, it's overwhelming sometimes!

Eventually you'll go into *samadhi*. Samadhi is a very advanced meditation. You dissolve in the clear light of eternity, again and again.

The experience of enlightenment. (Tomorrow night.)

How do you meditate? We're going to do a meditation technique. And I'm going to go through it now and we're going to do one. You will find that they will build over the evening.

We're gonna do three of them. This will be the first one. I'd like you to listen carefully. They seem very simple, and they are. That's why they work. But they're extremely powerful.

Tonight as we meditate together, I'm going to be moving in and out of different planes of attention, and taking the kundalini and surging it through you in a lot of different ways, to show you inside what it feels like to meditate.

Naturally when you're here, there's lots of wonderful people, and they've got lots of wonderful energy. And so you'll feel a lot of different things.

But the true test of how the experience was—what it did for you—was how you feel when you get home.

Go home, have a little bite to eat. Relax, and look around you. *See* the energy.

See how you feel tomorrow. If we did a good job, you'll be pretty gone. [audience chuckles]

What I'd like you to do is, to—in a moment … stay relaxed—in a moment, to sit up straight. It's good when you meditate to sit up straight.

Normally, when you practice meditation, you can sit in a chair, which I wish you would tonight.

Please don't sit in the aisles because there are fire laws you know. I don't know. Fire has problems with it. [audience chuckles]

But you can sit like this. You can sit—I don't know, any way you want—as long as you sit up straight, and your back is … the spine is straight. You should be comfortable. It's good to wear clean loose clothing when you meditate. You can meditate naked if that's what you're into. It doesn't matter.

The main thing is to learn to be still.

Now so therefore, why all this music when you're trying to be still?

The music is used as a backdrop. We have a lot of people together. A lot of different energies, and it gives us something to focus on a little bit.

And I take the kundalini, and I play against the notes with it.

I kind of, do a light show, inwardly and outwardly, with the energy—with vortexes of energy—as you sit there.

Opening you up. Opening up different parts of you, that maybe you haven't felt since you were a child. It's no big deal. It's just what I do.

What I'd like *you* to do, is to do a meditation.

During this experience—the next 10 or 12 minutes while we're sitting here and feeling in new ways, new energies—you're storing something.

MEDITATION AND KUNDALINI 87

Don't be looking for the flashy experience. It may happen.

But if it's strong enough, you won't realize it's happened until much later, when you start to come down from it.

What we're looking for here is ... storing power. You're accumulating energy. The kundalini.

So I'd like you to begin this evening, just for a moment, by taking your hand and touching the area around your navel. Just take your hand and touch that area, OK? And you'll know how much weight you need to lose. [audience laughs] The holidays are always devastating.

OK. This is one of the *nadis*. This is one of the places where the kundalini hangs out.

So what I'd like you to do is—while the music is on—I'd like you to practice a simple exercise, maybe 4 or 5 minutes. Then you can stop the exercise, and just go. And leave the driving to us.

What I'd like you to do, is to focus your attention here [navel chakra], and you will feel surges of energy. You don't have to touch that spot when you do this.

And I'd like you to feel the energy moving. We're going to move that energy from here, to the center of the chest.

Now touch the center of the chest right here [gestures]. This is the heart chakra. This is the navel chakra [gestures]. These are two primary energy centers.

The heart chakra is a very pure luminous energy center.

The *shushumna* is the tube that the kundalini passes up in the subtle physical body, and one side is the little guy called the *ida,* and the other side is the *pingala*.

We're going to move the kundalini from the solar plexus region [navel chakra]—where it stores—right up into the heart center, which purifies it, and connects the two halves of the being.

This is the central chakra [heart]. There are three above the heart chakra—throat chakra, third eye and of course the crown chakra. Navel center, one half way down, and then one all the way at the base of the spine.

So to start with, we're going to do a simple exercise, but it's strong.

Focusing here [navel].

And then what I'd like you to imagine—because imagination is power in the inner world. When you use your imagination, you are creating a movement of energy. It's not arbitrary. It's not daydreaming. Well, daydreaming is energy.

What I'd like you to do, is to sit up, relax—feel this area of your body—and feel energy or just imagine it, moving from here [navel] to here [heart].

Like a little surge, like a little fountain, going from here [navel] to here [heart].

If it goes further, fine, don't worry about it.

And so you just sort of feel energy, kind of going from here [navel] to here [heart].

Then you're going to come back down again, and bring it from here [heart] to here [navel].

Little circle.

Then you're going to come back down again, and bring it from here [heart] to here [navel].

But at this point, we're not taking the energy so much in a circle, as just bringing it up.

And I'd just like you to repeat this for a few minutes. Four or five minutes.

And as you do, you'll notice your attention level changing.

Thoughts will come in and out of your mind at this point, please just ignore them. Don't try and fight with them or stop them yet. Just ignore them, relax.

And just keep this focus.

After doing that for a few minutes, stop. Let go.

And just let the music absorb you or the energy absorb you.

The energy changes will be very [Rama claps his hands], very [claps] fast [claps], very quick.

I'll snap [snaps his fingers] you through a lot of different planes of attention, [snaps] very quickly.

If you feel uncomfortable, relax, it'll go away in a moment. You're trying too hard. Relax a little bit. Lighten up. Have fun with it. Smile a little bit. If it gets too intense, just sit back.

You might meditate with your eyes closed—normally that's the easiest. Once in a while it's fun to meditate with the eyes open and gaze forward without a particular focus. We'll talk more about that later.

To stop thought, you have to go above it.

So we're collecting energy, and then that energy—when it's freed it's like a flood. And the water will rise and rise and will take us above a certain level.

And then there's no thought. Then we're in altered states of attention. That's how the kundalini works, one of the ways.

So I'd like you to focus your attention here [navel], and then just very gently—as you sit there with your eyes closed—just bring the energy from here [navel] to here [heart].

Just imagine it. You don't have to see a picture in your mind. Just feel it.

Focus here [navel] then feel here [navel].

Then here [heart].

Then here [navel].

And just feel it rising up, and as you do, you may feel a sensation, kind of like you're floating. You may see visual colors—particularly if your eyes are open.

You may see colors. There'll be certain light changes that they're doing here.

But aside from that, you may see subtle changes in the subtle physical. Maybe no phenomena. It doesn't matter.

You're absorbing energy. You're absorbing power, which you'll take with you, when you leave this evening.

So let us begin. If you'd please sit up nice and straight.

Relax. Close your eyes. Focus your attention—navel center.

We'll be meditating for about 10 minutes, so just have a nice time. Don't fall asleep. And just let yourself go. Let yourself wander.

You're thinking, "What am I supposed to do, what's going to happen?"

Who knows? I don't know. That's what makes life exciting. Just let go. Ignore thought.

Feel. Just practice feeling. Feel the energy shifts in the room.

MEDITATION AND KUNDALINI 91

Ride the music for a while. Ride the energy.

Go beyond thought. Feel love. Feel peace. Don't think about tomorrow or yesterday. They don't exist.

Yesterday's gone, tomorrow hasn't happened. We only have this night and this night is eternity. Good. Let us begin.

[Zazen music plays and the meditation begins. It lasts 14 minutes.]

Please sit back and relax.

There are many, many ways to meditate. Essentially, in the very beginning, when you meditate you're learning how to feel again.

When we're very young children, we know how to feel. It's innate. But as we lead a lifetime, we pick up so many thoughts, impressions, feelings, ideas, that our sensitivity goes away.

Now little children don't meditate perfectly. Don't misunderstand me. Some children are perfectly horrible. [audience chuckles]

But their subtle physical bodies are perfectly intact.

But as we grow up, as we're exposed to hate and greed and anger and jealousy, and peanut brittle and all kinds of things, our subtle body erodes.

The subtle body must be intact to transmit the kundalini, the life force. As the subtle body wears we get sick and that's why eventually the body dies.

It's because something happens to the subtle body. The integrity of the subtle body is totally important. Think of the subtle body as the framework. The veins, capillaries, organs, everything is required for the body to function.

The subtle physical body also is made up of many different strands of luminous energy, and energies are flowing through them constantly in the etheric plane that supports—of course—the physical body.

Above the subtle body is the causal body, and then—of course—the soul, or whatever you want to call it.

That which we are. We're the universe. We're all-intelligent.

So what are we doing here? [audience chuckles]

Well, life is like that. You end up in the strangest places. They had a great brochure for this particular planet before this incarnation. You probably read it, too. [audience chuckles]

If you're starting to meditate, I suggest that you set up a schedule for yourself. It's good to meditate twice a day. If you're an absolute beginner, once a day.

If you can't get yourself to meditate once a day, then try once a year. [audience laughs]

Now you shouldn't expect as much, of course. Once a day is good to start.

The best time to meditate is when you first get up in the morning. Or evening, or whenever you rise. [audience chuckles]

What you want to do … Get up, wake up, take a shower or whatever, and sit down and meditate.

Most people have a little meditation table they sit in front of when they meditate, or sit in a chair.

And sometimes they keep large amounts of cash on it. [audience laughs]

MEDITATION AND KUNDALINI

And they hope that through the process of meditation, when they finish meditating, there will be more. [audience laughs] I don't know.

But, I myself have candles on mine, and some flowers.

The candles are nice because the light is very gentle. It's easy on the eyes. And sometimes a little incense burning.

Sometimes the rug, whatever [audience laughs] you're in the mood for.

The flowers are nice; they bring nature into our universe.

And then what should you do? It's a good idea sometimes before you start a meditation, to chant a mantra. A mantra's a very powerful word.

It vibrates like music does, only not just on this plane, but on other planes of reality. It creates a power, a force. It starts the kundalini moving.

There are many different mantras. The most powerful of all mantras, of course, is "AUM," spelled A-U-M or O-M.

It's usually chanted either silently, or out loud. But it's stretched.

So it's "OOOOOOOMMMM", stretched. [Rama chants for five seconds]

All mantras are always elongated.

The mantra for beauty is "SRING," S-R-I-N-G, to enter into the states of beauty.

And that's SRING, "SRRRIIIINNNNNNNNNG," and so on. [Rama chants for five seconds]

So if you would chant "OM," either silently or out loud, maybe seven times.

Seven, powerful numbers: seven higher worlds, and seven lower worlds, according to one philosophy.

If you would chant "OM" seven times, sit down ...

OK, woke up ...

[Rama mimics a slightly wasted but aspiring workshop-attendee. Audience laughs throughout.]

"Oh man, god, I gotta meditate, man, I can't take it man, geez.

"Last night man, that party, god I got so wasted! How am I gonna do it? Man, I don't know! Rama said I gotta do it, man, I'll do it.

"Geez, I gotta light the candles. Oh, I lit the flower man! God! Oh, bad karma man, like I won't tell anyone! I'll just put it back together. No one'll know!

"I'm gonna do this thing, man. I'm gonna sit here. I gotta do this OM jazz, man.

"Sounds pretty jive but I'll try it, man. I think I'll do it ...

"I hope no one will hear me, man, they'll think I'm sick! I'll go ... OM ! [a very short burst]

"That's good enough, man, he'll never know!

"Now I gotta do this, what do I gotta do, one of those exercises he taught us man.

"I got loaded before I went that night. It was pretty far out. I liked the music a lot. I don't know if I can remember.

"Let's see, what he said, something about the heart, man.

"I gotta like, focus! Like right here. I'm gonna put my attention. That's right. And sit up straight, man. [inhales]

"Oh, he didn't say I didn't have to breathe. No, no, you can do any kind of breathing."

MEDITATION AND KUNDALINI

[Rama returns to normal voice]

So what you're gonna do then ... [audience laughs].

We cut back to the present moment!

... is after you've chanted "OM" a few times, and sort of gotten yourself basically together, and put the flower out [audience laughs] you're going to sit there, and focus your attention in a number of different ways.

Any of the exercises that you start out with, will get the kundalini moving.

You don't have to stay with them for the entire period of meditation. You want to go beyond them. We want to walk through the door. Once we're through the door we're outside. We're in another world. But we need to get up and walk through the door.

So a meditation exercise serves that purpose. It's not something to stay with, because you'll fixate on it. We want to go beyond thought, beyond ideation, beyond feeling, beyond everything.

But we start in the physical, and in the mind.

We use the transitory to go to the eternal because they're really interconnected.

So you'll sit down in the morning, if you can't make it in the morning, try the evening to start with. Do the late show.

But you meditate best in the morning. Even though you may be a little tired, the mind has not been active yet.

Once you've been thinking—analyzing, talking, picking up energy, being active—it's harder to slow it down. Even though you're a little tired, the mind hasn't been moving. It's easier to make it still.

When you meditate in the morning, you pick up a lot of energy—focus, awareness—and that will be with you throughout the day.

You'll have a shield of energy around you. It brightens the subtle physical body, so you won't pick up as much negative energy from your transactions with the world. Your mind will be clear. You'll do everything well.

"Everything's better with Blue Bonnet on it." [Rama quotes from the ubiquitous 1970s margarine slogan and audience laughs.] Right.

So if you smear it all over yourself before you medi- [audience laughs].

Nooooo! Kinky! Boy, I'll tell you.

So sit there and meditate. Practice one of these exercises that I'm showing you tonight—or another one that you may know—to start out with.

Then what are you supposed to do? As I suggested, there are three stages.

If you're very new to meditation, simply practice the exercise for a few minutes, say five minutes, or as long as is comfortable.

Then after doing that for about five minutes or so, stop, just let go. Letting go is the hardest thing, isn't it?

Because everybody's so afraid. They're so afraid of eternity. They're so afraid of life. They're so afraid of what's on the other side of death.

There's nothing but light. Infinite light. Infinite awareness. God is everywhere.

So learn to let go. You do it a little at a time and you have small successes.

And those successes—in terms of mental clarity, feeling better, deep perceptions about life, developing your psychic abilities—whatever it may be.

The changes you go through. You become someone else when you meditate, you know. It isn't ... it isn't just a little technique.

If you really pursue it, you change radically, constantly, because you evolve. You can go through hundreds of lifetimes in one. You can experience so much. Feel so much. Be so much.

Or be nothing. Or everything. Or beyond both.

And it all starts with that daily meditation practice.

How long should you meditate? If you're very new to meditation maybe 15 minutes is fine. Set a minimum time. You'll sit there for 15 minutes.

Don't expect anything in the beginning. Just to do it is enough. It's like jogging. The first few times you do it you're not gonna suddenly be running marathons.

But if you do it every day for a little while, you'll find that time will increase by itself. It won't be as hard. It'll feel good and pretty soon you'll be amazed at what you can do.

Or in the case of meditation: not do, or undo.

If you've been meditating for a while—after a month or so if you're new to meditation, or two months—work it up to a half an hour. After six months or a year, maybe 45 minutes, twice a day.

You'll sleep less, have a lot more energy, and you'll begin to become conscious of consciousness, of awareness.

Meditation gives you personal power. You'll notice that people will treat you very differently—as you progress—because they can feel that power or that energy.

Naturally, it's the hope of those of us who teach meditation—particularly the release of the kundalini, which is a very powerful form of meditation—that you use that power wisely.

And if you search your heart, I think you will.

You'll learn through experience like everyone. Experience is the great teacher.

You'll have to go through the trials and tribulations—and the ecstasies and abandoned moments of wonderfulness—that all of us did on the way to enlightenment.

It's a great, great life we lead.

But it causes substantial changes in the way that you see life.

Because the way you see life is the way you've been taught to see life. You've been programmed, brainwashed to see life in very specific forms. Some of them may be useful forms, but still they're specific forms.

Life is endless. And we are a body of perception. We're an awareness … that's endless.

And as you meditate, you experience different parts of that perception. And as perception alters, the universe alters. Because the universe is only perception.

So in the beginning when you're sitting meditating, just ignore thought. Pay no attention. Shine it on.

Then after you're comfortable with sitting there—you've been meditating a month or two—try selectively eliminating negative thoughts.

By that I mean, thoughts that draw you into the world of unhappiness, that agitate your mind.

So rather than worrying about your exam that you've gotta take—or your career, or the person you're in love with, or whatever it may be—begin to have thought control.

MEDITATION AND KUNDALINI

You can practice it during the day, also. But start in your meditations.

And meditate and think positive thoughts. If you must think, think good thoughts, happy thoughts, constructive thoughts. You'll find that sometimes while you're sitting there, you'll get a lot of great ideas.

Now granted, you want to go beyond ideas and beyond thought, but that takes years of practice (if not lifetimes) to erase thought—even subconscious thought—completely, for extended periods of eternity.

So in the beginning, we're just stopping thought for a while.

But first just ignore it, then selectively work with your thoughts.

And then you'll begin to move into periods of no-thought. It'll just happen, and you won't realize it's happened until you've started to think again, and you'll think, "Boy, I wasn't thinking." [audience chuckles]

It's good to meditate in the early evening if you can.

Ideally one would meditate in the morning. Clear yourself. Bring in a lot of kundalini, a lot of energy. Go out into the day. Have an exciting day. Come back, slightly worn by the day, but feeling good, having learned in the school of life.

Come back. Meditate again and clear yourself again.

It's very easy to mediate at sunset. There's a doorway that opens between the worlds at the time of the setting sun. It's very easy to still your thoughts.

Sometimes it's fun to meditate outside. Be creative! Meditate at the beach. On a mountain top. In the desert. Wherever you're comfortable. Don't get hung up in rituals or routines.

How do you end a meditation session?

It's nice to chant a mantra again. Maybe repeat it a few times. It seals the meditation.

You'll notice sometimes after a meditation, I bow. Wonderful for the stomach muscles. [audience chuckles]

What am I doing? You don't have to do it that way, you can just do it inside. You don't have to give it physical form.

You're giving the meditation away. You have a meditation. You do your best, and then you just give it to eternity.

Don't judge your meditations. Don't rate them. The mind—the physical mind—cannot tell, how well you did.

So if you start to think, "Gee that was a good one, that was a bad one,"—nonsense. There's no such thing. The only bad meditation is when you don't meditate. As long as you're sitting there trying, something will happen.

But you will not necessarily feel the positive effect of your meditation experience, perhaps for a half an hour or an hour after you've ended the meditation.

Then suddenly everything will get very clear. You'll just feel very good; a sense of well-being. This is the preliminary, the beginning.

You don't stay with well-being, you move to ecstatic consciousness; perceptions about life, eternity.

You become the cosmos. It just depends how far you want to go with it. That's up to you.

Kundalini can be used in a lot of different ways. Essentially in the beginning, you're just trying to get it moving within yourself. Everyone has kundalini. It's already there.

But it's a question of waking it up.

As I suggested before, the subtle physical body must be intact. If there are problems with the subtle body, it's very hard for the kundalini to flow.

A certain amount of the kundalini is always floating through the ida and the pingala, these two little subtle nerve tubes, on either side of the shushumna—which is the central tube in the subtle physical body. And that's what keeps us alive.

When the subtle physical body is damaged, you'll begin to notice changes in your skin. When your skin starts to get kind of gnarly. Dry, problems with it.

Now I'm not speaking of acne. Acne is not necessarily a problem with the subtle physical body, it just means that you have a lot of kundalini which stimulates the hormones.

But when you see deterioration in the skin, or the hair particularly, you're having problems with the subtle body. You're taking in too much bad energy—usually from people—or you're thinking too many negative thoughts.

You're just on the wrong circuit. You're pulling an energy that is not suitable for the human life form.

The human life form vibrates at a certain rate, but all vibratory rates are not suitable for human life.

So it's very necessary to meditate on higher octave energy, on the clear light, on joy, on happiness, peace.

If you try and pull too much power through too soon, you'll injure yourself.

The kundalini can be transmitted. You're trying to awaken it—bring it through you—it brings you into other states of consciousness.

But it can also be transmitted. A person who is very adept at the kundalini, who has a great deal of it, who's gone through this enlightenment process, can transmit it—and that's, of course, what I do.

When you're sitting here, I'm taking the kundalini and moving it through you. Some of you—if you're sensitive, of course—you'll feel it. If not, you won't.

But it still has an effect. It's like a radiation. Whether you feel it or not, it's affecting you in a very positive way.

You may notice during the meditation, sometimes, I'm moving my hands and doing different things. What I'm doing is moving the kundalini in very specific ways.

It's kind of like reaching into another dimensional plane, and pulling the kundalini through, and moving it through you in specific ways and forms.

So you can transmit the kundalini physically when people are there, of course, long distance. It's energy. Interdimensional energy.

It's much easier for women to meditate than it is for men, innately.

And it has to do with the nature of a woman's subtle physical body. The subtle physical body of a man and woman is slightly different. Both a man and woman can meditate well. But women will just find it a little bit easier. They have to do a little less work. That's all.

Because their subtle physical bodies pick up the kundalini much more quickly. They vibrate at a slightly different rate, it passes very easily.

But that's also problematic, because a woman also picks up bad energy or negative energy. It affects her more—hate, anger—things like that affect her subtle physical more.

Sensitivity is a two-way street. When you're sensitive you can feel and appreciate, but you can also be injured more easily.

But women find it very easy to release the kundalini, and bring it through their beings.

The kundalini brings about changes—structured changes in the being. We're reordering the self.

We're made up of a series of awarenesses.

Beyond the subtle physical body we have something called the causal body. And that's more what we are.

We're a series of interconnecting awarenesses.

It's possible—it's like a molecular bond, a DNA, a double helix—we can change that. That's what self-discovery is.

Self-discovery is a very advanced art. What we're doing basically is screwing around with what you're made up of.

We're taking awarenesses—feelings, ideas, impressions—and changing them. We do that with ourselves.

As you expose yourself again and again to the power of meditation—to the kundalini—you're changing that, and refining it, enlarging it.

You have a house that has many, many rooms in it, but you've only seen a few. But there are so many. And then there's beyond the house. There's the outdoors. The endless universe.

You are sitting on this little planet—spaceship Earth. But the universe is very accessible to you. You don't need a spaceship to travel there. And most of the worlds are non-physical.

And it's all God, it's all eternity.

ॐ

I'm going to teach you another meditation technique.

This one is very simple. It's a focus on the heart center.

The heart center is the principal chakra. There are three above, and three below. It's the central axis of the being.

What I would like you to do—it's very simple—is to focus on this spot, and to feel love.

Now, how do you feel love? Spontaneously?

Well, you can think of someone you love, or something you love. A nice experience that you've had. Anything to get the flow started.

> The patient is on the table. Not breathing.
>
> We've gotta get that—We're gonna pound that sucker [Rama mimics a CPR chest thump and says, *"Pow!"*] to get him started.
>
> Once he's started—[Rama, *"Gasp!"*] you see, then the heart will get going again.

But we can do it more delicately.

What we're going to do is feel love. That's going to get something in us started. That's going to get our awareness moving. Light flowing through our consciousness.

So what I'd like you to do is simply to focus on this center. [Rama gestures to the center of his chest]

If you like, you might visualize a flower, or feel that there's a flower there. But it's like a rose, and it's all folded up.

And as you meditate, feel—you don't have to see a mental picture—but just feel the flower is opening. That there're all these petals—they're closed up.

And gradually they're opening up, and there's set after set of petals. And as each set of petals opens up, it's a little larger than the first set.

- ॐ The first set that opens up will kind of fill a small area. Real slowly and gracefully ... they'll open up. And light will go through your being.
- ॐ The second set will open up, and maybe it'll fill the chest area, very gracefully.
- ॐ A third set will open, and fill the whole body.
- ॐ A fourth set, the room.
- ॐ A fifth set, the whole sky.
- ॐ A sixth set, the universe.
- ॐ The seventh set, all of eternity and so on.

Endless petals opening up.

Each time you open up a set of petals, you're going deeper into the self. Deeper into nirvana. Deeper into eternal awareness.

When thoughts come in and out of your mind just ignore them.

You might try meditating that way with the eyes closed for a few minutes. You might try meditating then with the eyes open. It's good to learn to meditate that way.

We call it *gazing*. Just looking forward, without a singular focus.

And you can *see* the kundalini actually moving through the air. Other than the light changes, of course.

There are other changes taking place. As you watch my hands, you may notice energy flowing through them. It's going through you.

It's the transmission of the kundalini.

So we'll meditate again for about 10 minutes. And you'll notice that this meditation will be quite different.

Try and feel love. We're meditating on love this time. It's the strongest force in the universe.

Now we're just going to open ourselves up to it, and just let it carry us.

There're a lot of wonderful people here and we're all networking our energy together. We're getting high together. And they can't do *anything* about it. [audience laughs] So let's try.

So sit up nice and straight please. Focus on the center of the chest. Relax. Relax. Enjoy yourself. This is your life. [audience chuckles] Exactly.

And imagine a flower there, if you like, or just focus on that spot for a few minutes. And feel it unfolding. Let yourself go. Ignore your thoughts. And let's meditate.

[Live music plays and the meditation begins. It lasts 15 minutes.]

Please sit back and relax.

It's a good idea when you meditate, to avoid eating for a few hours before you meditate, because otherwise, you just feel your body too much. You really don't want to feel the body.

If you're very, very hungry though, you should have something to eat, because otherwise you'll just sit there ... and think of food. [audience chuckles]

Which is not the worst thing to think of, granted!

Kundalini flows in different directions. Some people are under the assumption that the kundalini just flows from the base of the spine up. That's not the case at all. It flows a lot of different ways. Kundalini also flows down. Downward.

You can take the kundalini from the crown center—which is an access point—and bring it down. You can bring it up, or you can stabilize them both.

When you stop breathing in meditation, the kundalini is stabilized.

When you go into samadhi, very often you won't breathe for half an hour, an hour, there's no breath at all.

The kundalini—the life force—is perfectly stabilized.

Usually they stabilize in the solar plexus area. You can stabilize it anywhere, actually. But that's the most common.

The kundalini can be used for a lot of purposes. Healing disease, obviously. Healing the mind.

More importantly, it can be used to help awaken someone—to life.

We're all asleep. This is a dream—that we're in this world.

We're trying to wake up.

We have this recurring dream—is that we're human beings—that we have bodies, that we're in time and space, that there's birth and death. We keep having this dream, day after day.

To awaken from the dream … of life—or to *see* endless dreams—or to go beyond the dream to nirvana.

To be conscious of eternity, and yet to be here, and to be aware. Of the moment!

Meditation. Never leave the body without it.

I'd like to answer a few questions, about meditation and the kundalini specifically, for a few minutes.

We'll be doing another meditation after a while. It'll be our final one for the evening. But that won't be for a while yet.

And if you have a question, I'd like you to raise your hand. If you could say it nice and loudly so I can hear you, it would be helpful, and I'll repeat the question for everyone else, because they probably won't be able to hear. So if you have a question, please raise your hand.

It's such a vast area—meditation and the kundalini. You may have specific interests.

When you meditate at home sometimes it's good to try very hard. You know, you just want to really just do your absolute best.

Now sometimes—some people say when they start to meditate—they get a headache when they meditate. It's because they're trying too hard. You're pulling in too much energy. It's like eating too much and then you feel sick afterwards.

So if you just feel any ill effects, it means you're trying too hard.

But tonight it's really not necessary for you to try very hard. Because there's just so much kundalini surging, that if you try too hard, it'll just get—you'll get in your own way. You see?

It's best just to let go, and leave it, this evening. That'd be the easiest.

To try and not to try. It goes back and forth. To strive, not to strive. There are different ways of talking about something that's really beyond words. It's an experience, which is why we meditate together.

You see, real higher meditation is not taught through techniques or words. These are the beginning steps. It's how we start someone. And everyone has to go through that process. Really. You have to learn the basics. One can never be too proud to learn how to begin, again.

But the real meditation experience is taught—it's either just learned, of course, through practice naturally—but it's taught inwardly.

In other words, you shift a person through different dimensional planes.

But they have to do the prep, for you to be able to do that, as a teacher. So it's necessary for you to meditate on your own, and just refine your consciousness. Tighten up your life.

You know, constantly examine your life and look for weak points. Are your relationships sloppy? Are your emotions sloppy? Or are they tight? Are you loving and giving, or are you being selfish and weird? You know, what's going on in your life?

As you meditate, you get clearer on that. You get clearer on the fact that you can shape and mold your life. You can be an architect of your own destiny.

Most people, they lead their lives like they drive their cars. [audience chuckles] And you can be more precise.

You can lead a life poorly or very well. So meditation gives you the energy, and also the insight to do that.

How should we meditate—hard, easily ... ?

Every meditation is unique. There is no absolute rule. That's what makes it fun. You have to feel out each situation and try as you go.

So if you're sitting there meditating one day, and you're meditating on the heart center ... it's been great the last three times, this time nothing—don't stay with it, switch.

Do something else. Be creative. Meditate on your navel center. Do another exercise. Switch it around. Don't be bound.

Stop for a minute. You're sitting there, it's just not happening. Stop, take a break for a moment. Walk around. Sit down try again. Try a different room. A different energy. Every place has different energy. Be creative in your meditation.

So tonight if you're sitting there, and you're trying real hard, and it's just not kicking over for you, don't try so hard, obviously. You see, every situation is different. But there's just so much energy tonight that it's not necessary.

Questions. Yes.

[Rama repeats the question]

How do you deal with the fact that you're meditating at home and sometimes you stop breathing. And your question is how do you deal with that?

[Rama holds his breath, gasps, falls down, to audience laughter]

How do you deal with it? Well, I don't know.

I can remember when that started happening to me about 15 years ago. And I wouldn't breathe, and then suddenly become real uptight because you're not breathing. Your mind says …

[Rama mimics terror, gasping] "I'm not breathing! I'm supposed to be breathing! God, I'm not breathing! [Gasp!]" [audience chuckles]

Then you realize, all you did was just bring yourself down from a nice meditation.

The trick is to meditate just a little higher and you won't even know that you're not breathing. So then it isn't a problem.

Because as long as you're in the plane where you know you're not breathing, you know you're going to think about it ...

Try not to think about an armadillo with a purple beret. [audience laughs]

Good luck! Here he comes now. [audience laughs]

Right?

So you know you're not breathing. It's good you're not breathing. You don't need to breathe so much. People breathe too much, listen. [audience laughs]

If everybody would breathe less, there'd be more oxygen on the planet. [audience chuckles] Rama's suggestion.

So you don't need to breathe. It's happening by itself. But your mind will tell you you do, because we've been conditioned to think that we need to breathe.

And you don't need to breathe so much. I mean, breathing is nice. It's OK. But it's nothing to get attached to. [audience chuckles]

It's a matter of just ignoring that whole experience. It's just another place to get stuck.

As you're meditating, you're stuck to start out with. You're stuck in your thoughts.

It's like your feet are in, you know, Bonomo Turkish Taffy or something. You know, "Ughhhhhh. " You're trying to get them out. And then you get one free, and then you get the other one free, and then finally you're going, but then along the way there are little things that kind of "Whoosh, ulp, ah!" grab you. See? And those are all your attachments.

You know, you're having a great meditation, thoughts stop, you're cruising along and then suddenly ... the love of your life comes into your mind.

He/she or it is sitting at home thinking about you.

[Rama mimics a greedy, snarling voice and audience chuckles]

> "Reaching out! Whoosh! Throwing a lasso of occult energy around things.
>
> "Don't go so fast there! Think about me!"
>
> [audience laughs and claps]

[normal voice]

Now, of course, if you're not experienced in the ways of occult power, you'll assume that you're just thinking about Susie or Bill or, you know, the armadillo or whatever you're into.

And you won't realize that they are—because human beings are very strong, and they all radiate kundalini and energy—inserting themselves into *your* thoughts. It's true. It's true.

It's a good idea, if you're going to have a really good meditation, to unplug the phone.

Because you'd be surprised. Boy, that's—that's one you learn early. Because just when it's finally happening, "Rrrring!"

[mimics nerd father]

> "Hi, son." [audience explodes in laughter]

Whatever it may be, right, you know. And it's like [mimics surprise, gasping] "Ah, ah, ah, ah!"

The energy crackles along the line. [mimics electricity crackling, audience chuckles]

Another question. Yes.

[Rama listens to a woman's question]

I would think so, yeah.

OK. So, your problem is, then, that you live in a—as you said—a multi-room dwelling where different people live, known as a rooming house.

And that there's a fellow who lives in the room next to you, who—as you put it very poetically—has a drinking problem.

And that when he starts to rave and scream, as you said, it—and like he puts out a lot of bad energy—and you're sitting in your room, and you notice … the flowers are wilting [audience laughs] and stuff like that.

So your question, then, is—I'm just repeating it for all to hear—your question is, How can you put out an energy that will kind of protect you from that experience?

Well, the obvious answer is "Move," naturally. [audience chuckles] That's the easiest.

Because when it's real serious, you know, it's gonna be a battle every step of the way. But if that just isn't in the cards—you really like the room, or you're just determined, or you signed the lease, or whatever, and you're stuck with it …

Then, you need to turn your room into a place of … Power!

[mimics a spooky voice] "Wooooo." [audience chuckles] Yeah.

It's a good idea to have flowers around, candles, incense. You know, happy things. Make your room a beautiful place.

I mean, you should always do that with your house anyway. You should have beauty wherever you are. Because life is so pretty.

And so just make your room really beautiful, and just keep it very clean. Impeccably clean. All the closets in order, drawers. Everything in it's perfect place.

And just turn on music, when he screams. That's the best, I think, personally. A walk-person, headphones. You know.

There's not much you can do, except feel that he doesn't exist.

Ah! This is the trick. What you can do ... Some people get this kundalini-sway business.

It's possible—now, I don't know if you can do this, but I can do this—it's possible to block out any noise.

Not by blocking it out, but by expanding your attention level—so that it's so vast, that it's just another part of eternity—and you do not apply a specific mental charge to it.

In other words, that particular sound or those vibrations that person is sending out, are offending you. They are offending your sensibility. They hurt your subtle body.

But it's possible to go up high enough where everything's sort of a white noise. Everything blends together, if you can do that.

In the beginning, that's pretty hard though. I'd move. That's my advice.

But just—if you don't do that—just make your own life as tight as possible.

Don't think badly of the person. Because what can they do? I mean this is his karma, right? He can't help it. He's got a weak subtle physical body, so he drinks.

Life hurts sometimes real badly. Who knows?

I mean, we should never criticize or judge a person who does things like that, because who knows what they've been through in their life? Some people have some pretty rough lives and he's just killing the pain. That's all he's doing.

But naturally, you're in a different place. You're vibrating at a different cycle. So you have to do something about it.

I'd move, or just try and be very compassionate and understanding and play music. Little things. Little practical applications.

But if you can—in your heart—understand what's going on, it's easier to deal with it. Because obviously this person has had a tough incarnation.

Question. Yes.

[a man in the audience asks a question, which Rama repeats]

Ah! Yes. So you're saying that sometimes, when you meditate, you're kind of going beyond the body, and then you notice that your body is just sort of tilting or falling, or something like that, yeah?

[audience member elaborates]

Yeah. Right. And that brings you back. So that's not a good thing. What you need to do is, learn to discipline your body to sit there. You can do this when you go into very advanced states of attention.

And the way you do it, is just by gently correcting yourself. When you meditate, your body shouldn't move.

Some people get this kundalini-sway business. You know? It's nauseating to watch them meditate. [audience chuckles]

[mimics barfing] OK, you get a whole room like that and it's like … [mimics more barfing, audience laughs]. You bring Dramamine to the meditations. [audience laughs]

So, the body should be kept still. And if you find yourself leaning during a meditation, then correct yourself. Gently, don't worry about bringing yourself down, that's fine. Correct yourself. You just have to do it a few times. You know, you make a little habit of it. As soon as you start to go off, bring yourself right back.

And you'll find after a while the body will know that and it will just stay that way.

The only time that there will be variances … in samadhi.

In nirvikalpa samadhi you go completely beyond this world, beyond the physical level of attention, and the body just, "poof". [Rama chuckles]

That's it. It doesn't stay, it's gone. Erased. [audience chuckles]

Doesn't matter. You don't care. But.

Huh?

[audience member asks a question]

Yeah. Your body is, yes. Exactly. Your body's distracting.

That's why I'm saying, if you take the time to—every time—observe your body for awhile, and correct yourself.

In other words, this problem could go on your whole life.

Better you should take a little time and correct it early, now, and just pay a little attention to your posture. Every once in a while, check yourself during the meditation.

And you might think, "Well, that's gonna bring me down." That's OK.

If you do it just for a little while, for a month or so, it'll become a routine. You'll never have to do it again. Otherwise you're going to deal with this thing forever. See what I mean?

So just use a little tighter physical attention on it, and it'll work out fine.

Question. Yes. There's somebody back over there.

[audience member asks a question, which Rama repeats]

OK. If your subtle body is damaged, how can you tell where it's damaged, and how do you repair it?

I wouldn't so much worry about *where* it's damaged. Because usually it's not a specific place. It can be.

But usually, it's just more of an erosion of the whole subtle physical body. It's just not sort of healthy.

What can you do about it?

Well, first of all, naturally you have to stop the harm that's being done to it. But even actually before that, you have to realize that there's harm being done to it. Let me give you an example.

Let's say that you go up in the mountains, and it's real cold up there. And you come into the cabin and it's just freezing, it's 10 below zero. Even some of the windows are open. They have to be boarded up. It's just a mess.

The first thing to do is light a fire. The first thing, light the fire. Don't worry about the windows. Light the fire.

Once the fire is going, that'll provide a certain amount of warmth. And with that warmth you can then take your time, and fill in the biggest holes to start with. The biggest losses. And the heat will spread and you'll get warmer.

Then you can gradually get the little ones, until there's no heat loss whatsoever. Also you can make the fire larger, whatever.

So with the subtle physical body—and with one's attention field—we start first by generating energy, the kundalini.

You've got to make yourself warm. You need energy and life force, to *see* and feel what you need to do.

Otherwise you're in a dark room, and you can't tell what's going on.

So to begin with, you just need to practice more meditation. That's the best thing you can do. And to meditate well.

Some people, they, you know—I talk to them, and they—"Oh I meditate for four hours a day."

And you look at their consciousness and it's like *"luuughh"* [Rama mimics gagging].

You meditate for four hours a day? You know, they're obviously not meditating for four hours a day, they're sitting there spacing out. They're not meditating.

There's a large difference between spacing out into the lower occult astral planes—just kind of this weird junky, fuzzy energy—and meditation.

Meditation is sharp [Rama snaps his fingers], clear [snaps fingers], precise, perfect, luminous, shiny, happy, etheric, cosmic, dissolute. It has various forms and formlessnesses.

But it's not this kind of spacey stuff, that then makes it difficult to orient to your life.

If that's your experience of meditation, you're not meditating. You're tapping into the lower astral planes, which is not a healthy place for human beings to tap.

So you need to have good, clear, sharp, precise meditations that are filled with love and light and energy. Then you can address questions in your life.

And you start with the biggest energy losses.

The biggest energy losses for most people are relationships, interrelations with other people. That where we lose most energy. Through our attachments.

Or just by opening ourselves up to people who may be very nice on the surface, but underneath they have a lot of problems.

And when we open our heart up to someone, that energy, of course, comes into us.

So you just have to start to examine the people in your life, and ask yourself if you're really having fun with them. Sometimes we keep relationships going with people who aren't what they used to be. They're not the people we knew and liked. They've changed. We've changed.

But we keep up this association because we're afraid to make a jump to something new. And we die inwardly.

When we're young, we were little kids—we'd change, we'd make new friends all the time—we're alive, we're growing. But we get scared as adults. We get too conservative. We die.

So begin by looking at your relationships.

And usually what you do is, you just take out a piece of paper—two actually—and on one piece of paper, just put down all the people you know and associate with, who you feel are adding more to your life than they're taking.

And then on the other piece of paper, put all the people you know—list them—who are taking more than they're adding.

You should also include people from the past. Just because you're not physically close to someone doesn't mean that there isn't an interaction of energy.

You may not have seen your ex-wife for 10 years. But there can be an interaction taking place.

Then what you need to do, when you find any that you feel are not happening—they're not generating energy—you need to cut those inside yourself.

At the umbilical region we actually network with people.

And so what you can do, there's a little exercise ... where you just can picture, if you want to ... that you're cutting these cords that go out to everyone you know.

And as you do that, you create a sense of detachment. It doesn't mean you don't love them. It just means you're cutting down on the negative energy pickup from people. The people who hurt you are the ones you love, because you're most open to them.

Then, of course, you have to look at your own thought forms.

Are you sitting around thinking a lot of negative thoughts?

These injure the subtle body. When you hate. When you're angry. You bring that energy through you.

Are you focusing too much on the lower occult? The lower astral? Are you contacting entities and strange low-vibe beings in weird worlds?

If you do that, you're accessing energies that are *very* bad for the subtle physical.

You should be focusing more on light—energy, storing personal power—whatever it may be.

But there's certain neighborhoods that are not healthy to traverse.

Then of course, it gets much deeper, naturally. Then we get into self-discovery. That's my specialty.

And that's dissecting someone inwardly. Looking at the different selves. Making changes in them and so on and so forth. It's what we call the Tibetan Rebirth Process.

It's a very complex process of changing levels of attention. Changing selves around and so forth. It's all done inwardly with the kundalini.

That's the art of self-discovery, advanced self-discovery.

But first you have to go through all those preliminary stages, and also there are obvious physical things you can do.

Spend time in nature. Get away from the city once in awhile. Go jogging down on the beach. The ocean is a wonderful place—you know, if there's not too many people around—to be.

To draw in a lot of prana, a lot of good energy.

Have a lot of plants in your house. Happy things. Plants generate energy. Make friends with them. Transact with nature. Nature is energy. It's prana. It's healing.

Drink lots of water—it has a lot of prana in it. Things like that.

Physical exercise—anything that's aerobic where you're moving a lot—jogging, tennis, swimming, long distance walking, hopping [audience chuckles], you know, whatever.

Be very careful whom you love. Not how much, but whom.

All the usual spiritual stuff, you know.

And then the subtle body will begin to return.

A lot of people trash their subtle physical body with drugs. Psychedelic drugs and things like that, while they do certainly give you experiences in altered levels of attention, you pay a price for it.

They create some awakenings, but they definitely screw up the subtle physical.

And so sometimes … Yoga's very good for that. Hatha Yoga, that's good.

Sometimes fasting, not excessively, you know, with … But that can be good.

Lots of things. Whatever, whatever makes you feel good.

You might be listening to music, things like that. Just find what makes you feel gentle.

What makes you feel still. And people who have that effect upon you.

I mean, sometimes it's fun to just be crazy with energy and laugh and be silly. Don't misunderstand. That can be very regenerative. But you need the stillness too.

What is the relationship between the kundalini force and the sex force? The sexual drive *is* kundalini.

Really, any energy within us is a form of kundalini, so it's a particular fragrance or aspect of kundalini.

Now, like all things, they're neither good nor bad—it's how they're applied. And I wouldn't even say the effect is good or bad, but there is what we call karma.

Karma simply means that there's a reaction for an action. There's cause and effect in the world of duality.

So the sexual energy then becomes problematic, if you use it to enslave someone, to demoralize them, to hurt them, to wrap them up.

In other words, the way most people use sexual energy is to hook somebody. They use it to wrap them, to get control over them.

Some people use the sexual energy—particularly during intercourse—to take personal power from each other. Or it's just a gratification of a physical sensation. You know, there are lots of ways it can be used. But those ways don't engender a rise in consciousness.

If you use that energy to love somebody, then it works a little better in terms of raising one's level of attention.

Some people say that if you have sex, you can't be enlightened. That's not my point of view. I think it isn't really so much whether you have sex or not, but it's what you're doing with your attention level during that time. That's the issue.

In other words, if you can meditate and be very high—regardless of what you're doing—then that's what you're doing. You're meditating.

But you have to be able just to slash through your desires to do that. Because otherwise, you get so caught up in physical sensation, you know—pleasure, this, that and the other thing—that you're distracted from meditating. So you have to have a very intense degree of detachment and determination to do that.

But then it can become a cosmic experience, you see, as everything is.

But the kundalini and sex are extremely interrelated. The sexual drive is part of the kundalini.

That's why it's funny because some people who have a lot of sexual energy—they think of themselves as being not spiritual, because they have a lot of sexual energy. And that's like, "tee-hee, how silly," … they're probably *more* spiritually inclined.

All that sexual energy is kundalini. That's all it is. They'd probably do really, really well in meditation.

But because in certain books they say [Rama mimics authoritative voice] "Well you know, blah, blah, you know … uuurrr," [audience chuckles] … uh, and you figure you're kinky, right? And you figure, what hope is there for me?

Well, from my point of view, you'll probably do better, because you have more life force, more energy, and it's just manifesting.

But what you need to do, is take some of that energy, and use it in some other ways, in addition to sexuality, you see.

It's a very healthy sign. It means you're alive. You've got a lot of life force.

So you're trying to give it away. [audience chuckles]

Nice of you! [audience laughs]

Such a guy! [audience chuckles]

Now if you're interested in developing the *siddhas,* the occult powers *("whoosh"),* all that stuff, you have to be a little more conservative—unless you're very, very far along—because there is a certain drop of a type of kundalini when you have sex.

So if you're into developing the supernatural powers, then it's a good idea to be a little more temperate.

Some occult teachers suggest celibacy. I don't know.

But in terms of spiritual development, meditative development, enlightenment, and so on, it's not a big deal whether you have sex or not, the question is more of who you have sex with, and what their energy is doing to you.

Because if you're having sex with someone who's not on the same frequency that you're on, it can be very problematic. Because the greatest transfer—karmic transfer—occurs in ... aside from meditating with someone ... in sex with someone.

Particularly for women, because women tend to open themselves up more.

And just because their subtle physical bodies are so much more sensitive, they pick up the total energy of the man they have sex with.

And so it's a real problem, because a lot of men hate women subconsciously, or just are very confused about them, or are afraid of their power, or want to suppress them, or, you know, the usual.

And so when they have sex with someone what happens is—on the one hand they're having a good time or they're trying to do this, or perform or whatever ... you know, it's Ed Sullivan, [Rama mimics making an introduction] "Hey!" [audience laughs] But ... gotcha ... yeah.

But the problem is, that ... it's not Ed Sullivan. And that's *somebody*. And you're affecting their attention level, incredibly.

And if you have a lot of problems inside yourself, they transfer. So it's, it's good to be selective and to love a whole lot and not be attached.

It's ... it's a very delicate balance. And the further along you go—the more delicate the balance—it's the razor's edge that we walk in advanced self-discovery.

So what I'm trying to say is, it isn't important what you do or what you don't do, it's how.

And by "how," I don't mean *Kama Sutra* Position Number 95 [audience chuckles]. You know, "Hanging from one foot from a large building."

[audience chuckles] You know, while chanting the mantra, "fwam!" [audience laughs]

But rather the quality of your love. That's what I mean. The quality of your attention. Your ability to maintain a sense of love and giving, without any ownership. Without any possessiveness. Without any jealousy. Without any greed.

A sense of the total sensitivity of this universe that you're colliding with, and trying to be perfect for that universe, without any egotism or vanity whatsoever.

It's the [makes *shuuuuu* sound] … it's a very fine line.

And if you don't do that, if you're not able to do that exactly correctly, it comes back on you, naturally. It's a very quick karma and your level of attention drops.

And afterwards you don't get along. You don't feel so good. You're energy's down.

That's because you didn't … it was not a transcendent experience, because you didn't care enough and give enough, and you got lazy, sloppy and selfish. Like most people.

But it doesn't have to be that way. You could be one in a billion, why not? What the heck? It's worth taking a shot at, you know. Practice. Keep me informed. [audience laughs]

Oh, one or two more, then we have to meditate.

Yes. Another one. Yes?

[woman asks a question]

Oh yeah, you wrap them up with your second attention. Yeah. Most people do.

Right. It's a habit, yeah. Uh, yeah, women are very good at it particularly. You men do it too, in a different way.

But women have really developed it as an art. They've had to, to survive.

You understand—the world the way men have designed it—if you can't use that power, then what else have you got? Right, you know?

So, but the problem with it is, it limits you. It puts you into a control situation. And even though you can control someone and it protects you in a certain extent, still you're in a controlling situation—in duality—it brings you down.

So what you really need to do is—I would suggest—is first of all, *watch* how much you do it. It's fascinating.

Because we're brought up and educated to do it. You know, it's … and then you need to be around people who aren't like that. I mean, people who have decided that there's another way to lead their life, and it's not necessary to wrap people up.

The reason you're doing it, is because you don't have enough power. If you had enough power—if you could unlock your own personal power—you wouldn't need to control others.

So you need to be around people who've learned there's another way of leading life.

And if you can find people like that—who feel good to you, and you're around them, and that's how they lead their lives—you'll find that it's catching.

It's a happy disease to get. And that's … You don't have to control people.

And you can—you can easily stop them from controlling you.

But you have to be able to *see* to do that. You have to develop your psychic abilities, and increase your personal power and, you know, all the usual things. But, yeah, it can be done.

But I don't have a simple technique for you. It's a way of life.

Some of us lead lives like that, and we have a good time. [makes a silly, happy sound]

One more. Uh-huh.

[man asks a question]

How do you, how do you … ? Let's say you're going to meditate. If you're very new to meditation—you're just starting—I suggest that you have a watch or a clock by you and set a minimum amount of time.

Chances are, what you're going to be doing is referring to it occasionally. Because after five minutes you're going to say, [mimics a cranky voice] "I have to sit here longer?" [audience laughs]

See, so you set 15 minutes, let's say, as a minimum. You're going to sit there and no matter what you think, songs are running through your head, you're thinking a million things you never would think, "This is never gonna work." Doesn't matter. Sit there. Do the 15 minutes.

After that you'll find, after a few weeks, that it becomes very comfortable and suddenly you'll look down at the watch and 20 minutes have gone by, or 25.

So what you want to do is, sit as long as it feel good. Once you've reached a minimum time and you've just gotten used to that, then just sit as long as it feels good.

Sometimes it's fun to set little hurdles for yourself. It depends. There are different ways to go about this. There's not one right way. Some people like to set hurdles, so then they'll try half an hour as a minimum time.

Other people would feel uptight if they did that. It wouldn't be a natural flow for them. So maybe it's better then just to see how long you sit. When it stops feeling good, you'll just find yourself stopping.

Sometimes you'll start out, you might meditate on the heart center, or in one of these various methods, you know, that I'll show you. Or rather as I'll show you another night, and—or that you've learned elsewhere—and you meditate for 15 or 20 minutes, it's wonderful.

Then suddenly, you'll feel your consciousness, logging back too much on the physical. The thing to do is, then maybe do a different technique for a few minutes. And what you're doing when you do that, is bringing kundalini through, and then you're riding that kundalini for a while.

A time comes when you don't have to use meditation techniques anymore. You just sit down and you're nonexistence itself.

So as far as time is concerned, just as long as it feels really good—once you've reached the point where you're past the minimum time. Good.

We're going to do one more meditation technique to close it out here. And this one will be the most powerful. So please listen carefully. This one's a little complicated. So I need your second attention here.

What I would like you to do—in a minute—is sit up straight.

And for the first couple minutes of meditation, I'd like you to focus right around the back of the neck. There's a chakra that a lot of people don't know about.

Most people are aware of the basic seven, or the ones in the hands or the feet. But there's some other more hidden energy centers in the subtle physical body.

There's one around the back of the neck—OK, it's just, just kind of, oh—around the top of the neck.

And put your hand back there, just for a second. Just feel that area, back there.

Feel your neck, sort of, then come up, just about to the top of it, where you're connecting with the head.

Never thought of it that way did you—good thing, huh? Yeah. [audience chuckles]

Right around there. That's where you're gonna be focusing. To start with.

What I'd like you to do, is to start focusing your attention right there, and then take that energy and feel that it's gonna transmit from there in two lines … to your hands.

I don't want you to move your hands, do anything with your hands. Just put them in a comfortable position. You might put them on your lap. Some people hold them like this. Or just any way you want.

But just *feel* that two lines of energy are going to move out from here to your hands.

And when they hit your hands, you'll kind of feel a warming sensation. And then from the hands, we're gonna bounce that energy right back to the heart center. And ground it.

We're taking a very occult or a very mystical energy, and we're shooting it through, then we're gonna bring it into the psychic being. And it's done in waves like we did before.

So we're going to start with the energy here, and then just feel it pulsing towards your hands.

You can visualize lines of light—if you like, or not—just feel it going there. It doesn't matter whether it travels in a straight line, or through your arms, whatever. It gets there.

Just feel the energy going there—and it's going right to the very center of the palms. And then it's going to bounce back.

This is a more advanced technique now, so it's a little stronger.

And then it's gonna bounce back, and go right into the heart center.

So it's just out and back. Out and back. Just do that in a rhythmic way, for just a couple minutes. And then stop. Let go. Go with the music.

Then open your eyes a little bit, and watch me meditate. Just observe, without looking too hard. You don't want to focus too sharply.

You just kind of, you want to …

You're not just watching me, the body. You're watching the energy fields, here.

You're relaxing your eyes, not looking too sharply. *Gazing.* You're just watching. You're letting go.

Then you might try closing your eyes again—opening them—you know. Whatever is comfortable for you.

So you're gonna start by focusing your attention back here for a few moments. And then just feel this energy moving into your hands any way you want to, as long as it gets there.

And then you're gonna feel it coming back from the hands, right into the heart, right into the psychic center.

And then it just dissolves. It radiates through your whole being there.

What we're doing is taking an occult energy, bringing it into a place—it's like an amplifier, it's amplifying—in the chakras in the hands, and then we are neutralizing it, and spreading it through the being.

And again the hands can be in any position. It doesn't matter. The energy flows. And that would be good.

So please sit up straight and close your eyes for a moment. And focus around the back of the neck to start out with. And let us begin.

[Zazen music plays and the meditation begins. It lasts almost 20 minutes.]

Could you guys stand up for a minute? Stand up. [audience applause]

Thank you. [audience applause, continuing]

On guitar, Joaquin Lievano! Bass and synthesizer, Andy West! A lot of synthesizers, Steve Kaplan!

Two Blisses,[3] lots of astral beings, lots of energy. Thank you very much. Good night. Get one of our free brochures on the way out. Hope to see you again.

Namaste.

---

3. Blisses are hand puppets which Rama discovered. He said these look like beings from an actual very high astral world, with bright colors, big noses, and very happy expressions, always delighted with life.

CHAPTER THREE

ENLIGHTENMENT AND SELF-REALIZATION

Good evening. Tonight we'll be talking about enlightenment and self-realization.

Well, good evening spiritual types. [audience laughter] Anybody who comes to a workshop in self-realization and enlightenment classifies as a spiritual type.

[Rama chooses music from a case and loads the player]

Sometimes I can look at these things for hours! [laughter]

Well, you know, on higher planes of attention, I mean, you can see eternity in anything. It's not necessarily so hard.

Well, tonight, uh … God, anything can happen.

And I'm glad you came! Aww, gosh, gee! So nice to see you! Kisses! [general laughter]

So you want to know about death, eh? I thought I would dress suitably for the occasion. We're celebrating your funeral. Coming soon to a theater near you.

Yes, everyone dies! It's a fact!

That sounded good, didn't it? That was like very intense, and right? Punchy. And good way to get ...

So everyone dies, it's a fact. And then you are reborn again! Big deal.

And then you die again and you're reborn again, and you die again. The average human being has something like 84,000 incarnations.

Yeah! Isn't that ... awesome? 84,000 incarnations. And you're having trouble with one. [great laughter]

So tonight, I thought I would make your life a little more difficult ... and we would discuss how—within a week or two, in your spare time—you can lose all of the good karma you've amassed over all those lifetimes. [laughter]

Now, I would guess that—chances are if you're here tonight—you've had at least 30,000 or 35,000 lifetimes, somewhere in there. Just ball park estimates. But ...

You want to know about [enlightenment]. You really want to know?!

You know what you have to go through? Don't ask.

If you ask, I'll tell you. It's a long, long, long explanation. But it's funny! That's the thing about life.

You see, the chances of *you* attaining liberation—no, be realistic for a moment, down to earth tonight—let's forget all the spiritual jazz and let's talk dollars and cents. [laughter]

The chance of you attaining enlightenment [Rama chuckles aside, audience laughs] ... is probably better than you realize!

No, it's true. Hey, why do you have such a negative attitude about yourselves? Why not feel, it could be you? It could be! ... I wouldn't hold my breath! [great laughter]

ENLIGHTENMENT AND SELF-REALIZATION 135

But it could be! It could be.

Krishna, you know—you've all read the *Bhagavad-Gita* and memorized it, I'm sure [laughter]—Krishna says, to Arjuna, at one point he says, "Arjuna, do you know where I can get a good strawberry shake?" [laughter]

That wasn't in your translation.

Krishna says to Arjuna, he says, "Arjuna, do you know what your chances of attaining enlightenment are like?"

And Arjuna says, "Uh, I don't know man, what do you think?"

He says, "Well, one out of sometimes millions—sometimes billions—attains a full liberation."

That's—I mean—that's a lot of people. Now, you could of course, take that very personally, and say, "What chance do I have? The lottery is a better shot."

But you might have a better chance than you think, because what he's saying is that most people aren't even interested in the subject of meditation, enlightenment and self-realization.

So naturally, they're out of the ballpark. OK, the first cut.

You've eliminated several billion right there. [laughter] So your odds have just improved dramatically. [laughter] See what I mean? So that's why you shouldn't be so negative.

We're talking, of course ... Through the whole Earth, you don't have a chance—but—most people on the Earth could care less about liberation.

So, then, how many are there? How many people do you really think are striving earnestly towards self-realization on this planet right now? Five? Six? No. But, how many?

Oh, thousands! Ten thousand, twenty thousand. Oh, there are many people in different religions and they pray and do things like that.

But they're not going through the training process—that's necessary—the training process that the universe puts you through.

In order to qualify—even to get into the pageant, right—you've got to figure, you've got to have at least 40 - 50,000 incarnations. I mean otherwise, they don't even look at you.

Then you get an audition. And we're talking, you've got to be … good.

Not necessarily. Ah! This is the good news!

You see, most people are under the assumption, that in order to attain enlightenment, self-realization—we'll talk more about those subjects in great detail … later.

But, in order to do that, most people think that you have to be really, really, really good. A sweetie. "Mmmwah!" In love with life, little birds, trees, flowers, everything, happy!!!

All the time! Blithering idiot! [laughter]

>Nuclear bombs? "Wonderful!"

>Pollution? "Good!"

"God is in all things." So, you know, dull-dull-dull.

I mean, God gets *bored* by people like that. Well, you can't have much of a conversation with someone like that.

>"How are you today?" "GREAT!"

You know, where can it go?

>"How's everything in your life?" "WONDERFUL!"

ENLIGHTENMENT AND SELF-REALIZATION

A little less cocaine please! [laughter]

So you want to know about self-realization. Well, you've come to the wrong place. No, the right place. It's someplace, we'll find it.

How do you do this? Well, there are different ways. You've got your (I'm sorry, I have to go through this, just bear with me) you got your Zen. Nice sounding word, isn't it? Zen. Bodhi Dharma started it out. We'll get him!

You got your Tantric Mysticism. Oooh, that sounds gnarly, doesn't it? Yeah, I like that.

You got your Bhakti, the path of love.

You've got your Karma, the path of Hard Work. [laughter] All those interested in the path of Karma Yoga, please line up on this pin over here. [Rama and audience laugh]

[Rama imitates a slacker]

> "Hey, man, like it's the twentieth century, man, like, you know, I can't hassle it, you know, it's like I got a lot to do, man, I just don't have time!
>
> "Wow! I mean, like, I gotta get dressed in the morning? That takes a half an hour, like I gotta take a shower, you know, sometimes I forget to turn the water on.
>
> "And then, like, just the freeways, man, by the time I get home, I'm too tired to like be enlightened, man, I mean it just takes too much energy. You gotta be wealthy, you know, to have the time to do it!"

[normal voice]

So, yes, it's true, enlightenment has become a tool of the wealthy and powerful. [Rama and audience laugh]

So yes, so you've got your paths, your four basic paths. Count them, four.

The path of love—this is ridiculous, I know, "the sermon on the couch"—the path of love [great laughter from the audience, Rama joins in].

Oh, sorry. Well, what do you want? Do you know a hill around where they're not going to hassle us?

You've got your path of love, your basic, right—Bhakti.

Selfless giving.

The path of knowledge, also known as Jnana Yoga. Knowledge, discrimination. And that's the real techy stuff.

And of course Mysticism.

Those are the big four.

Then you have the subvariants like Zen, which is the path of no mind, OK?

The Tibetan Rebirth Process, techy rebirth experiences in the *bardo*.

Oh, Tantric Mysticism which is sort of living in the world and seeing God in household products.

Oh, there are subvariations. I mean you've got Buddhism, for example, which is like a combination of various forms. Or you've got Raja Yoga, or there's the—you know, there are all the "-isms".

Taoism, the path of being wet. Sooner or later one can offend everybody. [laughter]

So, what does this all add up to? It all adds up to a very confusing thing!

I mean, imagine a poor little soul that went down to the Bodhi Tree Bookstore, that was looking for enlightenment, right?

ENLIGHTENMENT AND SELF-REALIZATION 139

You know, like we had a sincere one. Let's say one floated in from someplace, you know, Cleveland or something. They got off the bus in LA, right? They heard that LA was a hot power spot, you know.

It is, yeah. There's ancient civilizations used to exist right in the Los Angeles area. Mystical civilizations. A lot of spiritual practice going back a long time ago was here, long before the Indians. This is a power spot we live in here. A wonderful place.

So let's say somebody in Cleveland had a dream, right? You know, "Come to LA" So they take the plane, land at LAX and they ask, "Where's the spot?" And they say "The Bodhi Tree Bookstore". Right? [audience laughter]

Because they have, I mean, any path that there is, is in that place, right? They have books on it. So you go down to the Bodhi Tree Bookstore. And go inside, and you look around, what's the poor thing going to do?

[Rama mimics a young female voice]

> "There're so many books, so many teachers, so many paths!"
>
> "God! I can't even afford half of them." [laughter]

That's the books, right?

Well, I mean, what's ... It used to be simple in the old days. Really. You know, people couldn't read. [laughter, growing slowly]

(This is my Zen approach, you understand.)

So, then, what does it matter? I'll get you to that point by the end of the evening, where you won't care what I say—see, and then we'll be making ...

That's good, then we will have gotten into another level of attention.

Enlightenment. Enlightenment is absorption in eternity. To become one with what we call nirvana.

There are various stages that we go through in the process. We can discuss it, but you should always remember that any discussion of the process is in no way indicative of—at all—what it's like. Because we're just painting little tiny pictures of eternity.

Enlightenment is to become eternity itself. To merge with all of life, all of existence. Beyond definition, beyond form, beyond awareness.

But yet there is a defined way to do that. Life has a structure. Life has a pattern, it has a weave.

And when we understand that way of life, that eternal Tao, the movement of existence, of energy, of consciousness, as we pull back from the veil of maya, of illusion, we become aware of that which we are, and that is the Self, or eternity, nirvana, call it what you will.

How does it begin?

Well, we have to talk, of course, a little bit about reincarnation, naturally, if we're going to deal with such a lofty subject 'cause that's the general cosmology that usually is found in the approach.

Reincarnation.

There was a time—or there is a time occasionally—when there is no time. There's no life, there's no death, there's nothing but eternal awareness. The Self—God, the unmanifest, reality—is everywhere.

And then—it gets bored. That's what they say in the books. It gets bored. And so, to give itself some entertainment, right, it puts on a video. You.

(You didn't like that. OK, I'll try again.)

The Self creates—out of itself—infinite forms, worlds, realities, dimensional planes, multifarious beings. Everything that you could imagine—and more—is existence.

That existence will be manifest for a certain period of time. In the East they call it "the day and the night of Brahman," and the day of Brahman is the creation.

It's usually measured in yugas, which are long, long, long periods of time, and there are these different cycles within a cycle of creation and finally there's a cosmic dissolution.

Everybody goes back, the stage is cleared, the players leave. Everything is empty for a while, and it starts again.

But that's only one aspect of eternity. Beyond that is something else entirely. And within that is everything.

Enlightenment is the study of the particular—of the moment, of feeling, of being human, of having a body—of seeing the world around us. It's the exploration of interdimensional planes of reality. Thousands of them, endlessly stretching out.

It's discovering that we are not physical beings, but that we have *bodies of light* that stretch into these other dimensions, and exploring, discovering our different selves that exist in parallel dimensions.

It's the experience of samadhi. Samadhi means the entrance into the supra-conscious state.

Dissolving into the pure white light or clear light of the void. Being absorbed in that light.

Over and over and over until all of your impurities—not just the ones in the conscious mind, but in the subterranean selves—are completely washed away, and you're completely clarified.

There's no jealousy, no anger, no possessiveness, no greed, no hatred, all of these qualities are completely washed away, even on subconscious levels.

Eternity is a hard task mistress.

If you step forth on the pathway to enlightenment, then you must experience, really, a little bit of every part of life. And it's a wonderful, wonderful journey.

Meditation is always the key, regardless of the path that you follow. Meditation takes us there. It's a vehicle.

Meditation is stopping thought. Stillness. Erasing the perceiver. The one inside who's watching, who's observing the personality forms.

You are capable of everything.

But to do that you need something that you don't have now. Power.

The power of the kundalini energy which gradually rises through our being in the process of self-discovery.

Self-discovery is so wonderful, I can't believe that people can get through the day without it, because life is so empty, and horrible, and boring without it!

It's really terrible. You're out there, and you're alone, in this cruel world, and people could care less, and even when they care, it's mostly about themselves.

You know, we live in a world of wars, and war's alarms, they're building Star Wars technology so we can pollute outer space now. I mean it's ridiculous. The same old thing.

So it appears. But it's not really. And that's the exciting part. One could get very discouraged if you just viewed the world.

But the inner worlds *are* reality.

ENLIGHTENMENT AND SELF-REALIZATION

This thing that you see—life, where we're born, and we exist for a while and we die, and we experience some pleasure and some pain—is just an appearance.

It's just the outermost surface of all that exists.

Life is wonderful beyond comprehension.

But in order to experience that, to know that, you have to be called. ("Hey! Psst!") No. You have to be called.

Something calls you forth.

You're out there, perfectly content to just like, heavily sense out, and have a good time with your life, right?

And a hand—you know, like the Monty Python hand that reaches in—the big hand comes down and grabs you, and pulls you up and says, "You are going to follow the pathway to enlightenment."

And you say,

> "No way. Listen, I've heard all about that. This is not for me. Now, look, there's lots of people in the world. You know, you made a mistake.
>
> "It's the house next door. He's over there now. He prays, all the time. He's got beads, he does the incense, the whole thing, you know?
>
> "I mean you should, I mean, if I tell you what I do with my time, you don't want me! You don't want to know. I mean, we are talking Impure City.
>
> "Sodom and Gomorrah? That was just lunch! [great laughter]
>
> "I mean, what goes on in this mind of mine? Boy, I mean it could wilt flowers miles away. No, I'm just, I'm not the

one."

And then the voice says, "You!" [laughter]

You can argue, you can reason, I tried, we all try, it doesn't do any good. When your number is up, that's it. They get you.

You cannot beat God! It's worth trying. But you just can't. God has all the cards, God can change the rules on you halfway through.

You're playing under a certain system and you think, "Ha! I won!" They say, "Oh, yeah? Read your rule book." And you look it up, and it's been changed—while you're playing—in the book. [audience laughter]

You just cannot beat God, but you have to try, that's part of it. You've got to, you know, you just say, "Ohhh, I'm gonna resist every step of the way, I'll make it tough for you."

Go ahead, that's the sign of a good spiritual person, is you fight every step of the way, it doesn't matter. They get you.

So, I'd like to talk a little bit about what's going to happen to you. Because, obviously, if you've been drawn to a talk like this, much against your will, to listen to somebody like me, much against your will, obviously, your number is up.

It's clear. I mean, I just sit at home and meditate, and you know, put out an extremely powerful force, and snag people like you to come and listen, and get your consciousness expanded for an evening, and then you can go back and trash it, and drop the energy. It won't matter! [laughter continues]

They got you.

So, my job, they sent me in tonight to talk to you, because essentially, they wanted someone to explain to you what's going to happen.

You know, they're compassionate, they understand, the people who run the universe. And they know, they've been through it themselves.

So, you're like the new recruits. They just want you to understand what's going to happen to you, and it's really OK, and that God loves you, and … sometimes. [laughter]

Well, God has other things to do than just love *you* all the time. I mean, give me a break, you know?

But they just wanted to, you know, they grabbed me and said,

> "Look, it's your job, you go out and you just explain to them what's going to happen to them, and they'll feel better. They'll sleep better at night."

So I said,

> "Well, sure, I mean, I have nothing else to do, sure, you know, it doesn't matter what I had planned to do with my life, no way! No!
>
> "Sure, I'll go out, I've had nothing else to do but take my life and go up on stages and talk to people and have people out front who say [Rama mimics noisy gibberish of picketers. Audience laughs.]
>
> "Sure, it's fine by me, I don't care!
>
> "Get married? Doesn't matter, no, that's OK, I can give it up. Nah, it's alright. Have children? Nah, that's alright, I never liked kids anyway. Ummm …
>
> "You know, my career? Sure, sure, right, which one? Which one do you like? I gave up two, three careers, sure, no problem! For you? Hey, you're hot, I'll do it!
>
> "But—I can't be responsible for their reaction."

That's a difficult thing to explain to someone that they're going to die, not just once, but again and again and again.

And that it's wonderful, because every death is followed by a rebirth, and I don't just mean in the physical terms of death.

When you meditate perfectly, it's a kind of death.

And death is a celebration. It really is. People misunderstand death. They're so afraid of it. I don't know why. You've died many times. You don't look any of the worse for it, you know? [laughter]

There is no such thing as death, it's an illusion, it's a doorway that we walk through.

The question is, how can you beat death at its own game? Well, that's what I'd like to talk to you about.

The only way you can beat death is to die before it gets you.

Right. You understand. That's what a warrior does.

Wimps? They just, "Oh, snivel, snivel, Oh, I'm gonna die! Oh!" [Rama mimics sniveling]

The warrior, he's already dead.

That's what enlightenment is. Enlightenment is a kind of death.

You have to understand, it isn't the big lollipop at the end of the ride. What do you think you do, sit around in Glow City all the time?

Oh, sure, sometimes there's nothing but infinite light flowing through every atom of your being, you are that light, and you know, all the usual samadhi stuff. But …

Well, it is complete ecstasy most of the time. I mean, that's fact. I have to be honest about it, that is ahead of you.

I don't know how you'll do with it. It's pretty intense to be in ecstatic

ENLIGHTENMENT AND SELF-REALIZATION 147

consciousness 24 hours a day, 7 days a week, you know, and the whole bit.

[Rama sighs heavily, like it's a job, someone has to do it. Audience laughs.]

You get used to it.

Well, it's kind of weird when you glow all the time. I mean, literally, the kundalini just rolls off my body, and everywhere …

You just glow. You can never be in a dark room again.

Seriously! You think that I'm kidding. Just waves of energy just always come out, all the time.

What do you do with it? There must be a way to make money with this. [laughter]

Now, that part I've never worked out. Rajneesh does well with that, I must admit. He's got that part figured. We always run in the red. But what can you do? Anyway. So …

That was good, I thought that was a good bit there, that put you through a change.

So, anyway.

[Rama adopts a sneaky, conspiratorial voice]

"Now wait a minute, now wait, what is this, what's going on?"

I think we should meditate. That would be a good thing. If you'd sit up nice and straight, please, I'd like to describe the meditation technique.

Great.

When I meditate with you, I'm going to be going into samadhi. I'm entering into dissolution. I go away, I dissolve. I'm not much here anyway, most of the time. But not at all, then.

What will happen is a tremendous amount of energy—a volume of energy—will come through me to you.

And also all of these good folks here tonight are joined together, and we're linking our consciousness, we're creating a psychic network, we're networking our energy.

A few people can make a terrific difference.

People get very discouraged these days because, you know, things don't look too good on this planet.

But don't be fooled. A few powerful people can make all the difference. They always have.

Even sitting here together tonight, linking our energies in meditation, all these people with all these incarnations of stored power, is just waiting to come out.

We send out a force and energy that is part of destiny, too.

What I'd like you to do is to try and still your thoughts. We'll be doing several meditations tonight to music, I play electronic music to meditate to. You can ignore the music or just flow with it, whatever you prefer.

The first meditation I'd like you to do is the meditation on the third eye. The third eye or the Agni Chakra is located between the eyebrows and a little bit above, right here. [Rama touches his forehead]

If you just take your index finger for a moment and touch your Agni Chakra, between the eyebrows and about an inch above. Touch that spot, and just press very lightly and close your eyes.

Wonderful. OK, you can let your hand down.

ENLIGHTENMENT AND SELF-REALIZATION

The Agni Chakra is one of the seven principal chakras in the subtle physical body, or the body of light that surrounds the physical body. They are doorways that lead us into altered states of attention, into states of enlightened awareness. They all work differently.

I'd like you to focus your attention for a few minutes on the third eye, and just look at that spot. After a while you may see kind of a glowing light, it looks like the sun or like the moon. It might be different colors, you may see visual scenes, nothing at all.

But while you're focusing there, what you're doing is letting the kundalini flow through you more strongly. And naturally, I'm producing a great deal of energy, or it's coming through me, you might say, to alter your attention, to bring you into a spiritual state of attention.

Just focus for two or three minutes and then stop focusing, and just let go. And just let the energy take you.

When thoughts come in and out of your mind, please ignore them, just relax and have fun with it.

If the energy gets very intense, which it sometimes does, when we meditate together, just enjoy it, relax with it, don't try too hard. Let the energy work for you.

Don't try and accomplish any specific aims or goals, don't use a mantram or anything like that.

Just sit there, and feel the silence, enjoy the music, and just let the energy fields that emanate from my being spread through you and all of the energies from all of us here will network together, and we'll have a great time. Good.

We'll just be meditating for about an hour and a half. [laughter]

We'll be meditating for about, you know, 5, 10 minutes, something like that, and then we'll talk. Good. Great.

And we'll be meditating to some Tangerine Dream. So if you sit up nice and straight, close your eyes.

Later on you might want to open your eyes and meditate with the eyes open a little bit, but to start out with, focus on the third eye, please, you're all familiar with it.

And we're going to be looking through the spiritual eye vision at eternity.

Moving from time to the timeless. Don't try too hard now, let it go.

[meditation]

Enlightenment is not something that happens to you in one day. It's a very gradual experience that takes place actually over many, many lifetimes.

Some people are under the assumption that it's sort of a flash, bang experience. Not really.

It's just each day your awareness becomes more formless, you're less in the world of time and space, less in duality, and a little more conscious of eternity or eternality.

But enlightenment does not preclude the physical. That is to say, it isn't necessary to reject the world or commonplace events, because enlightenment exists everywhere, in all things, in all experiences.

Enlightenment is the awareness of awareness. Becoming eternally conscious. Waking to life.

And those wakings or spiritual epiphanies can occur in the darndest places. Sometimes they occur while you're seated in meditation, in a situation like this. Sometimes they might occur while you're shopping in a supermarket, or hiking up a canyon somewhere; in traffic; at work; with someone you love; in a terrible situation.

Suddenly a moment will turn on itself. It will dovetail, and it will become eternity. You'll step outside of time.

It's not just a question of being out of the body in the sense of an astral experience, but suddenly you'll become aware of the timelessness of existence, of the perfect beauty and stillness of life.

Those moments add up as we have them over and over again, and more frequently. Gradually, eventually, we *become* a moment like that ourselves.

Someone who is enlightened is like a hole in time.

If you're interested in studying, of course, if that's your bent, if you're interested in becoming more conscious, more aware, more beautiful, essentially—if you really like beauty and you'd like to be a very beautiful being—then there are a series of ways to accomplish that.

Traditionally, of course, in the books, they say that you should go seek out a teacher. Now, I always wonder about that because I figure these books were written by teachers. So, but, you know, who am I to buck the system?

So, I think that you just have to be yourself. That's the most important thing that you can do, in self-discovery, is to be yourself.

To not try and do your meditation—your experience—like anybody else.

There's some schools of self-discovery where they tell you that what you should so is, "Do this practice, and at 6 a.m. you get up and at 6:30 you wash, and you do ... and at 7 you do ... and at 11," they lay out your whole life for you, and I suppose that works for some people.

At a certain phase that can be good. You need the discipline, something like that.

But in the more advanced aspects of the self-discovery experience, it's really not necessary to do that. We have a much more fluid way of dealing with consciousness. It's no less intense or disciplined, it's probably more.

But what we're interested in doing is learning to become conscious.

Not in any particular structured way. As a matter of fact, it's a real pain in the neck for people who have gotten attached to structure.

A lot of people have problems with advanced self-discovery because they get so attached to the basic practices in self-discovery in their early years, that when you finally run into someone who is a little more demanding, and they say, "OK, now let's really—you know, you're interested in advanced self-discovery, great! Now let's do some things."

And you had a picture-perfect idea in your mind of what advanced self-discovery would be like—you figured you're going to sit around and eat bananas all day, or something, I don't know what. But you have ideas. And it's nothing like that at all.

It's different for everybody, but yet there are certain stages or experiences that everyone must go through. Yet your approach to them—the way they happen to you—will be unique to yourself.

Do you need a teacher?

I don't know, it depends on how you feel.

I think the most important thing is to have heart, to have a sense of love and well-being, and then everything will fall in place. If you don't have that, then nothing will really work out for you.

What matters is aspiration. You know, it's funny, people want everything, but sometimes they don't want to do the one thing they need to do to make it all happen or take place.

And the thing that you need to do is to love. To love, to love, to love.

In a new way, in a different way.

To love without strings, without something in it for you. It's frightening at first, I'll agree. It's a little scary, to not know where your life is going to go, to not have everything programmed out.

Also, of course, my experience, or at least the way I teach is, I feel that people have to be extremely well-grounded in the physical world.

Because having traveled the ashram circuit and that sort of thing, what I have observed is that most people get so up there in their second attention—they get kind of out there—that they lose contact with basic reality. They think they're being spiritual, and all they're doing is ruining their minds, and not making much spiritual progress at all.

A good sign of a person who has their meditation together is that their life is very successful also.

You're able to think and function in the twentieth century, or whatever century or on whatever planet you happen to find yourself. It really doesn't matter, because if you can't do that, there's something lacking in the system, you see?

So I think it's real important that you be versatile. You don't want to do the same thing all the time to the point where you get stuck in a structure.

You see, enlightenment is going beyond structure, it's going beyond "-isms". Religions are great, and forms of self-discovery are great, but the point of them is to take you beyond them. And not to get stuck in them.

You don't want to get stuck in anything, really, in self-discovery.

How do you do that? Well, the secret really has to do with erasing the self, erasing the ego.

Now, this is tricky because there is a need for a certain amount of self to exist in the world.

In other words, if you go down to the dry cleaners, and they ask you, "What do you want?" there has to be somebody there. [audience laughter]

To say, "My cleaning." [audience laughter]

Or suppose you're out in the world and somebody gives you a hard time. You know, you're just walking down the street, or you're in the store, the department store, trying to exchange … Somebody gave you some useless gift, and you're in there, and you're trying to exchange it and they say, "I'm sorry sir, but we can't."

Or someone starts to take advantage of you, because they sense that you're a "spiritual type". Commonly known as a push-over. So they figure, "Ah, here's someone I can manipulate and give a hard time to." So, if there's nobody there, you'll just kind of go, "Ah, ah, oh, oh, gosh, really? Oh, gee." [Rama mimics a babyish voice]

See?

So, then, we have to redefine our ideas, or forget anything we know about enlightenment and God-realization and meditation, and just throw it all away and start over. Every day.

Because we're trying to go beyond forms.

Yet, there's tremendous etiquette in the enlightenment process, it's amazing. It's amazing, the etiquette.

So what we're going to do then, is we're going to start out with the person you are now.

"Today, Suzy Q. Public, you are going to begin the process of self-discovery!" Various trumpets sound, you know, archangels descend and all the usual stuff. [laughter]

And you say, "Oh, really, me? How wonderful!" Sort of the Miss Piggy-consciousness. [more audience laughter]

So, then, great. The first thing, Suzy, it's your first day as a student.

"Hi, Sue, how are you today? Please sit down. Not too close."

Well, you know, right? You want to be realistic, you don't want to be that close to somebody's energy field, they're a beginner, you know. Who knows what's in there? It takes thousands of lifetimes to clear it out. [Rama laughs heartily] Gotta go slowly.

So you say then …

"Hi Sue, now look, this is the thing. The first thing we've gotta work with is your current self. Now Suzy, you have the good fortune of being a woman.

"However, your good fortune is a difficult fortune because you have been conditioned by the world to think that you are a powerless being who is not very capable of almost anything.

"Because you're a woman. That's the definition of woman in our society and our world.

"So, Suzy, your task is going to be even bigger than the task of the guys because you have more conditioning.

"The first thing that we're going to start with is the conditioning that you've gotten in this lifetime. Now, Suzy, I know that you've had a lot of incarnations in spiritual practice, otherwise you wouldn't even be very interested in meditation and you certainly wouldn't have found me, because I don't work with beginners at all.

"I mean, you may just be starting meditation in this life, but I only work with people who have had lots and lots of incarnations doing this, and clearly you have, because that's why power brought you here. OK, great.

"I know you've got it all inside you, and you're really frustrated right now, because you know you can do things that you just can't do now, and you know that these states of consciousness that you're in, and the clothing that you wear, is just not what you want. I understand that!

"You're not chic enough, inwardly or outwardly, but we can take care of that.

"But in order to get back all that knowledge that you've already got inside you, the first thing we have to do in the enlightenment process is deal with who you are now, and wash away all the conditioning from this lifetime.

"Once we clear how they've screwed you up in this life, then we can take on the samskaras, the deeper tendencies from your other lifetimes.

"But of course, every time we clear a level, lo and behold, you'll feel great, you'll feel wonderful. It's like getting a 'good' haircut. And you just walk out, and hey, they did it right, you see? So you'll feel really good, Sue. (This is LA talk).

"So, now the first thing I want you to do Suzy, is you've got to meditate every day. It's real important. It's more important to meditate for an hour every day than five hours every other day. Because you have to start to put little holes in time.

"Right now, Sue, you're in a world of desires and emotions and feelings and thoughts, most of which aren't even yours.

"These are thoughts, and ideas and impressions that were given to you—you were programmed by your world and your society—to feel.

"And it all starts with sex. They define you sexually. You're in blue or you're in pink. You're a little boy or you're a little girl. And now they're going to

ENLIGHTENMENT AND SELF-REALIZATION

tell you what that means.

"But obviously the people who are telling you don't have it all that together, because they're not exactly happy. They're not exactly enlightened, they're not having a great time with their lives. They're doing the best they can.

"But for some reason, power has brought you to this point, where you're having an encounter with someone who has gone beyond time and space. And who says that you can do the same thing. It's not that difficult.

"As a matter of fact, it's your destiny. But there's still certain things that you have to do to make it work.

"So the first is, we've got to set up a meditation schedule.

"You need that meditation every day because in that period of time, whether it's a half an hour or forty-five minutes once or twice a day when you're sitting there, gradually as you learn to stop thought, you'll open a doorway to another world.

"That doorway will not necessarily close at the end of meditation.

"That is to say, the light, the kundalini energy, the power, the beauty, the perceptions of God, all those things will continue to flood through you during the day.

"So, Sue, start every morning with meditation. Get up, take a shower, be clean, feel good, sit down and meditate. Because your mind hasn't been active all night, you see. After you've been out in the world and you've been thinking a lot, it's much harder to meditate. So always start the day with meditation.

"Then, run off to work, and during the day now, you've got to do some yoga. It's really important. Yoga means union. Union with everything.

"So what I'd like you to do is, watch your mind during the day.

"And every time you start to think about the past, don't let it happen. Because it's gone. And when you think about the past, you're identifying with a person whom you no longer are.

"Suzy, you're anybody you want to be.

"But you've already seen the movie that we shot about your past, and it was a good movie maybe. Maybe it wasn't. But we don't want to do a rerun.

"We want to get you in a new take, here, OK? So let's forget the past. Every time you think about the past during the day, push it out of your mind. Just say 'No.'

"That's your mantra Suzy, your mantra is 'No.' [audience laughter]

"Every time you start to think about the horrible experience you had when you were five, the wonderful experience you had when you were twenty, the mediocre experience you had when you were thirty—whatever it is—'No.'

"We're not interested, we've done it, we know—thinking about that Suzy is not going to make you any different. It's not going to change you.

"Let's not worry about tomorrow. Because we all know that tomorrow is going to be a horrible day [laughter]. Because every day is a horrible day on the planet Earth. It's a fact.

"So we know already it's going to be beat, so let's not worry about it. Let's just assume it's going to be terrible, but we're going to have a good time anyway.

"You know what Rama says, Rama says, 'Life sucks wherever you go, but you can still have a good time if you know how.' [audience laughter]

"And the reason it's going to be horrible, Suzy, is because those people out there who are not going to leave you alone. They're going to try and mold you and condition you and make you unhappy. They're going to try and

ENLIGHTENMENT AND SELF-REALIZATION

drain your personal power, and just reduce you to rubble.

"They want you to just be another automaton walking around there in a machine-like existence, because they're afraid of women with power! They're scared to death of them.

"And if you start to get powerful, Suzy, you're going to threaten, like, the whole male power structure.

"And we've got a problem there. So we've got to be discreet about this. We can't let them know."

"We must consider your wardrobe, Suzy. Real important, because the way people project energy towards you—which is half the battle to be honest with you—depends on how you look and how you dress.

"It's very, very important, whether you're a man or a woman. Because as an evolved soul, you're very sensitive, you're all psychic. And you pick up energy, more than you realize.

"Most of the thoughts inside you, Suzy, are not your own! They're from the people around you, but you're a psychic sponge. You've had thirty thousand incarnations, you've developed your psychic abilities in past lives.

"I remember you in Atlantis, you were the one on the left, in the temple, in the back. You gave me a hard time then! Don't you give me a hard time now. Now listen to me.

"This time, get it right, alright? We don't have time, you know, this is the Kali Yuga. The end of the world is not that far away, so we want to get it together and get out of here. We've got to beat feet.

"So look, we've got to do something—you look terrible, Suzy. Why don't you wear makeup? You're into holistic health. Big deal. What's that going to do for your enlightenment? Maybe it's nice for your body.

"Wear a little makeup, because if you don't you're going to be picked right out. Alright?

"Wear a little black, Suzy. It's a little more powerful. You've got to have a more powerful image as a woman.

"Your friend Bob over there? Maybe he should soften his image a little bit, a little more androgynous.

"Because maybe he's been defined, they brought him up in a way and told him that you're a guy and you should be, you're afraid …

> 'It's no good to be a girl. There's something wrong with it. Women are inferior, they're second class, "Bob, you can't be like that, don't be a girl, Bob! Be a man." '

Right? But they never say that to Suzy, they don't say, "Suzy, don't be a man."

"So Bob, maybe they've pushed you out in an extreme, too, and they've tried to make you into some kind of desensitized macho being that you're not. Sure you can be tough. Why not? You can be a great warrior. But still be soft inside.

"And unattached when necessary. Actually, you'll make a better warrior.

"Now, you've got to get this meditation going every day. Great.

"We've got to work on the wardrobe. That's fun, we'll go over to Bullocks, we'll get new clothes, that will be fun. Alright.

"New image. Now, I know what you're going to buy, you're going to buy the same old stuff again, no way. We've got to go with a whole new image here, a little bit of makeup, that'll be nice.

"How's your body doing? You should be getting more exercise.

"Because as you advance and the kundalini starts to surge through you, your body needs to be in pretty good shape. It's real, real important.

"Your subtle body is pretty trashed by your experiences in the world.

"You know, men project anger and hostility towards women all the time. And so you pick all that up in your subtle body, and it's like acid.

"Particularly when you have sex with somebody, you have to be very careful who you have sex with. Yeah, you can have sex, sure. But you have to be very careful, because people get very—men get very threatened by sex, you see.

"And it's not their fault. It's not their fault, but they were brought up to feel that they have to always be like the raper, the conqueror, the performer, you see.

"And so naturally, they feel all this power in you, because women are innately much more powerful than men are, and so this need to control.

"Now we know that you've been controlling *him* all along. That's obvious, and not letting him know.

"That's clever on your part, but the only problem with that, Suzy, is that—granted that he thinks he gets sexually excited but you're just pushing energy through him and not letting him know, and that male ego just goes for it—but the problem with that Sue, is that when you do that, you're putting yourself into a duality situation.

"And also, of course, when you're just pushing it out like that, then you get all this energy thrown back at you.

"So the sex thing, you know, do whatever you feel is right. But just try and be more unattached about it. And just pick people who don't have so many problems inside, because I can see you've run into a lot of them.

"Let's see, what else have you got to do?

"Oh, you've got to just be exposed to more highly evolved people.

"You should go someplace ... I know you're not a joiner. I don't blame you, I was never a joiner myself. I'm definitely a loner if I've ever met one.

"But at the same time I know that it is a gnarly world out there, with all kinds of people who aren't very interested in love and selfless giving, and so we evolved types have to stick together.

"That's the lesson that we've learned.

"Because when we don't stick together, they get us. Every time.

"When we stick together—and we network our energies—then our power is impeccable, and they just cannot trash us. They can't shoot us, crucify us, burn us, french-fry us, whatever it may be.

"They can't get us.

"But when we all go our own way ... I know you need solitude—you like to do your own thing—I'm all for it!

"But you've got to go find a group of people—what in the *I Ching* they call an organic community of people—who you feel good about. It doesn't matter which one. But pick one that you feel good about, and be with those people. You need the association.

"Now during the day you've got to learn to be kind to everybody, Suzy. It doesn't matter who it is. I don't care if it's the lady with the dry cleaning, if it's the person who cut you off in front of the freeway, you just have to learn to have more of a reverence for life.

"Because that reverence for life will make you very, very happy. Of course, meditating every day gives us the energy to do this, and the insight.

"But you've got to become more sensitive. That waitress, Suzy, you're a woman, you'd think you should know that being a waitress is the worst job on earth.

"And you go into that restaurant and she comes over and you treat her like she's just some kind of a robot or something. That is a fully sensitive being, a sentient being in evolution that's standing there taking your order. Don't look at them like they're some arbitrary being. That being has life as much as you do. Feelings.

"That doesn't mean you have to stare at them with a glassy look. But respect that being. Relate! Just because other people don't, doesn't mean that you shouldn't.

"But at the same time you have to learn to be inaccessible. Don't tell people you meditate. Don't tell people that you're involved with self-discovery. Because they don't understand. You think it's America, California, the 20th Century, Los Angeles. Doesn't mean anything! Look who they just elected for president, you know?" [laughter]

That was our political note. [laughter, Rama snaps fingers] Not that there was much of a choice.

"So, Suzy, life is fantastic, but you just gotta get your tush in gear here!

"What else can you do? Well, you could read spiritual books. Now, they're good. If you need to fall asleep and you can't fall asleep at night, read a spiritual book, you're out in a minute! [laughter] Zoned!

"Who do I recommend? Anybody who makes you high. But I think, you know there have been some genuine spiritual teachers. A lot of phonies, but there's some genuine …

"Ramakrishna. Can't go wrong. He's a little heavy with the Bhakti, get's a little carried away, but it worked for him, right? But he's inspiring. He was a nut, but he was a spiritual nut.

"Ramana Maharshi, now that's Jnana Yoga, it might be a little thick for you. Because you might want to run away, and you know, you just don't understand what he's saying yet. He was very techy. He was a good one.

"*The Way of Life* by Lao Tzu. Impeccable knowledge.

"Shankara, again more Jnana Yoga. I like that sort of thing. But you know it's the highest path, Jnana Yoga, it's a good path.

"The Tibetans are fun to read. It doesn't matter. Whatever you like.

"Yogananda. Whatever suits you.

"They were all trying to say something that couldn't be said in words. Most of them didn't write, because they were just too gone. You have to understand, Suzy, what it's like to be enlightened.

"I mean, most of the time Suzy, I don't even know. I mean, I'm not even here! I'll just be like sitting, I'm just gone.

"Samadhi takes you over, and I just dissolve in eternity again and again, you know?

"So it's tough. 'Cause how can you say—when you are everything—what are you going to say? You read the books where they describe it and it's real nice, but it's not like that. It's not like that. A few of them have written, because that was what they, that was just how the dharma worked through them.

"Most of them don't write, because if you're really meant to get there, when you're advanced, you will find someone who's enlightened, you'll be drawn to them, and you'll hang out together.

"They will … you will see each other from time to time. And a beautiful interplay will occur between the two of you.

"See, Suzy, if you really want enlightenment real, real badly, you probably won't get it. Let me give you a hint to start with here.

"The way to go about it is selfless giving.

"This is just my opinion. You know, you start out with love. You meditate on the heart chakra, you learn to love, and just feel the wonderful love flowing through you.

"But I think the hip way to go about it, is not to be so concerned with your own realization. It'll happen when it's supposed to. God's got a computer program worked out, your number's up at a certain time, *pow!* It'll just happen.

"What's important is not self-realization, but what you can do for others. That's the emblem of a person who is really ready. Who's in the ballpark at all.

"So, Suzy, what you need to do, is begin to think more of the welfare of others. Like what can you do for other people. And you say, 'Well, what can I do for other people?' and well, there's an easy answer.

"Smile more, be kinder. You know, you don't have to get up on stage in front of thousands of people and give talks about spirituality.

"Every life you touch is something. Every energy, every thought you send out affects others.

"You can be sitting in your room—Suzy, I can sit in my room, and I can affect thousands and millions of people when I meditate. They'll never know it, they won't know my name, that's fine.

"Who needs to? What's the big deal? I'm nothing anyway, I know that. But it has an effect. A good effect.

"Sometimes you don't believe in God, I know. Well, I wouldn't believe in God the way they describe God either. Sounds ridiculous.

"You say to yourself, what kind of a being is going to make a world like this? With all this horror and suffering? I understand! It's a difficult thing.

"But don't look at it that way.

"You've got to make friends with God. You know, God has gotten bad press. [audience laughter]

"Meaning, men have made God in their image. I mean, God is a man, Suzy, what are you going to do with that, right? Know what I mean? What a start!

"God's not a man, God's not a woman. God is *everything*. Everything.

"We're talking artificial intelligence here." [audience laughter]

We should do another meditation.

This time I'd like you to meditate not by focusing on any particular chakra or place. But I'd like you to meditate on something, and that something is light.

Light is our substance. We are literally made up of light, of energy.

When you meditate—when you meditate very well—you will just *be* nothing but light. You will see that that's all that there is—is endless light, timeless, ecstatic, perfect light.

And that this whole world appearance, it's just like a movie that you are watching.

And that you should be neither attracted nor repulsed by it.

Light and life is interesting, but the universe is endless. We're all endless. We are that light. You are God, in essence, and in substance.

I'd like you to meditate on light. Now, how do you do that? Well, just by feeling it. You don't have to picture it, you don't have to see vast rays of light shooting through your mind. It's not necessary.

Meditation is a very quiet, a very personable experience. Very subtle, yet totally powerful in the changes it brings about in your awareness and your attention.

So what I'd like you to do is just to close your eyes, to start with.

And then just to consider light. Just to feel it. And as we all do that together, we will invoke a great light. A great energy. It will transmute us all, it will change us all forever.

If you'd like to, if you do need a sense of focus, I would recommend focusing on the heart chakra—right in the center of the chest—which is the center of love. Sometimes it's very easy if you focus here to feel light spreading through your being.

Or you could not focus on a particular point, but just feel light. Imagine a sea of light, an ocean of endless light stretching in every direction endlessly, never beginning and never ending. Nothing but light, forever.

When thoughts come in and out of your mind, ignore them. Stop them if you can, but don't get too hung up in them. Just ignore them.

Let the meditation take you. Feel the energy in the room shifting. As we meditate together, I'm bringing you through a series of dimensional shifts.

Planes of attention are whizzing by you, one after another. You're out in space and you're traveling.

Some of you are more aware of it, some less, it's dependent upon whether you've developed your spiritual sensitivity. But just relax and let it go.

As you sit here, you're storing power. When you leave tonight, you will leave with much more power than you came in. How you use that power is up to you.

But an evening like this is an evening of great power.

So the best thing is just to have happy thoughts—if you must have thoughts—but try not to get too involved in them. Don't judge, don't wonder what you're getting out of it, leave yourself alone. Take a vacation.

Just relax a little bit. Think of light and just let go. And you will feel this energy, this light, pass through you and change you. Forever, actually.

Good, let's meditate for just a few more minutes.

[meditation]

Very good. Please set back and relax.

[Rama begins speaking in a cowboy twang]

> Put up your feet and stay a spell. Ahhhh-yuh. Hang out with that kuuuuundalini. Ahhh-yuh. All them chakras a glowin'. Ahh-yuh. Eternity just spinning around your fingers.

[Rama resumes normal voice]

So you can play with light, after awhile. You know, when you get up in the upper stages of attention, you can just manifest it, or it manifests you. It's all the same. And you can just, with the movement of a finger, change the tonality of the universe. [over a period of about 10 seconds, Rama breathes out several times]

The thing people forget—I think sometimes—about the enlightenment process, is how beautiful it is, how incredibly beautiful light is. We're made up of light, it's our substance.

And as you let go of your attachments—as you fall in love with light—that

ENLIGHTENMENT AND SELF-REALIZATION 169

light just becomes you.

And then of course, you can do some things with it. Some people develop the superpowers, the siddhas, where you can project kundalini, manifest light, create changes and alter peoples attention, and things like that.

Some people are just absorbed in nirvana, and that's enough.

There's no right and wrong in it. When you get up far enough, it's all the same. It's just the Self, it is that which you love, and it operates through all of us in different ways.

But you've got to get your feet off the ground. Low level flying. You've got to start.

And so many people get incorrect starts. Oh, there are some things to be learned from it. But there's no singular way. There's so many ways.

I'd like to answer some questions for a while that you might have about self-discovery, the enlightenment process, self-realization, it's such a vast field.

And so you may have some particular questions. So, if you would raise your hand, I will call on you and perhaps I can answer your question. Say it nice and loudly so I can hear you. I'll repeat the question, because doubtlessly lots of people won't be able to hear it, and I'll see if I can answer a few questions.

Just try and absorb this energy that's in the room. That's the main thing. The room is pulsing right now with kundalini. Just let it go through you. You don't have to do anything, it's just absorbing in you, and it will be part of you. It will help you.

So, I'd like to answer some questions. If you could just raise your hand—Yeah?

[question from a man]

> OK, uh, is enlightenment, or Buddha Nature that very living silence that's in between your thoughts, beyond thought … and thinking itself.

[Rama]

Right. Yes, it's endless light, and as you said, it's the nothingness that's between thoughts. That's very good. It's that absolute stillness, the satori, you see. There's no thought, there's no self, there's no jiva, no soul, no world, no god, no universe, all of this goes away. That's why we use the term nirvana. Meaning the extinction of the flame.

But at the same time, it's within the world, within the form. The stillness and the substance are really the same thing. We just use words to make them appear different in duality.

So it's wonderful because you can't categorize it. It just is. And sometimes it isn't, and sometimes it isn't/is at the same time. Right! I agree.

Yes. Yeah?

[question from a woman]

> These different selves that you talk about … are they like different life beings?

[Rama]

Ah, very good, yes. Very often when I talk, I say, "know your selves"—with an "s"—because there are many selves within the self. And your question is, "Are these selves, selfs from different lifetimes?"

Yeah!

Yes, in each lifetime you develop a self, and it never entirely goes away. It becomes part of the causal body, and so it's always there.

ENLIGHTENMENT AND SELF-REALIZATION 171

But also there are selves that aren't just having to do with, like, particular incarnations that you've had, but let's say they're just part of the structure of the unique being that is you.

They are deeper voices. Most people don't realize that the surface personality is actually controlled by the deeper selves, that are operative in other dimensional planes.

And coming to know them is fascinating, yeah. So, it's that and something else too.

Questions. Yes?

[question from a woman]

> When I'm out in the world, I kind of have a shell around myself to protect myself, especially driving in bad neighborhoods, against men's hatred of women.
>
> Other times, like occasionally, in my own home, someone will have a guest over. Or right before you came out. Someone made a comment and I wasn't protected, and I felt a feeling in my body, I feel like I'm kind of wasting my time.
>
> My thoughts keep going, what I should have said, what I could have said.
>
> Is there a way that I could preserve myself when that happens?

[Rama]

Yes, as a woman, you're in a very difficult situation.

You're in a hostile environment for women, where women are seen as commodities to be traded in exchange, to be used and abused. And the energy you pick up—particularly as an evolved woman, is—I mean it's pretty hard to ignore.

It's like living in the South, say 20 years ago, when you couldn't go into a restaurant, and you know, trying to pretend that that wasn't true, you know, it's pretty absurd.

You can just feel the hatred towards you, if you're black. Just because of your color, right?

So, it's the same thing being a woman.

Just constantly energy is being projected at you that just says you're inferior, you're not capable, or very often, you're just hated.

It's this understated anger that you've talked about, that's there all the time. What can you do to protect yourself?

Well, the best thing you can do is, first of all, become more powerful yourself.

You have to tap more deeply into your own power. Because if more power is generating through you, naturally, these things will bounce off more. You won't be so fragile.

Secondly, as I suggested, you have to begin to think about appearance. When you're running into people on a one-to-one basis, a lot of the reason they push you or give you a hard time or project energies like that, is because they think they can get away with it.

So there are ways you can remain a nice person. But you know, Christ said, "Be like the lamb, but kind of dress like the wolf, appear like the wolf."

You need to learn to be inaccessible. Not to let people understand your sensitivity unless they would really value that. And project a counter image that is an archetype that touches the consciousness of people and suggests a certain strength and power that people will just not bother with.

It makes a tremendous difference in the amount you'll pick up. Just in terms of, as you say, when you're driving through a neighborhood and you just feel like hostility and anger, what can you do?

The best thing is just to try and be at a high level of attention, maintain your sense of humor, and stay pretty grounded. I mean, you have to feel kind of tough, really, because you are.

You know, part of the illusion of the image of women is that they're not tough, you see. And you walk around thinking that, and then naturally you think you're not strong, and you can't deal with things, and you can.

You're very strong. The very aspect of the kundalini that manifests through you is raw power.

But of course, if you don't know that, and you haven't tapped into that, then you're operating on 1/10th of what you have, if that.

So, it's really, you have to redefine yourself and just learn how, of course, to plug more into that essential energy that's in yourself.

The same is true for a lot of men, too. There are a lot of men who are really nice.

But they, in being nice—in realizing that there's an alternative to just being aggressive constantly—sometimes go too much to an extreme, almost to make up for something. And again, they lose contact with their energy and power too.

You can be kind but powerful at the same time. You need to learn how to discriminate from a spiritual point of view to do that.

But it really has to do with just unlocking more of your own energy, and really redefining your image.

You have to go through your life. You have to go through the people in your life who are defining you in a certain way, even mentally. They're just holding an image of you, day and night.

And the closer they are to you, the more powerful that effect is. Not in physical proximity, but emotionally.

The people you love are the people who hurt you or help you the most. Because you're psychically open to them. So you have to take a real look inside the people you're close to, and ask yourself just what …

Do you know what's a good question to ask sometimes, of everyone in your life? What do they want from me? A real basic question.

Because if they're not enlightened, they want something. They may love, they may care, but there's another part in there. If that being is not enlightened—if they are not in a luminous state of attention twenty-four hours a day—then there's still residual karmas, residual selves in there that haven't been completely worked out. There are selfishnesses.

And so they want something.

And it's no problem, I mean, people are people, right? So you should expect it. It's just nice to know who you're dealing with. It's good not to be too idealistic about human beings.

They're all gods and goddesses walking around.

But it's nice to know the deeper structure.

So it's good if you could take a good psychic scan of everybody you know. And just ask yourself, "What is it they really want?"

And trust your intuition. That doesn't mean that they're not a wonderful friend, or that they don't love you.

But like yourself, they have their limitations, too. When you understand those limitations, you won't be hurt by them.

ENLIGHTENMENT AND SELF-REALIZATION

Then you'll say, "OK, of course, I don't expect them to be kind about this or understand this. They're working that out. But I'm not going to let them work it out on me."

Follow? Yeah, this is true whether you're male or female. I mean, it makes no difference.

You have to learn ... People are more powerful than you realize. And naturally, as an evolved person—meaning someone who's interested in meditation—you are going to naturally know and attract people who are more evolved. And they may not look any different than anybody else, but inside they are.

The difference—between a soul that's had 40,000 incarnations and one that's had a thousand—in power, is tremendous. In their ability to affect your attention level. It's astounding.

Most people's lives are molded and shaped by those around them, more than they realize.

So it's necessary to step back from everyone in your life—inside yourself—and just reexamine constantly. And ask yourself, is this person—do they love me, do they care?

If they don't, you really don't need them in your life, unless it's just on a business basis or something like that.

Do they understand what I'm about? Not that they should have some perfect understanding, but does it matter? You see, because if it doesn't, then you shouldn't expect anything, but a little negative energy once in a while.

Because they're just looking at their fantasy creation in their mind, you see, and it could be you, it could be anybody else. They'll just slip somebody into the fantasy creation model mode.

And then they will treat that fantasy creation in a certain way, and naturally when it doesn't live up to the impossible expectations that they have for it, then you get the abusive anger.

So, in other words, you have to downplay your expectations a little bit about human beings. Human beings are human beings.

This is a planet of beings in relative early stages of evolution, obviously.

There are also some beings—a small number here—who are in more advanced stages of evolution. This is not the way the universe is.

The universe has many lower worlds, where the beings are in even lower states of evolution—hard to believe, but true [audience laughter].

And many higher worlds, where there are beings who are all fully developed, who are all enlightened. There are worlds just of enlightened beings.

So don't judge the universe just by the action on this particular planet. It's not a good representation.

But you are in a unique position because, as I said, if you're drawn to a workshop like this—unless somebody handcuffed you and brought you—this means that you have some evolution. That's why you came. You came because of the energy, the power level.

The ads don't really matter, something drew you, it was an inner force.

And that suggests that you have a certain amount of evolution. So you are a stranger in a strange land.[4] That's your situation. You live in a world of people who are not as evolved as you.

And consequently some are more evolved.

But consequently you have to learn how to deal with that, and particularly as a spiritual woman, it's really tough.

---

4. *Stranger In a Strange Land,* Robert Heinlein, science fiction, 1961

You know, there is a way to deal with it.

But you have to be aggressive without being angry. I mean, you have to be a little bit militant. Just because the conditioning is so against you, and your back is so against the wall in every way, that you have to just be very, very militant and very strong.

But not strong in an angry way, because that just dilutes your power and energy. And you just have to tap into the kundalini more. And remember, this is the planet Earth, what do you expect?

Keep your sense of humor about it all.

Another question.

Yes, sir, back there a little ways in the middle—yeah?

[question from a man]

> In meditation I find myself getting to a point ... where all of a sudden I feel ... and open, and sort of hunger for more light. How can you maintain that on an every-day basis more?

[Rama]

You mean how do you keep that level?

[questioner]

> Yes.

[Rama]

So in other words, how do you stay in that?

OK sure, when you come and meditate with me it's easy, because I'm just putting out so much energy, you know, that if you're at all sensitive you just sit back and you just roll right out, right?

No, well, that's why you come. That's my job, that's what I'm supposed to do. If I do a good job, that happens for you, and it opens you up.

But also, of course, there's a structural change that takes place on an evening like this. With so much kundalini manifesting, it's creating a change, and creating openings for you, so it's easier for you to do this on your own.

How do you maintain that level on your own?

It's very, very hard. That's why people band together. But, there is something that I was talking about a couple of nights ago, and it's the psychic network.

There's a network of higher beings throughout the universe. On this planet, also. People who are highly evolved, beings who are highly evolved, and they network their energies. And that net is there 24 hours a day.

24 hours a day there is a high level intensity energy that you can tap into. I'm part of that network, every enlightened being is part of that network, you can join that network.

You don't have to pay any dues, fill out any forms.

Wherever you are, all you have to do is open yourself to the network, and just feel that there is this luminous edge of eternity, of energy that we're part of.

Naturally, of course, when you're around people all the time who could care less about light, all those thoughts and all those impressions—because you're somewhat psychic as an evolved soul—enter into you.

So you need to begin to discriminate between what's *your* feelings, and the feelings of those people in the apartment next to you, in the car next to you, in the city and so on.

And you've got to just go through this process of self-discovery, where you just will go back and go through and eliminate all the conditioning from this life. It's a fascinating thing.

But the network will help you, is what I'm suggesting. It's real, it exists. And I'm a subscriber. [audience laughter]

It's like getting the cable hooked in, you know, lots of channels. Lots! Lots! More than *you* can imagine. And the network is there.

So when you're out there during the day or at night, or whatever, and you're cruising around, just think of the network. Just think of it, that energy. And not just in this world, but throughout all of the universes, all the dimensional planes, all of eternity.

All higher beings are part of the network, this network of light.

And they understand the plight of the individual who is just trying to reach higher, and they help. Everyone on the network helps.

And if you reach intensely enough, then light will always be there.

That's what the network is for. And it's available to any being who seeks light. You need not be alone, even when you're supposedly alone.

There is no aloneness, because the network is always there.

But you just have to make the mental effort to think of it. To sit down, to meditate for a few minutes, or just driving your car, think about the network. You can feel it pulsing. Buzzing.

The net is always operating all the time. Through all the universes. And just light will come, and that will help a whole lot.

Another question, please. Yes.

[question from a lady]

> The people that, that they have in the thousands of incarnations, what were they doing for all these reincarnations?

[Rama]

Well, not everybody starts the game at the same time. In other words, in the process of reincarnation we say, well, somebody has a thousand lifetimes, somebody has 80,000 whatever, it's like school. Why, why, why are not all kids seniors in college?

Because new kids are starting school, or being born, and they're starting the process.

So new souls are formed, actually. They come forth from the infinite. They combine and they begin their journey.

It isn't as if there's one group that started at the same time. So we have what we call younger souls and older souls. Older souls just means more incarnations.

Now, more incarnations does not necessarily mean smarter.

But it does mean more powerful. That power can be used in good or ill ways. So, for example, you could have a dictator who oppresses a country, it's obviously a very powerful person who's had a lot of lifetimes. But those lifetimes have not necessarily been used in the quest of light.

Not everyone attains enlightenment. Not all beings do that.

You know, there are higher and lower tendencies, there are different pathways you can follow. And one isn't forced, really, to follow.

Questions.

[question from a man]

ENLIGHTENMENT AND SELF-REALIZATION 181

> Could you comment on the lokas? You talked about that in your tape, and multidimensional lives?

[Rama]

Well, lokas. Lokas are planes of awareness or attention. They're dimensions. And there are a number of different lokas. There are different terminologies. The Tibetans looked at it one way, the Indians another, and so on. But they're all saying about the same thing—there are different worlds.

This tiny world—when I say this world, I don't mean just the planet Earth.

But the physical universes are just one dimension.

And there are many other dimensional planes. They are endless in their size.

And in terms of the incarnation—you know—I believe that all our incarnations are happening all at once. They're not ... I don't believe in progressive time, in linear time. But everything is simultaneous.

There is no beginning and there is no end. Time doesn't end. Time doesn't begin. It's not like that. From my point of view.

Yeah?

[question from the audience]

> Does a higher intelligence or higher awareness permit or deny any particular goals in my path, or are you always the captain of your ship?

[Rama]

Well, that's a very good question. Does higher intelligence—the higher intelligence of the universe—permit or deny you any experiences that you might want, or are you always the captain of your ship?

Well, it depends. You know, I could give you lots of answers to every question. It depends which dimensional plane I'm answering them from.

So from one dimensional plane I would say to you, "No, you are always in charge. Absolutely. You are never forced to do anything whatsoever."

And that would be absolutely true. In that dimensional plane, that would be a true statement.

In another dimensional plane, though, I could say that there's only the Self which is the doer of all things. And we just think we have free choice, but there is no free choice whatsoever.

Then, in another dimensional plane, I'd say, well, there's both. The Self exists, but at the same time creates free choice.

The reason there are different answers is that there is no right answer, because the real answers to these questions lie beyond words. There is something that is understood in that twilight area that we call enlightenment.

Because you're dealing with such a process, it's so complex, the way that the Universe is run, that the level of attention you need to understand it, you have to be so expanded. In other words, you've got a great computer, with fantastic this and that, but you've got an operating system that can't handle it. It just can't process, you see.

So that's the situation you have with enlightenment.

But right now the operating system that you have can't process all of the information.

So what's necessary is to switch operating systems. And you just do it gradually, to a slightly more competent one, a slightly more competent one, and so on, until eventually your operating system is the universes themselves. All of it.

ENLIGHTENMENT AND SELF-REALIZATION

So, it's a little of this, a little of that. It depends what day of the week it is.

Yeah?

[question from the audience]

How can you use the psychic network to make money?

[Rama]

How can you use the psychic network—well, that's not—how can you use the kundalini to make money? That's easy.

If that's your interest, the more kundalini you have, all you have to do is work. [audience laughter]

I would suggest a career in data processing, as a good start.

And if you're just somewhat clever, you see, computers are fascinating because the mind set necessary to work with advanced structures and programming and in design, is exactly what we do in advanced meditation. It's exactly the same mind set.

So people who meditate, find computers to be the easiest thing, once they get into it a little bit. Particularly the more advanced programming. So if you want to make a lot of money, then obviously that's the area to go into. You'd be a natural for it.

But, you know, just work real hard at it, and you know, start your own company, and put in 20 hour days, and you'll make a lot of money.

I mean it's not hard to make money, if that's what you want to do. You just have to work twice as hard as everybody else and be clever. And have a lot of personal power, and you can make a fortune.

But it just seems to me like there are more interesting things to do with your time.

It's good to have a bunch of money, I mean, don't misunderstand me. But endless money, I don't know. Unless you have some great selfless plan that you want to help people with and you're inspired, I don't know.

I can think of more interesting things to do with the kundalini. But it's really not hard to make money at all with kundalini. You can take this energy and do anything with it. But the thing we ask ourselves is of course, what is right?

That's the thing. As you progress along the path, that becomes more important than the energy, "to do what is right."

And so we search the self for those answers, and if what you come up with is what is right is to make a fantastic fortune, and if that is what is truly right, then that's what you'll do.

Because once you ascertain what is right, a tremendous power is unleashed from within you that will accomplish whatever is necessary.

So what I advise people to do is, rather than worry about techniques of "how to," instead to inquire into the self and gain self knowledge and determine that which is right.

Because once you determine what is right for you, not only will it make you extremely happy, and will liberate you, but it will also give you the requisite power and knowledge to do whatever it is you seek to do.

Whereas, if you just learn the snappy techniques, you'll accomplish it, but *you* won't be any different. You won't have changed, and it will just be paper, just empty experiences.

But, obviously, the question answers itself. As you have more kundalini at your disposal, power finds a way. It will happen, whatever you want. Whatever you desire …

Always remember my friends! I should tell you this. There is a law in the universe, there's a number of them.

- ॐ One of them that you should know, is whatever you want, you get. So be very careful of what you want. Sooner or later, it'll come. If not in this life, then another life. So be very careful. The monkey's paw, here, OK? [5]

- ॐ And the other one, of course, is whatever you don't value, you lose. They go together.

Questions. One or two more.

[question from the audience]

[Rama]

OK. Well, recognition is liberation. Just realizing, that, of course, helps you sort, at least, and you can detect when suddenly you get in the … Let me tell you a story.

Some friends of mine—some students of mine—recently purchased a house, a married couple, and they've never had problems or disputes over money. They've always gotten along, it's no problem. Whether they had a little, whether they had a lot, it was never a big deal, and they've been married for many, many years.

They move into this house, right, and they haven't actually even moved in. They buy, and you know, they're fixing it up, and going over to the house once in a while, checking it out, putting new cabinets in, all that sort of stuff.

And when they go over there, they start to fight about money. Whenever they're there, they start to fight about money. They start to bicker about money.

---

5. "The Monkey's Paw" is a horror short story by English author W. W. Jacobs, 1902.

"Well, we shouldn't spend this much," she's saying, "goddamn it." He's saying, "But we've got to do it right," and you know this whole thing is going on, right.

So, they get in a conversation with the woman who, I guess, lives next door or whatever, and she says, "Oh yes, well you know the people who had the house prior to the tenant who was in here, they were renting it for a while because they couldn't sell it because the market was lousy, the couple, they had a divorce.

"The reason they had a divorce? Well, they fought over money all the time."

And the subtle impressions stayed in the house, you see.

Now, once they saw that, of course, then they said, "Ah, this is it." And then it was just easy to, you know, do your simple exorcism of the house and that took care of it. [audience laughter]

So, when you realize that you're being affected, it makes it a whole lot easier. When it's tough is when you don't know, and you're just sort of depressed, or discouraged, and you assume it's you!

And you don't realize that you're just picking it up from somebody else.

That actually you're a happy being. And there's not a darn thing in the world to feel bad about, but you're just picking it up.

So when you realize that, it makes it a lot easier.

Once they understood that fact, that helped a whole lot. And, it's harder in proximity. That residual vibration of the house, so what they did was just had it totally cleaned, repainted, and you know, did the stuff, and anyway.

But when you have somebody living near you that's putting out a lot of bad energy—this can happen at work. A person's desk next to you. It can happen where you live, it's more difficult.

If it's real bad, I always suggest that you try and get out of the situation, or move to a different place, or whatever. If you can't do that, that's not practical, then the best thing to do is just to strengthen *your* place as much as possible.

Make your house as beautiful, or your room as beautiful as possible. Put as much good energy into it. You're creating walls of energy. Keep your place impeccably clean, your closets in order. Everything in place.

That creates a force, a web, a network of energy around where you live. And of course by meditating there.

And then by being compassionate, and trying to understand that that person is just in a certain stage of evolution, and that's where they are.

That's about the best you can do, really. Just to try not to think about it too much, because if you get angry with a person, you focus on them, and more of their energy enters into you.

And there's nothing to be angry about. They're just doing what they do. That's the kind of being they are, that's the kind of operating system they have, for now.

So, try and feel compassionate.

If you can move, that's the best. If you can't, you try and be understanding, and at the same time, just make your place as strong as possible.

Put as much good energy into your home, or your place of power, as possible, and that will help a whole lot. That's really all you can do.

Yeah?

[question from the audience about conditioning]

[Rama]

Well, conditioning is everything that you've been taught. In other words, conditioning is sexual conditioning, that's where it starts. Meaning that you are a certain sex, and as a member of either the male or female sex, you are this and you are not that.

Conditioning has to do with language. It's thinking. The thoughts that you're taught. How you view …

> "Now this is a good person, Suzy, and this is a bad person."
>
> "Suzy, no you can't wear that dress, it's too short, you see, that's not right."

Conditioning is what your parents teach you, society, teachers.

But conditioning—that's simple conditioning. More complex conditioning has to do with the way or the nature of reality.

In other words, we're taught that,

> "This is possible, and this is not possible."
>
> "This is real, and this is not real."

We're given … Our whole framework in our minds is supported by our thoughts.

But there is another section of our being—the will—which has nothing to do with that, which is open to other worlds, other realities. Very few people ever tap that part of their being, and that's the part of your being, of course you tap to attain enlightenment, and higher planes of attention.

But conditioning is the way you see life. When you look at a tree, do you see it, or do just see your idea of "tree" that you were taught? Or do you *see* what it really is?

Do you *see*, in other words, the tree on other planes?

What I mean by conditioning is—those thoughts and impressions that keep

ENLIGHTENMENT AND SELF-REALIZATION 189

you limited, your consciousness structured to one plane.

You can look at a tree, you should be able to *see* its luminosity, it's life forms on other dimensional planes. The reason you can't do that is because you've been taught that it's not there.

So we're cut off from most of life by our conditioning. And so the removal of that conditioning is the first step, and then of course, the deeper conditioning—the samskaras, multi-life patterns—has to be dealt with also.

And the way it's really dealt with is just by absorption in the superconscious. The more you move into light, light just diffuses that, and washes that off, and of course the recognition that it's there.

You don't have to think about it a whole lot, but what you need to do is just move into higher and higher spectrums of kundalini, of energy. It's just as if there are layers upon you and they're just washed off, it goes away.

And, of course, you have to tighten up your life, and see where you're losing power and stop losing power, learn new ways to gain power, luminosity.

Refocus your life more on light, and God and truth and frogs, you know, things like that.

You see, there are two principal paths. One is the pathway of light, and the other is the pathway of power. Both lead to enlightenment and self-realization. But they are very different ways.

In order to follow the path of light, you have to be good. That's the path of the saint, the happy little soul.

But you don't have to be good to really get there. There's another way, that's why there's hope [laughter].

And that's the path of mysticism, or the path of power. And that doesn't really have to do so much with morals, as with power and its use, and its abuse, and the structures of power within the self. The systems analysis of power and its uses to change attention and regain luminosity, and things like that.

There are different ways to attain enlightenment. There isn't just one way. And different ways are suited for different people.

The question is, sometimes you feel that there is a blockage, as you say, a root blockage, within the self that you can't seem to get rid of, that's separating you from the light, or the self, or God or higher consciousness, and you don't understand why you should keep feeling that, because why feel the pain of it since you don't seem to be able to get rid of it.

Well, it can be gotten rid of.

And just because you haven't done it in the past doesn't mean that you're not about to do it. But obviously, in order to do it, you're going to have to do something that you haven't done thus far. Because if you just repeat what you've done thus far, you're going to get the same result.

So you have to … You know you have to keep hope in your life. You see, there's just so much discouragement in the world today, you just pick it up.

You know, we're entering a very dark time now. We're entering a dark age spiritually. And it really intensifies starting in 1985 and it will be really tacky from now until about 2015.

We're in a thirty year cycle now, in a dark age to begin with, in the Kali Yuga. Where it's just very, very difficult for things that would be much easier. That you would just look at and say, "Oh, what the heck, that's going to transform in its own time, and let me just work on a lot of happy things now, and light is going to take care of it," you see.

But instead we just pick up these very negative attitudes and impressions about how difficult it all is. And it's not particularly difficult at all.

ENLIGHTENMENT AND SELF-REALIZATION

Chances are we're discussing here a samskara, a multi-life tendency. And that's why it is harder to deal with. It's nice that you can feel it, because if you can feel it, that means that you have a sense of what you have to work on.

But now, what you need to do is turn your back to it for a little while. Because just to keep looking at it, it's going to frustrate you.

It's like trying to take an exam over and over that you fail, and after a while you're gonna get so discouraged, you'll give up the subject. Let's forget that exam for a while, and work on some things that will create a success pattern in your life, and give you more energy.

So that when you come back to it later, it won't be so awesome.

Let's let the Self work on it. Don't feel that you're the doer, that you have to accomplish this action. It's the Self that does all things. It's just vanity on our part to think that we're capable of anything whatsoever.

It's the Self that does everything. You take a sharp piece of glass and you throw it in the ocean, and it comes back two months later, it's washed up, and all the sharp edges have been smoothed perfectly. When I was a kid we used to call it harmless glass.

That's what the process of enlightenment is.

You've got a lot of sharp edges right now. But if you keep throwing yourself into the light, over a period of time, those edges will soften, but please don't expect that it should be done in the order that you like, or that you would prefer. Because you'll only be frustrated.

There is an order that's taking place, that's beyond your sight right now, and it's a wonderful order. And that's the order of eternity.

But you can open yourself up to it, or you can slow the process down. Largely based upon your attitude, to be honest.

And the worst thing you can to is to start to feel discouraged, and that it's some kind of insoluble … Nothing is insoluble. Nothing.

All things transform. That's the one thing, my friend, you can be assured of in the transitory universe. Nothing will remain. Nothing. It's just a question of when. So, the thing to do is to have fun in the meantime.

Because by having fun in the meantime, instead of knocking your head against the insoluble, you see …

Ramakrishna used to say, and some other saints, they used to say that they were really happy when life made them really miserable, because it made them cry more to God. And some of them used to just …

That's an interesting way to look at a situation, too. There are different ways that you can play it. You can play it as an opportunity.

But I would just feel that you haven't found the way yet.

There's a way to cut down any obstacle. You might try making friends with it. That's my method. I make friends with everything.

Because you can make friends with your opponents. Go out to lunch with them, you know. And you can make friends with your obstacles. You should see that that so-called obstacle is God, too.

It's just a question of perception here. You've got to loosen your perception up, it's too stratified. You're still thinking too much in spiritual terms. You've got to stop trying to be so spiritual, it's boring. [laughter]

Because when you're trying to be spiritual, you aren't. When you leave yourself alone, you are. You see, you're still in concepts of what is right, and what you should be and shouldn't be. Forget it. You're obviously not having enough fun with your life.

Good!

ENLIGHTENMENT AND SELF-REALIZATION

I'd like to do one more meditation before we close up the evening.

I'd like you to focus your attention at the very base of the spine. The kundalini resides—part of it—at the base of the spine. All the way down the bottom. What we're going to do is very simple.

We're going to take the kundalini energy, and just bring it all the way up to the crown of the head, straight on up.

But! Ha.

Once you get it up to the top, you don't want to leave it there. Because otherwise, you'll become top heavy and fall over. [audience laughter]

So what you want to do, is then you want to bring the kundalini all the way back down.

If you take something out, make sure you put it away. Don't leave it out.

If you just bring the kundalini up all the time—[Rama mimics a cuckoo whistling]—you will go clean out of your mind. [audience laughter]

I'm serious. The kundalini can destroy you completely. The kundalini must be balanced. And if there's too much up flow or down flow, it's check-out time. So, always bring it back. Be polite.

So what we're going to do, is just feel the energy at the base of the spine. You may not feel anything, that's fine, just go through the exercise.

And just, what you're going to do is imagine a streak of light, or energy, or power, moving from the very bottom of your spine—and just in a nice quick flash—to zoom it right up to the top of the head, a few inches above the head. If it wants to keep going, fine.

And then feel then, we're going to do the opposite. But when we bring it down, it's not so much a flash—it's like a gentle rain of golden light—trickling it's way down through our whole body, and our whole being. All the way down.

So we're going to go up fast, and down slowly. I'd like you to do that for just a couple of minutes, and then stop.

And that will have released a great deal of kundalini, then we'll meditate.

Ignore thought, or stop thought, or just pay no attention, and just let the energy carry you.

So for a minute or two, you're going to be taking energy—maybe do it ten or twenty times. Twenty is good.

Take the energy all the way up—imagine it going right up, and then veerrryyy very gently radiating just a beautiful light all through your whole being. Relaxing you, renewing you, and then we'll do that over and over again, just for a couple of minutes. Then stop, just let go.

You may feel light like you're floating, or whatever. Ignore thought.

Relax. Just let go. That's meditation.

[meditation finishes and Rama continues speaking]

So how's it going out there, OK? Good.

It gets intense, you know. [Rama chuckles]

But what the heck. That's what you're here for.

How do you attain enlightenment? I don't think you attain enlightenment. It's something that happens to you. It's the hand of cards you get dealt.

But there are certain things, you know, that you need.

When we're talking about enlightenment, we're talking about something that's very far out. We're not talking about good meditations, or even just experiencing altered states of consciousness all the time.

We're talking about merging with the universe consciously. Wedding yourself to it, being it's bride. It's a big step. You have to give up your humanity, your humanness. You're going to become something other than human.

You know, I have a lot of students and they all want different things. I give a lot of workshops to the public, and you know, I travel, go to restaurants, Denny's sometimes. I see a lot of life.

And I don't see people who want enlightenment much. That's not discouraging, it's just how it is. People want pleasure, power. Power is the big one, isn't it. That's what people really want. In this age, power is it. Whether it's power in the physical world or power in the inner world.

But how many people really want enlightenment? Because if you really want it, what you've got to go through—it's beautiful, it's not hard—but you have to want it very badly. And you have to want it more than anything. Want it so much that you're willing not to have it, if that's what's right.

That's not just a little cute trick you say in your mind, but that's how you feel. I mean, you have to be really clean. Inwardly.

You have to just have total integrity, work beyond the point of exhaustion, meditate with your whole being. Live a life that's just perfect.

Not perfect in a moral sense. That perfection will take itself in different directions. But perfectly true.

> "To thine own self be true. And it must follow [as] the day the night, thou canst be false to anyone."

You have to be true to yourself.

Enlightenment is not gained by techniques, by wishing, by hoping.

It's gained by loving and by giving and by serving. Things that most people really don't want to do too much of.

And they're missing all the fun. What's fun is not to lead, but to follow.

To be a servant of eternity. You know, when you become enlightened, all that means is that you're a servant, essentially. It's not an elevated position, it doesn't mean that you're the king or the queen of the land. It means that you've become a servant of all.

Because you realize that the real excitement, what's really happening, the techy stuff—from a spiritual point of view—is in service to others.

So you have to have a very strong mode of selfless giving. So I suggest that there's another way. The way of power. But even the way of power will take you through the same channels.

The difference is—when you follow spirituality—what we would call the Yoga of Love, the Yoga of Selfless Giving, Karma Yoga, the Yoga of Knowledge. You know, all of those different things. There's different paths.

In the beginning, you have to first be good. And then later you become powerful. Because the idea is if you become powerful first, you'll probably abuse the power, create a lot of bad karma for yourself, and just mess things up entirely.

So they tell you to stay away from power. And to just be good. Learn goodness. Learn humility. Purity. Integrity.

On the path of Mysticism—which is an equally valid path—I teach both, you know. I follow both.

But on the path of Mysticism, you do it the other way around. First you become powerful. You don't worry about being good. And then goodness comes after power.

It's a riskier path. But you can do it either way. You have to go through the same changes either way.

Enlightenment means taking the self that you now are and dissolving it. We're just going to make you go away. We're going to take a big eraser and erase you.

And then we're going to have another self that's similar, that's more evolved. A little higher tech. And then we're going to erase that one, and do it again, and again, and again.

Until we reach a self structurally, inwardly. I'm not talking about how you look or how you think. But inside yourself, in the inner worlds, in what we call the causal body.

Until everything is lined up in a certain way. Until you network with all of the universes. So you're an access point between time and the timeless.

Enlightenment is not an arbitrary thing. It's not just some state that can't be defined.

There are actual structural changes that take place in the being—the nonphysical being—in order for that to be.

And the process that you go through, causes that to happen. It can be done over lots and lots of lifetimes. It can be compressed. You can go through—what you would in many lifetimes—in one lifetime. And there are different approaches that you can take.

But the point is not to become enlightened. The point is to become luminous. Whether or not you'll become enlightened in this incarnation, who knows?

But you can become luminous. You can go very, very high.

Enlightenment is the post-doctoral stuff. It's pretty out there.

You have to be willing to take some very large risks, which most people are not willing to take. You have to be willing to face yourself. All the horror within you, all the beauty within you. And then walk away from both, and let yourself dissolve.

You can't be afraid of dying. You have to be willing to die many times in life, over and over, and go through this dissolution process. It's not for everybody.

Because all the things you want, all the things you love, all your attachments will swing up before you, each time you're about to go into samadhi. Everything you love is there. And you know that after samadhi, that self—that was there—won't be there again!

It's the darndest thing. You'll be somebody else. And so, if you're at all attached to any part of that self or anything—if you can't let go and just trust God or the universe completely—you just can't do it.

So you have to build up to that point. But even when you get to that point, the most difficult part is, as you become more advanced, of course, you kind of become powerful.

Maybe you can manifest a few psychic powers, you know. Create falafels in the air, stuff like that. [audience laughter]

And when you can do that you start to think you're hot stuff, you see. Big deal, they can do it down [at] the shop, you know. You go down to the Falafel Shop, they can do the same thing. And it doesn't probably take them half as much energy.

But the problem is the advanced, so-called "advanced spiritual seeker" is a real pain in the ass—to work with, as a teacher. Because they have a certain amount of power, so they're not willing to start over.

You have to always be willing to start over. You have to be a perpetual beginner. 'Cause that's where the fun is. The fun is being new.

The universe is new every day. It's just beginning. Every moment. And, but you see, as human beings, when you're into power—once you get power—you're afraid to lose it. Because it took you so long to get it. Big deal!

So what, if you're everything, who cares?

The point was to have a good time. We were only playing Monopoly! It's you who started to think that the money was real. [audience laughter]

So you have to go back to playing Monopoly. That's all life is, it's a big board game.

You know, you get the chance, right, you know that sort of thing, the Community Chest, and the heavy bucks come in. They send you to the clink for a while, somebody springs you—it's karma, right? And in each life you're accruing karma.

You are experiencing in this life what you accrued in your other lifetimes.

But you're not bound by it, because now in this lifetime, you're accruing new karma, which you will experience either immediately, or later in this life, or in another incarnation.

Enlightenment doesn't necessarily mean an end to lifetimes. Just because you attain liberation—I've attained liberation many lifetimes ago, and you know, you come back. (We're working on it though.)

But—there was this brochure, I keep telling you, they show me this brochure about this place. They said "Vacation Loka". Right.

You just have to put in a couple of hours once in a while, help a few people, right? Ha, ha, yeah. [audience laughter]

Last time I go to that interdimensional travel agent. But what can you do? You try and save a buck, you go to the cheap one [laughter].

"Bargain Vacation World," my foot.

That's why this is my last incarnation in this one. I'm beating feet. There are other places, and this one's going down, anyway.

But—you can't necessarily do that, can you? I understand. I'm sympathetic. To a certain extent.

Well, you got yourself into this mess. You can't expect me to get you out of it, hell. I can laugh about it, but what do you want? You're the ones that created the karma that got you into the mess that you're in, right?

But you're also the ones that can change that. I mean you can be next to someone who's imbued with light, energy, power, and it can all just fall "in one chakra and out the other".

Unless you really have figured out the error of your ways.

And the error of your ways is simply that you didn't love enough.

It's not what you do that hurts you, it's what you don't do. What you don't do is love enough. You need to love more.

You know, all the teachers say the same thing, and one ever gets it. It's so basic. You need to be wildly, madly in love with life. With God, with whatever part of life works for you.

But it's that love that frees and liberates the spirit.

You also have to learn the ways of power, of course. Otherwise, you'll be a victim.

You have to understand the structure and networking of the universes and interdimensional planes. Because you're subject to all of that, of course. It's a very complex subject, naturally.

But the thing that you need the most is to love.

And not to worry about enlightenment and nirvana. But rather just to plug yourself into doing good for others and advancing yourself.

In other words, you need a sound structure to start with.

You have to define your goals properly, in my opinion. Now again, I'm an old school spiritual teacher, you'll have to forgive me. But I believe that what you need to do is think about what you're doing before you do it.

A little self-analysis can go a long way. It can save you a lot of incarnations. And what you need to think about is—what you're here for. You took incarnation in this lifetime for a particular purpose. And you need to ask yourself, are you doing it?

And if you're not doing it, no wonder you're not happy.

The reason a person isn't happy when they're evolved—a person such as yourself—is because you're not doing what your soul wants.

Before you came into the incarnation, there were certain goals that you set. They're not like goals like we think of goals. Like, you know, producing 50,000 cars or something. But there's certain things you want to learn or experience.

But now we come in, and we're timid, we're afraid, we allow the world to beat us down, the descriptions of the world and so on.

And we don't fight hard enough. If you really love, you'll fight for light.

Not fight someone outside of yourself, but you'll fight inside of yourself so that you'll never settle for anything but truth and clarity inside your own mind. And you're willing to work hard enough, because it's fun to be liberated.

Every day you meditate, every time you care, every time you love—you take a step into a larger world. You become more of a citizen of the galaxy than a citizen of a very small confused planet.

There's a big universe out there, with lots of highly evolved beings who figured out the problems people are having here, a *long* time ago.

And you can be part of that world, or you can stay in this one for a long time. That's up to you.

And you don't have to follow a religious code, you don't have to follow a particular creed, all that stuff is very backwards. It's good in its place for beginners. But as you advance, that's not necessary. We move into the pure experience of mysticism.

You need the actual experience of the clear light.

Talk is great—what you need is to dissolve into that light again and again. That's what creates enlightenment. And also, you have to have a feeling of, there's more in it than just for yourself.

You have to want to put energy back into the system. Because if you don't, there can be no enlightenment. It's impossible. There's just not enough evolution in the soul.

Because an evolved soul knows that you are not just yourself, that you are all of "this". And every time you do something for "this", it's for yourself.

And that's just where the fun is, is in giving. It's that attitude that's necessary. Along with a tremendous sense of humor and a great deal of personal power.

And powerful friends help. You know, they always say that associating with the holy is part of how you do it. You burn away some of that—when they say the holy, they don't mean people who are walking around on Wheaties all day.

The holy are some of the weirdest bunch you'll ever meet. I mean if they're really holy. Meaning, not that they walk around with Bibles, but if they're really holy, meaning they're intoxicated with God-consciousness. You're dealing with spiritual teachers, the real ones, or just enlightened beings, or highly evolved beings are a weird bunch.

And they're funny, they're real funny. And they're all real different, they're characters.

And they're not particularly moral, nor are they particularly immoral. They don't follow any code or any creed. It's all been passed away.

Because once you've merged with that light, God is in everything, so what's the difference. You just let the Self direct you. Because you are the Self.

So, associating with beings like that, obviously, you pick up a tremendous charge of energy and inspiration from that. That helps a whole lot.

But the main thing is—you just have to ask yourself—what did you come here to do? You came here to do something. Not "do" in the sense of a project. But what did you come here to see, to experience, to learn? That's your project.

Anything you accomplish here will be washed away, everything is transitory in this world. But you came here to have certain experiences, to enlarge yourself.

To increase your heart.

You know, you want to be like the Grinch. You know, the Grinch who stole Christmas? The old Grinch is not too evolved in the beginning. He's going to rip off all those Whos. All that Who pudding and Who pie. [audience laughter]

He's going to go for it, the Grinch! But then something happens to the Grinch!

He has a little enlightening experience. His heart grows. You know that day he's up on the hill and he's got that poor little dog pulling his sled, and all the Who pudding and the Who pie and the whole bit and the presents are about to go over the cliff!

And the Grinch, suddenly it's just like his heart chakra goes "Whhhong!"

And he just realizes that there's more to life than just messing up the Whos' Christmas.

And I always cry at that part when—Boris Karloff is narrating it—and the tears come down, "And the Grinch's heart that day grew the size of 12 Grinches."

And then he pulls his sled back and he goes back and they have a great Christmas, and stuff like that. And then they shoot the Grinch. [audience laughter] They cut that part for TV.

Well, he needed to move forward to another life, I guess. I mean how far can he go, he's a Grinch, right? I mean, even a good Grinch. There's structural limitations upon a being.

Maybe he'll be a Who in his next life? I don't know. Is that a step up? Sally Who?

"Ha ho ha hoo!" [said in a sweet sing-song manner, audience laughs]

Those Whos were bhaktis if I've ever seen them.

I don't know about all that love stuff. I'd stay with power if I were you. [laughter]

Love—you can't trust it. One day you love, the next day you hate—stay with power, don't get involved with love. Love is the pits, love is the pits. Power is happening. Because when you follow the path of love, I mean, the dangers on the path of love are excessive.

They're just excessive. Because what happens is, you don't really love. It's just your self you're loving. You're not loving outside yourself. It's very selfish. You're loving all the time because it makes you feel good.

Whereas, when you follow the path of power, then you can do anything for someone. What can you do with love? Love is totally impractical.

I would love if I were you. I would always follow the path of love. [laughter] Love is absolutely the best way. Power has too many problems in it. You can be taken out by it.

Listen, this could go on forever, and it probably will, but what I'd like to do is end with just a very brief two, three minute meditation. But I want to really take you over the top with energy, OK?

This is the last public workshop in our series. I won't be doing any more until like next September in Los Angeles, so it's like nine months, so this is the last minute of it. So it's sort of the moment of power at the end of the series, 1985, the whole bit.

So for the last few minutes, I'd like to just sort of take you away someplace. Put you out for a while. Make it difficult for you to walk later, the usual.

Now, I'd like you—in this meditation—to at least part of the time keep your eyes open and watch. I'm going to be doing some of those mudras again.

And essentially what I'm doing is taking the energy of the kundalini. It can be done two ways. One can just sit as I was before, and be absorbed in samadhi and dissolve. I go beyond the form and the formless and just dissolve in eternity.

And you could say, "Why would you want to do anything else other than that?" Well, that's wonderful, and the kundalini radiates to everyone.

But there are other types of power that can be transferred to people—that will aid them in their self-discovery—that can't be transferred that way. And they're transferred through what we call the siddhas.

The siddhas are not just miraculous powers to dazzle and entertain, but the siddhas are the opening of interdimensional planes of reality, whereby certain energies—strands of luminosity—are brought through.

We actually open those interdimensional planes and bring energies through, and infuse them into people. That's really what spiritual teaching is all about. It doesn't have that much to do with words, but it's the transfer of energy and power.

So, when we do it with the siddhas, we use the body, because the body is part of the Earth, and these are powers of the Earth. They are of the material universe. They are high-tech spiritual powers. But they're of a different order than the superconscious.

The superconscious is just the absorption in nirvana, the stillness.

This is samadhi. Dissolution.

[Rama briefly goes into samadhi in order to demonstrate dissolution]

The siddhas are different. It's applied power. So that's what I'm going to be doing.

And the reason I have you watch is because what you're doing is focusing your attention, like you're aiming.

But never watch too hard, because you need to be meditating. Clearing your mind, but it's like daydreaming. It's what we call *gazing*. A different practice than meditating.

You don't want to look directly. If you look too hard, you'll focus too hard, and you'll focus too much on the physical.

You want a very diffuse gaze. You're just looking very generally at the stage.

I'll be doing a series of movements. Sometimes they look like—it looks like tai chi sometimes.

It's really what tai chi evolved from. People don't understand tai chi. Tai chi has very little to do with movements. It was originally energy transposition.

But things are forgotten in this age. It's leftover from another cycle.

And I'll be just bringing a lot of energy through—just for a couple of minutes—and then we'll say goodnight, and you'll have a good journey, I'm sure.

Why not? The way is Light, isn't it? So. Let's meditate for a few minutes, OK? Good.

Part Two

Psychic Development Workshop

CHAPTER FOUR

AN INTRODUCTION TO RAMA SEMINARS PSYCHIC DEVELOPMENT

What is it to be psychic? To be aware of all things, or just "hidden" things? What is it to feel another person when they're thousands of miles away? To look inside someone, perhaps deeper than they can see into themselves? How do you deal with knowledge of the future? Or knowledge of past lives?

Psychic Awareness can be the greatest of all gifts, or it can be a curse. It can create harmony or pain, trust or separation.

My name is Rama. You may have heard of me. I teach classes in Psychic Awareness, Self-Discovery, Mysticism, Meditation, Enlightenment and Magic. I've been teaching for many, many lifetimes. I was a teacher in the Temple in Atlantis, in the old Egyptian Cycle, I've had incarnations teaching in Japan, as a Zen Master, in India as a Jnana Yoga Master, in Tibet as a Lama. I ran very large monasteries. You might have been in one, in a past life. And I've taught in other worlds other than this world. I'm always teaching, wherever I go.

In this lifetime, of course, I've been teaching for about sixteen years. I teach people how to be free, how to go within and find meaning, purpose, to develop their strengths and talents; to find who and what they are in this crazy universe; to find peace, to meditate and enter into powerful interdimensional vortexes; to develop the psychic abilities, occult powers, the siddhas; and to deal with the world. A world that is not necessarily interested in refinement, inner peace, psychic development and awareness. It doesn't recognize the luminous spheres of existence and the higher beings in other planes that seek to network with those who develop themselves psychically in this world.

It is my belief that we are all psychic. Yet, some are more psychic than others. Psychic Development really depends, to a certain extent, upon what you have done in your past lives. The chances are that you have practiced self-discovery in other lifetimes. That's why I sent you this tape. You may not be able to recall that. Perhaps you can reclaim the powers from your past lives. There is a way.

Up until recently, I had about 800 students. I had some meditation centers in different places—San Francisco, Los Angeles, Boston, San Diego. I decided to let go of my students, to not teach them formally, as accepted students.

They've done very well, over the years, and I taught them the things that I could teach them in that particular way. Most of the teaching I do is through awareness. My own psychic and occult abilities are highly developed, and what I do is meditate with people. And when I meditate with them, I can enter into their attention field. And transfer knowledge, power and information.

This is 1985 and a great change is taking place in our universe. We're moving into a darker age. It's becoming harder to *see*. And people who are psychic and spiritually inclined are feeling that shift. Things that were easier before are more difficult now. The mind is more restless. It's harder to find that still center, to see the beauty in our physical environment. To be close to others.

There's nothing wrong with you—if you are experiencing these changes. This is psychic interference. The first thing to know is that you should not blame yourself. This is a shift in the planes of reality that is taking place in the interdimensional vortexes in which our world is contained. I would like to teach you how to deal with these changing times. In order to do that, as I mentioned before, I recently let go of my 800 students and closed my centers to devote myself fully to working with the public. I've been very reclusive for the last 4 or 5 years, only occasionally meditating with the public and just working extensively with my private students. But now the time really necessitates those of us who are teachers to step forward and help others, because the times are getting darker.

To be psychic is problematic. In the sense that while it's a great gift, you're also a kind of a psychic sponge. You pick up thoughts and impressions from everyone around you. And unless you've learned how to *see*, you probably don't realize that most of the thoughts in your mind are not your own. They come from the people around you—in your household; where you work; people you are networked to.

There is a strand of attention between you and anyone that you've ever loved, been close to, had sex with—and unless you know how to break that strand of attention you continuously pick up thoughts and impressions from those individuals, even though you may not have seen them for many years. They influence you. You're influenced by the place you live, and it's power. You're influenced by all those around you, and by psychic unseen forces.

There's a way to deal with all this effectively and powerfully. There's a way to increase your own personal power and knowledge. Psychic Development.

I've begun a series of workshops. They last for four evenings. Four evenings in Psychic Development. I'm holding them every other month in Los Angeles. They're never the same. I haven't assigned titles to the individual workshops. I feel that at your level of development, it's not necessary for me to tempt you with fascinating titles. You can hear my voice, close your eyes and have contact with me immediately and know what it is that I do, and whether I can be of any help to you.

The seminars are in Los Angeles, and they're designed to help you reach enlightenment, to develop powers. A place to come and laugh, ask questions and be in an environment with hundreds of other persons like yourself at different levels of development. Souls that have incarnated here from different worlds. I attract powerful people of all types. Many I've worked with as students, or in other lives. Many I'm just meeting for the first time.

The areas that I'll be focusing on have to do with psychic development, meditation, occult powers, astral travel, the enlightenment of women and men, of course, but with particular focus on the enlightenment of women, and the development of their powers. Since women have been so neglected over the incarnations, it's time to balance that out, isn't it? Mysticism and Magic.

The seminars last for about 3½ hours each, four nights in a row, Thursday, Friday, Saturday and Sunday at the Los Angeles Convention Center. We sit down in a room and the world shifts. What I do is not what I say, what I am is not who you see. My real talent is to shift planes of attention, to guide people through interdimensional vortexes. As we sit there in the room, I'll talk about astral travel and mysticism, developing powers, how to generate more money in your life using psychic attention. How to focus. How to deal with those who every day drain your energy and power. Who manipulate you and take advantage of you because you're a nice person because you're psychically developed. How to heal, how to channel energy. All of the topics in psychic development.

But while we're sitting there, what's really taking place, as any, of course, of your friends who have attended my meditations can tell you, is a psychic transfer. I go into samadhi. Into enlightenment. I am enlightenment. My attention field, that is. And I use the powers that life has been kind enough to share with me to aid you in your development. What will the effect be on you? I can't say. I can, of course, guarantee nothing. Since everything is dependent upon your receptivity. Yet I do what I do. I'm there to help you if I can. To make you laugh, to astound you, to shift the worlds in front of your eyes. Hopefully, if you're receptive, when you leave, you'll have a much broader perspective on life and yourself. You'll feel clearer and more energized. Most people attend my classes on a regular basis. Some come one time and that's sufficient.

What is it that you want? What is it that you seek? When you can shift attention, you change the universe. The first step is learning to stop thought. As long as there are thoughts in the mind, it's very hard to be quiet and still. Then you need to learn *gazing* techniques—ways of focusing attention so you can unlock your hidden psychic powers and use them. Naturally it's important to never use these incredible powers to injure or harm others. Unless, of course, they are doing the same to you.

Money is very important. In my opinion, as a person who is psychic, you need to realize and see that the times we are living in are about to change. The period of time from 1985 to 2015 is going to be a very upsetting time. And as a person who is psychic, and who will become more so—if you practice the methods, of course—you need to really have a very refined, beautiful and inaccessible atmosphere. So a great deal of the teaching I do has to do with money. That is to say, how to make more of it. How to use it more effectively.

I run a computer company in addition to teaching classes in meditation. One of the things that we do in the computer company is something called systems analysis. We look at and evaluate a system and we seek ways to improve it. And really my approach to self-discovery is very high tech. Essentially what I'm going to do is teach you how to examine your life and take it apart structurally.

How to look at every part of it, and then ask a question, "Am I *gazing*? Or am I wasting time? Am I stepping in other dimensions and opening myself up to the totality and seeing what I am?"

If you're not, it's because you're losing energy. And it's necessarily important to look at every aspect of your life and analyze it, and that's what we do in the seminars. I'll discuss how to look at every part of your life and determine whether or not you're gaining energy from it. We'll examine your relationships, thoughts you think, places you go. Every activity either adds to your personal power or detracts from it. And the sum total of your kundalini, of your energy, of course, determines everything that happens to you. So, in the seminars I sit up front and talk about all these things with everyone. There are periods of meditation where I teach meditative and *gazing* techniques from Egypt, Atlantis, Tibet, Japan, India. You practice these techniques with me and take them home with you, and continue to work on them, and they'll aid you tremendously. They're extremely powerful

The seminars intensify. The reason I have four nights, is that the first night or two is really just a clearing process. As we're sitting there and I'm using the kundalini—when we meditate—I'm clearing your subtle physical body. Washing away layers that you've picked up, and talking about all kinds of useful things—but the real transference takes place most effectively on the last two nights. I need the four nights with you to really do what I can do. The first two nights are a clearing and the second two nights are a transfer. Oh, the transference of course takes place each night.

I'm an architect of consciousness. I design, revise, take in, take out, change. The Seminars are designed for people who wish to not just have a superficial change, not just come to a seminar series and buy a few tapes and pacify themselves with the fact that they're doing something for their internal growth. They're powerful experiences in consciousness. They change you. All that energy changes you. How, who can say? And before attending a series of seminars I suggest that you ask yourself what it is that you want. Is your life really going the way you would like it to? Are you making the advances in awareness that you are capable of? Do you feel that there's a deeper you in there that's really longing to get out?

Well, let's do something about it! Needless to say, I can't do it for you. I can show you ways that when properly employed over a period of time will cause that to really happen, though. And we can meet again and spend some time together in this transformative process that we call life.

There really isn't any advanced registration process. I like to keep it simple. Just come. You can pay at the door. Use Visa Card or Master Charge if that makes it easier. I'll probably have a few tapes for sale which will be available before or after the workshop, or during the little break we take in the middle.

When we practice *gazing* and meditation, during those periods of time, I'll be playing some music, usually electronic music, which just makes it more relaxing to sit for five minutes or so in stillness while we practice these powerful transformative techniques.

Again, to be honest with you, I really am not in the mood to sell you. I'd like to tell you about these seminars. But the teaching I do is for very sophisticated people. The majority of people, of course, who usually come to my seminars are in either the high tech fields or in entertainment or law or medicine. And quite a few students. And I have been reclusive for many years now. But now I've let go of my students so I have time and energy to deal with you. It's an inner contract that we write. The outer form: you come, I'm there, you're there, we sit in a room with lots of powerful people, Rama talks, Rama meditates, Rama laughs, Rama does his "act", maybe he dances, who knows what Rama's gonna do next? I sure don't.

We have fun. But something happens. There's more going on, needless to say. In other words, psychic teaching is done in a different way. If I want to teach you something—I was an English professor at one time. And when I would teach Shakespeare or poetry I would naturally explain verbally. But in psychic teaching, if you're a real psychic teacher, the way you do it is of course psychically. You talk and answer questions and teach people how to become more receptive. But the material suggests an inner communication.

So the whole time on one plane of attention while we're sitting there and I'm talking and answering questions and discussing thousands of aspects of psychic development, occultism, mysticism, using the siddha powers, demonstrating the powers, and so on. And moving in and out of various enlightened stages of attention—what I'm doing is having a conversation with you. I'm really having that conversation with you right now. Not just on the tape, but psychically, aren't I?

I'm saying, "Greetings friend, life is more beautiful than any of us can believe, but it can also be exceedingly painful if you're not aware of how to use your psychic skills."

You may never reach your potential. You can be victimized by others who steal your energy, psychic vampires. Everybody's cruising for energy. And you as a highly evolved person are someone who attracts more of those people. They can take your energy from you in a million ways, and do. And then you look in the mirror and you're older and more tired, and you know that you just never reached that potential.

Well, there is something you can do about it. But you've got to be serious. Serious and happy. But serious. Life is going by. The incarnation doesn't last forever. I like to work with people like that. Not just the happy-go-lucky, "Hey, gee, life is great for sure!" type people. People who are serious and want to get down—in the transformative process. Who want to work with it now. You've taken the fun courses. You've seen the gurus, you've done this and that. Now you want to sit down and really learn it so you can actually experience the totality. You can really develop those powers, you can shape and form your life.

You've got to have a little bit of determination. Then I can teach you something. Then you're ready.

So come to the seminars. A little brochure accompanies this tape that may explain more. The tape is just here to say "Hi!" To tell you that what you've been experiencing in your psyche right now is not really your fault. It's just a way of explaining that there's a great shift, a great conjunction that is taking place right now in the inner universes. We're dropping—the Earth—into a lower level of attention. So there's just a lot more psychic interference, it's hard to be happy and perky, it's harder to have energy. I'm sure you've felt it.

But there's something you can do about it. Psychic Self-Defense. And Psychic Development. Learning to draw the occult energy in and through your being to deal with these changing times and have fun with them. It's also an exciting time, a wonderful time. The seminars are designed in four nights to aid you in this. I can't make you a guarantee as to what will happen to you, what will work and what will not. It's entirely up to you and your application of the materials.

And if our only contact is this tape, I would just like to wish you well.

Say, "Hi! How ya doin? This is Rama, life is eternal, the universes are changing and spinning, be excited about it all. Draw on your power. You can handle it all. It's not a problem, you just have to know how. Don't be discouraged by the world around you of wars and war's alarms, of people who just seek things for themselves and don't care about others. The Star Wars Systems, the generals.

"Don't be concerned. It's just illusion. It's just one dimension. The whole universe is not represented by this Earth. There are worlds with higher beings who are far more advanced, and you can join them. There's universe after universe. It's eternal, it's endless God. Infinite reality. And power is hovering."

I'd like to talk to you about places of power. *Dreaming*. How to astral travel. How to be still inside. But—whatever. Hope to see you if you can come by. I've made it hopefully easier for you the first time. I have to pay the bills, needless to say, and run a seminar series. But the first time by, half price. If it's your first four night seminar series, half-price. After that, the regular price. Just to make it easier for you. And our student price for full-time students 25 and under will be half-price also, if it's your first four night series. I hope to see you at the LA Convention Center.

Meditate for a moment after this tape with me. And look, let's look a little more for the beauty of the universe. And don't think about whether you should come or not, just see if power draws you. If power draws you, then we'll have a heck of a good time. And if not, I'd just like to wish you well on your journey. And urge you never to be discouraged. To always be joyful. And careful.

So this is Rama, wishing you well on your journey. Just touching base here in these changing times with you. Suggesting that it might be fun to go to the timeless worlds, since this show here is getting a little gnarly, on the old planet.

And it might be fun for you to sit in a room and network with other powerful psychic beings, and to meet some of Rama's nonphysical friends, who tend to drop by, never paying an admission charge, naturally, at the seminars. Meeting in Los Angeles, the city of Ultimate Power. An ancient power place, Los Angeles. Contacting other worlds, other planes, the usual. Infinite consciousness. Hope to see you.

Namaste.

CHAPTER FIVE

SELFLESS GIVING

Today is November 1st, 1985. It's around 2:30 in the afternoon.

I'd like to talk with you today about selfless giving.

People ask sometimes, what is the meaning of life? Why do we exist? Is there a purpose, or a reason or, did it just happen? Are we just an accident in the cosmos? Or is there a plan or an idea?

Is there a God? If there is a God, how could a being we refer to as "higher" create a world with so much pain, frustration, selfishness, and beauty?

Most people lead lives of frustration and disappointment. They enjoy temporary pleasures … and long-lasting suffering.

We live in a world where people fight wars; they kill each other. They rape the Earth. One nationality suppresses another, one religion claims to be the exclusive way to truth or God.

We see very few people who are satisfied. They say that the only ones who are really happy are the enlightened or the fools.

You live in this world for a short time. Ten years, twenty years, eighty years. Eighty years is not very long in cosmic time, is it?

We don't really remember where we came from and we're not too sure about where we go to. If we go, if we "are", after this thing that we call life.

There doesn't necessarily seem to be a whole lot we can do about it. You don't really have a choice. You are alive, you will die.

And yet, there are those who tell us that we can be uncommonly happy, even in a world of disease, a world of frustration and more than occasional disappointment. You can be uncommonly happy.

There are those who preach the gospel of life after death. In other words, if you do certain things now, then in an immortal land after you die you'll enjoy some kind of perpetual happiness.

And they posit that against hell and suffering, some kind of eternal damnation. If you don't do those things, or if you do their opposite, then you will experience eternal suffering.

There are different views—different cosmologies, ways of seeing life.

I personally don't subscribe to any particular cosmology or belief system … I'm a "seer".

My name is Rama, and I'd like to talk to you a little bit about my own personal experiences, because those are all I really have to go with or from. Now, I'm fortunate in the sense that I have pretty good vision. Sort of 20/20 in the inner world.

So, of course, I can recall my past lives, and other peoples' lives. I can *see* other times, other dimensions. Because I've spent many years and many lifetimes studying the science of being, the science of attention and awareness.

Now, what all of that boils down to—for me, and of course for others who have had similar experiences—is a kind of a *seeing*. And that *seeing* is a *seeing* of life.

That is to say, I see life not in just one way, but in a lot of different ways, because life is not one thing. If I put on a pair of rose-colored glasses, the world will be rosy. If I put on yellow-tinted glasses, the world will be yellow.

There are thousands and millions of dimensions. Other worlds. There are of course, other physical worlds, but there are realities that are mind. States of mind. Everything is a state of mind. Everything depends upon your level of attention or awareness.

So there are many views, many ways to view life. Is there one way that is infinitely more correct than another? I think so. In that I think that the way that is most correct is not to have a single way.

But one thing that I have seen, again and again, regardless of the method of apprehension of the dimensional plane that one is in—one thing that I've seen again and again is selfless giving and how effective it is.

Selfless giving presupposes something.

It presupposes that there is a luminous reality which is beyond sight, sound and mind. It is beyond the senses. It's within us and around us.

Some people call it God, some call it nirvana, truth, there are many different names, the Tao. Lots of names. The names don't really matter. I could call you Susan or Bob or Harold. That name doesn't ultimately change who or what you are, it's a description. It's something we affix in time and space.

The luminous reality is for real. Because I see it and feel it and experience it. Constantly.

One who sees and feels and experiences the luminous reality constantly, we say is enlightened. Simply meaning that they live in a state of light. They're always aware of that luminous energy that is life.

They're not simply confined to the experience of their senses—feeling, tasting, smelling, hearing and touching. They use a sixth sense to look where their eyes cannot see; to hear where their ears can't listen; to taste that which cannot be tasted with the tongue; to feel that which can never be felt, even in the most delicate caress.

To hear something more beautiful than all the symphonies that have ever been, and the most celestial voices.

Perfection—it's everywhere.

But yet again, looking at most of the people in this world, you'd say, "Well, where is that? If all this so-called perfection is around, people sure seem to be missing the boat! Why don't people see and feel it more?"

It's because they're stuck in their senses, they're stuck in their thoughts. They're stuck in a real limited way of seeing life. Which is based upon all kinds of things—karma, attention fields, descriptions of the world—but ultimately, everything that causes one's limited view of the world is not important.

What's important is getting out of it. And not simply adapting another cosmology. That's just as limited.

For example, there are many people who are pretty primitive in a limited way of looking at life. Our life is to be lived just for the enjoyment of the senses, meaning [that] eating, having sex, feeling comfortable, is a short path to annihilation in my estimation.

These things might be fun, but if that's what you base your life around, if your life is around just being comfortable, then you're never very comfortable, are you? You suffer quite a bit. Because in the realm of the senses there is not only pleasure, but there is pain. The senses, and their experiences by themselves, create emotional storms; passions surge through us, and those passions that are not fulfilled: we're unhappy, the desires, that is.

And yet, they say that the luminous reality is all around us, it's right in front of us, it's inside of us. There are those who are enlightened, who live in a perpetual state of bliss.

Now the truly enlightened are not necessarily very religious. Religion is a way of looking at life. It's a convenient description to take care of our fears, to pacify us.

Enlightenment doesn't have much to do with religion. You can be religious and be enlightened. You could not be religious at all and be enlightened. Enlightenment doesn't simply mean being happy. Nor does it mean being able to meditate well and having a pretty fluid level of attention.

It means something else. It's quite difficult to define. It means going beyond the human spectrum—as we know it—and merging your awareness with everything.

Enlightenment doesn't mean [chuckles] that you know everything; it doesn't mean you can fix the car. It doesn't mean you can speak in all languages. It doesn't mean that you know what's going to happen when you go out walking today. It's not a prescient knowledge of the future and all pasts, those are psychic abilities.

One can be enlightened and not see those things because you are so immersed in light that there's no one there to know.

In other words, we like to think of enlightenment as something that we experience. You will experience enlightenment, meaning you will stay basically the same and enlightenment is like some wonderful food that you will eat, and the eating of this food will make you feel great.

But it'll still be you that's eating the food. Enlightenment is the food that eats you.

It means growing up psychically, and seeing that there's a big universe around us, with countless planes of attention. That life is composed of lines of light, fibers of energy, pulsing, surging, still. Pure being.

Self-discovery is the entrance into all of that. It means leaving this world, not necessarily physically. It's a journey, it's a trip.

The trip changes you. Your life is the journey. You're on the trip now.

How's it going?

There are different pathways—to immortality—to this experience of enlightenment.

And remember, enlightenment is not just a final ending. That is to say, it's not something that happens to you just one day. You get a letter in the mail and they tell you you've been enlightened. And everything was horrible up to that day, and everything will be perfect after that.

That's not the case. Enlightenment is something that happens gradually over many years, over many incarnations.

And, you still suffer, after enlightenment. In the sense that the body still feels pain.

Thoughts still pass through the mind, emotions. But there's not really a sense of participation.

Anyway, let's not talk too much about enlightenment right now because we're talking today about selfless giving.

You and I are having a conversation. You're listening, and I'm talking. But I'm listening to you as I talk. I can feel you out there. You're a part of me. I'm a part of you, and we're all a part of this great nothingness.

So the question—the only one that's really worthwhile—is, "What do you want? Are you content with your life as it is?" If you are, enjoy it. Enjoy the transitory pains and pleasures of what we call the samsara, the world appearance, the way things are, life.

But, if there's something in you that wants enlightenment—that wants the experience of power, luminosity, attention, energy—that wants to go beyond the veil of suffering and seeing yourself simply as a person; if there's something in you that wants to go beyond all of that, and each day grow into something that's more beautiful, that resonates more with life, then you're looking for enlightenment.

It comes in different forms and different packages. There's no one way to go about it.

Oh! There I go, talking about enlightenment again. I don't really want to talk about enlightenment.

I'd like to talk about—having fun. Now, different people have fun in different ways. Admittedly. And no one way is better than another. I guess.

But I have observed—you may have had this experience—that most people who are out there having fun do not seem to be having a great deal of fun. [Rama laughs]

People go to beaches, they go to carnivals, parties. They participate in sports, they do all kinds of things. They drink, they smoke. They sniff. They do a lot of things. They follow religions. They meditate. They do japa,[6] they repeat mantrams.

[Rama imitates an Indian guru]

> "Oh, the Guru! He tells them the truth in the divine waaaay, but he is not necessarily so happy a great deal of the time, because his disciples, they drive him up the wall!"
> [Rama laughs]

[normal voice]

Yeah, I don't see that most people are exactly real happy.

---

6. Any meditation on a higher power (God or a form of God) involving focused repetition, e.g., of a mantra, a thought, a phrase, an image, or silently.

Even the ones who profess to be this, or that or the other thing.

But I know a way to happiness. Why do I know this way? Because I've been interested in finding a way for a long, long time. I know a lot of ways to happiness. I also know some pretty fast shortcuts to misery.

There's one way, though, that I know of, that leads to happiness which never fails. It's the one thing that at any stage in your evolution can raise your level of attention. Can make you feel better. Can add significantly to your life.

And that is selfless giving.

Selfless giving is friendliness. It's an attitude towards life, a reverence for life. And it is one of the highest of all ways.

As a matter of fact, just about every tradition that talks about enlightenment—the expansion of consciousness, all that stuff—they all talk about one thing in common, and no matter what their method is or their methodlessness or whatever the heck they've got going on, I notice that one thing is constant. And that's that all of them, I'm sure with a notable exception or two somewhere, talk about selfless giving as a means, a way of raising attention, purifying the being, getting through the day, paying off karmic bills.

They talk about selfless giving.

Again, I see a lot of talk about selfless giving, I don't see too much selfless giving, even among the people who talk about it—but ... technical matters, right?

I should point out here—it's important—that I'm really not setting myself up as a paragon of virtue. I have done a lot of different things in this life and other lives.

I've experienced most of what the universe has to offer on my journey to enlightenment.

But I still see what I see. That is to say, when I talk about people who talk about selfless giving, and I say they don't practice it too much, that's the truth.

I practice it, not because I'm remarkable, but just because I find it's terrifically fun, and I find that these people who don't practice it don't seem to have much of a good time.

So I don't in any way—in any of my conversations or dialogues with you—ever wish to elevate myself. In other words, I'm not saying, "Gee, I'm a great guy, and other people aren't as great." Not even by subtle inference. I have no need to put anybody down. But I still see what I see.

It's sort of like the emperor's new clothes. I can see no reason to say that emperor is dressed well if he hasn't got a stitch of clothing on. So in the same sense, I see no reason to say that a waffle is a carrot. Unless, of course, it turns out to be one. But anyway, let's not get into all that stuff.

Selfless giving. What's the point? Well, the point is having fun.

"Having fun," you say, "isn't that a little transitory? Really Rama, I'm just into liberation, I'm just so devotional, I aspire so much to—I'm so good, I'm so pure, I'm so ssssselflessss." [Rama has fun mimicking an uppity spiritual seeker voice]

That's sort of the Beverly Hills spiritual seeker. There are a lot of them everywhere. People who are "So-o selfless, Rama, oh, but I want to take as much time and attention and show everyone how important and how selfless I am." Right.

Again, I have no issue with that, they just don't seem to be having much fun. I mean, who's having fun out there?

"Mmm, the purpose of life," the intellectual says, "is not to have fun, Rama."

Says who? Why not? Why not have fun, why not have a good time. What, just because everybody else is having a lousy time, you shouldn't have fun? This does not make sense. You know, common sense goes a long way in self-discovery, as in anything else.

Selfless giving is a lot of fun.

And I think if you view it in that way—in other words, don't think of selfless giving as a unpleasant prescription medicine that YOU have to take so YOU can reach higher levels of attention and feel all that power and ecstasy surging through every cell in your body.

No. Not at all. Selfless giving is just plain fun. Meaning you're going to do something that's going to make you feel better than you feel at the moment.

Not necessarily because it's going to help anybody else.

[Rama playfully imitates an Irish priest]

> "Oh, Willy, now. This is Father Flanagan now. Today you're gonna go out and we're gonna do some work for the parish and you're gonna go out and you're gonna sell those little Christmas seals. You'll raise a lot of money, and Willy, it's good. Aye, the Holy Mother, she used to sell them too."

[normal voice, Rama laughs]

Well, Willy might go out and sell those Christmas seals and feel lousy. And even if he sold a lot and he walked back into Father Flanagan, and he expected the Father to really pat him on the head and say, "Oh Willy, aye, you sold more than anybody, you're a great kid. You ever think of joining the priesthood, Willy? We have nice cars, you know. You like cars, Willy?"

You see, Willy isn't really practicing selfless giving. Because he probably had a drag of a time going from door to door selling those little seals. And then even once they were sold, his ego got involved in the whole action.

What a drag being Willy. Willy was probably happier before he did any selfless giving. Now he's miserable because Father Flanagan ignored him, or the Father will say, "Oh Willy, you're such a good lad, Oh Willy! I had a dream about you this marnin', Willy. In the dream God spoke to me, and he said 'Willy, that Willy, he's OK.' You hear that now Willy?"

You see, so then, Willy will feel, "I'm wonderful, I'm better than others, I am superior." And his ego will inflate. Willy was better off before he did anything. He was happier.

Did you ever have that experience? You're happier before you started meditating and practicing self-discovery? I know a lot of people like that.

Oh, they've learned a lot, and they're more powerful now. But they're still not happy; actually, they may be not as happy.

Well, is that because there's something wrong with meditation and self-discovery and selfless giving?

No way. What's wrong is their approach. Meaning, they did not have fun. In other words, if you are performing: selfless giving, meditation, *gazing*, mysticism, occultism and all those exciting arts, and you don't enjoy them while you practice them, if you're like gonna go through the, "Oh, I'm gonna suffer, and it's gonna be hard, but boy, one day I'll have a swimming pool, and a big house and a camel of my own!"

If that's your attitude, nothing's going to happen, really. Nothing in particular, that is. Because while you may be able to lift weights all day long and get strong muscles, you can't necessarily practice self-discovery all day long and become enlightened.

It has to be done in a certain spirit. Because unlike other arts, it's not simply a physical practice that causes anything to happen.

[Rama playfully imitates an evangelical preacher]

> "You can chant those mantras all day long, and do those beads, brothers and sisters. And you can send in them cards and them letters and them pledges and them dollars. But if you doin' it for the selfish motives, you not goin' anyplace. Matter of fact, you may go down. So I'm tellin' you right now, you better get down with selfless giving. That's right."

[normal voice, Rama laughs heartily]

Hi, this is Rama, it's November the 1st, 1985, and we're talking about selfless giving.

Selfless giving is a great time. It simply means you forget about yourself and you go do something for someone else or something else. It's living life for the hell of it in a really nice way.

Got the blues? Life got you down? Things aren't working out the way you want them to—well, they never do, do they? Unless you learn not to want. In which case everything is OK, or it just doesn't matter. That's the condition of the enlightened.

But that doesn't do *you* a lot of good, does it? Well, then, what do you do? Have fun. How do you have fun? Most people have fun by doing things to please themselves.

[Rama imitates an Indian guru]

> "To gratify the senses. That's what they do. They study the holy books. And in the holy books, it says, we do not gratify the senses."

[normal voice]

Well, some holy books say that; you know, how do these books get to be "holy" anyway? Who are these guys who wrote these books? Well, that's another matter for another time.

Anyway, selfless giving is having fun.

That's what it's predicated upon. It's not supposed to get you someplace and burn off bad karma. It's just a way to have fun right away, right here and now. Pounding good.[7]

That's selfless giving. A great time. And you can do it in any situation. You don't have to be Mother Theresa over in Bengal working with the street people.

You can do it at your job, in your home, "in the privacy of your own bedroom". [Rama laughs] You'd be surprised where you can practice selfless giving. And I notice some people think they're doing a lot of selfless giving all the time. Particularly in that realm. That's not necessarily selfless giving. If you know what I mean. Wink, wink, poke, poke, nudge, nudge.

Well, what is selfless giving then?

[Rama affects a cartoonish voice for "Willy," keeping his normal voice to reply]

> "Gosh Rama, what is selfless giving? Tell us Uncle Ram', please, please, tell us, tell us!"
>
> Well, Willy, selfless giving is when you do something because it fits. That is to say, there's no special reason to do it. But yet it's special to do it. That is to say, it's fun. It's fun to do something for someone else.
>
> "Is it like Christmas, Uncle Ram, is it like Christmas? Oh, I like Christmas, I get a lot of things and I'm happy for about a minute and then I feel rotten because I didn't get the things I wanted."
>
> No, Willy, it's not like Christmas at all. Christmas is

---

7. "Pounding good," and "right here and now," from *The Talisman,* by Stephen King and Peter Straub. Suggested reading at that time for Rama's students.

supposed to be about selfless giving. But it's really not. It's about merchandising, Willy. And you can make big bucks when you grow up.

"Oh, Uncle Ram, I'd like to make big bucks."

You can make big bucks, Willy, when you grow up, being a merchant. Particularly at Christmas. You do over half your volume business.

"Oh boy, Uncle Ram, where can I study that?"

Probably at the UCLA business school or any other large management-oriented educational university. But, Willy, you'll be miserable.

"Oh, Uncle Ram, what do I do, what do I do, oh, oh."

Well, Willy, you've got to practice selfless giving. Now selfless giving means …

[Rama returns to normal voice]

… forgetting about yourself.

Selfless giving means forgetting about yourself. It means letting go and doing something crazy.

What's crazy?

Well, the craziest thing you can do is do something that has no benefit in it for yourself. Crazy according to the world view. Because it seems to me that everybody out there is just doing things for themselves. So if you don't do that, you've got to be crazy.

Crazy about selfless giving.

[Rama affects a pompous voice]

"But Rama, Rama, isn't selfless giving, isn't it ultimately just doing something for yourself so you can feel good? How could that be selfless, Rama?"

[normal voice]

How could it be selfless?

Because feeling good and being happy is the by-product. And who said it's selfish to feel good? I personally think it's a natural condition of the universe, and it's an extremely unnatural condition to not feel good.

So in my opinion, when you practice selfless giving, you're in balance and harmony with everything. Nature gives constantly to us—the Earth, the air we breathe, our bodies, our attention fields.

We as independent egos think we're important. Life doesn't necessarily think we're so important.

Ah! Selfless giving has to do with overcoming the ego. The ego makes us unhappy. When we are ego-free—sort of like lead-free gas—we feel great. Less pollution in the air. In the psyche.

Selfless giving does not imply superiority. Again, we're sort of doing the "do nots" today. Is nots. Shall nots. Will nots.

Selfless giving is about love.

If, when you give to someone, you think you're better than they are because you're giving to them, then you're not really loving, you're not really practicing selfless giving. You can tell, in other words, [Rama mimics a deep-voiced radio announcer] "The key, the secret to selfless giving revealed."

The key to selfless giving is that you feel good when you do it and you feel good afterwards. And if you don't, it wasn't selfless. Now, granted, in order to give selflessly, one often starts giving selfishly.

As Tiresias once said to Odysseus, "Honey, you don't get through hell in a hurry."

So in the same sense, you don't become selfless in a day, a week or a month. Even a lifetime. But you can become more selfless, meaning you're having more fun.

Selflessness implies fun. It is fun. It's fun to be free.

No one likes to be chained. Well, you're chained by the body and the mind and the senses, your conditioning and your thought forms.

Freedom is inner stillness. It's not being haunted by your desires and your fears and your aggressive tendencies. It's being cool, "Hey, mellow—being a mellow fellow."

In the universal oneness, refulgent light, complete absorption in nirvana. Gone without a trace.

Selfless giving means being nice.

And there are times we don't want to be. And there are time we're pissed off and angry and "grrrr, snarl". And so maybe you can't be too selfless then.

Then when you settle down and cool yourself out, go back to it. Be kind. You're only here for a while.

No sense of superiority. Just do things for others. It's really fun, it's the most fun.

Naturally, in selfless giving, needless to say, one does not allow oneself to be taken advantage of. Selfless giving doesn't mean that you let people walk all over you. You get a lot of footprints on your face that way.

[Rama affects a tough guy voice]

> "You know what I mean, kid? You don't wanna' let nobody

walks on you, no matter whats. Ya gotta retain that integrity and respects. If you don't respects yourself, then you don't respects nobody else, and you can't let nobody waste you, know what I mean kid?

"So waste them."

[normal voice]

No, no. Wait a minute, now wait. That's a waste of time.

Selfless giving does not imply giving everything up. It's simply having a good time.

Now, let's face it. It's no fun to let somebody abuse you. This is not part of our happiness journey. So, if you're doing selfless giving and you feel abused and used, then you're not really doing selfless giving.

What you're doing is being unhappy. And if you're unhappy, you're not going to practice any selfless giving.

Remember, the happiness factor is the key to the effectiveness—the "high-grade, Columbian" selfless giving, as opposed to the low-grade selfless giving—is measured by how good you feel.

Self giving should be obvious.

[Rama imitates a sneaky person]

"Where do you start? I want to sign up, I want to join, I want to do this, I want to have more fun, boy oh boy!"

[normal voice]

Well, you start in your heart. To be honest with you.

[Rama imitates a mean person]

> "Well I'm a selfish, mean sucker and I don't care about anybody, where do I start?"

[normal voice]

Well, you start in finding a heart. You're kind of like the old Tin Man, you know, in *The Wizard of Oz*, he didn't have a heart. You need to find one.

[Rama imitates a mean person]

> "Well I think that's a lot of nonsense. I just want power and energy, and sure, I'd like to feel good, I might try this selfless giving stuff, it'll give me a rush."

[normal voice]

Well, it might. I'm not sure you're a candidate, but you could be, you could be, who can say? That's what's fun about life.

Do something nice for somebody. Do something nice for God. Do something nice for the Earth. And don't expect anything in return. Because if you do, you'll suffer, suffer, suffer.

What a drag, can't do a good thing and leave it alone. Always have to take credit.

[Rama imitates the little Willy voice]

> "Me, me, see me, I did a good thing, oh boy, appreciate me!
> Oh, Uncle Ram, I did a good thing, oh boy, I'm hot!"

[normal voice]

And then you'll just suffer. Still, it's better to do something. Even if you're still attached to the results, granted. Because that'll get you going. Then you can work on the selflessness.

But then again, just to do that over and over won't necessarily make you selfless, it'll make you miserable.

Selfless giving. If you meditate each day and still your thoughts, it'll come to you. Not only is the spirit important, it's what you do. There's a dharma to selfless giving.

Dharma simply means the right thing in the right place, in the right space.

And to see that you need to have a clear mind. Meditation will clear your mind.

Meditation is the ultimate selfless act. Because when you meditate you're sacrificing your puny personality for the universal reality. You're dancing with life. Life's a celebration. Don't miss the party.

Selfless giving has a lot to do with what happens to you in the future, of course. There is karma, both good and bad.

Now, good and bad are ways of looking at something. Something terrible could happen to one person, and they might think it's pretty great. And somebody else won't feel the same way.

Good and bad karma are just ways of evaluating causal experience. For every action, there's an equal and opposite reaction.

Real karma has to do with an attention field that we're in. That is to say, what you do affects your awareness field.

So you can tell when you're on the money because when you do something selfless your attention field is more clear, more lucid, there's more light in it, more energy. A stillness, a beauty in your being.

When you do something—in quotes—"selfish," you'll feel constricted and restricted. You won't be happy.

You havin' a tough time, things aren't workin' out no matter what you try and do?

That's because you're spending your whole life just doing things for yourself. It's a very limited view of your being.

Everyone is part of you when you do something else for someone else—it's for you. When you do something for yourself—it's for someone else.

Attitude is the clear definer here.

Selfless giving. It's kind of like putting on makeup. We're covering something up.

What are we covering up? We're covering up a part of ourselves that's not very aware.

Is it just a cover-up? Well, the thing is when we take the makeup off, that part of us goes away. The selfish part leaves us. We're freer, we're clearer.

Selfless giving. Selfless giving involves time. It takes a bit of time to care and share yourself with the universe.

It also requires a great deal of spiritual sophistication to see that the end result of all things is nothing. But yet some types of nothing are more fun than other types of nothing.

Selfless giving reminds us that there is an eternally present spirit in all of us, that when revealed, frees us and liberates us from both the transitory and the eternal.

Both of which ultimately can be attachments.

The yoga of selfless giving is easy for anyone to practice. But the key—remember—is detachment.

To do something for your chosen cause, your favorite friend, for God, for flowers, for the environment—but it's the spirit, remember—not the action.

The spirit is unattachment to results. You're just doing it for the heck of it, just for the pure fun of doing it. And as long as you feel that fun, you're right on the money.

The final result of all life is your awareness.

Your awareness is existence.

The short way to happiness is through kindness and sensitivity.

The true hallmark of self-discovery—of how advanced a person is, or a being—is how they treat those around them. Not simply what they say or what they preach.

But the results they generate. How kind they are.

As you pass through this life, have you done all that you really wish to for others?

If you're not having a really good time with your life, it's because you haven't. You may have done many things, but you haven't done much for those around you.

That's the secret to enlightenment—is kindness and selfless giving. Without that it's just words, isn't it?

So be kind, be loving, be generous. Give of yourself, give of your time, and you'll be happy, you'll be free. It's the oldest secret. The one that is most often forgotten. And that's to have fun through giving. Not simply because it's noble, but because it's fun.

"From wonder into wonder existence opens." [8]

So have the courage to be selfless in a world where such qualities are not necessarily admired. Dare to be different—be crazy. Each day, try and go

---

8. "From wonder into wonder, existence opens." from *The Way of Life,* by Lao Tzu, trans.Witter Bynner.

through the day with an attitude of being a servant of the world.

You'll benefit the most. It's true. And the way will be joyous.

Selfless giving. The best discovery in the whole incarnation. Enjoy it.

CHAPTER SIX

DHARMA

It's around 4:44 in the afternoon, on the 4th of November, 1985. Today I'd like to talk with you about dharma.

Dharma is a Sanskrit word that means the way, or the law.

It has many other meanings. I interpret dharma in the universal sense and an individual sense.

The universal dharma is life, that is to say, the word implies existence as it is. The Earth rotating at an exact speed, the seasons changing. Each year in a proper succession. The Sun rising in the East, setting in the West. Molecules and atomic structures holding together by prescribed patterns.

All of these actions: birth, growth, maturation, decay and death and rebirth, all of the patterns of life, not simply the patterns themselves, but that which holds them together is dharma.

The universal dharma is simply the way things are. But there's also a more precise dharma.

For each individual, for each nation, for each world, for each dimensional plane.

Dharma in this sense means filling the proper absence. A door fits perfectly into a doorway. When you shake hands with somebody, the two hands unite perfectly.

So dharma is something then, that exists for every situation and for every being. There's a dharma for your life, the way it should be lived. There's a dharma, an etiquette, you might say, for every situation that you're involved in.

There's a dharma for meditation and people who meditate. There's a dharma for warriors and fighters. There's a dharma for poets, a dharma for accountants, a dharma for lovers, a dharma for the enlightened, a dharma for criminals.

For everyone, there's a way to be.

There's an ancient template, which few people are very much in touch with.

When your life is in harmony with your individual dharma, or when the lives of those in a particular world—like our planet Earth—are in harmony with their world, then life is very beautiful.

When harmony does not occur, that is to say, when the dharma is not lived properly, then life is in a state of imbalance. There is little or no happiness.

So, finding the dharma is the quest; living the dharma is the challenge. What is your dharma?

Now, dharma and karma, of course are interrelated.

Sometimes you'll hear a person say, well, that's your karma. Meaning that you're in a certain type of situation where something has occurred to you which was unavoidable. Unavoidable because at a past time or in a past life you created a certain type of situation where you generated some energy, you acted in a way, didn't act, you did or did not do something, either inwardly or outwardly, that created a series of causal events, a chain which eventually comes back to you.

Dharma's different than karma.

Karma's the law of cause and effect.

You could say "the dharma of karma" is action and the result of action.

But you can follow your dharma or not. If you follow your dharma, then you might say that you will generate good karma, and if you don't you'll generate bad karma.

I personally think that's sort of a simplistic way to look at it. From my point of view, dharma and karma are not really bound by good and bad specifically. Those are abstract concepts, concepts of good and bad that vary from person to person and culture to culture. I see these things in a much more analytic way.

So the dharma is doing the proper thing, thinking the proper thought, feeling the proper feeling.

Naturally if you're like me, you're going to ask at some point, well, who thought all this up? Who says there's a proper thought, a proper feeling, a proper action?

And I would think you might get kind of angry at the idea that if your life deviates from a certain course or form or etiquette that it's going to be exceedingly painful. And that when it's in that proper balance it'll be happy.

Now, I suppose logically, once you find the way to lead your life that makes you happy, it only makes sense just to do it. But I don't know about you, I'm an American. And we Americans, we feel restricted sometimes, even by things that are right.

Good karma, in other words can bind you too.

Doing what's right can be a real pain, if you do it all the time, because then you can get caught in the trap of thinking you're right, and of doing what's right, which is just really another ideation, another philosophical interpretation or way of seeing existence.

So I am very sympathetic for the individual who feels that they're bound by dharma, that it's frustrating.

But let me give you a little piece of advice here. I better not say "advice" because that immediately makes people uptight and they want to do the opposite.

Let me make a "vague recommendation" [Rama laughs] and my vague recommendation is that whether you like it or not, dharma is there, and when you don't follow the dharma, it hurts like hell, and life is miserable, and nothing works out pleasantly.

And when you do follow the dharma, everything is perfection. Why the dharma is there, how it got to be that way, no one can really say.

Oh, there are theories, cosmological explanations, but they're just a lot of words.

It just is. The same way a leaf is, a tree is, a person is.

You can say, "Well, a leaf is, because it came from a tree and it grew a certain way." You can say a person is, "Well, they grew a certain way and they evolved" but you know that doesn't really explain anything, does it?

It doesn't tell us why it really is, it just is a way of analyzing growth in time, and all these wonderful explanations only trap us into believing that that's all there is to it.

In other words, you can look at a person and think of them in terms of what they are. A person is the way they appear to be, you know that people come from other people, that people have sex and they produce little people.

You know the evolution of the sperm and the ovum, and how they form together to create a type of life, you know about the DNA, and the RNA, you know about Sears & Roebuck and buying shoes for little kids, and you know about cotton candy and circuses and Disneyland and going to school and studying Biology and going on your first date, and oh, boy, just getting a job and just trying to get … being sick, having the flu, having to sit around in bed, and oh, pain, and someone doesn't love you and you don't get what you want, and it's not workin' out, and there's just nothing exciting happening, nothing good is on TV, *ever*.

[Rama laughs]   And you get all these notions and ideas about human life and you look at a person, and figure, "Well, that's what a person is."

A person is someone who grows a certain way, develops a certain way, is made up of certain things, has the types of experiences that all people do within certain variable limits, and you think that's what a person is, or a leaf or a tree or a frog or Godzilla.

Well, let me tell you, that's not it at all. Those are ideas.

And they may or may not be true, but whether they are or not, to believe that that's all there is to life, and to think that that's all there is to a person or a leaf or a frog or Godzilla, is to not see existence, to miss almost everything.

So dharma, then, has a lot to do with perception.

In order to perceive—to perceive the proper dharma for yourself or for any situation—you really need a handle on *seeing*.

Seeing is a sense of availability. The cosmos is available to us in various ways, and we're available to the cosmos in various ways, so it's sort of a time-sharing program. Lend-Lease.

The dharma must be apprehended.

[Rama affects a cowboy twang]

> Hmm! We're gonna put up wanted posters, "Wanted, the dharma." We're gonna git it, we'll put it in every Post Office, we're gonna git that sucker, we're gonna offer a very big ree-ward! We're gonna find that dharma, then we're going to lock it up. We're gonna have us a necktie party!

[Rama laughs and resumes normal voice]

I never understood ties, neckties. But I suppose they're the dharma of business. Anyway, lets get back to the dharma here.

[Rama cowboy voice]

> "Now hold it just a moment there, pardner, you talkin' about this dharma, now you all tell me about this dharma, I wanna know. What good's this dharma gonna do me when my cattle die, when the water dries up and when my woman runs off with the camel that lives across the street. I heard of things that's kinky, but this is ridiculous. Now listen, pardner, I wanna know about this here dharma. Now, are you gonna talk about it buddy, or you're gonna be in big trouble!"

[normal voice]

I'll talk, I'll talk. I'll tell you all about the dharma. You don't have to apply any force, I'm sorry about your wife and the camel but ... [Rama laughs]—you may wonder at this point what's happening on this tape and whether it was truly worth the investment. Well, let's consider it for a moment.

What is the dharma of self-discovery? Now let's get right into it and let's forget all the waffle talk.

What is the dharma of self-discovery? What is *your* dharma?

Well, your dharma is to … (fill in the blank).

Meditate, find yourself, pull your power together, get the hell out of this world, find that mystical doorway that leads into eternity, learn to meditate perfectly, learn to be humble and stop being such an egotistical prig.

Settle yourself down and smile more and frown less. Learn to care more about others than you care about your sniveling, miserable old self.

If your dharma is self-discovery and psychic development, then you need to learn—within certain constraints—how to be perfect.

Perfectly nice.

Oh, we all house all heavens and hells within our navel chakras, I'm sure. I mean it's all in there somewhere.

But the real dharma—the true way—is obscured.

You may be familiar with the term *yuga*, y-u-g-a. Yuga is a measurement of time that they used—the ancient Indian philosophers used—and they say that there are four yugas in the cycle of creation. Yugas last millions and millions of years each.

And in the first yuga, when the universe is first created, it's easiest to see and practice the dharma. And in each succeeding yuga, the psychic fields of attention of the universe become more obscured, the vibratory rates shift. It's harder to see the truth, it's harder to be happy.

In the first yugas, it was paradise.

And then in each succeeding yuga there's more corruption, more violence.

When we reach the final yuga, which is the Kali Yuga which is the yuga that we're said to be in now, we're said to be in the time of greatest darkness.

When everything is inverse. When the ignorant rule instead of the wise.

When injustice is prevalent. When darkness covers over the land. When the wisdom of the teachers is ignored, and the insanity of the perverse becomes the common way.

So we live in such a time now. And at such a time higher souls come into the world, are born here, for a time, to re-establish the dharma. They bring truth into daily life.

We call these souls avatars, meaning that they're very advanced souls that come here specifically to teach.

They have already reached a state of spiritual liberation themselves and they come into this world to teach, to be of service to others, and also just to check the world out, 'cause they got the brochure that told them that this was a nice place to visit for a little while.

Sometimes the brochure, like the *Hitchhiker's Guide to the Galaxy*, needs a little updating though.

So here we are in the 20th Century in the time of darkness. People talk about a Golden Age. Don't hold your breath. It's not the dharma. This is the end.

Yet for every ending there's a new beginning and there is a golden age inside yourself. I wouldn't worry too much about a golden age occurring on the Earth.

If you can attain liberation, if you can reach high levels of psychic attention, then you'll see beauty wherever you go, and perfection is everywhere, and it doesn't matter what the age is, or what everyone else is doing.

Psychic people and occult people have learned to use attention, awareness, to focus, to reach other worlds, and to create those worlds within themselves. This is the dharma of the psychic.

As a psychic person, your dharma is to evolve your psychic abilities.

To visit the great teachers and learn from them, and see them whenever you can. The more time you can spend in the physical presence of the teachers, the better for you. Because the real teachers generate a tremendously high field of energy.

Whether they're giving a talk on psychic development or meditation, or occultism, or any of these things. Or they're just playing, throwing a Frisbee, going to a movie, going for a walk, doing their laundry, it doesn't matter.

Their souls vibrate at very, very high rates. Their dharma is to teach others.

But the real psychic teaching, of course, is not done simply through conversation. It's done through the psyche.

Being around that vibratory rate of a teacher changes a receptive individual, whose dharma it is to learn the psychic way.

The dharma of the psychic individual—which of course is you—is very, very different than the dharma of the individual who's not psychically developed.

I'm really not going to spend much time talking about the individual dharma of those who are not psychically developed. They obviously have a lot of things to grow through and work on, souls in earlier stages of development. So that's what they do.

They get married, and have babies, and learn through experiences of relationships, and families and careers. They go through hundreds and thousands of births and deaths, growing and evolving in each incarnation.

But you reach a certain point where you've kind of worked out most of that. Oh, you still go through it again in each life, but it's pretty simplistic.

Once you grow up a little bit and understand a little more of who and what you are, you realize that you're alone. The dharma of psychic people is to be alone.

You're by yourself and always have been. And the facade of family and friends, of career—of meaning, even—falls away. And you see that you are alone in the universe, in the universal attention, and that that's a very good place to be.

And while you may be alone on your own odyssey—developing your psyche, recalling past life fields of attention, becoming complete—at the same time you see that you are the universe, you are connected with all life forms, all beings are a part of your own self. You are all things and in all things.

So then there's never any loneliness. The universe is your constant companion, it's always with you.

But naturally growing up in the world, you've been conditioned. You've been conditioned to fear being alone, to fear, to fear everything just about.

You've grown to think of yourself as a person, with the definition of a person that people in this world and this society have, but I assure you that you're not.

If you're listening to this tape, if you're drawn to workshops that I do or others do in this area, then that automatically tells you that you have evolution. Your interest in these subjects tells you if you are an evolved being, and you need to remember that.

It's nothing to be egotistical about, it's just a stage of growth, a plane, a level in school. But still, you are what you are.

And if you forget that, then you won't command some of the personal power you have that will enable you to follow what is the dharma for you.

The dharma for your self is to evolve. To develop your psychic abilities. That's what we do as psychic people. We develop ourselves, and we also help others do the same.

We help the teachers with their work by helping them in any way we can, and learning from them, if you're a student, if you're one who studies these arts.

As a teacher, you teach, channel knowledge and experience, power, and you just exist in the world and vibrate.

And just your presence in the world elevates the attention field of the world. You're not special, you're just useful, that's all.

The dharma is to develop your self. So part of that dharma is to have a strong physical body.

If your body is weak, you will not be able to deal with the high level vibratory forces that come through the psyche as you develop it. When you meditate and begin to develop your psychic abilities, tremendous surges of kundalini will pass through you, so you need a really strong body.

Regardless of what your age is, you need to exercise. It's very important—run, swim, do yoga, tennis, hike, ski, walk—to exercise. Sit-ups, pushups, aerobics, it doesn't matter. If you're elderly, if you're handicapped, you can still do some type of exercise. Exercise those muscles that move. Walk, work with your arms, whatever you can do. It's very, very important, in any way you can to build your body up.

At the same time you have to build up your intellect.

The dharma for one who practices the psychic arts is to have a very strong mind. So it's important that your job challenges your mind. And it's necessary to do a very good job at your job.

The dharma is perfection for people who wish to develop their psychic attention. That means you can't cheat anyone, because you will only end up cheating yourself when you do. It means you have to be honest. As honest as you can be in all situations.

It means that you have to clear your mind and let go of attachments, let go of the people who you're trying to hold onto. Love and appreciate people, have friends, enjoy your family, if it's enjoyable.

But no one should be in your thoughts. If a lot of people are in your thoughts during the day, then that of course tells you that you're heavily attached, or others are pushing their way psychically into you.

You see, you're very receptive. As a psychic individual, you pick up thought forms and vibrations, and the majority of thoughts that are in your mind aren't even your own thoughts, they're the thought forms of others.

So the dharma for someone who practices psychic development is to learn to clear the mind of thoughts. Naturally the most immediate time that one does that is during the period of meditation.

It's essential, at least twice a day, to sit and practice meditation. To stop your thoughts.

When you stop thought, you cleanse the psyche, and at that time your receptors are turned on completely and you will be able to input the messages from the cosmos, from the galaxy, from other planes of attention, from higher celestial spheres and beings.

You see, everyone vibrates at a different rate. All of life vibrates. And the more evolved you are, the faster you vibrate, the faster you process. It's like a faster computer.

When you vibrate at a higher rate, that creates certain sensitivities and special conditions whereby you need to lead your life in a little bit different way than people who vibrate at a different rate.

Someone who vibrates at a different rate may be able to eat a kind of food that would make you sick, that makes them healthy. They may be able to go to places and do things that don't work out for you.

Yet you'll be able to do things—vibrating at a higher rate—that they can't even imagine. Have experiences, perceptions and understandings.

So psychic people—from time immemorial—and occultists have learned to lead a different type of life. Our lives are a little more withdrawn.

They're withdrawn into the self because that's where our energy is. That's where our realms are that we explore. We're voyagers.

Yet at the same time, it's necessary as a psychic or occultist to be able to effectively deal with the world, and not be afraid to go out and mix with people, have a job, work, be successful, make some money, have a good time, go to a good restaurant. The dharma for the psychic individual is not to hide away on the top of some mountain.

But to move back and forth between solitude and interaction with the multitude. Yet always to preserve a sense of separativity from all others. Otherwise your psychic gifts won't work well.

In other words, think of it as being an athlete. You want to be in the Olympics, right? So, you're going to spend many, many years developing and preparing your body. And each year the body will get stronger. Occasionally you may have an accident, you may have to take some time to heal, and then you start over. But it comes back more and more quickly each time.

Once you've been successful at something, it's always easier to be successful at it the second time, and so on.

So you are developing your psychic abilities. That's the dharma for a psychic person.

To not develop your psychic abilities, to ignore them is adharma. It's against the dharma. And that will cause you great pain and suffering.

To not lead a life that's suitable for a person who vibrates at a higher level, a faster pace—to try and pretend that that world doesn't exist, and that you're not part of it, to run away from it, to hide—will cause you tremendous pain and suffering.

God has given you a gift.

And that gift is your soul which vibrates at a certain level. And that gift is your evolution, your psychic abilities. To not develop them is to go against the dharma.

It will be very painful for you. Because you will always know that you failed, you will always know that you are chicken [Rama chuckles]. You will always know that you are unfulfilled.

And in your next life the situation will not be karmically very good either. You set yourself up badly for your next incarnation and it will be even more difficult than this one was. And so on and so on.

You know, you can go into a chain of devolving incarnations, incarnation doesn't always go upward. If you set up the karmic patterns badly, it might take hundreds of lifetimes to get back to a solid footing again, so it's most important to do it right in this life.

Dharma is fun, it's easy. But you must have the stillness. The stillness is where you sense that rightness. You know, the question of course with dharma is, "Well, Rama, you say that I should follow the dharma, but what the heck is it?"

Well, certainly I and others try and recommend what the dharma is, generally. You know, on the tapes and talks that I give.

Mostly the way I teach it is of course just by vibrating at a very high rate. That's what real teachers all do. Real psychics. I'm a psychic.

Seer. Visionary. Occultist. Enlightened Being.

And beings like that—others, others on the planet like myself—the way we really teach is through attention. By shifting your awareness.

As I'm talking on this tape right now, I'm shifting your awareness. Naturally I'm not bound by this little piece of celluloid that's zipping around inside your "Walk-person" [9] or car or tape player or stereo or whatever you're listening to this on.

I can touch you right now from where I am. I'm outside of time.

I really don't need ...

For example, let me show you something, show you a little trick. It's not a trick per se—it's an advanced maneuver in attention.

I'm going to transmit a block of attention to you right now, and if you listen to this tape again, of course, I'll transmit a different block of attention, or maybe the same one, who knows?

But I want to show you something about psychic development here. The way it's really taught.

So in a moment—this is what I'd like you to do. Needless to say, don't do this if you're driving in your car. Now listen.

I'd like you to close your eyes, and relax. Go ahead close them. Close your eyes, ferme les yeux,[10] close your eyes, baby.

Relax.

Stop the thoughts, don't think about anything, just listen to my voice for a moment 'cause it's going to stop in a second.

---

9. Rama liked to use this non-sexist nickname for the Sony Walkman portable tape player that was popular at the time.

10. French, "close your eyes."

I'm going to transmit something to you.

I'd like you to focus on your third eye, that is to say, the third eye is between the eyebrows and slightly above. So just try and feel that area.

You might want to put your finger there for a moment and press down between the eyebrows and about an inch above, and then remove the finger just so you get a sense of where the area is.

And what I'm going to do right now, is transmit something.

To you.

Wherever I happen to be at the moment, this tape is just going to be our interactive medium.

But I'll be somewhere when this tape is made, in the body or out [Rama laughs], someplace on the planet or off-planet, and when you do this, I'll feel you.

And I'm going to transmit a block of attention. Not a particular thought or an image, but a complex …

Of interdimensional lines. I'm going to transmit them to you right now. So focus on your third eye, feel that area.

Relax, and here we go—there'll be just a minute or so of stillness, well, not that long. I'm going to process something very quickly from myself to you.

Here we go, 1, 2, 3, zing. Go.

[silent pause for 20 seconds]

There you go.

Relax, open your eyes. Look at the nice world that we find ourselves in. We're only here for a while, enjoy it.

I've just transmitted a message to you—not a message to go someplace and do something. A message about life, an understanding. That's how psychics teach. Advanced psychics. Enlightened beings.

The way you really discover the dharma is, you have to learn to do this for yourself.

That's what meditation is all about.

> Sitting down and stopping your thoughts.
>
> Practicing *gazing* and concentration and meditation exercises.
>
> As I outline at the seminars and these tapes and in books or as others do, or as you've discovered for yourself.
>
> The key is to sit down each day for a half an hour to an hour, twice at least, twice is fine, and still your thoughts.
>
> Focus on your third eye, or your navel center, or heart center, or any place you want, or no particular focus, just open yourself to the cosmos.

That's your time when you're cleansing your psyche. Just like you take a shower every day, to wash off your body, so people who are advanced have to wash their psyches every day. Just like the athlete has to go out and work out for several hours a day.

So it's necessary to cleanse the psyche, because the psyche *is* your tool.

If you're dependent upon your car for your business, your car always has to be in good shape, if you're a racing car driver.

So in the same sense, if you're a psychic, your psyche is most important, that is your tool, and you have to take care of it, and you have to make it stronger and stronger.

So meditating is the dharma for one who is psychically developed. And to meditate with more and more proficiency, and love and abandon, and discipline. Each day, each month, each year.

To develop that psyche and make it strong as possible so that when you die, it will be a kite you will hook yourself onto that will fly you into other worlds and you'll be able to take flights in this life, too. You don't have to wait till death.

The kite of knowledge and power that we fly on, that we fix ourselves to, is our psyche.

So that's why the dharma is to groom your life, to slowly perfect it over a period of years. To not get frustrated and feel you have to do it all in a week or two. To not be upset by little failures that you may have, but to be patient.

The dharma is *patience* for all of us in this field.

We know that we live on a planet that's not very evolved, most of the souls here are not advanced. So it's very uncomfortable, sometimes extremely painful.

Psychic and occult people—spiritual people—are always misunderstood.

So we don't try and be understood. We don't tell people what we are, or what we do, we're very quiet and inaccessible. We know each other, and respect each other, even though our ways are slightly different.

That's the dharma, is to respect other people in the practices. In what we call "the arts".

And we never interfere with each other. That is the code, the dharma for people in the psychic and occult practices is to never interfere with each other. We never use our powers and abilities to do anything but advance each other. It's a mutual protection association.

We never interfere with each other, we don't get mad at each other, and if we do, we quickly correct that, because it is never the dharma to attack or injure a brother or sister in the practice.

Whenever you're angry with someone as a psychic person, you develop and project a field of energies.

As soon as you're mad at someone, you slam them with a wall of energy. As soon as you're jealous of someone, you slam them with a wall of energy. As soon as you focus on someone sexually, and you desire them, you slam them with a wall of energy.

So we don't go around desiring people all the time, 'cause we're just slamming them with energy all the time. It's a waste of attention. That's not the dharma for psychic people. The dharma for psychic people is to feel sexual energy when they're having sex, but not all the time. It takes too much of your attention up—eats up too much memory in the CPU. Don't need it.

Sexual energy's interesting, it's a very erratic kundalini. If you like sex, it's an interesting exchange of energies, it also causes a residual drop in energy.

When you have sex, it requires a great deal of energy, of life force, it expends it. So a lot of psychic, and occult and spiritual people do not have sex. Some do, they feel they have the energy to use.

But even so, whenever you have sex with someone you create a tremendously strong networking with that individual, a psychic bond that doesn't end when you get out of bed. Or off the floor, or whatever. [Rama chuckles]

The dharma for psychic people is to love and be *very unattached.*

To know that you're only in this world for a little while and that you come from other worlds, and that one day you'll return to them. But you will only return to them when you fully develop.

That's the karma for psychic people.

So that your challenge in this life is to develop yourself, through all the hardships, and adversities and beauties that you'll pass through in this life.

The dharma for you is to develop yourself.

To learn to be honest with yourself, and not lie to yourself. To know what your real motives are, and not feel bad about them. But at least be honest about them with yourself, with your selves.

To realize you're composed of many different selves. There are different voices, and not all of them are healthy. And to only choose to listen to those voices inside the self that are beneficial, that lead you to a good place, to a happy state, to a state of inner stillness. To avoid things that upset you, types of music, types of food, experiences, movies, places, faces in the news, places of power that over-amp you.

And to work on that stillness in developing the psychic abilities. You have to practice being psychic, it doesn't just happen. It's like exercising a muscle. You've gotta do it, and if you do it, it gets stronger and stronger and stronger.

Naturally, you don't have to be a strong person athletically to practice these arts. You have to keep your body as strong as can be.

But our strength is in our attention field. That's where were work our miracles. That's where we create universes and change our lives.

So the dharma for a psychic person is to be psychic.

To develop, to meditate, to be aware, to be kind, to be patient, and to know that you have a dark side and it has to be mastered.

It's not bad. The dark side isn't bad, it's another part of us. But it has to be channeled in a useful way.

You need to learn to be still. And all your answers will come from that stillness, and to try and spend time both alone and with other people who are psychically developed.

With teachers when you can. They're not usually that available. Because they spend a lot of time alone, and just send out energy throughout the cosmos, like stars shining, sending light in all directions.

But to be with your friends in the arts.

To be inaccessible and not let people inside you. In your psyche. To preserve your psychic integrity … and to be kind always.

This is the dharma, for someone like yourself. Of course.

The universe is always changing. Our lives are like water. We flow, not knowing where we've come from, not knowing where we're going, only sure of that which we are. We are not anything particular, we're attention. We're awareness.

Whatever your awareness moves into, you say that you are. So if your awareness moves into a body, you say "I'm a person" if it's the body of a person.

When you go into the astral worlds, when your attention moves into the astral, you say, "Well, I'm in the astral, I am the astral, I'm an astral being."

We are what we assume.

When your attention moves into enlightenment, you say "I am enlightenment", 'cause *you are,* because that's where your attention is. We are our attention, our awareness field, that is.

So as you expand your attention, you change. You become other things, other beings.

We are attention. Endless, infinite and perfect.

So take the time to develop your psychic senses and your psychic being. That is your dharma. And meditate upon dharma. Ask yourself, what is right? What should I be doing? Not just in a moral sense, dharma has nothing to do with the Ten Commandments.

It means doing that which comes naturally and spontaneously. But in order to know that, you must cleanse and purify the psyche through psychic development.

Meditation, selfless giving, and having fun.

And learning to store and conserve energy so you can reach those other worlds right here and now in this life.

And so that after this life you can journey again. To your home. Back to the world from whence you came. That that's the dharma—for higher psychic beings.

CHAPTER SEVEN

THE CARETAKER PERSONALITY

The Caretaker Personality. Today is the fifth of November. It's around 7:30 p.m. I'm sitting here in the middle of eternity, thinking about nirvana. Thinking about reality. Wondering how it all came to be this way.

Who are you? How do you think of yourself, do you think of yourself as a particular person, with a particular view on life? Certain things you believe in, other things you aren't sure about, other things that you definitely don't believe in?

How do you feel about sex, money, God, religion, politics, the president?

In other words, are you you because of what you feel and believe? Is that what makes you you? In other words, how do you differentiate yourself from someone else? I mean, what is uniquely *you*?

Let's say, for example, that you believe and feel exactly the same way about everything that someone else does.

Are you them? Are they you? Well, you would say, probably not.

"No, of course, we just believe the same things, and think the same things, but I'm still me."

Well, what is it that makes you you? "Well, uh, I have a different body." Well, how do you know that there isn't one being with two different bodies? Sound ridiculous?

Well, isn't the whole cosmos, all of eternity, all of the planets and universes and the beings the body of God? The body of existence?

What is it that is life in us? In psychic development, there is an explanation—in a way of speaking—for this.

Advanced perceivers have found that as they have dug deeper and deeper into that which we are, as you gradually take off the layers of clothing, you start with the overcoat which is the outer personality, then you come down to the shirt and pants, or skirt and blouse—which is just the way you feel about things that are very deep and unspoken—then you get down to the underwear level.

Your deepest and most intimate feelings and intuitions.

And then when we take even that off, there you are, naked as can be. What are you?

"Nothing in particular"—advanced perceivers say. You're nothing in particular, that is to say, that you are composed of and part of all things.

You're just made up of light, when you go in there all the way. You're nothing but light.

And the thing that you think of as being yourself, that part of your being is just like clothing. It just comes on and off. Most people wear their clothing for a whole lifetime. And actually they add to their ensemble, and they start out—just like getting dressed.

When you're very young, and you start out and you put on your first shell personalities, and then gradually they evolve and develop through experiences you have—through conditioning—all kinds of things gradually cause you to be or not be a certain way.

You're molded by life and your experiences.

If you believe in reincarnation, of course, then you feel that your experiences are not necessarily limited to this lifetime, but that actually your personality or something about you that's within you has been with you for longer than that. You've been you. Or formations of yourself for a long time.

And while no personality exactly repeats itself from one life into another, there are still certain carryovers that occur. Certain parts of us that definitely remain the same. Feelings, intuitions, emotional complexes that carry on from one lifetime to another.

And sometimes those tendencies will come forward more in one lifetime than another. In one lifetime, the shell personality—the personality that you pick up in that particular incarnation—may just dominate for the whole lifetime.

In another lifetime, that shell personality may be almost impossible to get through. The deeper tendencies—be they evolved or not—will just not assert themselves, or *they will*.

They'll come through totally at a certain age.

The shell personality will literally burn away, and then the deeper and more complex selves, the structures of those selves from other lifetimes will reassert themselves.

Advanced seers believe that we are not just one type of being. Rather, they believe that we are composed of many different beings, we have many different selves within us.

In other words, when you scrape the surface down, and see what we really are, we're nothing in particular.

Or you could say we all contain everything. There's a basic substance that is eternity. It's consciousness, knowledge, awareness.

You could call it God, or nirvana, or nothing, or anything you want to.

And that basic substance is the Universe.

That substance takes on different forms and formations.

That pure limitless awareness ... segments itself into particular frequencies of energy and light and attention.

> And those particular frequencies of energy and light and attention form self-awareness.
>
> That is to say, the part of you that says, "I am."

Psychic development is a process that an individual engages in, in which they gradually work their way through the shell or surface personality that they've developed in this life.

The reason that you would do this is because you feel that it's a limited personality, as any personality is. There are deeper and more developed aspects of your being which this surface personality structure that you've evolved in this lifetime is blocking.

A surface personality structure is fine to start our life off with. It gives us a description of the world, we're able to function as normal human beings in a civilization.

But gradually it has to fall away ... so that the more advanced and developed essence of our being can come forward. That's when we begin to become more knowledgeable, more aware and hopefully funnier! [Rama chuckles]

The Caretaker Personality.

Well, if in fact we are all made up of ... if you go all the way inside yourself, past the personality of this life, and let's say then even past the personalities of other lives which you've developed.

And we get all the way down in there. What will we find?

Again, I suggest you'll find light. Energy. Essence of existence.

And within that essence of existence is everything that you're looking for.

It's birthless, it's deathless, it just doesn't take on any particular character, yet it has all characters, and contains all things.

It is life. That's what we are, we are life. We are really all of life. All aspects of it. And it's quite wonderful when you see and understand that. Not just as an idea, but as a living reality.

Almost all religions point to this ideal. They point to this idea that we are all things, all existence.

Some separate it. Some say, "Well, God is all of that and we can never be all of that."

But the more advanced religions, more sophisticated religions—particularly the Far Eastern religions—suggest that we are all God.

We are all that substance. That universal attention. And at the moment, we're not really aware of that.

And psychic development, vis-à-vis self-realization, is that process. But it's a really complex process, because we're not just discovering that we are that one undifferentiated substance which is God, or nirvana, or the totality.

Because that substance, on the one hand while being pure and infinite, and free of all conditions and limitations, yet at the same time it creates and houses endless universes, endless dimensional planes, realities beyond counting.

So the substance that is the universe, this universal essence, is not just consciousness.

But it also becomes manifest reality.

Planets, stars, people, flowers, dogs, cats, nonphysical beings, other universes, time, space, other dimensional realities that have nothing that resemble anything in these dimensional realities. Some in which time and space don't even exist.

All of it. That's all part of the universal reality too. We can't separate the form from the formless. The spirit and matter are one. The body and the soul are one. The body may fall away from the soul—the soul being that essence, that substance of the universe—but it too is part of this dream of existence. Its molecules, its atoms are life also.

Life is an inexplicable mystery. God is a jigsaw.

Those individuals who have had many, many past lives—uh, usually around 30,000–40,000 lives—are drawn into the study of psychic development and self-discovery.

Up until that point, we don't know who we are, or what we are, or where we're going, and gradually we're drawn deeper and deeper.

We're drawn to other people who are searching and questing also.

We're drawn to teachers. But I must say that ultimately everything we do, we do ourselves. That is, a teacher is good, but a teacher cannot possibly bring you the deeper understandings of truth.

A teacher points the way. If you have a powerful teacher, the teacher can shift your attention field, because they have enough personal power to boost you temporarily into altered states of attention.

And when they boost you into these altered states of attention you can *see* and feel and experience them. That's what I do.

But then eventually you will return to your normal, everyday attention unless you then practice the methods that the teacher shows you. If you employ those methods as the teacher did, him or herself, then over a period of time you will store enough personal power so you can access those higher dimensional planes, you can get to those deeper selves, or beyond them, to the totality.

That which is beyond explanation. The limitless freedom and perfection that is pure being.

Many people make a mistake. They go to a teacher, or guru, and expect that the teacher or guru can do it for them.

They want an authority figure to rebel against, they want someone to love them, to protect them, to answer every possible question, to do all the work for them. No one can do that.

No one can work out your liberation for you. It's a nice idea. People can help, higher beings can help. But no one can cause you to see the truth, it's something that you have to see yourself.

In the process of looking for the truth, you become stronger. And there isn't just one truth. There's countless smaller truths, eventually leading us up to what we call the Truth with a capital T.

Which is the same to say as, "What is the truth?" Well, it's the totality, it's nirvana. Again, we get into that nameless perfection. God, that infinite reality.

We talk about saints, and seers, and gurus, and enlightened beings.

Then we make kind of differentiations to say that, well, one is more evolved, one is less evolved.

I would simply say that the one who can reach all the way into the totality and merge with it is enlightened.

Some can do that for a few seconds, some just do it two or three times in their whole life and it changes them forever, and they talk about it forever. And they become saints and inspired beings who tell others.

Others can go into those realms for hours, days, weeks, months.

The more you step into that realm, every time you dive into the luminous attention fields in the inner worlds, the more you change and transform.

So psychic development is really the technical study of how you do that. And how you deal with the changes that are taking place.

There's a big swimming pool out in the back yard. It's like the swimming pool in *Cocoon*.[11] It's filled with some wonderful substance. First you just put your toe in. It changes you a little bit. You feel different. Next day, maybe your foot. Eventually you jump in just for a second. When you come out, you've changed. You feel better. Everything is clearer.

Life is shinier. You're seeing more. You begin to realize that you weren't seeing most of life. You can step back from fear and pain.

You jump in again and you stay in longer and you see that there's no death. There's never anything to fear.

Because you see that what you are is something that doesn't die. It's not just an idea. But when you move into other dimensional planes, you can actually *see* your essence, *see* that it's eternal, and know that this body is just like clothing that comes and goes.

Naturally, as you progress in psychic development, your lifestyle changes.

You learn that there are things that you can do that cause you to save more energy, so that you can sustain yourself in more levels of attention simultaneously. You can be more of what you are.

---

11. *Cocoon,* movie, 1985

THE CARETAKER PERSONALITY 271

There are ways you can lead your life that cause you to lose power. In which case your attention field is very low and limited to the physical.

You learn that there are people who use powers and forces against you.

Some people don't want to deal with that. They just like to live in a fairytale reality where no one hurts anyone else. But you know, and I know, if you looked around the planet, that's not true. Visit a prison. Visit a mental institution. Visit a war.

No one ultimately kills anyone, and that luminous, infinite self lives on forever, yes, it's true. But it can sure crimp your style.

So there are people who can use the powers in other dimensions to limit you. I'm not talking heavy paranoia here. It's true! Actually, almost everyone uses the power of attention to manipulate each other.

So as you become more aware and more conscious, as you rise up into higher and higher levels and strata of being, as you jump in and out of that pool more frequently, you find that you can see that.

You can *see* what they're doing. You can *see* into those dimensions and prevent anyone from injuring you.

You can also stop yourself from injuring others.

Harmlessness? It saves energy. The energy used to manipulate and dominate others.

The energy used in hating and being jealous, being angry and judging, and all these things is a waste of attention. You need all the attention you have, all the energy, all the consciousness, to open yourself up to those luminous worlds and merge into them.

So that at the end of this life you will merge with the realities and shift yourself significantly so that you can stay in those luminous realities forever.

Or go anywhere you want to, any world. If you have enough power, you can do that. Or come back and be what you'd like.

So the study of psychic development opens us up to worlds that most people don't even dream exist. They don't understand life out there. They just live in the senses, in the maya, in the illusion.

You may decide to be different, you may become a voyager.

Again, *no one can do it for you.*

As much as you'd like some all-powerful father or mother figure to come by and just say, "Hey, I'm gonna take care of it for you," anybody that tells you that is just taking you on a journey that's not very good.

It's fun to do things for yourself. That's independence and freedom.

Yet, associating with beings who are enlightened, or just advanced, will help you. They vibrate at a higher rate. A luminous energy comes forth from them, particularly from someone who's "way up there" so to speak.

When you meditate with them, you absorb the energy. You feel what it's like and it helps you in your own journey. And they can teach you a great deal.

But then you have to go put those teachings into effect.

I cannot stress that enough.

I've been a teacher for many years, many lifetimes. Even in this lifetime, I've taught for 15 years.

And so frequently people have heard what I've said, and they've watched me use the siddhas, meditate, change their lives, their attention fields, but they have not applied what I have taught. Because there's just so much energy around me. They ride that energy.

But naturally if I disappear, the energy goes away, and they're back where they started.

Not exactly, they've changed. They've seen something, but they don't know how to get back to it themselves. So it is most important—I'm not a guru—I'm a teacher. Someone who points the way, and can sometimes give you a boost with energy to help get you there.

But you must do it yourself.

The caretaker personality.

In the process of doing it yourself—with help of course, from the Earth, from plants, from higher beings, hey, take help any place you can [Rama chuckles]—but still remember, *you* have to do it. That's the fun, that's what defines you, is the struggle.

You realize that you aren't anything in particular.

Being not anything in particular is fine, but then again, how do you fill out the form for your next job if you're no one in particular? How do you talk to people, how do you exist, if you're just luminous energy?

So in advanced psychic practice, you learn about the caretaker personality.

The caretaker personality is like shopping for clothing.

You were born without a personality. It's not something that's intrinsic. You developed one, step by step, and you can also dismantle the one that you have, step by step, and choose another, or choose several—my recommendation.

There are different caretaker personalities for different occasions.

Just as you'll dress one way to go to work—another way to go to a party, another way if you're going to go out and work in the back yard, another way if you're going to go swimming—so there are different ways to appear in the world, and we call these caretaker personalities.

The caretaker personality is a personality that we actually develop and utilize, since the realization is that we aren't anything in particular. So if I'm not anything in particular, I can therefore take on any personality I want. Use it for as long as it is necessary, and then discard it. Or file it for future use.

Everyone already does that to some extent. You do that. You know that you shift your personality around. At work, you're a little bit different than you are with your family, than you are with your friends, than you are when you're alone.

You already do that, but you're more—at this time—probably *modifying* the basic personality structure that you have. You're not just *totally changing* personalities.

It takes a lot of power to do that, it takes a lot of energy. So if you meditate, and you set up your life properly, so that you draw more energy into yourself, you can do that. You can shift personality structures whenever you want to.

Now this is a little different than schizophrenia, in which you have no control, sort of the multiple personalities, you change back and forth.

Actually what schizophrenia is, are different selves fighting. You know, we have all those selves from all those other lives in there, different personalities. And sometimes a little war goes on between them as they try and get control. Or sometimes a person can be possessed by an entity or a force, and it struggles with the personal form.

So that's what we call schizophrenia.

And that's not what I'm speaking of at all.

Rather, a very advanced Tibetan psychology, in which we realize that we are not anything in particular. Therefore, we can be anything. Many different things.

THE CARETAKER PERSONALITY 275

Since we are intrinsically one with all of the universe, we can use any part of the universe, since it is us.

Some basic caretaker personalities are:

- ॐ the child,
- ॐ the warrior,
- ॐ the friend,
- ॐ the student,
- ॐ the sage,
- ॐ the saint.

The child is a caretaker personality that's very lovely to use when you deal with meditation. In other words, you become a little child: happy, spontaneous, a good kid.

> So when you sit there and meditate, you're very childlike in your meditations as you approach the infinite.
>
> If you have that childlike feeling, then the infinite will be very kind to you, very gentle, very compassionate.

When you deal with life, the caretaker personality of *the warrior* is good. You develop a warrior's personality.

> So you go out and do battle—victorious battle.
>
> You're tougher, stronger, more aggressive.

The student is a good caretaker personality to develop.

> Someone who likes to learn, who loves to learn.
>
> Likes to be around people or things that they can learn from. Is eager to learn, that's a nice one.

The sage, the knowledgeable one. This is a caretaker personality that you use after you've dwelled in the house of enlightenment for some time.

It's actually a series of interconnected personality structures that have no definite form, and vary from moment to moment, it's the most fluid of all the caretaker personalities.

You can be and are anything, there isn't one singular way that you are ever.

You can step in and out of any structure, yet there's another structure in addition to all those individual ones which is a fluid structure, that defies definition.

You are a little bit of everyone and everything and yet you are things that are not human, that are beyond understanding.

The caretaker personality.

How do you construct a caretaker personality? A little at a time.

First, a good thing to do is sit down, take out a pen and a piece of paper, and write down: the ways that you are.

Make a list to begin with. Perhaps try it after this tape is over, or when you get a chance, sit down, a little formal writing is always fun, just a list. I'm a great believer in lists, a lot of power in lists.

And write down all the ways you are.

Well, what would those be? How about trying: things that you like and things that you don't like. Attractions and aversions.

Make a list of things that you like and list them. If they're foods, types of people, places, all those things—then put down fears, things you don't like.

Make another list—after your attraction and aversion list—of things that you want to do.

Not so much just things that you're generally attracted to, but things that you definitely want to experience, before you die. Between now and death.

What is it that you really want to experience? Write it down! Places you might like to go on the planet, experiences you might like to have, list them.

You might even list them, if you want to get techy, in order of preference, those things that are most important, those that are least.

Write down, now do another category—category four—a percentage of happiness.

Let's say, how happy are you? Give us a percentage figure. To start with, just generally. How much of the time are you happy, content, at peace, having a good time? 10% of the time? 20, 30, 40, 90? List it. Be honest, it's just between you and your selves. [Rama chuckles]

Now, write down the times of day that you are happy.

In other words, let's do a chart. Morning, afternoon, evening, early morning—if you stay up late, or get up real early. And let's see what percentage of the time you're happy or unhappy, during those times.

Does it vary? You might be surprised by what you see.

Make a list of things that you regret having done. And once you've made the list, throw it away.

Never regret having done anything.

Life is acting in you and through you at all times, and any experience that you've had was definitely on your journey, and you can use that experience if you know how.

You can draw energy from that experience and use it to free yourself ... from limitations.

There are no bad experiences. There are only poorly handled experiences.

And even if something is poorly handled, if you look back on it, you can learn from it and grow from it. If you have an understanding and patient attitude with yourself.

Now, now that you've made that list, let's take out another piece of paper and make another list.

And that's of your darker side.

You are interested now in writing down the tendencies and thoughts and feelings that you *don't really like to deal with.*

Do you manipulate others? If so, write down who. Whether you do directly or psychically.

Do you hate? Are you angry with others?

What is it that you really want?

Power, domination, control, don't be afraid to put it down, no one's going to know but you, and you already know. But you're trying to draw things out of the psyche from the deeper selves.

Write down the dark side, and write down the light side. Don't be afraid of either. We're all a mixture of both. [Rama chuckles]

In psychic development, you simply learn to control the dark side, it has to be controlled, you know. Why? Because it's sloppy. The dark side wastes energy. It needs to be channeled.

It's the part of your personality that every once in a while goes on a binge and spends all the money that you've worked so hard for, and you have no money.

Those tendencies—when controlled and directed—are good. The energy of the dark side isn't necessarily bad. I mean, dark [or] light is just a way of talking.

I define the dark side of our being as the inefficient part, the part that wastes energy. I don't necessarily have a moral or religious point of view here.

And the part that conserves and utilizes energy to extend your awareness, or the awareness of others, I consider the light side.

I'm not doing *yin* and *yang* here, by the way.[12] It's a little more basic.

Now that we've listed all that out, OK, that's who you are, Yay! Now you know! [Rama laughs] That was easy wasn't it? Now let's try something a little bit different.

Let's think of some different people we could be.

Write down on another piece of paper the kind of person you'd really like to be. List the things that that kind of person would like or wouldn't like; would do or not do.

That's one kind of person you can be.

But if that's the only caretaker personality you evolve, you'll probably be pretty miserable, because there are other parts of your being that will think that your description is much too idealistic, and they really don't want to be like that.

So now, let's do some variance. Let's write down another personality.

Try the warrior.

If you were to be a real warrior, and just deal with life effectively, let's list your characteristics—efficiency, courageous.

Write down some situations in your life. Take a situation: going out and looking for a new job. And let's think of how the warrior would approach

---

12. "Yin and yang" is an ancient Chinese philosophical framework for describing the opposing but complementary energies present in the natural world.

that, as opposed to the person you listed before when you wrote down all of your current qualities.

You have to start by visualizing what you want to become. Imagination is a wonderful thing. It's not just a little creation of the mind that's hallucinatory. Of course there are no hallucinations, are there, there are only visions of different realities. Surprise!

But with imagination, one creates all things.

If a person couldn't imagine a house, it would never be built.

If a person couldn't imagine anything, nothing would happen, so imagination is a direct power in the inner world.

It takes more than just imagination, then you have to make it work.

But it starts with imagination. Imagination is creating a psychic attention field and focusing on something.

Now, there are those who take these little mind control courses out there who just figure …

[Rama adopts an "aw shucks" voice]

> "Well, gosh, I can get everything I want if I just focus.
>
> "Now, they taught me the creee-aaa-tive visualization, I saw the man on television, he sold me the cassette set, and said right there,
>
>> 'Just write down, Bobby Sue, what you want, and you just imagine all the time, all day long, and you're gonna' get that swimmin' pool with the great big ocean liner in it, and you're gonna' get them interdimensional beings to come have lunch with you.'

"They're particularly fond of that there fondue, I understand. Choklit fondue?

"So, I'm just gonna sit there in my room, and I'm not gonna do a stitch of work 'cause I know it said in the book if I visualize this stuff all the time, then I don't have to ever worry about it, it's all gonna' just come right true, I read it in the *Enquirer,* and if it's in the *Enquirer,* it's gotta be true. Y'all know what I mean?"

[normal voice]

Unlikely it will ever happen.

No, instead, it's necessary to begin with visualization, and then move from visualization to action. But our visualization helps us store the power to then go into action.

So if you want to make a structural change to a new personality, write down the kind of personality you would like to be.

But give yourself a couple of variants. Because otherwise you'll get too idealistic, and you won't do it all at once. You'll get frustrated and give up.

Let's start with maybe several stages of the evolution of a new caretaker personality: gradual improvements in who you'd like to become, finally working up to some kind of ultimate something or other, which isn't very ultimate, that's just the way you see the ultimate at the moment. Once you get up there, you'll see there are many levels beyond that one.

Then, each day, think of that person. Each morning you should, of course, always meditate and practice some visualizations to clear your mind before the day and store power. And at that time, ponder, or look at that piece of paper and read over the qualities.

And even if you do that for a month or so, every day, just spending a minute or two each morning going over that, without doing anything about it, it'll start something.

Then you have to do it, then you have to act, and start to make those changes.

If you're meditating each day, and practicing *gazing* and visualization exercises, you'll store more power that will enable you to make these changes.

So the person who just imagines—wants to make the change, and may even know what the change is—but they don't have enough personal power ...

whereas the person who practices psychic development

> does the exercises that create the power, the kind of inner cash flow,
>
> and they plug up the holes in their life where they lose energy,
>
> and they find new ways to create energy.

So that suddenly, and basically, without endless effort, you can make major structural changes—well, that came about because you learned the science of the conservation and creation of energy.

The caretaker personality.

Create a new you. Not just one, but many. We contain multitudes, as Walt Whitman once said. We are all things.

It's not necessarily hard to do, to step into those other worlds, those other dimensional planes.

In each dimension, did you know that you're someone else or something else? Did you know that you exist in multiple levels of attention, as multiple beings?

On this tape, of course, I'm just scratching the surface. The first few levels of psychic development. But you need to go through those before we can get to the next ones.

To see your totality, your infinite selves, stretched across the universe, yet all present.

So many things to be, and yet we're nothing.

What a riddle, yet how true.

Another favorite way to evolve caretaker personalities, is to watch others. Look at other people and how they set up their lives. Decide which are successful and which are not, according to your definition of success.

And you will find that you will begin—in a good way—to emulate those individuals. If you want to learn how to make a million dollars, spend time around people who have done it.

Not only do you learn the methodology, but you learn the vibrational pitch necessary to do so.

If you want to be a saint, be around the saints and study the lives of the saints.

If you want to develop your attention and learn how to be in multiple dimensions, then observe those who do that.

On a daily basis, our life brings us into contact with many, many beings, all of whom have had countless lifetimes, and they're not just necessarily the way they appear to be.

Start to probe into people.

As you meditate and practice your *gazing* exercises, you'll become more and more psychic and you'll be able to see beyond the surface, within people.

And you'll start to understand, on deeper levels, how they work. Examine their personality structures.

In other words, everybody has evolved one—if not more—caretaker personalities already.

There are nothing but caretaker personalities, there is no real personality.

And once you realize that, it's easy to change; from one personality form to another. It's fun.

So begin to look at the caretaker personality structures. In other words, don't view another person as just a person.

They are just a caretaker personality that they have woven in this lifetime, or has been woven for them, that they wear. They may have several.

And inside, there's something else entirely, it's just a cover.

> So look at them and *see* if there's anything you like in them. And if there is, add it to yours.
>
> If there's something that you don't like in others, you probably don't like it in yourself, and delete it.
>
> Be an architect of your own being. Design a new you. It's fun.

And probe even deeper beyond the caretaker personality into that absolute reality within.

That is your essence and your substance, from which all things come forth and to which all things return. That's what we really are. The luminous totality, nirvana.

Meditate on that. And you will be free!

THE CARETAKER PERSONALITY

There is a particular meditation technique that will help you do all of this, and I'd like to describe it to you. It's pretty simple, and if you practice it once in a while, I think it will help.

When you're sitting down to meditate, relax, sit up nice and straight, in a chair or on the floor, or any way that you're comfortable—the back should be straight.

And start your meditation.

> Then I'd like you to close your eyes, and visualize the sky filled with stars.
>
> Now, this is a little astral travel.
>
> Imagine that you're going to leave your body, and go right up into the stars, and as you go through the stars, you're going to change.
>
> Your earthly personality is going to fall away.
>
> And now your etheric self will be there, your subtle physical self, your astral self.
>
> Now you're going to go above the stars into other dimensions, and you're going to go through them really quickly, one after another. They're all going to be different colors.
>
> And you're going to kind of zip through them, and just feel yourself going through them.

Needless to say, this is not just a visualization, you're actually doing it.

And as you go through each one, more and more—of the self that you've been—is going to fall away, and your being will get clearer and clearer.

As you go through these dimensional planes, the parts of you that are from them will go back to them.

Finally, you'll get above all the dimensional planes, and you'll enter into a flux, a kind of a gold and luminous light that doesn't really move nor is it still. There's no direction, no dimension.

And you're going to go right into that. It's like going into the heart of the sun, and merge with that, and be that.

Feel yourself in that, get lost in it.

Study it, be it. Stop your thoughts, be still.

Just hold yourself in it with your whole psyche and all your power as long as you can, and then gradually feel you're coming back down—after a couple of minutes, or a few seconds—as long as you can be in that totality. Just imagine it.

Come back through those dimensional planes, and as you do, you're going to come back shiny and clear.

As you pass through each color and each dimensional plane you're going to take on new qualities, new hope, new belief, new power, finally down through the stars and onto the Earth, a strong new radiant self.

The right self will come back with you. The right caretaker personality. Don't worry about what it is, it'll just be from then.

Visualize that, practice that. It really works. Spend about ten minutes on it, fifteen minutes each time you do it.

Five minutes going up, maybe, five minutes there, five coming down. Or whatever, you don't have to time it.

Maybe even just a minute or two to start with and increase the time. Eventually it will become timelessness. Good luck! Have fun!

The caretaker personality.

CHAPTER EIGHT

PSYCHIC SELF-DEFENSE

Psychic self-defense.

Today is the 30th of December, 1985. It's around 1:30 in the afternoon. Today I'm here in Massachusetts, talking about enlightenment. The enlightenment of your being.

Enlightenment is really divided into two parts—the search for knowledge, illumination and power.

One part of course are methods and ways of stopping thought, making the mind quiet, and learning to be introspective. Gaining access to deeper stratas of being, of mind, of the universe.

These methods are taught, can be learned from teachers, fairly freely. It's helpful to be around people sometimes who practice. Those things that can be inspiring. Or to have a teacher.

But in a way, at least an equal, if not a more important part of the study is psychic self-defense.

Now, what's psychic self-defense?

Well, very simply, it is maintaining the integrity of your own awareness.

Life is a happy thing.

Unless someone interferes with you, or of course, unless you interfere with the happiness of others.

It is natural to be happy, to be strong, to be at peace.

Certainly there are other conditions, other awarenesses,

but the most important realization for you to come to, in my opinion,

>is that life is a state of mind.

Everything is colored, completely, by your perceptual field. If you're happy, you could be in hell, and it wouldn't matter. If you're miserable, you could be in heaven, and it would be horrid.

Your perceptual field actually is what creates heaven or hell.

As someone once said, "Nothing is either good nor bad, only thinking makes it so." Well, that's right! Not simply thinking as we understand thinking. But also awareness.

Thinking is a simple way of saying what we're aware of, our awareness field.

We're made up of life energy—boy, we are!

And that life energy is electric, it's filled with power and beauty.

And whenever our awareness field touches anything, we perceive it.

Our awareness field shimmers and shines, and moves, it's made up of the kundalini energy. Plasma energy. And other forces.

Our life energy is radically altered when it touches other energies. Some energies affect it more than others. The energy of other human beings affects it.

And there's lots of nonphysical beings.

The energy of plants, trees, rocks, places, all of these things affect our energy field.

Our energy field naturally determines our awareness. *It is our awareness.*

And if your energy field is high, strong, you perceive yourself wherever you go. That's what you're seeing all the time, are endless reflections of your self. That's all there is.

Psychic self-defense, of course, is the opposite of psychic manipulation.

In psychic manipulation, what someone is doing is seeking to gain your life energy. Pure and simple. [Rama chuckles] Or impure and simple, depending upon your point of view.

It is possible to tap into someone's life energy, just like you can lift out money from their wallet, if they're not aware of it, just like in the old stories, the vampire can drain blood from the victim and weaken them, and the vampire could finish them off and just take it all at one time, or they can keep coming back day after day.

Just like you can have someone who always gets money from you who causes you to feel sorry for them, when they could go out and make money themselves. And they make you sympathetic, when you shouldn't be.

And they feed off of you.

There are two mentalities in our world, and lots of spots in-between.

One mentality I have referred to, of course, is the coyote mentality. The coyote mentality is simply the mentality of the predator.

And then there is another mentality that we don't see too much of in this particular world, on this planet Earth.

And that is the mentality of the magical being that doesn't seek to feed off of anyone else per se. That doesn't seek to enslave anyone else.

These are happier, freer beings. And some of them wander on the Earth, and of course, in other worlds, there are more.

There's no right or wrong in this, I suppose, it's just a point of view.

But even the coyote is a little concerned about the pack of coyotes feeding on him, because that happens here.

The universe is wonderful, the secrets of life are fantastic, if you get to them.

And if you want to, you should be able to. It's not intrinsically hard to have a strong and powerful mind.

Granted, we live in a world of constant change. Success is followed by failure, failure by success, life by death, death by rebirth. But still, you can dance along with all those pairs of opposites and have a wonderful time.

It's not necessarily so hard, when you know how, like anything,

> unless someone or something is interfering with you.

In my opinion, everyone is interfered with—to an extent—by others.

People want your life force more than you realize.

Now, of course, at this point one can become extremely paranoid and start to blame everything that you don't succeed at in your life—or every problem that you have—on others who are taking your life force, which is just a wonderful way of excusing yourself and not doing those things.

So here you have to be very careful to perceive properly when you are being manipulated and when you are just trying to blame others.

And if you search your heart, you will really know. That's about all I can say on that subject.

Why do people want your life force, and how do they get it?

We need to understand how the predator works before we can prevent them—we need to know their strategies. You need to *see* the designs of others.

Well, naturally, if you're just very, very psychic, if you develop your *seeing* very well, you can just *see* it. You can *see* someone who's smiling at you and pretending to help you, who's taking the luminous lines from their subtle physical body and pushing them into your subtle physical body and draining your energy while they smile.

The chief device of a manipulator—meaning someone who doesn't want you to know what they're doing, because their purposes are contrary to your own—the chief device that a manipulator uses is to keep your energy level low.

Because if your energy level is high, you'll be able to just naturally *see*.

Just as your body recoils in pain, if you were to touch a flame for a moment, and it does that because it's part of its natural defense system, to let the intelligent being in there know that it has to, if it wants to preserve their body, keep it out of the flame—so you have a natural psychic self-defense network within you, that reacts completely sensitively to psychic manipulation and people draining your energy.

And if you would listen to it, you would always know exactly what to do. There's no need to be afraid, you'll just sense immediately—danger.

Withdraw yourself from the situation.

But—we live in a world where we've been taught to not pay attention to our feelings. And instead to always use reason and logic.

I love reason and logic. I write computer programs. Love reason and logic.

But that doesn't mean that I think reason and logic are the only modes of perception for dealing with life in the world when I have more.

That's like saying "I love my little Chevrolet, but I have five other cars, and I'll never use them. I won't drive the Mercedes, I won't drive the Ferrari, I won't drive the Jeep," that sort of thing. How silly.

We have many modes and levels of perception. They are us, we should use them. To protect us, to give us a good life.

But we've been taught not to believe and trust our most basic feelings.

So what a psychic manipulator does, is they seek to keep your energy level low.

If they can lower your attention level, you won't *see* what they're doing, and obviously if you don't *see* what they're doing, they can keep doing it.

Which is feeding off your energy.

Psychic manipulators work in a couple ways. They want your life energy, or sometimes, just for the hell of it, they're not that interested in your energy, they just want to screw you over.

They derive a malicious joy, just from injuring. Just from seeing people not succeed. Or, because they haven't succeeded at something themselves, they don't want anybody else to. It's a threat to them.

It's like in the middle ages when the Church would burn so-called heretics who were scientists because they didn't want to hear about the fact that the Earth wasn't the center of the universe, and so on. They didn't want to have knowledge, because if people had that knowledge, they'd look at the theories of the Church and say, "You guys are nuts! You're not going to run the world anymore. Your theories are not in touch with what is real."

So the answer on our Earth when you come into something knowledgeable that is at all a threat is … destroy, kill, suppress.

Shoot a Gandhi if you don't like what he says, shoot a Kennedy if you don't like what he says. Shoot a Lincoln if you don't like what he says. It's a threat to your little private economic establishment, your belief system … destroy, kill, mutilate.

Welcome to the Earth, environment hostile.

Now, I really don't want to get into a philosophical consideration with you as to whether this is a good or bad planet, I don't think it's either. I think it depends on your perceptual state.

But to try and pretend that fear and domination, control and manipulation are not the operative modes in this world—among the people who populate the planet—is nuts.

Talk to the people who have been in concentration camps. Talk to anyone who's been in a war, a prison. A family. A business.

Needless to say, this is not the only place in the universe. There are places where [Rama chuckles] actually it's a little bit worse, and it's a lot better too.

But it can be better in your own state of mind.

But to not see these things, and pretend they're not there opens you up for total manipulation.

Just 'cause you think you're trying to be positive, forget it. Be neither positive nor negative. Just *see*, and if you can prevent yourself from being manipulated, you'll have enough energy to see wonder in all things.

But I've seen too many individuals in the so-called spiritual fields who think, "Oh, that's a negative way to think. Oh, you'll just draw negative energy to yourself." And I watch them gradually weaken and fall apart. Unless they just have a tremendous amount of personal power.

You need to know what the bad guys are up to, in other words.

So, anyway, manipulators come into your life, they want your life energy, or they just don't want you to succeed for the hell of it, or whatever it is. And they operate in fairly simple ways. It's not all that sophisticated, but it's quick.

The psychic manipulation game is the fastest game on the planet, next to the enlightenment game. Which is a little faster.

And, what a person will do is get you to think about them. This is the first and most important step.

When you think about someone or focus on them, or you think about a place, or another world, or a God, or a being, or whatever it is, your life energy touches what you think of and focus on, psychically.

So what a manipulator wants you to do, is they want you to think of them.

And any way they can get you to think of them—any way they can get contact with you, that they can get into your life or get some control over your life or cause you to think that you need them, that they are important—will enable you to lose energy from their point of view.

In other words, they've got to have you thinkin' about 'em. Feeling you need them, you love them, you want them, that they're necessary. That you're afraid of them. Same thing—attraction or aversion. Any type or expression of control.

Needless to say, there are magical beings—enlightened beings, beings of power—who seek to do the opposite. Who would be happy to show you how to free yourself.

Who want nothing from you, who don't need to take life energy from anyone else, because they've learned simply how to create it, by stepping into other levels of attention in other worlds.

And they will teach you to be free.

There's both in the universe. But you don't have to worry about them. We don't really have to talk a lot about them.

If you meet one, if that's your good fortune, then trust them, after making sure that they're that.

But we do need to pay attention to the "coyote net" out there.

So the manipulator seeks to get your attention. Now, some of the most obvious forms of manipulation, domination, and control are

>sexual manipulation,
>
>manipulation through fear,
>
>manipulation through love.

Sexual manipulation is easy to understand. You're not particularly interested in having sex with someone, you know, a particular individual, they pass you on the street. And they project a sexual field of energy towards you, which everyone can, that hits your plasma body, your subtle body, you feel it, it creates a level of excitement if you let it, you look at the person, you desire them, they've got you.

Now, they're in your mind—and even if you only passed them in an airport, in the office, for a few seconds, and you never see them again—if you dwell on them, then they'll have what we call an energy line into your being, your attention field.

You've created a link between yourself and that person, and they can walk back across that link psychically, later, when you're not physically together, and draw energy from you.

The tease is a popular method of sexual manipulation.

Someone doesn't want to have sex with you, but they want you to desire them like mad. Actually, if you have sex with them, that will end the desire for a little bit, or you might get so close that you don't want to have anything to do with them. It's a control game.

So all they do is project a lot of sexual energy. And you feel it, and they're saying, in effect, "Come on! Let's jump into bed and have a good time." You feel that. But then when you come up to them, look at them, they pretend just the opposite, that they have no interest, or there's something wrong with you for even thinking that.

Therefore you get very frustrated because your body is feeling what they're really saying, "Let's go for it." But, they're telling your mind, "What's wrong with you? That isn't my intention at all." So, as you get frustrated, you focus on them even more, and of course they drain your energy even more effectively. It's a control game.

In terms of sex, the most difficult time, of course, aside from these that I've mentioned, is when you have physical sex with someone, it's a snap to drain energy and life force from them.

During sexual intercourse, there is usually a moment when a person will kind of abandon themselves—unless they have great control—to the ecstasy of the physical experience.

And as soon as they let go, they drop the defense shields. [Rama makes a snapping sound] You can snap their energy.

You can drain them.

Once you create a line, particularly through sex, it's very easy to drain someone's energy.

Now needless to say, it's also easy to raise their energy. That's the tantric sexual concept, because such a strong line is created during sexuality and after, that you can also raise someone's attention that way.

If you're powerful enough. Because having sex with someone breaks through so many barriers.

But it can be used either way. Depends on one's state of mind.

Naturally, one can have sex and not be manipulative. Of course.

One can go through life and not be manipulative. We're all manipulative. Meaning we all want things, and we use our power to get them.

But when I'm saying manipulative, again it's a point of view, I'm saying manipulative in the sense that you're trying to injure or hurt another or limit them.

One who tells you about the truth is manipulative, too.

In the sense that they're trying to bring your awareness towards truth, and you may not be interested in truth. So they use a variety of manipulations to help awaken you. To draw you to the study of truth.

You're glad later, because you have more power, and they teach you to be free.

We all use manipulation. We've had thousands of incarnations where we've learned very subtle methods of mind control.

There are very few new souls on this planet. Remember that when you deal with them. You're not dealing with who appears to be there. And the better the deceiver, the more they can mask their talents and abilities.

We all have some occult talents.

ॐ

The dream plane. A very sensitive time is when you're asleep. When your conscious mind is there, you'll know if someone's trying to break into your house. When you're asleep, they can sneak in.

So, it's very important to be aware of that. If you wake up feeling really drained, instead of refreshed, it means that you got hit during your sleep.

So it's good to meditate a few minutes before you go to sleep, bring a lot of energy into your being, read a book that inspires you, whatever.

And then when you wake up in the morning, and you feel very drained, just meditate for a while, recharge yourself, and review in your mind, who—you just feel—did it.

Again, your body knows. There's something inside you that knows. You just have to trust your feelings.

Then, if you break connection with that person, if you figure out whatever method of manipulation they have, to get inside you, what level of control they've gotten of your life or your emotions, or your time, if you eliminate that, they can't really bother you.

People can only manipulate you and come into your dreams and things, if you create an opening. If you want them, fear them, think you need them, trust them—they have to create an opening in your attention field.

Somebody could live three houses down from you, and you don't know them. They really will have a heck of a time infiltrating your attention field.

It's the people you know who manipulate you.

And the more you trust a person, the greater the possibility of manipulation.

That doesn't mean everyone you trust manipulates you. But those are the most likely candidates. Christ had twelve disciples, he trusted them. One betrayed him, and he died. In other words, you can have eleven good apples and one rotten apple. Don't worry about the good apples. They won't hurt you. But the one rotten apple, if you miss them, can cost you your life—energy.

Manipulation occurs through fear. If someone can get you to fear them, they get another line in.

That's why it's important to be absolutely fearless.

To realize that you are an eternal being.

Fire cannot burn you, water cannot drown you, you're birthless and deathless. When you see that, when you meditate deeply and see that, you become fearless.

But people will inject fears in you. Specifically, psychically, they'll push them into you that are antithetical to your nature. They're not how you feel.

Psychic manipulation is very, very complex.

It involves taking thoughts and ideas that the manipulator has, or wants you to have, and they can psychically push them into your mind.

The majority of thoughts that you think are not your own. They're either thoughts that you're psychically feeling from people around you that are coming through you, or they are the conditioning that you received growing up as a child. The way that you were taught to think and feel about life in the world. The description of the world that you have.

Parents particularly create a description of the world in which you'll always need them, want them, where you fear them, love them.

So it's necessary to find new ways of *seeing*.

New descriptions of the world that do not open you up to manipulation. Where you can view things just as they are, and maintain the wholeness and integrity of your attention field.

People have the ability to make you sick. They can enter your attention field, they can project energies.

Just like a magical being can project a field of light into your attention field and raise your awareness and lend you personal power for a while, give you a boost ... so it is possible for beings on the other side of the force, the dark side of the force, the Darth Vaders of the universe—as opposed to the Yodas and the Obi-Wans—to project negative fields of attention.

If this is happening, you'll begin to notice the signs.

The first place you see these things happening—where you're picking up negative psychic energy—is in your skin and your hair.

Your skin and hair will become very dry, your hair may start to fall out, we're not talking about male pattern baldness here. Diffuse hair loss. Change in texture.

These are signs that you're being hit by abrasive psychic energy.

Your skin becomes real dry, then of course more serious diseases will develop.

I always think, of course, when you see any manifestations or signs that something is happening with your body, even if you know for sure it's psychic manipulation and occult energy, and though the doctor can't do anything, I think it's good to see the doctor anyway.

Just to check, and get the doctor's opinion, and see if they say it's something else. And then, of course, when they say, "Well, gosh, you know, you're just getting old," or "We don't know what it is," or "There's nothing we can do about it," when they can't find another physiological cause, you know, of course, what it is.

And the only way to get better is to remove yourself from the awareness field of others by learning to be inaccessible, which is another topic for another tape.

So manipulators work through getting you to desire them, to need them. You're smart, you're intelligent, you can figure it out. But someone makes you think you need them. Your banker, your lawyer, your accountant, your lover.

People get into your life and they start performing simple tasks that you used to perform that you actually enjoyed, and empower you. And they act like they're doing you a big favor. Gradually they infiltrate your life, and you become weaker.

It's very important to do things for yourself. We derive a strength from it and an independence. Watch out for people who want to help you. Who want to come into your physical life. That's what I mean by help.

Because, again, if they can get physical proximity, it's easier to drain you. It's easiest to drain someone when you have physical proximity.

Next is just an emotional connection, or if they can get you to fear them.

If you fear your boss, if you fear the loss of the job, you've put someone in a position of control. With that control, they can drain your energy, lower your perceptual field, and take that energy into their own bodies.

We see, of course, you know, there's the older man, younger woman syndrome—where the older man is with the younger man or the younger woman—and he drains her energy as they live together and grow together, and he takes that energy into his own body, she never realizes it, of course, and he puts it into his life, and into his career, and becomes successful.

And then when her energy level is starting to lose it, she looks suddenly a lot older, her skin begins to fade, the hair, which means that her life energy is low, he goes and finds himself another young woman to use as a power base.

Women do the same thing with men, too, of course. But that particular manipulation we see more through men.

Men do that of course by causing women to think that they're weak and they can't be economically independent, and so on, that they need them.

Women do the same thing, only they use sexual energy.

We call it "wrapping".

I discussed it before, where you're projecting fields of sexual attention and getting someone to think that they're interested in you, and you could care less.

If you fall in love with someone who is just not your type of person, what do you think's taking place?

The most dangerous of all manipulations is love.

The most frequently used. Someone will get you to love them, or think that they love you.

Human beings have this crazy need—and the need is not necessarily there, it's just part of the way of *seeing* that we grew up with, that people taught us, but that isn't necessarily intrinsic to our being—and that's a need to be loved.

I don't really believe that we need to be loved. If no one ever loved you, you could have a perfectly happy life.

I do think we have a need *to love*.

And loving brings us into higher states of attention and makes us stronger.

But we don't actually need to feel anybody's love to be happy. It isn't feeling someone's love that makes you happy. Someone can love you and you can be miserable if you're not in a good state of mind.

But when we love, we are happy, we're strong. And we take a step beyond the limited self, and we see the other. But love creates the greatest possibilities of manipulation. Love and ego.

You see, a good manipulator can scan you psychically, they can look at you and feel your fears and feel your loves. And then they play those.

They will then mold themselves into someone who appeals to you, and they will pretend not to be interested in the things you're not interested in. And they will pretend to be drawn to the things that you're drawn to.

People have this ability. Believe it!

I mean, just consider yourself. How sensitive are you?

Can't you look at another person, and after talking with them for a few minutes, or even just glancing across a room, get a pretty good idea if you wanted to, about how to get into their life?

Couldn't you go over there and talk to someone and flatter them, get them to have lunch with you tomorrow, gradually work your way into their life and be a friend, just by—you know, you could feel their weak spot, you know what they want to hear.

And you know what they don't want to hear.

Well, don't you think other people can do this to you? Maybe they have, and they're already in your life.

Now, you may say, well, gosh, do they really know consciously that they're draining my life force? Yep, they sure do.

They know what they're doing. They're predators. We *all* have that side. *You* have that side. Don't pretend for a moment that you don't.

The only difference is, as you evolve into higher levels of attention, you control that side.

If you don't think you have that side, then you're a terrible manipulator. You're one of the worst. Because you're now manipulating not only others but yourself into believing that you don't.

Everybody has a light and dark side. Because we're all reflections of the universe, which contains all things.

Begin by admitting that you have that side.

Naturally, of course (I'll come back to that in a moment), but naturally, of course, when you manipulate others, you create a line, between yourself and them.

Which they can use too, to draw energy from you, it's real funny.

But once you create a line between yourself and someone else—you may create a line to manipulate someone, you play up to them, you want their energy, you want to be around them because they're powerful, they're successful—they can take that line, and when you're not aware of it, if they're manipulators also, they can take that very line that you've fastened on them and pull you in with it, and drain you.

That's why I advise people, don't manipulate, don't drain.

There's enough energy in the universe for all of us.

And you know, when you drain life force from others, it doesn't stay with you. It will empower you temporarily, or you can be like the husband with the young wife, or the wife with the strong husband, who's draining him, and feed on people on a daily basis, and you know, you'll have a little more energy every day.

But of course, from the advanced perceiver's point of view, you don't really want to drain energy from someone, because when you drain energy from someone, you also pick up their thoughts.

And if you're interested in becoming really powerful, you can't have anybody else's thoughts inside you.

Because no matter what, they're not going to be enlightened thoughts. The people you're draining can't be that powerful. They can't have come into their own yet. Because if they have, they'd *see* what you were doing. Follow?

So you're draining like a Grade B life force, which most people are content with, since they don't seek enlightenment and total power. But if you seek that, if you seek to go beyond this world, then draining won't do it for you, gang.

Learning to meditate, focus, learning the occult and mystical arts, this will teach you how to create more than enough energy for yourself, and even to give to some others who may need energy in their quest.

But draining energy from others accomplishes nothing.

Love is a manipulation. We're convinced that we need people to love us. We are lonely. You might be lonely. God, loneliness opens you up to every kind of manipulation there is.

You think that you need someone. The prince charming, the princess, the wonderful child, the strong lover, the good friend. Every one of these things opens you up to manipulation.

You have to reach a point of certainty within yourself which comes through introspection. That you don't need anyone. You can *enjoy* everyone and all things. Don't ever stop *enjoying*.

But if you feel that you need something outside of yourself, then someone can come along and feel that need and play it, and drain your life force.

Everybody drains life force, literally on the Earth, all the time, it's a continuous game that no one admits to. But if you're psychic, you can *see* it. And if you're very psychic, you can avoid it.

The way you avoid manipulation is by doing everything you can, for yourself, that is possible. By setting up your life so that you don't depend on others. You can work with others, but you don't depend on them. There's no one in your life who you don't feel is replaceable.

By never telling all your secrets to anyone, never opening up completely to anyone.

If you need to open up completely to someone, open up to a tree, a squirrel, a frog, a celestial being, a magical, enlightened being.

Release yourself to God, to the sky, to the Earth, whatever.

But not to another human being who hasn't crossed over that border into the world of magic where they never seek to manipulate others for disadvantage.

Never open up completely to anyone, because of course they have a lower nature, and of course they'll act on you.

Learn the ways of inaccessibility. Don't let people know what you care about, what you think. Because they can weave their way into your thought patterns.

It's good not to let people know where you live. You know, when you invite somebody over to your house, you walk them around the house, you show them your bedroom, they fix that place in their mind, and it's much easier for them to come back there psychically, if they want to.

That's like saying you're opening up your mind to them.

But people will come back there, because they'll feel your life energy there, and they'll drain it.

Surround yourself with good and happy things to restore yourself. Go to places of power, practice the arts that increase your energy, have lots of plants in the house that emanate a sympathetic vibration with a human form. A pet can be a real good friend, if you need an emotional outlet.

It's real fun to come home to your cat, dog, bird and give them a nice hug and have them waiting for you. All they're interested in is the next can of cat food or dog food or bird seed. Or they just love you.

And then sometimes you won't go open yourself to that human being, who you didn't really want to open yourself to, but you just felt this need.

Of course, if you meditate, you'll feel light, ecstasy, energy. You'll see that you're the whole universe, and you won't feel the need to look outside of yourself. Again, you can enjoy, more than ever, all things.

But remember, as you're drained psychically, as you're manipulated, you won't even see life well. Life is beautiful wherever you go. But when people are acting on your perceptual field and draining your life energy, when you look at the world, it will appear gray to you.

A day won't sparkle. The night won't shine. Nature won't seem as beautiful as it did when you were a child. A painting won't look as good as it used to.

That's because your perceptual field is lower. Nature hasn't changed, the painting hasn't changed, your perceptual field has dropped. You don't have as much energy. Things don't sparkle because your attention field is low.

Meaning that you need to do a systems analysis of your energy flow, which I'll talk about with you perhaps another time. You need to chart your energy patterns.

So what should you do? Make a list. Make a list on one piece of paper of everyone in your life who you feel empowers you, and another list of everyone who drains you.

Eliminate everyone in your life who drains you, and if you don't eliminate them completely from your life, eliminate a need or a fear or a love of those people, 'cause they're abusing you. Just feel indifferent.

Draw your mind into places, other than people. Don't dwell and think about people. Think about power places, think about art, read books, don't focus so much on people. That's what they want.

It's a good idea to keep track of who you think about and how much.

Once a week, maybe on Sunday, sit down, keep a journal, and write down who you thought about that week and how much. You can even do percentages.

And if you keep a little journal, you'll begin to see after a while a correlation to how well you felt that week.

Or you might just jot it down each day at the end of the day, because you'll forget.

Then, practice not thinking about people, and you'll notice if you think about fewer people, your attention field will be higher and brighter. You'll see a correlation to your success. You'll make more money, you'll get a better job, because your energy lever is higher.

When your energy level is low, you don't draw good things to you.

But also, as your energy level increases, as you become more powerful, you become of more interest to manipulators.

So as you become more powerful, as you follow the psychic study, inaccessibility becomes more and more of a factor. If you're poor, nobody wants to break into your house, no one wants to kidnap your daughter. When you're rich, they do. So, naturally, with wealth and power comes a certain knowledge and responsibility.

Don't be afraid of manipulators.

But they're everywhere, they try and act on you and work on you. The most important thing that you need to do is first just to put this in your mind. To be conscious that this is all really taking place, taking place on the Earth, twenty-four hours a day.

And just begin to think about these things. Begin to look at people and ask them, how do I feel around this person?

The only way you can tell is after you leave somebody. When you're with them physically, when you're around them, it's very hard to tell how they're actually affecting you. It's very difficult to know. Because they can fool you. They can dazzle you, they can make you actually feel more energized for a little while.

Then they can inject a lot of energy and make you feel sick, and drop your attention field so that you didn't see what they were doing. It's a quick game. It's like the pretty coral that attracts the fish. The fish goes to it, and then it stings the fish. It slowly injects a kind of a chemical into it that paralyzes the fish so it can't swim away and then gradually feeds on the fish.

Someone attracts you to them, they dazzle you, then they weaken you and keep you around. Make you need them, want them, love them, fear them, and then they gradually drain you.

They inject doubts into you that you can't do it yourself, that you can't be happy, that you can't be mentally strong, clear and free, nonsense!

Anyone can develop a strong and powerful mind. Anyone can learn to be independent if you follow the ways of magic and mysticism. You can learn to be happy and free without depending upon anyone.

But that's your battle. That's your struggle, is to gain your freedom.

From those around you, who—through manipulation, domination and control—seek to take your life force and energy.

So be brave, be courageous, and you'll succeed.

Keep meditating, and you'll succeed. Be fearless, and you'll succeed. Don't lose hope, and you'll succeed.

And keep looking, keep watching, they're everywhere! [Rama laughs]

Good luck from Rama!

Chapter Nine

PLACES OF POWER

Places of Power.

The Earth is a place of power. It's alive. Most people think of the Earth as an inanimate object. It's alive.

Some people think of it as growing and changing—volcanoes spew forth lava, new islands and continents are created, old ones fall or drift. Civilizations come and go.

But the Earth is alive, meaning it has awareness.

Different types of awareness in different places.

Just as you have different awarenesses in different parts of your body. But your body is not a total reflection of your awareness, is it?

So the Earth, what we call the Earth is a body, but what is its awareness? Invisible like your awareness, yet you're aware of it, you perceive through it just as the Earth does.

The awareness of the Earth changes from place to place.

Some places on the Earth are places of power—places of power for human beings.

Some places are the opposite—they're places of negative energy, reverse charge, where you lose energy, you lose power, you lose consciousness.

It's better to die in some places than other places. It's easier to move from one world to another. It's better to live in some places. It's better to be born in some places. It makes a difference.

Places of power.

What makes a place of power a place of power? No one really knows, it just is.

Yet places of power attract powerful beings who live there, visit there, meditate there, *gaze*, jump into other worlds from that spot.

And that increases the velocity of the place of power.

Places of power, like people, can be drained.

Some people go to a place of power, or live near it to access its energy. But they pollute it. There can be a beautiful lake—clear, crystal, pristine—people go and they live by the lake, they build houses on the lake and they throw their garbage in the lake and they pollute it, or their sewage, with their thoughts.

And soon, the lake is no longer a pure, crystal lake. It's something else, isn't it? It's a reflection of the attention field of the beings who live there.

Well, people do that to places of power.

You'll notice that wealthy people live in places of power, parts of New York City, parts of Beverly Hills, and every other city has its wealthy area. Did you know that that's a place of power and the reason those people live there is because they draw more energy from there to stay rich and famous? That's why it's so expensive to live there.

Some universities have more power than others, and of course some people.

The Earth is alive. If you could see the Earth through the eye of *seeing*, then you would *see* that the Earth actually changes colors. It's kind of like color graphics on some of those computer games—when the hero is out walking around from place to place on different landscapes and they change colors? It's very much like that.

Kind of like infrared photography that shows up heat vis-à-vis color? Well, if you could *see* then you would know that there's power everywhere and different types of power in different locations.

The Earth is alive, it has an awareness.

Now, when you move from one place to another you cross different "power lines".

The Earth is made up of a series of lines that interconnect different dimensional planes. The Earth is like a gateway between dimensions.

And everyone follows those lines, whether they're conscious of it or not, from the time they're born to the time they die.

When you can *see* the lines of power that someone is following, you can predict everything that will happen to them, in a general sense.

Most people never change the lines they follow. It is possible, of course, that's what mysticism and self-discovery are about.

They're about developing your mind. And making it powerful enough, having an enlightened mind, an awakened mind, with which you can consciously choose—or let power choose, life choose—which lines you'll follow.

You can switch, but you have to *see* them first, naturally, and know what your options are. And of course you need to have enough power to make that switch.

The place you live in naturally is the most important. It's where you spend most of your time, and it's where you sleep.

And when you sleep you're very open to lots of different psychic forces, and it's a time when we recharge ourselves. We renew ourselves.

So if you live in a place that isn't a good place of power for you, then you won't be renewed when you sleep, and your life will be very difficult.

So, the first step for someone who practices the advanced arts of self-discovery and psychic development, as a person who wishes to develop an awakened mind—a mind that's clear and free and *sees* — is to pick a place to live that has the right power for them.

Not based upon necessarily how much it costs, but how it *feels*. Not based upon the aesthetics of the house, or the apartment or the condominium. But how it *feels*.

Because you will draw most of your energy from the place you live. Or the places you live.

Not simply when you're there, but when you're off at work or on an adventure.

You create lines of power to that location and you draw the energy from that location. You store power and compress it there also.

You can draw energy lines from other places too, and from other worlds, not just from this Earth.

But the primary location is the home. Wherever you happen to be sleeping. That's our definition of home at the moment. [Rama laughs lightly] Wherever you're dreaming.

So, then, you have to pick a spot, how do you do it?

Well, you start with a city. Different cities, or the country that surrounds them, have different power accesses. One isn't right or better, you have to find the one that feels most comfortable to you.

How do you know which?

Well, make a list of, say, the 12 or 18 cities in the United States that most appeal to you. Now simply meditate for a while, still your thoughts, put your finger on each one on your list. Write 'em down, natch, close your eyes and feel each one.

And you'll probably be able to real quickly go down to about four which feel the best.

Naturally, if you're new to this, you should think about it and decide intellectually also if these are wise choices, I mean, you could just make a mistake here. But if you're truly psychic, this will be easy.

If not, then of course think about it all.

Before acting on any intuitive decisions, always think about it and say, "Is this wise?" Use common sense always as the common denominator for filtration of intuition.

It should make sense to your mind too.

Good intuitions are very sensible things. They're not far out or weird or nebulous. They're based upon common sense. It's just a faster process for understanding and making intelligent decisions.

Intuition.

It's that creative spark inside all of us that gives us the right answer at the right time—mysteriously.

Sometimes we get it when we wake up, we found it in *dreaming*, sometimes during the day.

We walk around in different states of mind.

>That's all there is, there are states of mind.

>We see our mind wherever we go.

So, then, narrow it down to four, then write the four, or whatever number on another piece of paper, bigger letters maybe, and do the same thing again. Until you find one.

Or visit the four, or get a poster of each one and look at it or whatever you want. Figure out which one is right. Then visit it, and enjoy it.

You'll know when you get there. Actually, when you get off the plane, when you land? You don't even have to see the city.

As soon as you get off the plane, then you'll know. As soon as your feet touch the ground in that place, that place of power, that city of power, or that countryside, you'll know.

Your body will say, "Ooh, this feels good, I want to stay here," or you'll just figure, "Gosh I could just get back on the plane and go." You'll know that it's not the one for you.

Now there's another interesting method, one of these strange Rama methods that I've evolved to deduce the changing level of attention in different cities.

It's very hard when you're in a city to tell how it affects you because after you've been in a place for a couple days you become a part of it in a way and it's very hard to get a clear delineation, you know, to really *see* clearly, to determine whether or not that particular place is influencing you.

Places have influence, just like people. So, how do you know?

Well, let's say you're trying to decide between three or four cities. But you realize that after you've been in a city about an hour or a day, it can almost hold you, it has a power of its own, and influence you.

Well, what I found is, if you're really serious about this—and you have a little money or a credit card and you can afford it—get on a plane and go to your two possible choices, or three, and see a movie!

Go to the city, spend the night in a hotel, or visit a friend, whatever, camp, [Rama chuckles] and see a movie.

Then see the same movie in each city. Can't be a different movie, has to be the same movie.

And when you're in the movie—allowing for differences of the people who are sitting in your particular theater, the vibration of the theater itself and the quality of the projection—notice how different the film seems, how it affects you differently. It's the same film.

And that's a way of determining. It's a reference point for determining the different attention level of different cities.

In any case, pick a city, suburb, countryside, whatever feels good to you. Then break it down into neighborhoods, which neighborhoods feel the best. Naturally it has to be something you can afford, and then start stalking. Start looking around. Visiting real estate agents.

When you pick a place to live, it's very important, before you sign the lease, to see it not just one time. Put a refundable deposit down if you want to or whatever.

But after you've looked at it once, look at it again.

Because the real estate agent, the landlord, the place itself can influence you; can almost manipulate you into taking a place that maybe you don't want. Now don't get paranoid at this point and think that all places are trying to get you.

But places and people have power, and they want to rent it and you're there, it's called good old American salesmanship.

So it's good to go back another time, maybe the next day, and even best to go back at a different time of day 'cause, of course, places feel different at different times of day.

When you select a place to live, you're not only selecting a location, but of course you're buying into the people around you, the person who owns the place—if you're renting, their energy lines are there obviously, and you'll be feeling them—so you should like your landlord.

If you don't like your landlord, don't rent. Because you're going to be feeling their attention all the time.

Good idea not to live next door to the landlord, unless you reeeally like the landlord, because they're going to be thinking about you and focusing on you a lot. Pick carefully!

But don't be afraid to pick one. Take the best of what's around. You can always change, but we have to be practical.

Pick a spot, and it's good to look at it at night too, if you want to. You know, just drive by it and park in front of the place before you sign that lease for a minute or two and look at it and see how it feels at night.

You know, it can be reeal different. It can be better, it can be worse. Who knows? Have to look and see.

Same is true when you look for a job. Get the job that sounds the best, but it shouldn't be in a place that drains you.

If there are two or three job possibilities, if one pays a little less, but the place feels ten times better, go for it.

Because ultimately, if you're drained, you won't be able to move on to a better job or a better position whereas if you feel good about where you work and whom you work for, that means your body's telling you it feels good—again of what's available.

How great can it be? They're paying you, right?

But still, pick the one that feels good.

When you drive to work, follow a power line.

Drive along the road that feels right. There might be one route that takes ten minutes longer, but the power line is better for you along there.

There are lines that run along the Earth, invisible lines. They're invisible until you can *see* them. Drive along those.

In terms of movie theaters, places you shop, supermarkets—everything is on a different place of power.

Don't let convenience run your life. *You* run your life.

Shop at places that you feel good.

When you come home from shopping, look in the mirror. See if you look drained. Examine your attention field.

Naturally, it's always draining to a certain extent to interact with a lot of people and places, but some places will pull you down more than others. Just like people. Some will renew you. Some will be fun to shop in, and some are exciting!

Also, don't wear a place out. It's very important to keep moving.

Not only because people find you and focus on you—when you stay in a physical place too long—but simply because you become too accessible to a place or too accessible to people.

Don't go to the same restaurants all the time, the same movies, you won't pick up any new power lines.

In other words, if you want to change and store power, great. You live in a nice place, you found nice shops, nice restaurants, you go to, you know, good places for vacations, good power spots.

But after a while you're just going to keep drawing the same power into yourself, and if you don't switch to new places, you won't be drawing new energies into your body.

So all you'll do next year is repeat what you did this year, pretty much. Follow me?

Find good things, but then don't wear them out.

Touch life lightly. Look for new places of power, new friends, new shops, new experiences.

And naturally, of course, power changes, the Earth shifts.

Power lines sometimes become weaker, some are stronger. So sometimes a place will feel good for a while, because it is. And then the power shifts.

And if you stay there, then that place can feel bad and drain you, that once empowered you.

Same with people, right? People change.

You can change. A power that used to work for you when you were in college doesn't work now. If you lived back at the college that empowered you, and made you feel great, or you tried to lead the type of life that you did then, it won't work for you now.

So, the places you spend most of your time are what we're really concerned with. Since every place is a power spot of one type or another.

A power spot isn't just some place you hike out to in the desert or mountains. I mean, how often are you going to be there?

The really important ones are the places you spend your time. Houses, cities, shops, freeways, department stores, apartment complexes, people you visit.

Always trust how you feel.

And if you're not sure, look in the mirror. Look in the mirror before you go someplace and *see* how your attention looks, and then look again when you come back.

Sort of gaze, don't focus on any part of your face but look at your whole self. It just takes a few seconds, you don't have to spend minutes, and you'll kind of get a sense of, "Gee, is there more light and more energy?

"Do I look good, do I look younger or do I look older?" [Rama laughs lightly] That sort of thing.

Places of power.

Today is the 29th of December, it's around 5 o'clock in the afternoon, now. The sun is setting here in scenic New England, a place of power, Boston. Tremendous, tremendous mental clarity here. Wonderful place to live and work.

Now, here's an example—lines of power change: Massachusetts, where I'm making this tape right now, had one of the highest unemployment rates in the nation just a few years ago. Today it has the lowest of any state. What happened? How come suddenly they went from one of the highest to the lowest?

Obviously, the power shifted here, which is why I happen to be here speaking to you, today.

Because the power here is very strong and very good. So I thought, "What a fun place to come and visit for a while."

Because the power here is very strong, something very good is happening. Particularly, obviously, in the computer industry. But what a fun place!

It could change again.

Employment is not necessarily an indicator, but it could be, anything could be. But you should see some kind of reflection in the economy, in the way the people are.

Everything is a state of mind, but our states of mind are radically affected by where we live and with whom we associate, and whom we think about. Even if we haven't seen someone in years, and we think about them, we touch them psychically, and that affects us.

So the person who seeks to find their totality, to become free, has to be extremely concerned with where they live, where they spend their time, who and what they think about. Because at every moment, you're gaining or losing energy. Your attention field is rising or falling.

And the strongest effect for most people on their attention field is produced by the Earth.

And the people they know.

One day when you move further into other planes of attention, you won't draw quite as much from the Earth, but you'll also draw from other realities, and you'll be affected more by nonphysical beings than physical beings.

Of course, there are other places of power. Places of power that we go and visit, places of power where we go to be enlightened, renewed, healed.

Where we gain energy.

These are usually places, of course, that are not exhausted.

The places where human beings live are relatively exhausted 'cause they're drawing the energy there all the time to make their careers successful, to make their lives successful, to make their sexual experiences more exciting, whatever it is.

Everybody wants energy. They all want to feel like they did when they were 16 or 17 or 18 or 19. Everybody's seeking energy, seeking power. They want a certain *feeling*, they want to feel great, they want to feel wonderful, they want to feel in control, whatever it is.

So people don't touch the Earth lightly, they live in a place, they draw all its power, they don't leave any over. And then of course, a place that felt wonderful a few years ago is today a trashed lake.

And we see that in some of the most wonderful cities in America and the world. They were great places of power and they've been drained.

Oh, if humanity went away, they would renew themselves in time, just as a forest will grow back over the concrete in time.

But with humanity spreading and covering every inch of the globe, soon the Earth's power field will drain lower and lower and of course, then there are certain consequences that have to come from that.

But in the meantime there are still a few good power places left around!

Naturally, they tend to be in more inaccessible places. So it involves more driving, more travel, that's why the guru always lived on top of the mountain, or the saint went out to the desert.

Because there were places of uninterrupted power where there were fewer thought forms, of course, from people.

Less people, easier to meditate.

But also the power lines there have not been interfered with. Everybody is not tapping into them and putting a lot of diffuse, "desire plane" energy into them.

Desire is the primary pollutant of power places, people go there to have their desires fulfilled.

But if you're seeking the other worlds and the mysteries of power, you don't really want to be near all that energy, it confuses you.

So there are lots of good power places looking for you, but there are also negative places of power that can drain you.

Let's stay with the positive places first.

There are places of rest and renewal, places of more direct healing, places of enlightenment, places of vision, where you can *see* particularly well, places of, of course, power, where you store power. There are different types of places out there in the wilderness, in the deserts and the mountains. By the seashore.

Wherever there aren't too many people.

How can you tell one from the other? Only by experience.

You just need to go there and walk around and be sensitive, meditate as you walk, your body will direct you.

Just find an area that you feel good about and go for a drive.

When you feel like stopping the car, stop. When you feel like getting out and walking, walk.

Naturally, in the wilderness one must always be prepared, and bring whatever you need for survival in the wilderness. Be cautious always. Particularly if you're not used to being out there and hiking around.

It's good for most people to visit places of power during the day and avoid them at night.

At night everything is intensified in the occult worlds, the power is different.

The power lines run differently.

Plus, just walking around in the dark you might hurt yourself. [Rama laughs lightly]

You don't really have to go to most places of power for very long. As a matter of fact, if you spend too much time at them, you can overcharge yourself, and kind of burn yourself out.

But once a week, maybe on a weekend, take a drive, or every couple weeks, and the whole journey is part of the experience.

Your preparation for it, packing for it, getting everything ready, getting your car set, it's very important to do each thing impeccably and perfectly because if you don't you won't set up your lines right when you get to the place of power—you won't be focused.

It's important before visiting a place of power to tidy up your life, all the details of your life should be set, so that

> *if you never came back, that would be fine.*

If you were to step into another world out there, you would have left your affairs in good order.

Your will's made, your check book is up to date, the house is clean, any important calls that you needed to make were made, anything you had to resolve with anyone was resolved as best you could in the time frame that you had before you went.

So that when you go, you go free. You can forget about your home, your life, and just go there and look at other worlds.

Other visions.

You're seeking a vision, a vision of reality, of yourself, of your mind, you want to know which way to go, you need information, you need renewal, many different things.

But your spirit has to be trimmed in a certain way. So that when you go to these places, it works. Otherwise you can just go and walk around and gain nothing.

And of course if you're not careful, it can work in reverse. Because remember, whenever you deal with power, there is danger.

There is enlightenment, but there is danger too.

That's the nature of power. Power is powerful, you have to handle it quite carefully, with respect and with knowledge.

So always prepare for your journey properly.

Spend a day or two thinking about it. Unless you just spontaneously wake up some morning, and, of course, are just drawn, then just do it. Don't worry about everything else.

But if you live your life as an ordered life, it's always in a state of preparation so at any moment you can just go.

I mean, your life shouldn't really be that messy that you have to straighten it up, it should just be tight all the time. But we can even make it tighter, and then we go and forget it all.

You need complete control in order to have complete abandon.

In order to let go completely at the power place, you need to have your life in complete control.

So then you hop in the car, you might bring a friend, you might not, and head out on the road.

Drive to the power spot, go out there, hike around, find it.

Now, of course, as I said, there are negative power places, places that can drain your energy and attention.

How can you tell?

Well, there are different colors, if you can *see* them. If you can *see* in the subtle physical.

Try to avoid the places that are red. They have a reddish-orangish hue in the subtle physical. There's a good power there, but just not for people.

There are places that are kind of a yellow-gold, or a white, or green, blue, those are better vibratory forms for humans.

There are no bad places of power, per se, but there are some that just don't work with a human life form, with its vibratory energy.

If you go to them, you can be drained, lose your energy.

There are also beings, naturally, that are hangin' out at the local power spot, nonphysical beings, and they can act on you and drain you, or they can empower you.

So it's important to go to the right neighborhood.

Go to the right neighborhood, you meet a nice person, have a great time. Go to the wrong one, you might get mugged. It's no different out there in the wilderness.

And just let your feelings guide you. You don't have to be able to *see* the colors.

Just if you don't feel good in a certain area, keep walking [Rama laughs lightly]. If you do feel good, sit down and enjoy it.

Places of vision, of course, are usually on top of hills, or overlooking mesas, or a high mountain.

They're places where you can *see* with extreme clarity. Now, they don't have to be physically high, usually they are.

Sometimes it's by a river, by a stream, by water.

Water is a reflector of cosmic energy.

Then there are places of renewal. When you're tired, you just need renewal.

And if you lie down in such a spot for an hour or so, or sit there and meditate, you'll be renewed.

There are places of power where you really store a tremendous amount of power. You shouldn't stay in those too long—hour, two hours, three hours. It's more than sufficient.

And what do you do when you're there?

You walk around in the wilderness, you find a spot you like, you sit down on your little mat or whatever you bring with you.

Well, naturally, what's important is what you think about.

If you think about negative thoughts out there, or fears, they'll all be amplified by the place of power. If you think about positive things, that'll be amplified. If you don't think at all that's the best.

So it's important to meditate there.

You might bring your journal along and write a few thoughts down, write a poem.

You might, of course, camp there, and practice *dreaming* there. But be careful!

You have to feel very good about the place because it changes at night. And when you're out there alone, unless you really know what you're doing, you can be a target to all kinds of forces.

Places of power, particularly in the desert and high mountain areas are very strong. If you're just going to your local forest, I wouldn't worry about it, camp and have a great time.

But in the very remote spots in the desert and high mountains, in rocky areas, you must be concerned. I think it's a good idea to not do it by yourself but to bring a buddy. Someone to give you a reality check.

And then you can practice *dreaming*. But you can practice that at home too.

Be cautious, always, when dealing with places of power. They're good, but they're best taken in small amounts. It's like eating a wonderful dessert. It's good not to eat every bit sometimes, but stop when you could have one more bite, and walk away.

That control is very necessary when dealing with power, or otherwise you can just amp out and gain too much power and start to think strange thoughts and have strange ideas.

Monitor your thoughts when you're in a place of power and if suddenly you start to get depressed or paranoid, or become obsessed with fears, it's time to get up and move!

That's how you tell if you've found a good spot or a spot that will drain you.

Watch your thoughts. Monitor them. Don't be concerned about one little strange thought. But if you see a pattern, it's time to move. You're being influenced in a negative way.

Try and avoid thinking about people you know when you're out there, or on the trip there. You don't want anybody else's attention in your attention. You're going there just for the energy, just for the experience.

If your attention is tight, you'll *see* other worlds there, you'll pass through magical doorways into other dimensions.

You can step from one world to another if you have enough personal power, enough control of your attention. If you have an awakened mind.

Places of power.

It's very important to travel.

The Earth, as I said, has different levels of attention. And a place can hold you and act upon you.

If you find that you're just not traveling a lot, it may not be because you wouldn't enjoy it, it might be because the power of a place is holding you or the thoughts of the people around you are holding you.

That's why they invented the weekend. The weekend is a good time, from a strategic point of view, to go on a journey.

Pack your bags, it's not necessarily expensive! Stay in your local Best Western Motel or whatever your favorite is, doesn't have to be fancy, go camping, and get *away*.

Also, people tend to get particularly weird, human being types, on weekends. Normally they're very focused during the week, they're going to work, they're running their businesses. But then when they come to a weekend, they tend to get depressed, because they don't have anything to do.

They try and find joy in their pastimes, but they expect too much. They expect Friday or Saturday night to be a most wonderful thing, or the weekend to be this or that.

So it's a good idea—if you study mysticism—to be particularly focused on the weekend, because the same applies to you, if you're working Monday through Friday. Then on the weekends, suddenly you don't know what to do. That's when people get into trouble.

You need a focus.

And you need a biscuit, right? [Rama speaking to his dog, Vayu]

So, at that point it's good to go to a place of power. Even if it's just for a couple hours, even if it's just local, even if it's just a little place of renewal that's around the corner, a local park.

But try and get about 20 miles away from the area you're normally in.

Power lines rarely extend more than about 20 miles.

Even if it's to go shopping, even if it's to go to a movie. Travel, it's good for you. Go away for a weekend, visit somebody. Drive, drive. That's why they invented the wonderful automobile. Get out there and drive.

Go someplace you've never been, or a great place you've been, get on a plane and travel. It doesn't have to be expensive.

It'll shift you. It's easier for you to shift your attention.

You can also assess how much people are affecting you. Your environment is affecting you when you're outside of it. When you're in it, it's very difficult to tell.

And also, you'll find some new places.

Then—power places.

Then during the week when you're at work or at home, think about the power places you've been to.

Keep a little journal, write down your experiences there, and you'll draw power from those places when you're not there.

So when you're at work, and you're working at your computer terminal, or whatever it is you may do, you can occasionally take a "power place break", instead of a coffee break.

Sit down, visualize a spot. Hey! Take photographs of the place, what a nifty idea, and keep a couple around the office. Have them blown up, bring them down to the local Fotomat,[13] or whatever, have them make an 8x10, frame it, you don't have to tell everybody in your office it's a power spot, they'll just think it's a nice place you like.

And access its energy. Think about it, feel what it was like when you were there. Travel there psychically. Places of power are power you can draw on at any time. Sort of like Eveready Batteries, you know, power to spare.

Don't tell people about power places, as a rule. You might want to bring a friend or two.

But if you tell too many people, suddenly it'll be the next polluted lake.

If somebody's supposed to find a power place, they'll find one themselves. They'll be drawn. And your power place might not work for them.

It's good to be discrete about these things, and inaccessible.

Also, it's good if people don't know the power places you go to 'cause then they can focus on you when you're there, and draw power through you or try and control you.

It's good if people don't know where you live and where you are all the time, otherwise you become too accessible to them, they focus on you and they exert a level of mental control over you.

Inaccessibility doesn't mean you're scared or running away, it just means that you don't want everybody to know every detail of your life. [Rama

---

13. Fotomat was a chain of drive-through kiosks which provided overnight film developing, popular in the 1970s.

laughs lightly]

And so it's good to be inaccessible about the special power places that work for you. Keep them to yourself, or just share them with one or two very close friends,

> but don't share all of them with *anybody*.

Always keep a part of yourself just for you. It's not selfish, it's quite sensible in my opinion.

Places of power.

There are quite a few beings, of course, who stay at places of power.

Very strong places of power are interdimensional vortexes. You can pass from one world to another at these places. When you know how.

In ages past, on the Earth, it was actually possible to even physically step from one world to another at a place of power.

But the density of the universe has somewhat changed, and now it's more difficult if not impossible—well, I wouldn't say impossible—it's more difficult to do that, but it's not necessary.

Your attention can go from one world to another.

And when you go to a power place, sit down, meditate and just feel the other worlds, and let your spirit wander.

And when you wander in the desert, you know, you may actually even physically *see* the other worlds if your *seeing* is developed.

And the beings that are there.

I wouldn't try and seek out the beings necessarily, unless you feel pretty strong. Just let them come and go on their own.

If you feel very strong, of course, you can seek one out—a magical being or being of power that can aid you and empower you. But you have to feel really strong, your life has to be very tight for such an encounter. Otherwise it can be a little bit tricky, dangerous.

Most beings don't have interest in human beings. Nonphysical beings. They could care less.

They have their own worlds and their own pastimes, but there are some that act upon people, that either empower or drain, but most are neutral.

And they have to be sought out, they have to be found. Usually you have to look for them, they don't really look for you.

Some people are all kind of—they're very concerned about nonphysical beings draining them, taking their energy, I really think that that's unnecessary paranoia.

The only things you have to be concerned about are either your own thoughts or human beings' [thoughts].

And nonphysical beings really don't care what happens to people. You have to actually seek them out and find them.

Convince them to aid you.

But there are some that can act on you in a negative way in the wilderness, so it's good to be cautious, as I said, always just trust your feelings, and never be afraid of anything.

Something can only gain power over you if you're afraid or unaware.

Always feel that you can do everything necessary in your whole life yourself, under your own power.

Or your power will bring any assistance you need.

If you need to develop power, just meditate, practice stopping your thoughts.

You gain power from *gazing*, focusing on yantras, pulling in energy from the other worlds, that's where power is gained, from visiting power spots, leading a tight life, avoiding situations and energies, and people that drain you.

Having fun, being happy, generates wonderful energy!

Being strong, putting energy back into the system for others.

Higher occult principles.

So power is important. Without it we don't live, our attention field falls apart.

Places are alive.

And they affect you much more than you realize.

Take the time and put out the effort to visit places of power on a regular basis, and of course, to select a place to live, to work, to travel through, stores to shop in, just the little everyday things in human existence.

Select places that have a good energy, a good power. One that works for you. If it changes, change.

And visit places of power in your mind. Psychically travel there.

And you'll have a magical life.

Also, on an editorial note, try to put energy back into places, not just take it out.

Whenever you leave a power place, thank it. Feel good about it. Don't just walk away. Thank it.

It helps recharge it and renew it so that when the next person comes there, that good feeling will be there.

Don't dwell on negative thoughts in a power place. You'll just leave those impressions there. If you can't think positive thoughts, or no thoughts, leave the spot.

Don't leave your litter about a power place, inwardly or outwardly.

Leave it stronger ... by going and having powerful and exciting experiences there.

When you go to a power place, of course, you can sort things out at certain places. Make important decisions in your life, things like that.

But once you've made the decisions, feel good about them, and always thank the place.

Thank the spirits and forces that live there, that drew you there ... that draw you through life and one day will draw you to your death and beyond your death, to your next life.

That thanking—that putting energy back in the network, and that touching life gently—will cultivate a higher awareness in you, and you'll *see* much more with that awareness than most people do.

Places of power, enjoy them, and keep them to yourself!

So this is Rama, somewhere in Massachusetts enjoying this great place of power. Massachusetts, with its clear energy and cold weather, it's wonderful.

One of many fine places on the planet to visit.

Always consider yourself a tourist of the planet Earth. Just here for a while, read the brochure, incarnated here, just checking it out, want to see the best spots while you're here, avoid the worst, and then off you go!

We're a tourist of the universe, we're wandering through different states of mind, wherever we go.

We are awareness.

See you later.

CHAPTER TEN

SEEING

Seeing.

Today is the 29th of December, 1985. We're at that in-between point in the year. We're between two years.

The dawn of one year, the twilight of another. We're between two places. Neither here nor there. Almost not in one year or the other.

In America, it's that week between Christmas and New Year's. The time when no one seems to be quite sure what they're doing.

A good time to *see,* to practice *seeing.*

Naturally, anytime is a good time to practice *seeing* but some times are better than others. Some places are better than others to practice *seeing,* to *see.*

Some people are better at *seeing* than others.

In the old days, of course, we'd call them, strangely enough, "seers".

People who had that special second sight. That ability to look where most people are simply afraid to look.

On the other side of the universe.

Beyond the realm of the senses.

What is *seeing*?

Well, *seeing* is a direct, immediate knowledge of something.

It does not imply any kind of judgment, or moral system or philosophical outlook or religious viewpoint. *Seeing* is *seeing*.

Right now I'm looking out a window as I'm talking, and I'm here in Massachusetts, there's a lovely big tree and a small forest, and there's snow on the ground. The sky is a very pale blue with wisps of white clouds.

It's early afternoon. I see these things.

Because they're there and I'm here.

Now, I could decide that I don't like snow, or I could decide that it's the most wonderful thing there is.

That's not *seeing*, that's reaction and interpretation.

Emotion based upon conditioning—maybe I've had pleasant experiences with the snow, maybe unpleasant experiences with the snow. It has nothing to do with *seeing*.

I could decide that the woods back there would be great to knock down and build a nice housing development. I could think that from a conservationist point of view, that's the worst thing you could do.

But that's not *seeing*.

Now, if I saw that they were going to knock the woods down and build a development, that would be *seeing*.

But being concerned about it one way or the other has nothing to do with *seeing*.

Seeing is just direct vision. Not, of course, physical vision.

What is there to *see*?

Well, to begin with, when you can *see*, you can *see*, of course, inside yourself. And you will *see* that you are not just one self, or one person, but you are kind of a conglomerate. You are composed of many different selves.

We like to think of ourselves as one continuous being, we're just one. But actually, we're many. Many aggregate selves are within you.

Many different feelings, many different voices, many different personalities.

If you could *see* more deeply than that, of course, you'd *see* that there's something beyond those selves, and that is light, energy, power, nirvana, endless eternity.

And that part of you is really networked with all things and all beings.

It's not separate.

The only separation exists within your own mind, when you categorically—through thoughts—think "I'm separate from everything out there, or everything in there." That's just an idea.

But if you can *see*, then, of course, there's no idea. You're part of all things and all things are a part of you.

When you can *see*, you can *see* inside others. Obviously, you can *see* their thoughts, their ideas, *see* their plans, this is useful! [Rama laughs]

Because their plans might be to injure you, their designs. Their plans might be to help you, and you don't really need the help.

You can *see* those designs.

Their plans might be to—who knows what they might be? You might be able to help them with their plans, because you can *see*.

Not that you can carry out their plans for them, but sometimes people don't even know what it is they want, and when you can *see*, of course, it's very apparent.

They're trying to figure something out, and you can just stand there and say, "Hey, wait a second, I *see* what it is you're having difficulty with."

They'll still have to do it, but you can lend clarity to someone's state of mind. That's why people of course used to go to "seers".

They realized that we live in a world that has a lot of confusion in it.

It's hard to *see* in this particular plane.

It's a "relative plane" that we live in, meaning that its a place where everything changes all the time. Conditions are in a state of perpetual flux.

It's getting harder and harder to *see* on our planet. Much harder than it was, say, a thousand years ago, let alone, several million.

In the days of brave Atlantis, it was much easier to *see*.

In the days of the ancient Egyptian civilization, or even a thousand years ago, it was easier to *see*.

Why? Well, primarily, because there were less people on the Earth, for one thing.

If you think of each person as a radio transmitter, and there were only a few million on the Earth not that long ago, each sending out a signal, a vibratory pattern.

Oh, animals, plants, rocks, everything sends out a vibratory pattern—non-physical beings.

But the ones that we are the most affected by are the ones within our own cycle. Human beings.

Now there are billions, like McDonald's hamburgers, billions of people on the Earth.

So there are billions of frequencies on this tiny little planet. And they project the population of the Earth will double again in about twenty years and then double again.

So, it's getting harder and harder to *see*.

It's also getting harder to *see* because the Earth is in a changing cycle.

We're moving into a new age. Moving into a mental age, and leaving the physical age.

Today, what determines personal power in the world is not how strong you are physically, as it was maybe 400 years ago—how many people you could beat, you would be the toughest guy or the strongest woman—but today it depends upon how smart you are.

The mind is the strength of this era, so therefore we're moving from a very physical age, an age of physical consciousness and brute strength and survival, to an age of the mind.

Now, an age of the mind is a complicated thing. On the one hand, we, you know, we'll applaud it, and say, "Hey, this is great! Boy, our time has finally come."

You're interested in psychic development, meditation, consciousness, so obviously your strength is the mind, so this is *your* time. What a great time for you.

It's not as good a time, perhaps in a certain way, for the person who just relies on their physical strength.

So this is a great time for someone who is psychic. But, of course, the mind is a complicated thing.

[Rama adopts a thick Irish accent, with a hint of conspiracy, passing on a secret]

> "Aye, it be true, ya' know, the mind is complicated. It is not only filled with the good and happy and cheerful thoughts, aye, but the mind is where all the doubts reside, they hang out there. They get together and have small parties. Aye! It's true.
>
> "In the mind is confusion, in the mind is illumination. So in the age of the mind, we get a little bit of everything. Aye! That be the problem."

The mind brings about all things. Everything is part of your mind.

The mind contains all hopes, joys and fears.

Of course, when I say mind, I don't simply mean the physical mind that thinks. Mind. You know what I mean.

Perception—awareness—is mind. There are different levels of mind.

How many of those levels do you *see*?

Seeing enables you to understand what it is that *you* want, or just to see different parts of yourself.

Seeing allows you to *see* the designs of others.

It allows you to *see*, of course, into other universes, other dimensions. Or even other physical universes.

Seeing allows you to *see* the designs of the universe itself.

The universe, the physical universe that you see is only one aspect of mind. There are others.

And everything that really happens here in the physical universe is caused by a certain "template" or design in other worlds, in other dimensions.

When you can *see* those templates, well, it's just wonderful, it's wonderful to *see* them. They're extraordinarily beautiful. But also, of course, then you can know what there is to know.

Seeing.

How do you *see?*

Well, the way you *see* is by stopping thought.

Stopping thought *is* a kind of *seeing*. But it isn't all that it takes to *see*. Let's say that it's kind of a pre-requisite. Certainly slowing down thought helps. In other words, mental control.

The reason you can't *see* is because your mind is filled with impressions and images, feelings, desires and ideas.

So a great deal of tranquility—and in my opinion—happiness (although some might differ with that) is required to *see* well.

One of the first things you have to do, on your way towards *seeing,* is eliminate the thoughts and impressions and the conditioning—that's been placed upon you by this world and by others—from your mind.

In other words, your mind is probably not very much your own mind. [Rama laughs lightly] Your mind is really a reflection of other minds.

Your mind has been conditioned. OK, by that I mean that when you were born, your mind didn't work in a particular way.

Oh, that which is you—which was born, which had other lives, in other worlds or in this world—had a certain awareness or attention. But the mind, the physical mind was blank.

Certain intuitive capacities are in the mind, certain archetypal feelings, uh—racial history, the body knows things stored in it through the DNA and the RNA are there.

But the actual pathways of thought and impressions in the mind are clear.

It's like a computer that hasn't been programmed. The hardware is there, but there's no software yet. Maybe there's an operating system. But no software. Nothing to run yet.

So, your mind is taught to *think* by whoever is around you as you grow up.

Your mind learns to think and perceive—though, not simply physically, that is to say—most thinking, of course is taught through language.

Through language we're taught a sense of values, good and bad. This is right, this is not right. Do this, don't do this. This is a good action, this is an improper action. You might be taught physically, you were hit, because they didn't like the way you behaved. You were rewarded if they liked the way you behaved.

The dominant impression, of course that's taught in this world is fear.

Fear is the thing that moves people in our world most.

We're taught to fear the unknown, to fear those who are bigger than we are, to fear those who are smarter than we are. [Rama laughs lightly]

We're taught to fear everything.

We're taught through pain what not to do, more than through love. Our governments tell us that if we don't behave in a certain way, they will lock us away.

Fear.

Fear is the dominant theme, at this time, in the evolution of this particular planet. It's the primary conditioning device, certainly not love. Love exists, but here we see a world of fear. Everyone's afraid of everyone else, of everything else.

You adopt the fears of your parents, or of those who raise you.

The conditioning that's done is not simply done vis-à-vis language.

Most of the conditioning actually occurs from a kind of psychic transfer. The mind of an infant, of a child, is very sensitive. And simply being around people, it will catch the impressions and thoughts that are passing through their mind, and they will be recorded.

It's kind of like when you are going to transfer information from one diskette to another in a computer. All we do is put a diskette that has the information that we want in slot A and then we transfer it over to slot B, to a blank diskette, we format it, and transfer it.

Well, that's really what happens.

Your mind is a reflection of the minds that you've come into contact with.

Until, of course, you start to overcome negative, and even positive conditioning. Which is another story for another time.

But in any case, in order to *see* properly, you've got to get everybody else's mind out of your mind.

You have to kind of go out of your mind to come into your mind.

And this is a process that's done over many years, a little at a time each day. It's not done all at once with a sudden burst of willpower.

There are many sudden bursts of willpower along the way, but it's done a step at a time. That's how all great accomplishments really occur.

Sometimes we see the last part of an accomplishment where it comes into manifestation. Dostoevsky writes *The Brothers Karamazov,* Shakespeare writes *King Lear.*

Somebody designs a building, builds a supercomputer. Whatever it might be.

But the way they did that was by living their whole life.

Everything in their life created a field of power or attention that one day allowed them to sit there, and maybe even they banged the book out in a month.

But it wasn't that they did it in a month. Their whole life is in that book or in that supercomputer.

Your whole life is in everything that you do at every moment. The sum total of your personal power, of your attention, of your awareness, is what causes everything to happen.

You can gain awareness, and to an extent you can lose it. Just like a battery can gain a charge or it can lose a charge.

Psychic development, of course, is the study of how you gain energy, gain power, gain awareness, gain knowledge ... and move towards a conditionless condition—that is neither above, below, within or without—called enlightenment.

Seeing is an integral part of doing all that.

It's a skill that has to be developed. Just like driving a car is a skill that you learn. Driving a car isn't essentially "hard" once you know how, is it? You take it for granted. But the first time you ever got in a car it might have been a little bit complex.

Flying an airplane isn't necessarily much harder. There's more things to calculate.

Seeing is similar to both. Because there's a sense of movement in *seeing*. *Seeing* is not a passive experience necessarily.

It has a certain volition, a movement to it. It has a sense of going someplace, that's why I compare it to flying or driving. Or even walking.

Seeing means that there's a sense of destination, a sense of where you are now. We're taking points within an infinite universe and creating a mind-set of a type, a kind of geography, star map, points of reference.

In order to *see*, you have to have points of reference. Well, what are the points of reference for *seeing*?

Well, the ultimate point of reference is the level of your own attention or consciousness.

In other words, *seeing* is, to a certain degree, based upon comparison.

How do you know that your *seeing* today is more accurate than your *seeing* yesterday? In a relative world, where everything changes all the time, it's hard to know. You could wake up today and not feel as well as you did a month ago, but not realize that.

Because consciousness is fluid, your awareness changes all the time. And there isn't necessarily a sense of how much it changes. We forget who and what we were an hour ago.

When you can *see,* as I can of course, or others who are seers can *see,* you can *see* how much people don't *see.*

Naturally, all of us can only *see* as much as we can *see,* and we don't know what we don't *see.*

So it's always good to assume, even if you think you're a pretty hot seer that there might be some things you don't *see.*

A little humility takes you a long way in *seeing.*

Consciousness, as I said, changes. It moves.

But it tends to forget where it was.

You may remember where you were yesterday, physically, or the people you saw, but can you exactly define the state of mind you were in five years ago? How do you know that the state of mind that you're in now is vaster?

Well, you need a comparison point. In navigation, or when you're driving your car, OK—but let's think of navigation. You're out there on the big ocean and you can't see any land. How do you know which way to go?

Well, naturally, you have to get a point of reference. A North Star, then you know where South, East and West are. The sun setting in the West, or rising in the East, something like that.

You need points of reference in *seeing,* too.

The points of reference in *seeing,* though, are a little different. They're not physical locations.

The inner navigation is rather accomplished by a sense of association with awareness.

By that I mean you have to be able to gauge what level your awareness is.

Now, let's not assign levels. Some people like to think of awareness in levels. They, in other words, they want to make a list of the different levels of consciousness and stuff like that. I think that's an interesting practice, but it's just another idea. You can't really chart awareness, in that way. I mean you can give it names, but so what? They're just names you made up. That doesn't mean they're true. [Rama laughs lightly]

But you can tell, without having to name it, when your awareness is shifting.

So, what you need to do, is—Step One in learning to *see* —is to find yourself a few places of power.

These are places where you will store and recollect shifts in your awareness. You'll map the ever-changing you.

Now a place of power, in my opinion, a good one, usually has no people around it, or as few as possible.

In other words, it's some land that still has some energy in it.

It's not necessary to go thousands of miles, to the top of a mountain in Tibet or way down to Central Mexico to a little hill someplace.

There are places of power everywhere, in every community. It could be a park. And there's a little quiet spot in that park that just feels good to you. It's good to pick something that they're not going to build on. [Rama laughs lightly] So it'll be there for a while.

It's good to pick a spot in a Nature Conservancy or a park, or something that's going to be around for a while. It's not free land that they're going to build on. You can still use that, but it's more of a hassle.

Find yourself a nice little park, or nature area, or a nature trail, but hopefully something that's, again, owned by the state or federal government or in some kind of private reserve and it's going to be there.

And go there. Have a couple.

And just go there and sit for a while. And look at your life, and look at the world, and look at your *awareness*.

Notice how you *feel* when you're there. What your awareness is like. Step outside of yourself for a moment and look.

Are you happy, is your life going well, are you unhappy, what are your goals? You know, just sort of think about your life for half an hour.

Walk around, look at the trees, look at the grass. Look at the snow. [Rama chuckles] And then go on with your life. Forget about it.

Then you should try and come back to that place about every six months, every three months, every month, every year, every two years, it depends.

And only in that place will you really be able to tell whether you're *seeing* more or less clearly, whether your awareness is actually evolving or devolving.

Because when you're out in the world among people, you can't tell. Because everyone is psychic. *Much more than human beings realize!*

Everybody is busy thinking almost everybody else's thoughts all the time. Just no one knows that 'cause hardly anyone *sees*.

But when you go to that little nature area for you, it's special. It's a special place for you.

And you create a kind of a field of power for the short time that you're there, and you're walking, or sitting, or whatever. For that short time, you're creating a field of power there, it's your spot.

Other people may come and go there, that won't affect it being your spot. But it's definitely your spot because you staked it out.

And when you go there, you'll *see* your awareness. You'll *see* how much luminosity you have.

You can be drained by others. They can act on you and drain your energy. You can be drained by the thoughts of others that enter you. You can be drained by your conditioning. There are so many things. And you can be drained so far that you don't realize you're being drained.

It's happened to me at times.

I think it happens to literally everyone on the path to knowledge.

So the only way you can tell—the easiest way—is to go to your spot and *see* how you feel. *And you will remember how you felt there before.* See what I'm getting at?

Normally you can't tell, because you're so in the flux, you're so in change. But it's like going to nirvana for a brief vacation. You're stepping outside of the circle of your life and you're examining your awareness. It's like taking your pulse. Going to the doctor and having a regular checkup. No one can do it for you, only you can do it.

Oh, there are simple ways to clock your awareness. My favorite is the mirror.

Mirrors are interesting things. Look in a mirror. And don't just look at your face, and think to yourself, "Gosh, I have more wrinkles, I have less, I look wonderful, I don't."

Again, that's not *seeing*, that's interpretation based upon some kind of expectation or desire.

Look at yourself in the mirror. Meaning look at your awareness.

Stand back from yourself and don't just look at the nose. [Rama chuckles] Look at the total being.

We call it "scanning", in occultism.

Look at yourself and scan yourself—without focusing very intently on your physical body—gently let your eyes look over your whole being, just for a minute or so.

Sometimes it's good to do that once or twice a day. Particularly after you've been through an experience you're trying to understand.

> You go out with a friend. You go to a movie. You come in from the office. You come in from hiking out in the power place, whatever it is.

And take a look in the mirror. Don't wait too long.

You will *see,* 'cause it's hard to know how you feel, it may sound ridiculous, but think of it this way ...

> You get up in the morning, you meditate for 45 minutes, clear your thoughts, you're in a nice state of attention.

> Then you go out with a friend.

Look at yourself in the mirror just before you go out. Don't be paranoid, just glance. Get a sense of your awareness. You've been meditating, you look good, you feel good.

You're trying to determine what effect the person you were with has upon you.

If they were a good manipulator, you may not know. Good manipulators can act upon us, take our energy and so on, and they can actually leave us feeling better, never realizing that we've been drained.

If you look in the mirror when you come back and you look *really terrible,* well, guess what happened? You were drained.

Unless, you yourself, of course, were doing something that would put you in a negative state of attention.

On the other hand you could meet someone who has a very positive effect on your life, and you might not like them. [Rama laughs]

Or you might not like the experiences when you're around them.

So at that point the best thing to do is to again check in the mirror. *See* how you look. Scan yourself. Is there more light? Is there more energy in your face, in your eyes?

Sometimes we can be going through a difficult time in life, when we're not really happy in a way, we're struggling, but we look great. Our energy's up.

That's what you're looking for. Not the immediate momentary happiness. That's wonderful.

But we're looking for a continuous progression, a gaining of energy in your life.

Naturally, your physical body, as you get older, will deteriorate. That has nothing to do with your awareness level, though.

In other words, you body can get wrinkled, because it doesn't have as much oil as it did because your glands don't produce as much. But that has nothing to do with your awareness.

Your awareness can get stronger and more powerful, more energized, more illumined, provided, of course, you're leading the type of life that causes that to happen.

It doesn't just *happen*. It's like cash flow. Money comes, money goes. We can save it, we can lose it. We can make more, somebody can take it, and steal it from us. Somebody can give us some.

So it's the same with energy. And there's a science to the study of energy which we call mysticism or occultism, synonymous words.

There's a certain approach to self-discovery, to enlightenment, to life.

Through energy analysis.

Seeing is a large part of that process. If you can't *see* if someone is taking your money, then of course, it'll be gone.

It's necessary to *see*.

If you can't *see* that you have money that you didn't know about, forgotten bank accounts ... if you can *see* where the gold is in the ground, then you'll know.

So with energy, with parts of ourselves, it's the same thing. You need to be able to *see*, to know these things.

Seeing involves getting people out of your mind, and sometimes out of your life.

There are people around you, since this is the planet Earth, and the operating mode of the planet Earth is fear, manipulation, domination and control. That's what we see here.

But we see moments of self-giving and love, but if you *see*, and you're not emotional and you don't want to play goody-goody and pretend that something is here that isn't, if you really *see*, you'll see that we live in a world of power.

All worlds are not like this. Not simply planets, but all dimensions. God is vast and infinite. This is one aspect of Her being. [S]he has many forms, countless forms.

This world's one of them. Yet, in this form, in this world, meaning the world—the world, you know, the world!

The world is a state of mind like everything. Life is just a state of mind.

That's what we're talking about is your state of mind. Trying to *see* it for what it really is, and maybe change it.

Changing your mind? Like changing your clothes? Changing the place you live, changing directions, changing your mind.

You can change your mind—anytime you want to—no matter what

anybody says. You just have to know how. It's not hard to learn how.

You need to *see*, though. *Seeing's* the trick.

A lot of people would like you to not *see*.

Because we live in a world that's on "fear net". Manipulation, domination, control.

If someone can cause you not to *see*, by draining your energy, by making you feel ill, by keeping you hassled, then they can do all kinds of things. They can enter into your life.

So it's necessary to *see*, to understand the designs of others.

But people will feel when you're about to *see*, and that's when they'll get in an argument with you, and by drawing you into an argument, your power level will go down. They'll cloud you with emotions.

> The young woman is about to leave her husband. The young husband is about to leave his wife.
>
> 'Cause he knows that something's goin' on that isn't right here, he's not happy, it just doesn't work, say what you will. He or she wants out.
>
> That's when suddenly they become very romantic, kind, they bring you the present. They get you in an argument over something that doesn't really matter.

Your energy is drained by that. They get you in long conversations—avoid long conversations with people. They can act on you too much.

Because those people can *see*, obviously, to a certain extent. They can read your thoughts. You've become too accessible to them. They can *see* inside you.

Seeing can work two ways, remember?

Someone can see inside *you* and know when you're about to make a big shift.

And if you allow somebody to *see* inside you, since many people have what we would call from a certain perspective "impure motives", what they would call from the predator's perspective [Rama laughs lightly] "most excellent motives".

Then they can *see* that shift that you're about to make, and try and block it. And sometimes they can.

Your whole life can be in slavery to others, and you never even knew it, because you couldn't *see*. You didn't see the other possibilities your life could have.

You see in this world, there is the predator, and there's the prey.

And then there are magical beings.

And there's not a whole lot in between.

Oh, there are non-physical beings that have different volitions, and no volitions, sometimes.

But in this world, there are those who seek power, and energy, and life force.

Some of them are nicer than others, I suppose. "Nice" being an idea that we've evolved, having to do with goodness and partialities. But most are just predators.

You have a cute kitten. From the coyote's point of view, it's a fine lunch. From your point of view, it's your cute kitten you'll protect from any coyote. Who's right, you or the coyote? Or the kitten?

Hard to say. Point of view, I suppose. The coyote doesn't think it's bad for him having a fine lunch from your kitten. The kitten wouldn't like it too much. You wouldn't like it.

Is the coyote wrong? Not from a coyote's point of view.

Well, in this world we see mostly coyotes on this planet, in this state of mind.

The strong feed on the weak, the weak try and get together—a whole bunch of weak—and feed on someone who's strong.

Then there are magical beings.

Magical beings are people who have come to *see* and understand their totality, they can *see* the designs of others, and avoid them. They live free, their minds are unconditioned.

They have power. They give power to others sometimes. They're free. They don't need to be predators.

Because they've *seen* that there's more than enough energy in everything in the universe for everyone. But they still recognize that very few beings *see* that way or feel that way.

So they live inaccessible lives where they avoid the negative designs of power of others and just enjoy how wonderful it is to be. In this great universe, to be alive, what a magical thing it is.

That's a great philosophy, it is true, for magical beings.

But the rest on this planet?

Coyotes.

Coyotes can change. The coyote can go through a mystical change and become the roadrunner he chases, yes? Beep, beep. That's what a real smart coyote does. They figure this coyote business is slow. A roadrunner has a better time. But most coyotes don't see it that way.

So you need to learn to *see* to even know that that possibility exists, and that's of course where meditation comes in.

Stopping your thoughts and doing a systems analysis of your energy patterns. Many topics which I talk about on other tapes.

But, immediately what can you do to improve your *seeing?*

Well, naturally, practicing thought control.

- ॐ Thought control means that at least twice a day you sit down to meditate to stop thought.
- ॐ Practice *gazing,* for say half an hour, twice a day, forty-five minutes, fifteen minutes.
- ॐ Start at fifteen, move to half an hour, go up to forty-five, even out at about an hour. After perhaps a year or two.
- ॐ Sitting there learning how to practice the stopping of thought.

There are lots of methods that you can use. Loosely we call it meditation. But there's both meditation and *gazing,* different practices.

You start with concentration, by sitting down and focusing on one point.

- ॐ For half an hour, just looking at a dot on a yantra, a candle flame, whatever you want. A pretty colored rock.
- ॐ You just look at it.
- ॐ Blink when necessary, sit up nice and straight.
- ॐ When thoughts come in and out of your mind, you just ignore them.
- ॐ You just try and focus on that image more and more.

After a while, you'll get good at it. Your mind will develop muscles, just like your body does when you exercise it.

Take it slowly, have fun with it.

Look in the mirror afterwards or before, and you'll *see* an amazing difference. You gain energy from doing it. That's where you get energy.

You don't have to steal it from people. There's tons of it in the second attention. But you have to gain access to the second attention.

So twice a day you practice that, then what you do during the day, well, lots of things.

There's two parts of your day: when you're awake, when you're asleep. Of course the other part is when you're practicing *gazing* and meditation. That's your third part.

So before you go to bed at night, practice *dreaming*.

Give yourself a task in *dreaming*.

Go visit someone, go to your place, think about your special place that you would like to get to. The practice that Don Juan gave Carlos, try and find your hands in your dreams, and look at them, and then look away, and then look back.

Gain some level of control.

Think of a place you'd like to go, someone you'd like to meet, think about that for a minute or two before you go to sleep. Don't get frustrated, it might take months or years. It took me years before I started to find my hands in my dreams, or to go to places I wanted to.

You're actually traveling.

As you gain more control in your daily life, you'll see more control in your dreams.

During the day, well, start scanning.

See. Look at people. Don't judge them, but look. Remember, they're going to present a front. But that isn't necessarily the way they really are. So during the day look. Don't look for too long, you'll pick up too many energy patterns.

Look at your thoughts. Ask yourself, are these thoughts my thoughts, or are they coming from someone else? How can you tell? Well, just say, is this the way I really feel in my heart? It might be. It might not.

Take a good look at your parents or the people who you grew up with. Remember them. Remember, your mind is an impression of theirs, of your teachers that you had in school.

Gradually begin to dig into yourself and ask yourself who and what you are. Probe yourself, never be satisfied with any answers.

Go to places of *seeing*. There are certain places that you'll find, if you want to, out in the wilderness that are places of *seeing*.

Others are places of enlightenment. Others are places of renewal. Others are negative spots, of course, where your power can be drained.

Trust your body, the way it feels, it will always tell you what's going on if you bother to listen to it.

When you go to a place of *seeing*, it's easier to *see*. You'll know you found it 'cause it's easier to *see*.

Step back from life more and look at it. Investigate it. Ask questions about everything.

Don't be afraid of anything.

Eventually you'll be able to *see* beyond life and death, beyond time and space, beyond matter, and then to the heart of life itself.

You'll *see* your own luminosity, your own perfection, your own infiniteness, your own power, your own completion.

Be around people who can *see* well. That's where you learn of course. A lot of *seeing* is taught in the same way that you were taught not to *see* so correctly.

The person who formatted you or the people who formatted you—parents, teachers, friends, TV shows, whatever it is, that caused your mind to think the way it does—formatted the diskette one way.

It can be reformatted if you meet a magical being, of course. If you get to be around one. At all. Just being around their energy patterns is helpful.

There are other ways to *see*. There's not one way to *see* that's right. You just don't want to get stuck in any way.

And being around a magical being is useful. If that's your fortune. If you store enough power, you'll meet one.

They'll come into your life for a period of time. And teach you a little bit about *seeing*, perhaps. And then you can continue practicing on your journey through time and space and eternity.

Never be afraid to *see* anything. Life is *wonderful*. The universe is wonderful.

But there are also beings that would view you as the coyote views the kitten. They'd be glad to eat your life force, your energy and control your life. There's lots of them in this world, don't be afraid of them. When you can *see*, you can easily outwit them.

Put your time into *seeing*, meditating and developing your mind. Your mind is everything. Devote your time to it. Keep your body healthy enough to give you a place to walk in [Rama chuckles] and work on that mind. It's the best thing you have. Develop it.

Don't be discouraged. If other people don't do it, it means nothing, you do it.

Develop your psychic abilities. Develop your mind, develop your attention. Become strong. And you'll have a wonderful life.

So this is Rama, wishing you well in your *seeing*.

Part Three

Rama
Live In LA

Chapter Eleven

CONSCIOUSNESS EXPANSION AND DESIRE

This evening I'd like to consider ways of expanding your awareness that are legal. [laughter from the audience]

And to try and consider what the totality of awareness is. I suppose tonight's talk is a primer for people who aren't sure if they're people anymore. And I'm not sure if we'll be able to solve any of the great riddles or mysteries of the Sphinx tonight, but—we might!

You all know the riddle of the Sphinx, right? You don't know your Greek Tragedies. You don't know the riddle of the Sphinx. Why did the Sphinx cross the road? [burst of laughter from the audience] That's the riddle of the Sphinx.

'Cause a moron threw him out the window, right? It's an old Zen joke. [laughter continues]

Tonight we have a great show. [laughter]

We're going to bring out the Astral Sisters a little later on in the evening, and, uh …

There are basically five types of spiritual seekers. [laughter—the audience is clearly enjoying the dialogue]

One type is represented here tonight! [Rama cracks up, the audience joins in]

No. Seriously. There are basically five types of spiritual seekers. I was talking to a friend about this earlier today. So that's how I know it's true. [laughter]

Well, how else do you know if something is true? I mean, I figure if you talk to a friend there must be some truth in it, 'cause it's a friend, and you wouldn't tell a friend anything that wasn't the truth, right?

There are basically five types of spiritual seekers.

One type is the spiritual seeker who is absolutely infatuated with eternity. I mean, they literally glow all of the time. These are extremely rare.

The second category would be a person who enters into that phase of spiritual discovery from time to time. All of you at one time or another have reached that point. But these are persons who, on a relatively regular basis go in and out of that very high, totally aware state.

The third type of spiritual seeker—I suppose we could say—is the average, only because they come in the middle. And that's the person who is conscientious, meditates, cares about others and tries to do a good job with their life. They have moments of inspiration, they have moments of depression, frustration, hope, joy, and they're very wonderful people.

Then we have the person who doesn't really enjoy spiritual seeking, but they do it anyway. [laughter]

They feel a kind of a moral obligation to try and realize truth, because they know that it's the thing to do. Or they're afraid that if they don't do this, something bad will happen to them, maybe in the afterlife. They still believe in an afterlife.

Then there are those, of course, who seek not really because they're interested in spiritual seeking, but just because it's an opportunity to show off their knowledge to others.

So a person who goes to a party not because they want to have a good time, but they go to the party just so they can cause others misery, in a sense.

Which type of spiritual seeker are you?

Well, let's consider tonight the first three, because I'm sure nobody falls into the other two categories.

In the first category, we're dealing with a very, very small percentage of persons. These are people who have reached—after many, many lifetimes—a kind of a spiritual oasis.

After meditating and seeking and striving, they've reached a point of tremendous purification and one-pointedness. Where all they really want anymore, you could say, is God, or nirvana, or truth, or to be of continuous service to others.

And it comes naturally. So it looks to the observer.

It never comes naturally. But it might look that way.

It just seems that this person is in a flow of light. They're always inspired, they always glow. You see, they just have this aura, we could say a very saintly person. They've worked out all the basic problems in their own life, and now they're trying to be of service to others.

But at the same time I don't simply mean that in the sense that they're a balanced person who is trying to help others get through the day. But they've actually developed their spiritual body—the body of light—to a very, very high degree. They're very pure, in other words.

They're always in a high state of awareness. Whether they themselves are happy or unhappy is unimportant. They've recognized that one's personal happiness or unhappiness is irrelevant. That happiness, unhappiness, pleasure, pain, frustration, joy, all of these things are transitory. These are states of awareness that come and go. One day it's cloudy, the next day it's sunny. You know, there's a hailstorm; there's nothing but sunshine.

And they're not particularly put out by any of these conditions. They accept—with an even mind—all of the conditions of existence.

But that even mind is not bored at all. They're very excited by life, by the spiritual process, by the birth and death process, by eternity itself.

So we're not dealing with someone who's necessarily just in a kind of a detached state who just watches the world go by without emotion. But rather we're dealing with someone who has become—in a sense—the cosmos. Perhaps not completely, but they're certainly aware of their own eternity.

This does not indicate that they don't feel pain or pleasure or things like this. But they have simply become balanced enough to deal with their life, not simply in the simple categorical sense—that most people do—of shopping. You know, selecting a good show on TV.

But rather they've turned their focus to eternity, realizing that eternity is all that matters, and all that ultimately brings liberation.

They no longer want to be trapped by their own frustrations and desires and limitations. Yet they realize that eternity exists not only in space per se, but in the moment, in time, in this world, in all things, in all people.

Such individuals are very rare. Obviously beyond this category we have enlightened people and stuff like that.

Now, what we see more of frequently, are people who reach that plane of consciousness for a time and they go in and out of it. And this is quite a natural process. This would be kind of our level—what I call Level Two.

In the Center. That is to say people who, for a period of an hour, a day, a week, maybe two weeks, will be in a state of consciousness where they're absolutely "on".

They've pushed aside the maya, the frustration, the self-indulgence, the jealousies, all of those things, and they're living in clear joy. Clear ecstasy. They're absolutely in love with life and with eternity, and they radiate that completely, with a tremendous sense of poise and humility.

Again, a person may not be in that phase of consciousness for a great deal of time. It might just be for an hour, once every year.

But for that hour, they're in a kind of a perfection, you might say. About as high as a perfection as one can attain short of very advanced self-realization.

And that hour or that minute isn't really an hour or a minute, because it's timeless.

They've moved beyond the boundaries of time and place and space and condition as we know it, and integrated their awareness with eternity.

And there's a sense of freedom, a sense of wakefulness, of "Oh, this is life! I'd forgotten!" There is no fear, there is no hate, there is no derisiveness. There's only eternity and it's matchless and perfect and shining.

What a waste of time to argue, to be unhappy, how silly to fight wars. When there's nothing but eternity, and each lifetime is so short—briefer than we realize—to enjoy, rather than to waste.

This is something that we all touch from time to time. And it's important that we touch it. Because even though you can't stay in that level of consciousness until you've really refined your being tremendously, still those moments—those wakings, those little spiritual epiphanies—cause you to remember eternity.

It's—this is my theory of the spiritual process to some extent, or one aspect of it—and that's that you're out there walking around in the valley. It's real smoggy.

And suddenly you climb up on top of a mountain and you get on top of the mountain, and you look around you and you can see, you go above the haze. And you sight your direction, "Well, gosh, I want to keep going north, now I can see that's the way."

So you kind of get a fix on your direction, then you leave the mountain, go back down into the valley, and continue on your journey.

Every once in a while you'll reach that clearing in the maya, that displacement where eternity comes closer and you remember.

Now, when you're back in the maya, when you're down in the valley in the smog again, you don't have to forget what it was like. You may not be able to hold that moment in front of you perfectly, but yet we do have the function of recollection of memory.

We can remember, "Well, gosh, yes, the way was that way." And even now I may kind of forget which way I was supposed to go, I may be confused, but if I remember back, "No, I remember the way quite clearly."

So that to me is the spiritual process. That's meditation.

Meditation is the epiphany, it's the awakening, it's coming to consciousness for a moment, for an hour, however long it may be.

The time spent isn't important. What's important is that you stop all thought.

Or that you so detach yourself from your thoughts that that breakthrough occurs. Each time you meditate, in a sense, you're climbing that mountain.

And in that meditation, which is a lifetime, or an eternity—even if there's only in our world time, ten seconds, perhaps at the end of that meditation period, when everything becomes clear and luminous—that ten seconds dovetails into eternal time.

There is no time then. For that moment you move through the veil of maya and everything becomes clear again.

So while we can say that there are these moments, or time periods—maybe once a year for a day or a week, or several times you'll have that level of clarity—yet in a smaller way within each day we have those moments of clarity.

There's a period of time each day when you have an epiphany, a breakthrough, a waking.

Or within each meditation there's a moment of stillness or silence when everything becomes manifestly clear.

So it's necessary to learn to cultivate these moments.

To make these moments into your life. To focus more and more of your time on these waking moments, because they inspire you and actually you can draw on them.

This is, as you know, why I suggest that you all keep a journal of these moments. That every person on the way should do that. You don't have to write down everything that happens to you in your life. But you should write down those moments, because they're fleeting.

Whether the moment came in a dream, in a meditation when we were together, when you were by yourself, when you were with someone—they can come at any time. Physical condition has nothing to do with one of these moments.

But it's necessary to record them, in my estimation.

Not at that moment, but in recollection. And the recollection should be fairly soon. Because if you wait too long, in a sense you'll lose it.

You see, the world is constantly imprinting us. It's imprinting us with ideas, beliefs, vibrational forms, all kinds of things.

And the imprinting is so constant and so powerful, that it's necessary for "we" to allow eternity to imprint ourselves in a slightly different way.

So when we have one of these moments, the longer we can meditate upon it, the longer we can keep it in our cumulative consciousness, the stronger in a sense it will become. Because the moment is not really a moment.

Rather, it's an entrance into another plane of reality, and that plane of reality is always available.

For a moment you walked through a doorway into eternity. You walked into a land where there was no time, there was no space, there was no condition. What was there may be difficult, if not impossible to describe.

But you can certainly describe what led up to that moment, what it felt like to walk through. Perhaps a little bit of what it felt like, and certainly any changes you noted in your awareness afterward.

Because later, in recollection, when you read over those moments—when you recollect upon them, at that time—you will find the doorway again.

It's not that you're trying to go back to that exact experience. But rather, through the doorway.

You bumped into it by accident. The doorway is invisible. You were walking in the world and suddenly you walk through an invisible doorway. And you have this marvelous experience. You become God. Perfection.

Then suddenly you slip back through again. But the doorway's invisible, and you can't find it, although you may look everywhere.

Well, remember, the doorway *is* everywhere.

So, recollection is something that we use to help us back to that moment, that doorway. And the way we do it is by imprinting it on our conscious awareness. It's kind of like learning Braille. I mean, we're blind, and so we have to learn, we have to touch and feel something new and we have to do it repeatedly in order to learn. Once is not enough.

So, what occurs is, we imprint ourselves. We have a spiritual experience, then we write it down. And in the writing of the experience, we imprint it.

We go back over it again. We bring our field of awareness, and we direct it again to that doorway, and our awareness again becomes familiar with it, and even in writing it, you will to some extent, go back through that doorway.

In rereading that experience, perhaps a month later, or six months later, reviewing your journey, your spiritual sadhana, you'll feel that doorway again.

There are other ways you can do this. When you leave a spiritual meeting, if you leave a Center meeting,[14] and you're riding with friends, if we go out to the desert to a place of power, and you're returning.

If on the return journey you discuss what occurred on the journey, let each person tell the tale, let each one be the Bard for a while and recollect and share their experiences—without egotism, without criticism, just observation—then each person will have the opportunity to recollect along with that person.

To not even listen to their words per se, because they perhaps were there, too, and saw, and felt the same things, or about the same things, but as they listen to the words—psychically, intuitively—they will feel that doorway that that person walked through to have that experience.

That's why I like telling experiences, spiritual experiences, and very often I'll have you, after a meditation, share your experience.

---

14. The Lakshmi Center was the name of Rama's teaching organization at this time.

CONSCIOUSNESS EXPANSION AND DESIRE

Not so that we can hear what was said, we all know what the experience was, but so we can feel the doorway again.

Because you can't always be at that peak moment, at least not yet.

But even if you're not at the peak moment, if you're a little further down, in a relative way of speaking, even if you direct your attention to it, you'll become absorbed in it.

And to be absorbed is life itself.

Spiritual absorption is not something that comes easily.

Spiritual absorption is something that comes with time. Time spent in specific ways. Focusing your conscious awareness on eternity.

We all have fields of awareness. Each one of you has *a* field of awareness, which you focus on something. And whatever you focus it on, you become.

Whatever you idolize enters into you, and you become. Whatever you hate enters into you, and you become.

So one learns, passing through the bardos—skipping through the bardo, skateboarding through the bardo—not to be attracted nor repulsed. Just to observe.

I'm sitting alone at my home. I'm absorbed. There's nothing, there's no one. There's no world, there's no Earth, there's no eternity.

There's a knock on my door. Someone comes in the house.

They come in. A world has entered my world. They sit in front of me and we talk. They tell me all of the good things that are happening to them. And I listen with happiness, I go, "Oh! How exciting!"

They tell me the terrible, awful, hard time they had, and I get soooo sad! Oh, sad, sad, pity, pity, unfortunate! [Rama mimics a sad, high pitched tone]

Hey, your heart goes out! You see?

Their joys become your joys; their tribulations, your tribulations. [Rama mimics the emotions. Audience chuckles.] And you identify with that. Then later they leave, and there's nothing. There's no one. Not even eternity.

So with your own mind—when thoughts pass through the mind—enjoy them. Thoughts are the decoration of life.

Listen to your thoughts.

When you have happy thoughts, be excited! "Oh what a good thought!" [Rama mimics excitement] "Boy I like that!"

Terrible, mean, ugly, jealous thoughts. [Rama's voice gets lower and darker] Oooww! It's like going to a horror movie on a wet Saturday afternoon when you're a kid, you know, and the creepy crawly things are there. Oooww!

But don't pay too much attention to your thoughts. They're interesting, they come and go. But they have very little to do with eternity.

When they leave, like the guest leaving the house, there'll be nothing, as there was nothing before. Or everything, you might say.

Be neither attracted nor repulsed. Enjoy them! Have emotions! Feel, love them! But remember, in this world, everything comes and everything goes.

Do the same with people. Someone comes into your life! [Rama's voice is very excited] A friend!

A loved one! [back to normal voice]

Always watch out for them. [Rama chuckles; audience laughs loudly]

A meeean person! A corrupt individual. A mediocre person. Is there such a thing? I'm not sure. I don't think so.

Enjoy them! Watch out for them. But don't get too involved. Everybody comes and everybody goes in this world, what's the difference?

Eternity existed before them, eternity will exist after them, and since you're eternity, what's the difference?

Emotions come and go. You get excited—"Our side! Our team! Yaaay!" [Rama mimics excitement] Flag waving! Super Bowl.

The opposition. Terrible, awful. Darth Vader.

Don't get too excited by your emotions. They come and they go.

Interesting. Observe them. Enjoy them! Be excited by them. Be horrified by how awful you can be. How vain, how selfish.

But don't be too excited. Let it come and go.

Life and death—

God! You're born! "Wow! Here I am! What a place! I can't believe it!" [Rama speaks excitedly]

You're growing up. "God! My feet are getting longer! They're further away! Whoa!"

Adolescence. [Rama laughs freely] "Who is that over there? I want them!" [audience laughs]

Maturity. Filling out tax forms.

Old Age. Realizing you blew it. [audience laughs loudly]

And then suddenly you're dying!

You'll see it all happen. Don't be too excited by life and death, these things come and go. Eternity remains the same, eternity isn't too concerned.

So you see, if you'd be eternity, if you realize that you're eternity, then these things really aren't a big deal. You kind of enjoy them, you watch them pass by. Today you're the hero, tomorrow you're the devil. Hey, it's all the same.

Ultimately.

Enjoy the play, but remember, it's only a play. After the play is over, the theater lights go down.

Somebody comes out and sweeps. And then *they* go home. That's the moment I like. If you stay in the theater and everyone leaves, and then you sit there and feel—absence.

Because eternity exists both in absence and presence.

So it's necessary to have a balanced perspective on your own spiritual aspiration.

You may be in what I call the Level Two.

That is to say, you're in that day, or that week, or that month of just intensive aspiration, and oh, exciting, exciting!

Atmananda [15] calls you up on the phone and says, "Come to dinner! Let's go on a journey." 'Cause as you know I like to be with people who are on that phase, because that's—they're ready for something else I can do for them. So whenever anyone's in that phase I spend more time with them, you see.

Then, you're not in that phase, and the call doesn't come.

Sad! Sad! Hours at home sitting in front of a cold meditation table! [Rama mimics a theatrical sad voice. The audience laughs.]

---

15. In 1982, Rama still used the name Atmananda. "The Last Incarnation," in *The Last Incarnation,* 1983, describes his later name change. "Eternity has named me Rama," Atmananda said. "Rama most clearly reflects that strand of luminosity of which I am a part."

"Oh! Sad! I've fallen, I've fallen. Ah, before I was so high, and now I'm so low."

Nonsense! Come on, vanity, vanity! Give yourself a break. Everybody goes up and down.

Don't be too excited by your so-called successes or too put out by your so-called failures. They're neither success nor failure unless you decide to label them that way.

Eternity does everything perfectly, in and through us all.

Whenever you're supposed to get there, you'll be there. (I always say that when I arrive late.) Whenever you're supposed to get there, you'll be there. [audience laughs] Eternity does everything perfectly, right? I mean ...

You need to learn to live with all of the divergent selves inside yourself. Happily. You need to start out and make friends with all of your different selves. And it's good if they can all like each other.

Because otherwise, it's very difficult. The different parts of your being are at war with each other. It's very hard to follow the spiritual process.

Because part of the spiritual process is all of your many selves—and there are so many of them, and they're so variegated—learning to like each other and get along harmoniously with each other.

Tolerance and acceptance of your self.

To learn to love each of your selves—the happy self-giving self, the pure and humble self, the selfish self, the slothful self and the self that you don't know yet. All of the sides of your being, to learn to love and embrace them all.

The question is, of course, who's loving, and who's embracing? The deeper self.

The deeper self is love. You can tell that it's the deeper self when you've arrived at that level of tolerance.

Who's acting through you at that moment. You've reached a deeper strata.

So in the spiritual process, then, in my estimation anyway, you will go through tremendous oscillation.

You'll have periods of time that seem relatively flat.

You're out walking on the plain, not much is happening. It might seem. That doesn't mean that's the case. It's just the relative mind that's telling us, "Not much is happening." That's why you're on the plain. There is no plain.

It just means you're stuck in the relative mind at the moment. One good meditation and you can leave the plain immediately and be on the highest hill.

But the hills, the plains, the mountains, all that stuff is still relative. That is to say we're still within the world of form.

There's the world of form, there's its opposite—the formless, or the void—and then there's nirvana.

Now the worlds of form have lots and lots of gradations, as you know. So for example, there's the physical. And then above the physical there's the subtle physical, what we call the astral.

And then there's something even a little thinner than that.

There are worlds in which beings live where there's almost no time. Almost. There's still time. But let's say their life span might be billions of our years.

There are worlds where incarnations take place so fast that a millisecond would be eternity.

There is the void. The void is the mat that the picture is hung on.

Even the void comes and goes.

All the worlds come forth from eternity, from nirvana.

They exist in the void. The void is that infinite space of consciousness—which we call awareness.

Then they return to the source.

Then, like the Phoenix, they rise again out of their own ashes.

Eternity comes, eternity goes. Don't be too excited by it. Be absorbed in eternity instead. Be eternity.

Be the finite, be the infinite. Be the void, but fix your eyes on nirvana, for that farthest shoreless shore.

So nirvana exists—a word we use—for that which is beyond both form and formlessness.

And when your awareness is integrated with nirvana, then we say, of course that you've gone beyond birth and death.

There is no one to be born, there is no one to die.

Because as you know, the operative definition of nirvana from this world is as follows:

> No one can enter into nirvana. It's a house that no one occupies.
>
> No one can leave nirvana.
>
> Because in order to enter into nirvana, you can no longer *be*, in the sense that we know being.

So a human being—or whatever we are these days—can advance through all the spiritual planes, subtle planes and all that jazz.

Meditate, become perfect, but still, as long as there's a sense of a separate self—of a finite awareness that's advancing, becoming and being, having experiences in the bardos or whatever—there can't be nirvana.

It's only when that person is erased—if we take the eraser and erase them—then that's absorption.

Now, death is different, as you know. Death simply means that you walked into a different room.

Right now we're sitting here at one room in the Neptunian Women's Club in Los Angeles. There's another room around the corner.

If we go in that room, we still are.

So birth and death, they're just different rooms.

We're in this room for a while, we go into the room of death for a while, we come back through rebirth into this room again.

Or perhaps a different world. You don't have to incarnate in this world.

Then there's the dreamer and the dream, of course. Another way of looking at it. All of life is a dream. It appears to be, but it's not.

> We see the rope on the street, you know, it's night time, we stumble over it, we think it's a snake. That's the classic explanation.
>
> And of course, in the light of day, we see that it was just a rope.

Of course, eternity is a rope of sand. If you try and hold onto it, it dissolves in front of you.

So, self-realization, then, is waking from the dream of life. Right now we're all in a dream. You think you're listening to me, but it's only a dream.

When the dream fades and vanishes, something else remains.

So when the dream of life and the dream of death—the dream of paradise, the dream of hell—when these things fade, eternity remains, nirvana remains.

So begin to identify, no so much with birth, death and rebirth. Not so much with this world. Not so much with other worlds.

But with absorption. Erase yourself. (Interesting!)

The problem is—if you're erasing your self—what do you do when you get to the last part? [audience laughs] Who's going to erase the last part?

That, that, that's the problem. That's the hook, you see, that most people have trouble with at the end.

Because you get to a certain point where you're doing and seeing these great meditations, and you've meditated for many years, and you've gone through all the different steps and you've become pure and humble and free, and aware. Kind to others, good to small animals, all that sort of thing. [audience chuckles]

And you're on the verge of realization itself!

Like the moon. When the full moon comes out, that's the ego.

And then lifetime after lifetime, the moon, you know it becomes thinner and thinner each day. Until finally there's just a tiny, slim, sliver of a moon left.

So as you approach realization, the ego gets smaller and smaller until there's just a little bit of ego left. Just enough to get through the day. No more, no less.

Not enough to hurt anyone else, or to hurt you. Just enough to get you through, to do what you need to do in the world, as long as you're still in the world.

Nirvana is the eclipse, of course. But an eclipse that never ends.

So people have trouble with that last phase. It is difficult, I admit. But when the time comes, it works out.

> You're standing on the edge of the cliff, looking down, and it's a long way down. Below you is the ocean, the rocks, and you want to jump, but you're afraid.
>
> But one day you jump, but you never hit the water or the rocks.

That's absorption.

I did that for some friends when we were in Hawaii on the volcano, I took a rock, and I said, "Listen! I'm going to show you what absorption is."

And I took the rock and I threw it up in the air and it never came down.

That's absorption. Or a very good right arm! [audience laughs heartily]

So, with all this great knowledge that we've now unfolded, all these higher dharmic truths, you see, now you can all go out into the world … and liberate others. [Rama laughs! The audience laughs, too.]

It's not that funny. You might be able to! It could happen! I mean it's possible. Don't put yourselves down, you don't know what you can do yet.

And remember, its very exciting what happens to people who liberate others.

Well, Christ had eleven disciples. Twelve actually. And they studied with … You know he had only three years with them? And then they went off to liberate the world.

No, really! They were very sincere. And you know what happened to them. Eleven out of twelve died horrible deaths. Not that death matters, remember, it's really not a big deal, it's just another thing you go through.

I think you need more than three years. [audience laughs]

Now, should we pay attention to the eleven—or the twelfth one? Ah! A question! I wouldn't even pay attention to the question if I were you. [laughter]

So, again, here we are still back in eternity, trying to figure it all out. And I think it's good to figure it all out, it's very constructive. [Rama exhales]

Now let's try it again. I'm sure we'll get it right tonight, and we'll all be liberated and we can skip the rest of the incarnation. [laughter]

Hmmm. OK, let's try it from the point of view of Zen, how's that?

As you know, in past lives I was a Zen teacher. So I'll summon up the Spirit of Zen Past. [laughter]

Zen again … right? [laughter, audience, then Rama]

> Once upon a time there was a Zen. And he grew in the garden. He grew for a long, long time reaching up to the sun, but he never got there.
>
> What was his name?

Or …

> Two roses. Fell.

Or …

> The Zen Master was driving his Toyota. One day. Down the freeway. When he ran. Out of gas.
>
> Was his tank empty? Or full?

Clearly, Zen is not the way tonight, I can see. [audience breaks into huge laughter]

They're laughing, that's good.

I had a meeting with some of the people who are kind of on the staff, the other day. I say "kind of," because I'm not sure.

But one of the things I was telling them was, it's always good to feel that you'll never attain enlightenment, particularly if you're working for a spiritual organization in any capacity, because it's probably true. It keeps you even.

The other thing that is good to remember is that anybody who studies with me must have had terrible karma in a past life. [audience laughs] Because otherwise you would have never gotten such an exacting, mean, disciplinarian. [long silence]

Well, it's true! I'm one of the toughest, meanest, hardest teachers you'll ever meet.

I mean, let's consider it. There are no rules. Now can you think of anything more difficult than spirituality with no rules?

In the beginning it sounds good, "No rules! He doesn't have any rules, Whoa!" [Rama mimics someone getting away with something. Enormous laughter from the audience.]

That's in the beginning.

> Then you come up to the teacher and say, "Well, gee, Atmananda, I ... What should I do? I just, uh, I, well, gee, I ... I'm not sure, I mean, should I, should I ... I have this opportunity to go to college here, or I could go to college over here, what should I do?"
>
> And I'll say, "Well, how about the first school?"

CONSCIOUSNESS EXPANSION AND DESIRE 387

And you say, "Well, gee, I'd really like to go there, I mean it's a beautiful place, and they're going to give me a scholarship and you know, all this stuff, and granted, you know, it's in the middle of, you know, Cucamonga, and I won't be able to come to Center meetings. But I really am inspired to go there, and I just know it'll be good for my spiritual practice."

And I'll say, "Well, that sounds very good."

Then you'll say, "Yeah, but you know, gosh, there's this part of me that really wants to stay here right now, because I know if I have that *contact* now ..."

You know, with "that *contact* ..."? [Rama mimics *contact* in a pseudo-hip 'valley girl' slang style. Audience really laughs.]

"I gotta make breakthroughs in my inner life!"

And I'll say, "Well, yeah, that's true too."

And then you say, "Well what shall I do?!"

And I say, "Well I don't know."

And you say, "Well, didn't you agree with me the first time?"

And I'll say, "Well, of course I agreed with you. It sounded terrific to me."

"Well, then, didn't you agree with me about staying?"

And I said, "Well, of course I agreed. I'll agree with *anything* you say."

You see, there are no rules. I have to agree. Why shouldn't I agree? Who's not to agree with? I'm friendly.

You want to do something? I think it's wonderful! You want to do something else, I can swing that way too. What's the difference?

You see, no rules.

Then one day of course, you say to yourself,

> "Now wait a minute. Something's going on here. Who is this guy anyway? [laughter]
>
> "He's telling me to do anything I want. That can't be spiritual. He must have another motive." [Rama laughs]

I have no motives at all. That's why I can agree. I'm friendly. I'm a cheap date. Listen, take me to a movie, give me some popcorn, I'm happy. [audience laughs loud and long] Leave me at home, I'm happy. Doesn't matter.

I've often thought that spiritual teachers are ... well, I don't know if I should talk about spiritual teachers, maybe later. [laughter]

Let's stick with you just for a minute.

So ... how can we get out of this? We're in a paper bag here, we can't see the light of day, it's very tough. Hmmm. Hmmm.

There are no rules.

Well, that means ... what? It means that you have to figure things out on your own, doesn't it. It means that you have to work a lot harder. It means that you have to become honest.

It also means that no one is going to give you the opportunity to rebel.

Ah! Tricky, huh? It's easy, you see, when the going gets tough to say,

> "Why, that so-and-so, he said something — *hmph, hah, foomf, foomf!*"
>
> Stomp, stomp, stomp, leave, leave, leave.
>
> [all said in a deep cartoonish voice]

CONSCIOUSNESS EXPANSION AND DESIRE 389

But if somebody's saying—if someone is not only admiring your great spirituality, but—

> Opening up the door for you to leave and saying, "Thanks for coming!" [laughter]
>
> And then you turn around halfway and say, "Oh, but I should stay!" and then they'll look at you and say, "Oh yes! Stay!" [Rama is comically theatrical]
>
> And then they'll look and say, "Oh no, I have to go, you're awful."
>
> You say, "Oh, I'm awful. Oh, you should go!"

It becomes very confusing! I'd be confused by that, I wouldn't know what to do. Which is precisely, of course, what I hope.

You see, it's like when people, when people think that … People sometimes think that if they can only do something, it'll all … it'll be wonderful.

So of course, they don't do that, so they can always think it'll be wonderful. That's basically what sex is, I think. You see.

You see, if people ever indulged and gave way to all their fantasies, they'd be extremely bored. So the idea is, of course, to not quite go that far …

But I think you should give in. No, I do! I think you should give in! To whatever you want. Enjoy it. As a matter of fact, I think it would be wonderful if you went *overboard* for a while. [audience laughs loudly]

No! As long as it doesn't hurt anybody else, of course, I mean that's just being a good person. But I think you should go overboard! Do, explore what you want to.

Of course you won't, because you're all scared. And also because you don't even really want to.

Ahh, you see, that's the thing. People don't really want to do what they say they want to do. They just want to torment themselves, so they set up things that they want to do, that they never quite do. So they can make themselves miserable. No, this is human nature!

You've got to understand the nature of the critter, if you're going to work with it. Or if you're going to work with yourself.

So I think when there's something you really want to do, you should do it.

And then you'll find that you're the same, it didn't matter a bit. Before the orgy, after the orgy, there was eternity.

Really not a big deal one way or the other. It's only a big deal if you decide it is. And of course it isn't.

Pleasure-pain, heat-cold, good weather-bad weather, it's all the same, you see.

So wisdom, then, is getting out of the trap of fooling yourself into thinking that life has a meaning and a purpose.

The truly wise people know that life has no meaning and no purpose whatsoever.

Because as long as you think that life has a meaning and a purpose, you're going to try and figure it out. And of course, since it has none, you never will.

Therefore, you'll spend all your time trying to figure out the meaning and purpose of life and never know life itself. Because real life is beyond meaning and purpose. Meaning and purpose are but intellectual partialities. Ideas in the mind.

Whereas existence itself is perfection. Rather be absorbed in perfection, and don't worry about partialities. Don't worry about trying to put into words that which is beyond words. A silly occupation.

So human beings have this constant flow of desire. Where does it come from? Where does it go to? I don't know. But it comes and it goes!

And what happens is—you're sitting there, in perfect being. This is the parable, this is what, you know, the Eden thing was all about.

You're sitting there in perfect being—Eden—in terms of consciousness. And a desire comes by *whoosh!* A bird flying by, *whoo*.

Now, if you just kind of watch it and don't pay too much attention to it, the bird passes by. Ah! But suppose you see a bird you like. You reach out and grab the bird. *Squwak!!* [audience laughs]

Take it home, tame it, make friends with it. The bird bites you. [Rama makes a biting sound] But gradually you tame it and make friends with it.

Then you and the bird have what we call a relationship. [audience laughs] No, really, the bird lives in the cage and you live outside. You see the bird in the morning, "Hi bird!" "Chirp!"

Basic communication is developed. The bird learns your routines, you learn the bird's routines. You think that the bird is your pet. The bird thinks that you're its pet. [audience laughs]

And you coexist. Two bits of consciousness put next to each other, you see. And you have transactions.

You bring a friend to see the bird. And the bird bites the friend. Or the bird runs off with the friend. Ah! [laughter]

Now one day either you die or the bird dies. Unless you're into Zen, of course, and if there was Zen, there was no bird. [laughter]

So, there has to be a funeral, because, I mean, funerals are things that are established. Thousands of years people have had funerals. You're going to go against the tradition?

So you have an elaborate funeral for the bird. You call up all your friends, and if you don't have many friends, you can just take a phone book and make random calls. And invite them to the funeral of the bird. [laughter]

You could advertise in local newspapers or maybe even in *Life Magazine* about the funeral of the bird. You could have famous photographers fly in. We could even get it televised!

And the bird would be buried. You'd stand there, people would come up, "Sorry about your loss, Jack. Tough. You ought to take a little vacation, now, you know, maybe think about getting another bird."

[Rama changes to a female voice]

"Oh, Harry, I'm so sorry to hear about your bird! Oh, he was so beautiful. Oh, it's a tragic loss, but he'll be alright in heaven!" [audience laughs]

[Rama changes to a raspy male voice]

"I never liked that bird anyway, and I thought the two of you made a lousy couple. You're lucky he died when he did! It's a blessing you two never had children!" [Rama laughs and laughs]

"Think of the suffering that's been spared."

'Cause then the drunken Zen Master walks in, who's drunken without having to drink anything, of course.

And he walks up, grabs the bird—in front of all the guests—gives him a big kiss on the beak. Throws him into the air, the bird disappears, and he lies down in the coffin himself! [raucous laughter, scattered applause]

Zen Masters are totally unreliable. [more laughter]

Well, after the funeral, anyway, you collect all the clippings from the papers about the big event and stuff like that. You go home, and you experience the absence of bird.

Now, tell me, are you any different at the very end than you were at the very beginning?

No, you were nirvana before and you're nirvana afterwards. You see? But that's desire. You get all wrapped up.

So an *enlightened* person just watches the birds fly by in the sky. They don't feel the need to trap them. They just watch them. That's more than enough.

A *liberated* person doesn't watch birds anymore. They are one. They're flying. Of course the *self-realized* person runs a bird store. [laughter]

Which brings us back to self-realization, I guess. Now, I keep trying to figure this thing out, and I know we'll get it sooner or later, and it might be tonight.

You know, sooner or later the world is going to disappear and we'll all be absorbed, and we won't have to concern ourselves. And I just figure if we come back every Wednesday night and keep trying, sooner or later we'll get it.

Absorption.

So you find yourself on the Earth, collecting birds. Some birds it goes well with, some it doesn't go so well with.

Then one day, of course, you look beyond. And you see eternity. You see, suddenly, for some reason, out of the maya came that epiphany, that crystal clear awakening, when everything becomes clear. And shining and perfect.

And you see eternity. You feel light. No longer do you wish to collect birds. What birds?

You're not even looking. Oh, there may be flocks of birds all around you, but you don't even notice, because you're so absorbed in perfection.

Then, of course, suddenly, you're catching birds again. That's life. For some. There is an alternative, though.

The alternative is to direct your attention endlessly towards perfection, and to go through this process which you have decided for a period of time to engage yourself in.

In which every part of your being must be trained.

I spend a majority of my time addressing your nonphysical being. We talk, chat, while away the hours. But while we're here meditating together, there's another show going on.

The show of words, of actions, of belief systems, has very little to do with what's occurring. While we're here ... we're absorbed in meditation, and my nonphysical being of eternity is addressing your nonphysical being and communication is taking place. The light is being transferred to all of you. That's what a spiritual teacher does.

Some spiritual teachers don't even talk. They just sit and meditate and their students come.

And that's more than sufficient. Some like to talk. Some feel that it's good to address what Don Juan refers to as the *tonal*. And to address the *nagual*. It's good to address the physical being. The part of the being that extends itself into this world. The iceberg. The part that's above the surface.

But as you know, the larger part of the iceberg is below the surface. You don't see it, but it's there. So the larger part of one's being is below the surface, and most of the work that I do is below the surface.

We need to address the outer being, too. The outer being must become happy, balanced, orderly.

But our real work is on the other side.

That's why you can come and we can talk about birds flying through the sky, or great spiritual principles, the latest movie. It really doesn't matter.

Because our real conversation between myself and each one of you, or between any of my students and myself, or just anyone who meditates with me or any enlightened person—self-realized person—is an infinite conversation that is not bound by time, or days, or hours or ways.

Think of a person like myself as not existing. Or again, there's just a thin sliver of a moon, just enough left to exist. No big deal. Basically a harmless person. On the surface, very often like a child. Very childlike, very silly. As I said before, a cheap date. Popcorn, a movie, happy!

But below the surface entirely different. Below the surface eternity. Abilities, powers—like an aircraft carrier. Planes always landing and taking off.

So carrier beings [16] constantly moving in and out between the teacher and all of the students.

Not the students who are simply physically present but all of them, all over the world. Between the teacher, and beings on different planes. And so on and so forth.

You see, you have to look beyond the veil of maya, beyond the curtain. There may be a curtain, and we see what's going on in front of it. But in meditation we part the curtain and see the other side, we see eternity.

So all of you really need now to begin to try and address yourself—openly—to the nonphysical side of your teacher, because that's the part that's of most help to you.

Now again, I think the way you do that, is first by balancing the physical side. And the nonphysical sides relate automatically. That's why you came

---

16. See "Gods, Goddesses and Carrier Beings" in *The Lakshmi Series,* Rama - Dr. Frederick Lenz, 1982.

and you study here. The physical side didn't bring you, believe me.

The nonphysical did, and then it convinced the physical that it was a good idea. [In a deep voice] "Fill out the application!" [audience laughs]

You see, the thought is in the mind, but where does the thought come from? It's generated by the inner being.

But now it's necessary for you to try and make a breakthrough between the two sides of your being, and see them as one.

You see, the problem is that we think that there's two sides. Now, some people are not even aware of the second side, the larger part. They're just aware of the little physical self in the mind. They have no realization that the inner self goes on and on and on.

So then we begin and we show you the inner self. We show you it's various sides, aspects, dimensions, and so forth.

But then there comes a point where we integrate the awareness so that there's no difference. You see, there is no difference between the inner being and the outer being. There's just being.

So that's what we're working on now.

But you can help in the process a lot. Either by not thinking about the nonphysical communication at all and just letting it happen, if that suits you, or by focusing on it very intensely, if that suits you. Either way works fine.

It's just a question of balance, of seeing which is the best for you. But I—or any person like myself—is available, seven days a week, 24 hours a day, we get no vacations. We don't need them. We *are* a vacation.

But it's necessary to address that, to utilize that.

You see, in spiritual discovery, you have to—this is the sad, sad, sad news—you have to change.

You know, I've told you before, *you* can't attain enlightenment. Not one of you here will ever attain enlightenment. That is the God's truth, even if you don't believe in God.

None of you will ever attain enlightenment. It's impossible.

Remember the Road Runner and the Coyote. The Coyote can't catch a Road Runner in that cartoon, because Coyotes don't catch Road Runners in that cartoon.

So you have to become something other than you are now.

The self that's here listening tonight cannot attain enlightenment. It has to go away. Pack its bags, shake hands with all the old members of the staff and faculty at the college, get their gold watch and go off into the sunset to where old, tenured faculty go. Shangri-La, or whatever.

And then a new self will emerge. That one won't attain enlightenment either, but it'll go a little further, you see? It'll be younger, more pliable. And then that one will fade away. And so on, and so on— you'll go through self after self—again the moon getting thinner, and thinner and thinner. 'Til finally, one day, there's the thinnest, tiniest self left.

And then even that goes away, and when that goes away, life goes away, death does away, the world goes away, Adidas tennis shoes go away, Pac-Man goes away, Ms. Pac-Man goes away.

Everything goes away—which does not mean that there's nothing.

Now here's the problem people have with nirvana. They think that, well, gosh, nirvana must be nothing. Emptiness. A desert. You know, barren, emotionless, horrible.

No, not at all. There's simply no way to describe it.

When we say everything goes away, it doesn't mean everything goes away.

> One bird flying through the sky attracts your attention.
>
> [Rama mimics a theatrically impassioned voice]
>
> "Oh God! If I could only have that bird. Oh I want that bird, oh it is the most beautiful bird. Oh Daddy, Daddy, please can I have the bird, please can I have—look at that bird. Oh! Oh! It flew away! Sad, cry, miserable.
>
> "Oh! Here it comes again, here it comes again! Oh wonderful bird! Oh bird of light do visit me!
>
> "Oh, it's going away again! Oh, he didn't call. I sat up all night waiting. He didn't call, he was the one, my soul mate, my opposite flame."
>
> What nonsense! [Rama normal voice, audience laughs]
>
> "Oh! Oh! Ooh!" [Rama impassioned voice, then back to normal voice]
>
> You know, give me a break, right?
>
> You see? One bird can do all that! Amazing, the power of a bird. That's why I'm a member of the Audubon Society. [audience laughs] Birds have power.

Now, again, for one who's absorbed in nirvana—what Shankara [17] calls "liberation while on the street", [Rama laughs] ... no, that's an "in" joke—"liberation while living".

(They didn't go for it, oh well.) [referring to no laughter]

To one who is absorbed in nirvana, there could be thousands of birds all around you. You wouldn't notice.

---

17. *Shankara's Crest Jewel of Discrimination;* Rama's recommended translation is by Swami Prabhavananda and Christopher Isherwood.

CONSCIOUSNESS EXPANSION AND DESIRE 399

You see, the thing is not getting rid of the birds—it's getting rid of *you*.

Ah! You in your current form.

You see, that's all the thing with the funeral for the bird. You're the bird.

Of course, as you know, according to the Zen Master, there was never a bird to begin with. However, the Zen Master would definitely agree there was a funeral. The funeral was for nothing. [laughter]

"How to lose students fast." [more laughter]

I try to do that all the time, you know! I'm always trying to get people to leave the Center. I say the most silly things I can, to discourage people. You know, hold the door open. "Go away! Bye! Bye! Thanks for coming."

I even give excuses so they don't feel bad when they leave. You know, as you listen to the series of lectures that I give, seriously, I will build in rationalizations for people so they won't feel bad.

It's part of the service of being kind to people. So they can walk away and say, "Heh, hmph, ha, no way!" [Rama theatrically mimics dissatisfaction]

I'll be the first to agree.

I love it when people go away. I love it when people come. What people? [audience laughs]

I tell you, there are a lot of birds out, and they're flying everywhere all at once. Nothing but birds, what a wonderful thing. I love birds, you know, you just see them everywhere. Pelicans. Lots of pelicans.

You see, nirvana! [Rama laughs]

(I'm not going to say it.) Nope. You're all so serious! And you think you're gonna attain self-realization? Oh, come on. [audience laughs]

How many times do I have to tell you, you have to die. Christ said it, "You must die before entering the kingdom of heaven."

Or, when, you know, different spiritual teachers talking about, "Every day I die a thousand times."

I mean, the self is going in and out of nirvana. You see, come out—pop!—here you are again. Liberation while living. What? What's going on? Here I am! Whoops! Fwump! You're gone!

You're there again. But there's no sense of gone, since there was no one to be gone.

How do you know you haven't been for a while? [laughter]

(Stttreettch that awareness, stretch that awareness, stttreettch.)

There is no end and there is no beginning. Is there a middle?

No, I'm asking you straight Zen questions, really. This is serious stuff. I'm glad you're laughing. But this is a very formal training session tonight. [laughter after a long pause]

So I've been pondering this thing about the birds for a long time. The bees were never of much interest to me. I respect bees. But no, the birds are the ones that fascinate me. (This could go on for a long time. You might as well sit back and enjoy it.) Now …

How the heck … [laughter] … are we going to get you out of your present awareness—which is limited—into eternity?

I mean, that's, you know, if we could take a crow bar and sort of try and pry you out. No, I try all kinds of stuff. Really! I use different forces, powers, dissolve myself in front of you just to show you it's a good time. [laughter]

Talk about birds, take you out to the desert, do miracles. I mean, I'll do anything to get a person to enlightenment. I'm not proud. I'm committed.

(Yeah, I know you think I should be.) [laughter] But seriously, I'll go for it.

But you see, I need you in the Level Two. See, you're all hanging out one level down from that.

As I said, remember in the beginning of the talk, there are five?

The first is what we call, well, the "levelest" level. That's you know, very advanced spiritual seekers. Well, I don't have to deal with any of those—yet. No, I'm looking forward to it, whether it's you or someone else.

Again, if that particular type of bird doesn't come by that's alright with me too, I like the ones that are here.

But if you transform into those birds, that's fine, too. That's somebody who's always "on". Who is always ready for liberation. Who will give everything to be of service to humanity.

And while being of service, is completely absorbed in eternity—who wants nothing but God. I mean such people are rare.

You are those people, eventually.

But we have to deal with today. You know, it's great to address—you know—the commencement of the sixth grade class. [laughter]

And eventually, they'll be the ones who are, you know, graduating from the university, but in the meantime, I mean, you're still stuck in time and this world and you've got to deal with the commencement of the sixth grade class.

But what you are capable of doing, in my estimation—if you try a little harder—is moving into Level Two. See, remember the concept of the fluid Level Two in the Center, is that you are capable of—for a period of time—moving into that state where you're just totally "on".

Your self-giving is happening, your meditation is happening, your life is happening. It doesn't matter what's happening *to* you. Whether there are a few birds or many. It's irrelevant.

No excuses. You're just living completely. Then you glow. Then I can do some neat stuff for you, you know? I mean I have a whole, whole bag of tricks then that I can use, things I can teach you.

But until you come up to that point, you see, I can't show you what's over the horizon until you come up to the top of the hill. We have to keep dealing with what's down on the bottom of the hill. Which is good, important stuff. Earth.

But right now, most of you ride that middle level, which is an accomplishment in itself. I mean, that's good. There are billions of people on the Earth, and not that many of them are even in that middle level. Most of them are in the fourth level—religion.

In the sense that most people mean religion. Idolatry. Worshiping statues of birds. As opposed to the birds themselves. [laughter]

So you're doing OK in my estimation. But if you could just get into that Level Two more often, you see. Then, of course, the idea is you make these little excursions to Level Two and you find out what it's like.

And, of course, it puts you down a little bit. I mean, you have to change. Suddenly you confront Light, and you see all the things that have to go. Like yourself, yourself and yourself.

But you do it. You do your homework, and you get rid of some selves, and some new ones come in and some old ones go out, and some new—it's like birds. They come and they go. You know, birds can come and go at night and you'll never know? [laughter] Yeah. It's a fact.

So, how are we going to do it? I mean I keep trying. I don't know what else to do, except to keep doing the same stuff. There must be a way. Hmmm. Hmmm. Hmmm.

[long silence, about ten seconds]

You know what I think the way is? I think I figured it out. [laughter]

You've got to do it. [laughter]

'Cause I'm doing the best I can.

You've got to do it. It's up to you. You've got to reach it on your own. With all the help people like myself can supply—nonphysical beings can supply, your own inner being can supply. But *you* have to do it. That's what I've concluded.

So I've decided to be patient. And if no one asks me out, I'll stay at home at night. That's the part I was talking about—spiritual teachers—before.

Spiritual teachers just sit at home at night waiting for someone to ask them out.

And if no one asks them out, they stay at home. They try and look their best—you know? [laughter]

No, really! I mean, you try and look attractive, put out a nice force, you know, stuff like that. But you just wait by the phone. [laughter]

It's true! You're waiting for somebody who's happening. Who's glowing, who's ready to really go along. On a certain level.

I mean you're out there doing the best you can for humanity, but another part of you that could be doing things, just has to wait by the phone.

And you'll know if somebody calls, immediately. [Rama snaps his fingers] The student pops into your consciousness. Pow! They're there. Even if it's for an hour. What the heck! [raucous laughter]

But you see, I'll be the same after you've all gone. I'll be the same forever. So you're all phantoms to me. You all come and go.

All the selves that I see here will not exist in the future, because I *see* the future.

But one day you won't be a phantom anymore, you won't be a shadow. You see, when you move into that height of aspiration and spiritual seeking, then there's just Light. No shadows.

Even the Light must be transcended eventually, but that's an awful good start. We can't show you how to transcend Light itself until you at least become Light.

So I wait at home nights, whiling away the hours. Thinking about birds, watching them fly through the night. Because I can see them at night.

Waiting.

I've considered getting aggressive. "Liberation of spiritual teachers", we call it.

Just going out and saying, "Hey listen, whatch ya' doin' tomorrow?" [laughter] Yeah, I've even tried that. Yeah.

But … you're better off to stay home. That's my feeling.

Really. People misunderstand, they don't treat you well. They think you have the wrong motives.

I tell you, we live in a structured society. Better to sit at home. And wait. And if no one comes … [in a secretive whisper] it might be better!

Because then you can sit with the birds all over your living room, and have marvelous conversations with them, and talk to them. And no one will know, will they? Because they didn't come and find out. You see the problem? You get my "drift?"

You see, you'll never know unless you reach a little bit more than you are. You're doing fine, but I'd like to see you reach more.

CONSCIOUSNESS EXPANSION AND DESIRE 405

Into eternity itself, in this lifetime while we have—who knows how much time we have together? I don't know.

I bet the birds do, but they would never say.

But if you reach a little bit more, it's endless. I'm trying to tell you that life is so much better than you can imagine. That eternity is so complete, that nirvana is so perfect and shining—but you're just skimming it. You're missing it.

And that's a part in the process.

But if you just reach a little more. If you just extend your self-giving—your love—a little deeper. If you just try a little harder in your meditations—it's endless, it's perfect, it's beyond anything that you can imagine.

And I would like that for you. It would be quite wonderful.

But you'll never know. You might even think that you know. But you'll never know.

Unless of course …

Just some thoughts on a Wednesday night for you. For your scrapbook. Should we meditate?

[meditation for several minutes]

Question please? Yes.

[a male student asks a question]

Your question is quite apt, I think, and that's …

There are different levels of mistakes. And if I make a serious mistake, I'll lose my way, and it may take a long time to get back. How do I deal with that?

And the response is, well, first of course, if you can avoid making a mistake, that's always the best. Or even if you can catch yourself halfway through and stop, you can minimize the damage.

And then again, if it's gone too far, all you can do is recognize what you did, so hopefully you won't do it again. Or do it again a minute later. You know, you have to stop the process.

And then you have to move to a kind of a middle ground, and gradually work your way back up.

But before we even do that—this gives some people problems—the idea of mistakes.

In one sense we can say everything is the dharma, and even if you make a so-called mistake, wasn't God working through you? And wasn't that destiny? And so maybe there aren't any mistakes.

Now, I don't believe that for a second, to be honest with you. Not in *this* world. If we're dealing from the perspective of other worlds, I would agree.

But that's not going to help you get through the day. In this world, you have to feel that you have freedom of choice, and that you make decisions.

Because if you don't, you become a very confused person, in my estimation.

So, it's necessary first, then, the way you avoid this problem is to assess what is dharma. Because it's my belief that once you know what dharma or truth is, be it dharma in its larger sense, or in an individual situation. Once you know that, you're bound to do it, it'll happen.

Once a person has seen truth clearly, then they have to follow it. But as long as they can shine the truth on and pretend that they don't see it, they don't have to follow it. Again, that's just my perspective.

So, I think, then, the place to start is with seeing truth. Truth is a very difficult thing to see.

And I don't believe that you should present too much truth to a person at a time. No more than they can handle. Because if you do, all it does is destroy people. It discourages people.

So, for example, tonight I presented in our earlier talk, dozens of different spiritual concepts. I literally threw them at you. Hundreds of them, just bombarding you with lots of different things for you to consider.

Now, those were all leads. It's like want ads. I gave you a lot of want ads before, and you can call up on any of them, and see if they're available, or you can ignore them if you want to.

I'm not going to force anybody into the truth, that's not the right way. Because you *can't*.

You can't force truth on people. They have to be ready for it and want it.

You can encourage them, you can drop little hints. That's what I was talking about before when I was referring to sitting at home at night waiting for somebody to call you to go out.

That's what a spiritual teacher does, you present ideas—waves of light—but people have to follow up on that.

So, and when they don't follow up on it the way you might like them to—or if you don't find yourself following up on it—you have to be very patient.

And you have to realize that you have many selves—which are not always in harmony—and if one self acts to do something that makes you suffer, you have to realize that that's what happened.

There's absolutely no shame in it whatsoever. But that if you continue to do that, you'll continue to suffer.

So you have to bring another self in to take over. See, the horse that's leading the sleigh loses it's way, and the passenger is lost in the woods.

So now you have to have a ... put a different horse on the sleigh, and the horse will take the sled, perhaps he knows the way a little better, you see.

So in the maya, it's very difficult to know the way.

That's why we have a weekly meeting, so you can sit here once a week in proximity, in an energy that you simply can't deny, and assess what truth is. In other words, this is your *correction*.

Let's say you're going to correct ... You have a compass, but maybe it's gone off, so we want to correct it.

So if you're sitting face to face with me—or with any person who's in the superconscious—the force is so strong, if you have any sensitivity at all, that you see it, and it confronts you. I mean, it's not what your mind is confronting.

Your mind can sit here and think all the million discontinuous thoughts, different emotions can pass through you, it doesn't matter worth a fig about those things.

But again, what I was discussing before, as you're sitting here, and I'm sitting with you, on another level—on many other levels—we're having conversations.

Not conversations like we have in this world, we're not exchanging ideas.

First of all, I'm exchanging solid power into you, to give you the ability to follow dharma. Or, if you've lost the way, to pick yourself up. That's the least I can do as a service to you.

Then secondly, a recognition is taking place. As you look at me, you see nothing, you see an absence because I'm merely an absence. I'm a doorway, you see, the absence that you walk through. That's all any teacher can be.

Once you walk through—then you don't even need to look at the doorway—you're in the other room. So I'm merely an absence.

But if all you're seeing in your life is presence, then it gets very confusing. There's so many things swimming around you, so many people, so many ideas, so many emotions. Where does it begin and where does it end?

So what I do, is try and bring you to a still point inside yourself.

And once you find that point of stillness, then you'll see correspondence. Then suddenly the way will be known. Then you'll understand things I have no words for.

So that's really what we do.

And even if you've made a mistake, or if you've totally lost your way, still you have to find your way again, anyway. I mean, it doesn't matter.

You're walking along a pathway. And then you go off the pathway and you're lost. Well, you have to find the pathway again.

I mean, there are no degrees of lost. There is lost and there's lost. I mean, there's no "little bit lost" or "very lost".

Again, I'm a very strict spiritual teacher, so you have to understand, I'm very old school in my ways. You know, I believe that there's enlightenment and ignorance and there's nothing in between.

And that people can talk all they want to about their great spiritual experiences. As far as I'm concerned, it's refracted maya.

There is enlightenment and there is ignorance.

There is maya and there is nirvana.

So that a person can't be a little bit lost. They're all completely lost in my estimation. From my point of view everyone's a shadow, still.

If you remember the analogy, you're on the bank and the river is flowing by you. And in the river you see all kinds of people flowing by, and they're all drowning.

So you try and reach out to those, and have somebody take your hand. You try and pull them in. But sometimes when people are drowning, they're so disconcerted that they pull *you* in. They're very confused.

So you have to be very careful, because what you're dealing with is your self and your self is drowning. Yet at the same time your self is trying to pull you in.

And you have to be careful not to pull in the self that's trying to help you—into the whirlpool, into the vortex. That's the main thing.

And the way you do that, is not by worrying about mistakes or being lost. But by, again, realigning yourself with the dharma. That's how it's done.

You focus on light. You spend time with spiritual friends. And you don't overdo it either. You take it in little pieces, a piece at a time that you can assimilate. And then you move forward.

You'll see eventually, there are levels of truth and reality a million-fold, beyond your current perception. As there are layers of ignorance—a million-fold—beyond your current perception.

So you're somewhere in the middle of the maya right now, and we're trying to get you out. And it's done little by little—with love and care and concern—as you cultivate humility and purity, integrity and truthfulness.

As you learn trust, and you learn not to mind screwing up once in a while. Because you know you'll always rise to the surface again, 'cause you've done it before and you'll do it again.

And it'll actually take less time—each time—to come back again. You'll find this. That's how you know it's working, what we're doing is working.

And then the day comes when you just smile much more. That's how it's done.

So be patient. It's a *long* journey. But it's a fun journey. It's an exciting journey. It's all we have to do with our lives, really, is to journey. Remember, there's no place to go. It's just the journey itself that matters, and the journey is endless. We're always journeying one place or another.

So just live in the moment of the journey, and just enjoy the journey. That's what don Juan says. All paths lead nowhere. So it really doesn't matter which path you follow. Just follow a path with heart, because the way is happy on a path with heart. A path without heart, the seeking is miserable.

Just follow a path of heart, and then the way is always happy.

And whether the way is nirvana or the way is maya. If the path has heart—even in the midst of the maya—you can be happy.

Because the way is light. That makes more sense to me.

CHAPTER TWELVE

REINCARNATION AND THE TIBETAN REBIRTH PROCESS

Tonight we're discussing the sophistications of the rebirth process. Looking at reincarnation from many different points of view.

Reincarnation is a cyclic process. It's a big circle. We end up where we begin, in a sense. Where we begin, though is not this world. We're not really indigenous to this world. This world being a temporal plane of reality.

You might say that we're all light. We're all composed of light and that there are many dreams that are available in existence, and this is one particular dream that we find ourselves in now. What we call this lifetime, this evening, this moment.

Birth and death are stages of transition, but life is a continuous transition.

Reincarnation is an apprehension of a movement, and the movement occurs in time. Without time, there is no reincarnation. Reincarnation is a reflection of time in this world. There are, of course, many people who do not necessarily believe in reincarnation. Their sight is confined to one particular structural lifetime.

They'll be surprised.

Pleasantly, I hope.

Reincarnation in the large sense of course, is the progression of the soul or the jiva, or the anatman, if you prefer, through a cycle of lifetimes of incarnations.

The idea, of course is essentially quite simple. And that's that we are all part of the source. We are all one with God. We are eternity, and a part of eternity, as in that marvelous poem by Andrew Marvell, *On a Drop of Dew*. Just like a little dewdrop separating itself from the cosmos, we separate ourselves from existence for a while, or seemingly so.

And we enter into incarnation, into a temporal plane where there's time and space, the world. We have a body.

We pass through hundreds, thousands, perhaps millions of existences. In each lifetime we're exploring another part of our own self, which is eternity, our larger body is eternity.

Eventually, we return to the source in its undifferentiated form, in its absolute form, which is both form and formlessness.

But we exist in that sea all the time. You could think of us all as little boats. And we're taking a great journey across an ocean. We're on an odyssey. Each one of us is on an individual spiritual odyssey. And we have, like Odysseus, many adventures in our return to Penelope, which is the source, I suppose, ultimately.

Reincarnation, though, is not simply a logistical game plan of existence. In other words, reincarnation suggests that we have many lifetimes, that there's a particular progression of that lifetime, which we'll be discussing a little bit later. How it works, I suppose. The different fields of attention that we pass through, the different cycles of birth and death, karma, the sophistications of the rebirth process.

But at the same time, reincarnation has a value. In the sense that simply the knowledge of how something structurally works doesn't change anything. So, for example, we know that one day we're going to die, or at least so it appears. That doesn't really necessarily help us, that knowledge, per se, it's just an objective fact I suppose, if you still believe in objective facts.

So the knowledge of reincarnation by itself—or of any belief system, no matter what it is—doesn't necessarily help us. Maybe it makes us feel better.

Maybe when we're lying in the hospital and we're at the moment of death, suddenly we feel better because we feel that in our next life we might be a tomato or something. Maybe we had an affinity for tomatoes in this life. I don't know.

There's a sense of continuance. That life is an endless process. We're eternal.

There is nothing to fear, unless of course you think that life is not something that you like particularly—in which case it would be terrible to know that you're eternal. There's no escape from living. Death doesn't even end it.

So this knowledge by itself doesn't really mean a lot. And again, it's a structured form, it's an ideation. When we meditate and we enter into the superconscious, we see that it isn't exactly the way we explain it. There are no words to explain the cycle of existence. But we do our best with words.

But what is of value is what we call the Tibetan Rebirth Process. The idea is that we are an aggregate. A human being is not one individual self. We're composed of many, many, selves, and that these selves are growing and progressing within us.

As Walt Whitman said, "I contain multitudes."

His perception, as a bit of an American poetical mystic, was that we're not one individual. We're everyone. We're all one. We're all connected. Not simply as a theory or intellectualization where we say, "Oh, yes, I can accept that perhaps our life energy is all connected." But rather we are one. This is a dream. In the dream we see multiplicity. We see multitudes of people, of beings.

Crossing Brooklyn Ferry, one of Whitman's poems, where he's just—remarking on just this continuous movement, the progression of humanity—the birth, the growth, the change, the death, this marvelous cycle that we see in the diurnal world, the world of change and transition.

And yet at the same time we're eternal.

That's the wonderful mystery, is that, on the one hand, while there is this part of us—this body and this mind that comes and goes, which will never be the same again—which I suppose makes it all very precious, and kind of poignant at times. Yet at the same time, life is a cause of continual celebration in that we recombine in new ways, like a perennial plant.

We just come up again season after season. The winter of death comes by and spring rolls around. We pop our heads up above the ground and look around, and see what a horrible world we've been born into. [laughter]

But nevertheless, it's something that perhaps we can add a little bit of beauty to, hopefully.

The world itself is quite lovely, as you know, it's only people who are the problem. And people aren't actually the problem, they just think they are, which is why they create a problem. Just another passing dream.

Buddha called it, "the nightmare of the day".

So the Tibetan Rebirth Process, then, is the awareness that it is possible for a human being, a sentient being, to go through hundreds or thousands of lifetimes within one incarnation.

The Tibetan Book of the Dead, naturally, is a guidebook which teaches us to some extent about the bardo—that is to say, the states that one passes through between death and rebirth. This is referred to as the bardo.

But, as you examine the more esoteric, as opposed to the exoteric side of the *Tibetan Book of the Dead* —which is really understood only by a few initiates—we come to see that what the *Tibetan Book of the Dead* is, is a guide for the living, not the dying.

The popular use of the *Tibetan Book of the Dead* today—I don't know if it's all that popular—but [laughter] the popular use of the *Tibetan Book of the Dead* is instruction for a person who's dying.

And the idea is, that if you're properly prepared at the time of death, it's possible to seek a higher birth through a knowledge of the after-death states—the states between birth and death—like Arkansas and Mississippi [laughter]. I think humor has its place in reincarnation, but I suppose it has to be better. [more laughter]

So, then, the *Book of the Dead* initially appears to be this guide—sort of like a Motor Club TripTik—so that when you die, you can say,

> "Well, Alice, where are we gonna go now? Uh, let's uh look here, there's, uh … this, this world got a very good rating, it got three stars. [laughter]
>
> "It looks good, uh—but they say you have to make reservations in advance, and you have to have meditated for several hundred lifetimes in order to get in, uh, I'm not sure if we …
>
> "Now, the next one is only two and a half stars …"

You see, that sort of thing.

So the *Book of the Dead* prepares you for the bardo. But that's not really the purpose of the *Book of the Dead,* that's the popular use that it's fallen into.

The idea behind the sophistications of the rebirth process is that *this is the bardo.*

The bardo is not a *place* that you go to at the time of death. The bardo, or the bardos, are the levels of awareness—fields of attention—that we pass through.

And we're in them right now.

The mere fact that you have a body, is not discontinuous at all with being in the bardo. That's just an objectification that our mind produces, or our thoughts produce.

In other words, you're already dead. You're passing through the bardo right now.

And the Tibetan Rebirth Process then becomes of interest, because the idea is that within one given lifetime—again and again—we can dissolve our form and reunite it into something higher, something purer, something more conscious of its own eternality.

And this is the path of, of course, Tibetan Mysticism and Secret Doctrine.

But before we move into that world, let's step back to the overall theory of reincarnation.

Theories of reincarnation abound. Reincarnation has certainly been the most popular philosophy in the history of the world. Certainly more people believe in it than any other single philosophy if we look at it on a world population basis.

In the most ancient of civilizations, there was a belief in reincarnation, of course, Egypt, Atlantis and other places. The systems vary that people have. And I don't think that that should be a problem for us. In other words, we'll read one system of reincarnation where a person says, "Well, this is the rebirth process. This is what happens." Someone else will say, "Well, this is what happens." And the two versions will differ a little bit. But as far as I'm concerned, those are like different types of Christianity. They're all suggesting the same thing, but there are different interpretations. But if we look at what they're really trying to say, the message is the same.

There are simply no words for all of the complexities of the process, as we'll find when we move more into the Tibetan Rebirth Process. So this is kind of an amalgamation, then—this particular map that I will be presenting to you—of a lot of different ways of looking at it. Sometimes it might appear to be contradictory. It usually is. That's what makes it interesting.

As I suggested before, the thought is that we are all part of eternity. That at one time, before time—which still exists, of course—beyond time, there was nothing but luminosity. What we call God, or truth, the dharma, nirvana, satori. Different names for the same thing.

And that this infinite self—the supreme reality—sends forth parts of itself on a journey, on an odyssey. And that it's kind of a spiral.

We begin by taking incarnation, some people hold, in very basic form. Some people feel we go through the material world first—in the sense where we have incarnations in the mineral kingdom, the plant kingdom, the animal kingdom—then we progress into the human kingdom. It's a very orderly progression.

It reminds me very much of the philosophies in the Renaissance, "The Great Chain of Being". Where they had this long, long, explanation of every aspect of creation—all the way up into God, down to the devil, and everyone in between—was seen in this great chain, this very orderly process.

Other views of reincarnation suggest that some of the initial incarnations we have may be extremely advanced—they may be in other worlds. Nonphysical worlds.

There are countless worlds. Countless planes of being and reality. The world we're in now is just a small fraction—as we know if we've watched Carl Sagan—of what existence is. Well, beyond Mr. Sagan's wildest dreams [laughter] there are other dreams.

There are the nonphysical worlds, beyond the quasars and just on the other side of the black holes. And they're endless.

We call them lokas—planes of existence—where there are beings, energies, awarenesses, things that are somewhat like us, or our field of attention. Things that have nothing to do with us. Our opposites. Different dreams.

Many of us have had lifetimes or incarnations in those nonphysical worlds—before we took our initial incarnation here.

Sometimes, people will incarnate through a succession of different nonphysical worlds and they might come to this world just for one incarnation. Sort of a vacation. It's like going to Disneyland.

Others will have their first incarnations here, and will go through a very long progression.

But the word "progression" is reincarnation.

It's like going to school. Where we're going from first grade to second grade and so on, through high school, college, graduate school perhaps, perhaps teaching—or something else—with no thought that one aspect of reality or one level of attainment is better than another. Everything is equal in the eyes of God. Yet things are different.

So, on more of a cosmopolitan basis, we find ourselves here in this world, in the twentieth century. We're born in America, or another country, but something has brought you here tonight. And we find ourselves dealing with a society, with a family, perhaps, with a career, with a body, with smog alerts, with the world.

And yet reincarnation suggests that just over the horizon is eternity. And that all of the things you see here are transitory. They don't last. The only constant in this world is change.

And that human misery occurs because of attachment and ego. A sense of individual self. We feel that we exist. That we are something special.

And it's the sense of being special that interferes with the flow of light. Or you could say that it's a flow of light in a different direction. But perhaps a painful one.

Reincarnation shows the way beyond pain and pleasure. Which does not suggest that one won't feel pain and pleasure, it's just that there'll be no one there to feel it.

Reincarnation is the dissolution of the self. It's like going swimming in the ocean, and no one ever comes out, because one has become the ocean. Or what does emerge is something far different.

The goal of reincarnation—if it has a goal, I'm not sure, but that's a way we like to look at things sometimes—is not the cessation of being. Some people feel that nirvana is the end of existence.

There is no end to existence!

How can that which doesn't even exist, end, or how can—to say it another way—that which *only* exists, end? The purpose of reincarnation is not an ending. If you see that you are one with all things—both material and spiritual—then how can there be an ending? And after the ending, then what, what's the next movie, after we've seen the first show?

The descriptions of reincarnation suggest that you should look beyond the descriptions. That's their purpose. They're designed to give you a central orientation. Here you are now—on the map.

It's like one of those roadside stands that they have when you're driving across the country, and you pull into the little map area, and you're looking at this big map of whatever state you're in and all the highway networks. And then there's this one little sign that says, "Here you are now." And an arrow points down to it. And that gives you a sense of well-being. You've found yourself at last in the big universe out there.

Now what's on the other side of the map—what's beyond the edges—so that's the nagual, the unknown.

But we can't worry about that. Certain things one shouldn't dwell on. So we'll concern ourselves with the map and that sense of well-being that we get when we finally know at last that we're safe. Because we know where we are! [laughter]

So that's what reincarnation provides for people, a sense of well-being. Because you finally know where you are. [laughter] But don't think about what's beyond it.

Karma is not a receipt of a physical experience, because of what someone has done. There's a popular conception about karma. And that is that as you sow, so shall you reap. That's only true if you're a farmer. [laughter]

If you just buy produce, like I do at the local store, then you sow what others have reaped.

Karma has to do with fields of attention, levels of awareness. Each one of us is a composite of energy. And this energy seeks a particular level—or it is a level.

Imagine that you're a circle. You are everything contained within the circle. But the circle is empty and it contains different things at different times.

So each one of us has a "field of attention". That is your awareness, your consciousness. Your field of attention tells you this is, and this is not. Beyond the boundaries of your field of attention, you don't know. There's only the thought that there's something beyond the boundaries of the field of attention.

Karma means changing planes of reality or changing fields of attention. There will be, perhaps, a resulting physical action stemming from the change of these fields of attention.

Graphic example.

Let's suppose you're in a good mood, and the day is going well, and suddenly you're on the freeway, and you're driving along, and someone cuts you off. And they almost kill you. They just miss.

You get very very angry at that person, and you find that there's a traffic jam ahead. It's rush hour. And as fate would have it, your car is about to roll up right next to theirs. And they have their window down. [extended laughter]

And the radio is blaring, and they're just hanging out. And they don't even realize that they just almost ended your life. Completely oblivious. You pull up next to them.

A motorcycle passes between you. [laughter] That's a liberated soul! [laughter] Not bound by the finite rules of traffic. Probably an old Zen Master.

So you pull up next to them, and you roll down your window, and you begin to curse them, using a variety of vocabularies from different incarnations. [laughter] Then, very satisfied, you pull away.

Except that something has happened.

Your anger has caused you to drop into a lower field of attention.

Now, most people won't be aware of this, because most people live where they are. [laughter] That is to say, their field of attention is limited to the moment and they immediately forget where they've been. If you go to the dentist, and you're sitting in the chair, and the dentist is probing away, and the dentist touches a nerve, immediately your body contracts with pain. And for that moment it's a terrible, terrible experience. Then you leave the dentist's office, and no matter how intense the experience was, it's forgotten in the evening's activities.

Most people live in the moment.

REINCARNATION AND THE TIBETAN REBIRTH PROCESS

What we're trying to do is live outside of the moment. In the moment there's very little awareness.

So our friend who is in the car will not really be aware that they changed planes of attention, because all they'll see is what's in front of them, and a kind of marvelous maya occurs when we change planes of attention.

We forget where we were.

It's winter in California and it's raining. It's rained for three or four days in a row. And as you sit looking outside of your window, you feel that it's always rained. The rain is forever. We've had 250 days of continuous sunshine, and now, in four days, it seems like it's been always raining.

And it has always been raining, actually, in the world where it rains, because there is no time. But within the structure of time, it hasn't been raining, only for a few days. So maybe you're right after all!

Anyway [laughter] …

Our friend in the car—who has probably made it a few exits further down the freeway by this time—is angry, and doesn't feel as well. And has changed planes of attention. That's karma.

Karma means that your intent produces a resulting change in your conscious awareness. Karma doesn't mean because you do something nice for someone, you give someone a gift, that two days later or in another lifetime, someone is going to come and give you a gift. It has nothing to do with it.

Karma simply means that whatever type of energy you project—or you allow to pass through your being—you will become. For a period of time.

So those who hate, those who are violent in nature, live in a world of hate and fear and violence—inside themselves, inside their minds, inside their awareness. Those who love, and who have a sense of purity, live in a very luminous band of awareness.

If you'd like to think of it in a linear way—just as an example, it's not necessarily this way—just imagine a great chain of being again where we have levels.

The ocean.

And down at the bottom of the ocean there is very little light, hundreds of fathoms down. Then as we come up, if we segment it, we'll find that maybe 50 fathoms up there's more light, 50 fathoms up there's more light, eventually there's a great deal of light and finally we break through the surface into the air itself.

So these are planes of attention, levels of awareness. A human being will normally change planes of attention many times a day. But they're very, very minor changes.

When you're born into a particular lifetime, your being is somewhat fluid. From about age 1 to about age 4 you start to think, really, it's a very viscous state of awareness.

But then as we're conditioned by the world and society, by our families, by our language, by the vibratory fields of energy that are generated by the beings and the world that we're in, we begin to harden into a form.

And our attention fixes at a particular level. Which, of course, is also an outgrowth of our past life activities.

So we stratify. And within that point—within that frame of reference—a person will change. So we'll have a high water mark and a low water mark.

The high water mark is what we call being very happy—the happiest you could be, or you have ever been. That's the high water mark on your scale of consciousness. Be that in a happy, jovial sense or in just a very placid, deep sense, if I can use the word happy in a wider spectrum of ways.

On the other side, of course, we have the darkest, deepest depression, the greatest hate, the anger, the frustration—when we feel absolutely miserable.

And within those two points we will oscillate throughout our lifetime. And most people will never go further than their happiest point from childhood, or lower than their deepest depression from adolescence [laughter]. And if they do, it does tend to be a rather downward movement or motion.

When we meditate, what we do is change the spectrum, whether that meditation is an active meditation or a passive meditation.

Passive meditation—which is not particularly passive—meaning sitting and meditating, stopping all thought or slowing them down, and letting go of the description of this world that you now have. And going back to your original form. What in Zen they call the "original face".

Active meditation is selfless giving. When we work for the welfare of others. For humanity, for our friends, family, ourselves, whatever it may be. But without seeking a return on our investment. Just for the joy of giving.

These are the two forms of meditation that one can practice.

So when we meditate—and of course we go through the Tibetan Rebirth Process—what we do is change levels of attention radically.

In a particular lifetime we fixated—from age 4 to age 14. The personality hardens, and we'll have that small range that we'll go back and forth in. We may become more knowledgeable, we may become successful, we may become powerful, we'll have a variety of different experiences in life. But those really do not necessarily extend the basic emotional tonal range that we have, and beyond the emotional tonal range, our conscious awareness.

The Tibetan Rebirth Process, which is ultimately meditation—in variant forms—means that while we were in the ocean and we were going up and down in our little bathysphere, our little submarine and we picked a certain level, uh, 500 fathoms. And now we're going to alternate between 500 and

600 fathoms all our lives. That's all we'll do.

It means that we're going to change that. We're going to step outside the structured self and dissolve that. And actually take on an entirely new form.

We're going to move to a completely different level. A higher plane of being, where there'll be much more light.

It is also possible to move in the other direction. To go downward. And drop 200 fathoms, and then just stay in a small range there.

Nirvana, of course, is beyond any ranges or descriptions. What we call self-realization. It means that one exists within all ranges, and at the same time is unaffected by them.

The Tibetan Rebirth Process involves what we call "the caretaker personality". Now, again, in short menu form, on our screen here, the Tibetan Rebirth Process is the microcosm, reincarnation is the macrocosm.

Reincarnation is this long, involved process where we're dancing our way through thousands of lifetimes. In each lifetime moving to a higher level of attention, as in school, one step at a time, until finally one day we reach a point where we have absolute knowledge or awareness.

We start from the darker side, you might say, and move into absolute light. Although we started in absolute light. It's a circle. We come back to where we were.

The Tibetan Rebirth Process is—instead of taking thousands of lifetimes to do this—we'll do it in a few. We'll have all those experiences—that we could have had in many lifetimes—in a few. We'll speed the process up. It's very, very intensive.

The idea being that if we speed it up, we will not eventually come to an end, but we will become endless, and beginningless.

We'll move beyond the confines of life and death, which does not preclude reincarnation. It just means that we will step beyond what being human is—and the limitations of being human—and become limitless. In one program, it will take you eighteen years to finish your education. In another, one year.

In the Tibetan Rebirth Process we use and develop what we call the caretaker personality. The idea is that we really aren't a person, we just think we are. We think we're people because we've been told we're people.

Since the advent of our existence in this world, we've been told that we're a person, and we've been typed. If you were a little boy, you were given a blue blanket, and if you were a little girl, you were given a pink blanket. We were sexed. And someone said "This is what a little girl can do and cannot do." They gave us a description as they did for a little boy. And they tell us, "This is what a man can do," and "This is what a woman can do."

That's not necessarily true at all, but we tend to believe it and not look beyond the parameters of our education.

Self-discovery is validation. Seeking validation. It means that we're looking ourselves, and not discounting what we've been told. But under the theory of the scientific method that one can repeat an experiment and get the same results, we're experimenting with our awareness, and seeing if what we were told is true. And if not, seeing, well, what is true?

So we don't really have one particular personality. That is to say, we don't have to be limited to it. You may be. You may be in a very structured personality right now. It's like living in a house. And you're just living in one house. And you may feel that you have to live in that house all your life.

And when you started out as a little boy or girl, that house was very small, it was one room. Gradually, you've expanded, and you've added rooms as time has gone on. There've been new aspects to the personality. But essentially the structure hasn't changed all that much. It just has gotten a little bigger, and there's just more to keep clean. And the taxes have probably increased.

In the Tibetan Rebirth Process, we sell the house. Straightaway. And then we begin to explore other houses, and we live in other houses for a period of time. But we don't feel that we are the house we live in. We feel that we are awareness, we're the thin air, we're eternity.

And we can take any form. And we begin to explore different forms. Now, naturally, in order to do this [it] takes a great deal of personal power.

You're fixated in a striated world, in a limited field of attention. And what you're trying to do is jump out of it. You've lived so long in one place, that you've forgotten that you could live anyplace. You have great reasons for staying there. And those reasons defeat you. Because the house is not too expansive. It doesn't have that much light. Not too many windows. Hard to grow plants. So, we begin to shop around.

But in order to do that, we have to realize that we are *free*. And that's what meditation is for. When we meditate, we come to see that we're not a particular person, in the way that we think of a person. We're not a personality. We have one, but it's like clothing. We can change it. The same is true of the body.

So, in reincarnation, then, we change bodies, from lifetime to lifetime. But the aggregate of our self really stays the same. It recombines, but it stays the same and we find ourselves in another lifetime.

In the Tibetan Rebirth Process, we're not so much concerned with changing physical bodies, but with changing personality structures and fields of awareness.

And in order to do this, we need not die physically.

Rather, what we do is meditate and find we are light.

We are not a reflection of this world. We see ourselves in terms of this world, and we're not the world at all.

As we meditate, we see that we have attachments. The reason that we stay in one house, even though it's not a very nice one, is because we're attached to it. So we see that the attachments are really not helpful, and we let go of them. And we see that eventually we would die anyway, and the house would be gone. So why be attached to it? Why not let go of it now?

Because when we're attached to the house, we always live in fear. Fear that it will burn down, fear that something will happen to it. We identify with it. We think of ourselves as the house.

But we're not, we're vast, we're infinite, we're eternal awareness, eternal joy. We're not limited by the body or the structured personality.

So the person who practices, then, the Tibetan Rebirth Process within a given lifetime, sees that all lifetimes exist within a given lifetime.

And what the individual does is to assess themselves, to meditate, to step outside of the house for a while and just see what that's like. That's meditation. We go up in the sky.

It's amazing. We can be wrapped up in our little world with our problems, our decisions, our careers, our relationships. All of the things that matter to us, that make us happy and unhappy. Our private heavens and hells. And then we'll go to San Francisco or Denver. We'll get in an airplane and we'll go up above Los Angeles and we'll look down, and we'll look at all these millions of little houses and buildings and in each one there's a person who's chained to it.

Living out their life of despair and frustration and transitory joy. Notice that there's two. You've got the despair and the frustration, and only one on the other side—the transitory joy. And even that's transitory. Seems to be weighted in one direction.

So we go up in the plane and we look out the window, and suddenly our problems don't seem as big because we realize that there are lots of other people who are miserable, too. [laughter] They all have mortgages, or rent payments or whatever it is. And they're all going to die—sad!

Maybe it's good. Be awful crowded in this world if we all lived forever.

Things are only what you make them. Nothing has a value until you assign it a value.

> The Ferrari is parked outside. A person doesn't care about cars. They walk by it, they don't notice. Someone's wanted a Ferrari all their lives. They've thought about it, grown up reading *Car and Driver* magazine.
>
> When they walk by the Ferrari, immediately images come to their mind. They see themselves driving it. The wind in their hair, sitting next to that perfect person. [laughter] It's a Hallmark Card. The tape player is blaring, you see.
>
> So when they walk by that Ferrari, they stop, and they look at it. They think about perhaps touching it, but they're not sure because there may be a very profound alarm system. [laughter]
>
> The other person didn't notice!

Well, we assign the values. That's what the caretaker personalities are all about—assigning values and creating a structure within ourselves.

When you meditate very well and stop all thought, the world dissolves. This world goes away. Time goes away, space goes away. Life and death go away, you become eternal existence itself. Formless, conscious. There are no words for it, just arrows that point in that direction.

But in the world, we do need a personal form. It is necessary to dress when you go to work, unless you work in a nudist camp. It's necessary when you interact with the world to have a personality structure. Nothing wrong with it.

You don't have to kill the personality in order to attain enlightenment.

Well, actually, you do, that's not true. Actually a lot of times—but—you get used to it.

The idea is that your personality was given to you. It was created and you had no choice in the matter. It was structured for you by your parents or whoever was around you in basically the first seven years of your life. It was then modified by educational systems, advertising, cultural thoughts, languages and so on. You didn't have a lot to do with it. No one asked you at three what kind of caretaker personality you wanted for the rest of your incarnation. Of course, unless you grew up in the Himalayas.

So what you're doing is deciding yourself.

We're going to go shopping for cars. We're going to go look at the Chevys, the Fords, the Maseratis, we're going to see which one seems appropriate for us at this time. Because we've been driving the old clunker for a while, and it's startin' to rattle and we just know that something's going to go wrong with it soon, if it hasn't already.

So we're shopping for a new self.

Types of Caretaker Personalities.

Well, first we have to dissolve the old one. But sometimes we don't want to dissolve the old one 'til we know what we're going to. You see, that's the safe method. People do that in relationships. They're not going to give up the person they're with 'til they find the next one. So we'll go shopping.

Well, what are some of the caretaker personalities? Well, let's think of them.

> A good one, one that I like, that's very healthy, is the *student*. The student is one who is always growing and learning. There's not a sense of superiority but of progression, and joy and learning. Eagerness. Enthusiasm.

> Another caretaker personality of course is the *warrior*. The warrior is the person who is fighting their way through life. Not in a negative sense, but in the sense that they lead a warrior's life. They lead a very tight life. It's very circumspect. There's power in it. There's joy and efficiency and abandon in their actions. Their lives are not sloppy. Their thoughts are not sloppy. Their emotions are not sloppy.
>
> The *child*. Having a sense of awe and wonder. Looking at life as a child does.

Different caretaker personalities that we put on and take off as the occasion seems fit.

What I'm suggesting is that you can lead your whole life another way. That you don't have to be the person that you are. 'Cause you're not, anyway. You just think you are. That you are far beyond personality. But you have become locked into a particular personality structure.

And that you can change personalities. Not just for a period of time in terms of months or years, but sometimes you can go through many personality structures in a day.

> If you're a nurse and you go to work, you put on one outfit. At home, you may be relaxing in your casual clothes, then you might go out to dinner, you see. You might go skiing, swimming, you'll change your clothes accordingly, rather than try and wear one thing to all places.

So you can modify and change the personality structure in advanced meditation to suit the occasion.

But of course in the context of the Tibetan Rebirth Process, we're not simply modifying it for social occasions.

But we're continually moving to an upgraded structure of being. We're

REINCARNATION AND THE TIBETAN REBIRTH PROCESS 433

becoming more conscious of our own luminosity, of what we really are, which is eternity. We're overcoming fear, anger, jealousy, hostility, anxiety, hate, things like that. Things that limit us and bind us to this or any world. We're becoming cosmopolitan beings who flow through existence both in timelessness and time.

How do we do it? How do we break through the confines of our structure of our life. How do we change levels of attention?

This is the subject matter of self-discovery. Self-discovery is a very, very vast thing. There are many paths in self-discovery. Many ways, many languages that are spoken. But ultimately they all say the same thing. And that's silence.

Meditation is the way that we change levels of attention. When we meditate, we bring a power, an energy, a force from within ourselves into our current awareness field. It's also the way that we bring our past lives out.

There's some popular methods right now of past life discovery, and they're neither good nor bad, I suppose, it depends how they work for you. Some people use hypnotic regression to go back and see their past lives. Some use *dreaming*. There are many different methods.

As far as I'm concerned, it really doesn't much matter what you did in a past life. It's a movie that's already been shown. Sometimes it's fun to see the movie again. But we've already played that role. We acted in that particular film, and it's fun to move on to a new challenge.

But it is nice if we can bring forward the experience that we gained in the last movie that we acted in. In other words, if we developed our craft of acting before, and we can bring that knowledge with us to our next project, we'll do better.

So it is valuable, then, in my estimation, to bring forward the powers that we've developed in our past lives. You may have had a thousand lifetimes. You may have practiced self-discovery before. You may have been in the ancient Egyptian cycle. Atlantis. Other worlds, where you were much more developed than you are now, in terms of your field of attention, your spiritual powers.

The way we bring those back is three-fold. Or four, actually.

One, of course, is just meditating.

Two is encountering a powerful individual who has the ability to project us into those fields of attention. What we call an enlightened person, a spiritual teacher, something like that.

Three is by going to locations where in past lives we have been and stored power. Places of power that are places of power on an individual level. Not simply revisiting where we lived in another life. But if in another life you practiced the mystical arts, and you were aware that one can store power—and you did—you can go back to those places in this lifetime and draw that power back.

And when you go, you'll change. You will go one person and come back another.

After a while, there are many selves inside you. All the different voices from all the different lifetimes. Not in terms of personality or thought, but awareness. They blend and merge, because all of them are us. All the people, all the things, all the beings we've been are still there, because ultimately everything exists forever.

There is no time in the sense that once time has marched on, that which is behind it dissolves.

Every moment exists forever. All incarnations occur simultaneously. That is to say, everything goes on all the time.

It's like reruns of *The Tonight Show*. It's on videotape somewhere, and you may see it again. But what is necessary, since we've already seen it, unless

REINCARNATION AND THE TIBETAN REBIRTH PROCESS 435

you're just fond of it, is to become aware of what's happening now. The live show. Or so it appears, or to go beyond it all.

The fourth way—of course—of bringing back the awareness from past lives

> aside from meditating,
>
> being with a person who's able to generate strong fields of attention and causing us to become conscious—not simply, again, of where we've been or what we did—but to bring back that which we really are,
>
> or of going to a location where we stored power—which is not something everyone has necessarily done—that's only if you practiced advanced mystical arts in other lives …

is *luck!* [laughter]

It just happens sometimes. There's no reason. Or if there is, we sure can't put it into words. Just one day you're walking along, and you remember. You change. For no reason. It just happens.

So, then, lets consider a little bit, how we invoke that which we are. Under the assumption that there's a lot of money for you to inherit if you can just remember what your name is, and you can go and say, "Hey, my name is so and so," and they'll give it to you. You see, there's all this marvelous stuff coming to you.

Now, we're not assuming that you have all this terrible karma coming. [Rama chuckles] That's kinda like hate mail.

That you're interested in exploring your own infiniteness. That that's the raison d'être of your life.

Then it's necessary for you to become a student of two things. That which is off the map, and that which is on the map.

Going back to our cross-country drive—which we're all on I think—and we found that map where there's a little arrow pointing and saying, "You are here." Well, we have to explore everything here, because everything is contained in everything and nothing is contained in everything and everything is contained in nothing.

On the other side of the map, beyond the perimeter, well, that's existence too. But it doesn't exactly work in the same way. One is the known, one is the unknown.

Not known in the sense that it's someplace we've been and we've explored before. But known in the sense that it's comprehensible to our reason. Our internal software.

That which lies beyond the known we call mysticism. Mysticism is that exploration of various fields of attention. Finding out that we're more than just a human being, that we're limitless awareness. Things that there are no words for. *Experiencing* that. Having direct experiences where you dissolve in light. You become the dharma. You exist simultaneously in thousands of levels of attention. And you still have the same shoe size.

So those are our two fields of awareness that we're dealing with. And they have very different languages and very different methods. The two are ultimately one. But that's confusing at the beginning. I think it's better to think of them as two to start out with. It's easier.

In other words, simply because the map stops at a certain point on this big billboard where they're saying, "You are here," doesn't mean it really stops. Everything keeps going. But we've segmented it, 'cause we really don't want to look at a map of all the universes, and quasars, and other dimensions and lokas and aspects of nirvana. It's just enough to deal with the map. That's all we need right now, to get to where we're going. Why worry about celestial existence?

But then there are times when we become very concerned with that, and that's when, of course, we dissolve into the other planes of attention and we become our other selves. We see that we are a construct of luminous awareness, and that that can change when we open ourselves up to the forces of existence in a specific way, which is meditation and self-discovery. And that's when the fun really begins.

So we deal with both. We deal, in other words, with the pragmatic physical world. Career, family, friends and mostly with the internal software. With our own ideas, our thoughts, our concepts, our attachments, our opportunities.

Then on the other side we have that world of mysticism. Which is not reasonable or logical. Which is existence. Countless worlds, planes of reality, beings, forms. It lies just over the horizon.

And we go over the horizon. We go through the doorway into eternity. And then we come back again. We go back and forth countless times. That's what an advanced spiritual person does. They're not limited to this body or this world anymore. They don't have to wait for death to be liberated. We call them *jivan mukta* — liberated while living. The guy on the motorcycle who doesn't have to get stuck in traffic.

I'd like to drop back to karma for a moment, if I can.

Some people use the term in a negative sense. When they say, "Oh, that's my karma." You know, they just had a car accident, they're being audited by the IRS. There's always a sense of fear that runs through the audience whenever you say that one. [laughter] Something that they consider bad happens and they say, "That's my karma."

And karma, in America has gotten this sense of something bad that happens to you, and it's not at all.

Karma is the way out. Karma is opportunity. Karma is the ability to change fields and planes of awareness.

The idea is, that certainly there's certain things you cannot control. You're here in this life now. You weigh x pounds, you make x dollars a year, some people like you, some people don't. OK? And let's say that there's certain circumstances that are out of our control.

We may be able to modify them eventually, but right now they're out of our control.

It's going to rain, let's say. Now while we can't ultimately stop the rain until you become very advanced with the siddhas—but most people can't stop the rain—what you can do is be happy in it, or be very sad in it. You do have that control. That's the ability of a perceiver.

So then, one study is how to be happy in all situations. Happy not meaning sort of running around in a mindless euphoria giggling at the misfortunes of others. That's not what I mean at all.

Happy meaning being very grounded and having a luminous awareness. Being in the world, but not exactly of it. Not limited by it. So if it rains, that's nice. If it's sunny, that's wonderful. Seeing beauty in everything.

That's what spiritual awareness gives us.

As we clear ourselves out, as we rewrite the internal software—that's the caretaker personalities—we move to higher and higher forms of attention. There's more light in our being, or let's just say we're more aware of what there really is. The various selves from our past lives come out. The strengths, the powers.

We also can see the limitations that we've gone through, and avoid them. Retrospective knowledge. "I made a mistake, it wasn't pleasant, I'm not going to make the same mistake, I'll go on to a new one." This is a learning process.

Then, of course, all that's great—we put the world in perfect order, we understand everything. But we're still not satisfied as beings. Because we're eternity. While its wonderful to have the limited and perfect order … we want the limitless.

We want nirvana, we want enlightenment. Our heart, our being wants to be free. To be what we really are. That's what reincarnation is for. To do both.

> To be in the finite, in the world, and gradually—over a succession of incarnations—to have different experiences and perfect ourselves. To get a great education.
>
> And at the same time to go back home.

I think that was ET's central appeal personally. ET is this metaphorical journey, this strange Odysseus from another world who just wants to go home. Obviously, home must have been better. [Rama laughs]

And we're all trying to get home. And it's a long, long journey. But the journey *is* home. Home is not a defined place. Nirvana is not a location. There's no zip code. Unless it's 0000.

Infinite awareness is everywhere. *This* is the bardo.

All possibilities are open to you right now. You can move into any field of attention. Once you know how. Once you've cleared up a few old bills and learned to meditate perfectly. And developed humility and purity through selfless giving and caring about the welfare of others, more than your own welfare.

Then you're at the core of life, as Lao Tsu would say. You've understood. That the purpose of life is not to attain enlightenment for ourselves, but to be of some service to others without a sense of inflated self-importance or that we're ultimately necessary.

And if enlightenment is a useful experience—if in some way, as we develop through our incarnations, or within an incarnation if you progress—you can do more. If you have more money you can be selfish with it or you can help others out.

So then, karma is this opportunity. It says that, yes, certain things in life are fated. Are destined. But yet, within that framework there is freedom.

This is what the *I Ching* is about. Freedom within limitations. That we have both. You are on this planet, at least at the moment, for a while anyway, or so it appears in this dream.

But there is something that you can do. You can be active. You can change things. You can move to higher levels of attention. You can understand that which is truth—that which is right. And come to know your essence.

So that's why I find reincarnation ultimately the most happy philosophy. Because it suggests not that we're fated prisoners in some bizarre process that was cooked up in some other world, in a think tank.

> You see, when they were figuring out how to run the universe. These guys were sitting around and they said,
>
> [Rama mimics a vaguely authoritarian, slightly humorous voice]
>
> "Well, yeah, let's, let's, let's give 'em a million lifetimes—and uh—run 'em ragged."
>
> [audience laughter] You know.
>
> "Why just give 'em one? And what's time anyway?"
>
> [normal voice]

That reincarnation is a process whereby we can become conscious.

And the trick is to do it before you die. Not after you die. Because after you die, you'll be dead.

And then you'll just be reborn again, and you'll forget. You have to go back to the starting point, and you don't get to collect the two hundred bucks, you see.

So reincarnation suggests that you are able to change your destiny. That destiny is just the way you see life.

And that the choices you make—you do your best with—but you actually have many more choices available to you than you realize. But within the structured self that you now have, you only see, "Well, I can do this or I can do this."

So to step outside of that and to become something other—to go beyond the limitations of what we call being "human," and at the same time to enjoy the things in humanness that are enjoyable—that's what this study is for.

That's what the knowledge of reincarnation gives you. Not simply a map, and you are here, and this is where you're going. But that the journey itself is wonderful, and that you can use karma—intent—to do *anything*.

That what you project to others is not what you'll get back from them. That's not true. You can love others, and they can hate you.

Look at Mr. Gandhi, who lives a life of service for others and he gets shot for it. You see. The world is not necessarily kind to you, just because you're a nice person. Quite the contrary, usually.

But what it does suggest, is that every time you think a positive thought, you give of yourself, you meditate, increase your level of awareness—that *you* will become happier, more complete and more aware. And thus can do more for others, or just enjoy being.

But to do that, you have to change.

The parable of the coyote and the roadrunner saves us at this point.

You all know the Coyote and Roadrunner cartoon. With the little roadrunner who runs around beep-beeping. And this coyote, old Wile E. Coyote, is always trying to catch him. It's one of these karmic relationships that they have. Clearly they've been doing this for many lifetimes. Probably they switch from lifetime to lifetime.

So in this lifetime, they reincarnate in the cartoon world. Which is quite a world to end up in. Many possibilities, many variables. And in the cartoon world, of course, there are certain operable laws, as there are in any world. As long as it's a world, it has laws. Why, I don't know, that's just the way it is. In nirvana there are no laws.

So in the cartoon world, the laws are very simple. "Coyote does not catch roadrunner." Or even if he grabs him, somehow that roadrunner is gonna get away. Because otherwise there'll be no cartoon. Once the coyote gets the roadrunner and eats him, that's it. Then we have "The Coyote Hour." [laughter]

So, the roadrunner can't be caught. Now, why can't the coyote catch the roadrunner? Well, this is a Zen question, I suppose. It's because he's a coyote. Because under the definition of coyote in that structured cartoon world, coyote does not catch roadrunner. Can't do it. Roadrunner is always gonna outwit him.

Now, the roadrunner is basically a brainless critter. That's his strength. He doesn't know anything. He just runs around all the time. And he's this happy little thing.

This coyote is an intellectual. He reads Hegel [18] at lunch. [laughter] This is a smart coyote, see? It says—if you've ever read the cartoons, it says—"Wile E. Coyote Genius" on his mailbox. This is one smart coyote. He's got a Ph.D.

So what this coyote is trying to always do is figure out how to catch the roadrunner. And impeccability for the coyote is trying to catch the roadrunner as best as he can. And not being discouraged knowing that he'll never catch him—because it doesn't matter—because in that world it's

---

18. Georg Wilhelm Friedrich Hegel, 1770-1831, German, one of the most important writers of Western philosophy.

always happening.

Keats wrote a poem. And it's about some dancers on a Grecian Urn. I think it was Keats, it might have been Shelly—but "Ode to a Grecian Urn." And, on the urn (it's one of these long romantic poems where they're sitting around languishing, which they liked to do in that period), and there are the dancers that are on this urn.

And, he's saying, well, it's so great, because here they are, and on this urn, on this big pot, there are these painted figures. And the guy is chasing the girl, you see. And she's sort of dancing away. And he's saying, "How great that he'll never catch her, because they'll always be happy this way."

Once he catches her, they'll move to the suburbs, you see? [laughter] And they'll get a Kenmore washing machine. And probably get talked into the service contract.

> "It's a good deal sir, you know if we have to come out one time, it'll cost you a thousand dollars. Whereas for forty dollars here … "

So he says, he says, (you know, the romantics loved that stuff, they loved to just sort of look at life that way, their aesthetic modality) and he's saying, "This is great. They're always going to be happy on this vase. Not like us." You see, that's always the understatement, you know, in all the romantic poems.

So that's the creation of the coyote and the roadrunner. It's in a new form. Coyote is happy trying to get that roadrunner. And he never gives up.

How could the coyote catch the roadrunner? If he wasn't a coyote. He has to change. So if he took a "quick course" in the Tibetan Rebirth Process [laughter] he could change forms and no longer be a coyote, and then he could grab that roadrunner. But maybe, in the process, he'd learn to be a nice guy and leave the roadrunner alone. Then the roadrunner would chase him. That's karma. [laughter]

And, of course, I've always held that the coyote is a siddha master. You know the siddhas, these are the powers: the ability to project your body to different locations, to manifest things, to walk on yogurt, to do different things like that. These are the siddhas. To reconstruct your body, things like that.

And the coyote is a siddha master because whenever anything bad happens to him, he gets blown apart, in the next scene he's back together. So clearly he's a master of many, many occult powers, but in spite of these occult powers, he doesn't have what the roadrunner has, which is enlightenment. He's mindless. [laughter] Idiot. Roadrunner. Running around. But then again, what would the roadrunner do if the coyote didn't exist? Be happy probably.

[Rama laughs, then the audience]

So the Tibetan Rebirth Process essentially is the transition from the human phase into the supra-human. It's the transition that you will make when you go beyond the human fields of attention into the supraconscious and move through the various stages of enlightenment.

And it's possible to do that within a given lifetime. Naturally, one would have had many lifetimes of advanced spiritual practice before that lifetime in which you made the final transit from the human world to enlightenment. It won't happen in a first birth, certainly.

But after a number of lifetimes where

> you've practiced meditation and self-discovery,
>
> and you've strengthened your field of attention,
>
> you've worn off your rough edges through service to others,
>
> you've learned to be kind and loving, and so on,

then it's possible within a given lifetime—through meditation, through working with an enlightened person, going to places of power, pilgrimage, and with a little bit of luck, or grace, whichever you prefer—to do something uncommon in existence.

And that's to go off the map.

What's out there? Who knows, it can't be described. But that's the journey of existence.

CHAPTER THIRTEEN

MEDITATION

Tonight I'd like to talk a little bit about a timeless subject, and that's meditation.

I don't think there's a way we can really define meditation. I think it's easier to say what it's not, and perhaps come at a definition that way.

> Meditation is not being caught in time.
>
> Meditation is not being limited to any condition of the mind, body or spirit.
>
> Meditation is not being fixated, even on the avoidance of fixation.
>
> Meditation is not the awareness of eternity, although in the process of meditation we certainly become aware of eternity.
>
> Meditation is not the avoidance of this world and it's people, places and things.
>
> Meditation is not impractical or unrealistic, nor is it difficult to integrate with any lifestyle or any age, in that it's timeless although it occurs in time.

So meditation, then, is something that is very hard to categorize, which is what makes it useful to us. Because we live in a world of categories, of things that are very definable, and that's what we're used to, and meditation offers us a doorway to a world or worlds beyond "that which we can easily define".

There are ways we can talk about meditation, but in doing so, we should try and keep in mind that they're only ways. The exciting thing about meditation is that we can't pin it down.

And while there's an innate urge in all of us, I think, to try and pin something down—that is to say, to limit it or restrict it in the sense that we want to quantify it and be able to feel, well, this is the parameters of meditation, these are the parameters—because I think we feel indigenously more comfortable with something then.

We feel it's sort of under control. But that control sometimes usurps the very thing we're seeking, which is awareness.

So meditation, then, is essentially something that's indigenous to the heart.

Which makes it, I suppose, hard to talk about—but I think that's its very point is—it's something that we don't necessarily need to talk about too much, other than to get a sense of the practice and the tonality that we're dealing with. And then best leave it alone and just do it and see what happens.

Because too deep an understanding of the subject precludes the study itself. If we get too, too involved with it's practicality, we'll get so caught up in the rhetoric of meditation that we'll miss the point, and the point was to go beyond rhetoric.

So I think there's an in-between place, and that's what we try and seek. That's always the hardest, is to be in the middle. It's easy to run to extremes on either end.

Meditation, for convenience sake, I think, can be divided into three sections. Intermediate, advanced, and of course, beginning meditation. The principles involved in all three aspects of meditation are really not so different regardless of the stage of meditation.

The chemistry is really the same in the sense that, I suppose, when we go to school, graduate school is essentially not so much different than first grade or high school or college. Each involves class experience, home study, things like that. While the level and intensity of the material may differ, still the experience is somewhat similar.

So I really think that there's not all that much difference, in a way, at least in terms of approach.

Now, there are definite schools of meditation. In other words, there are people who say, "Well, there is a definitive way to meditate and this particular way or method is the best, ultimate, supremo, fantastico way." I don't think that's true.

I think that there are many, many ways to meditate. Styles of meditation are like languages. I don't feel that Italian or French or German or English—I don't think one language is better than another. Each has its own beauty. But the point of the language is not simply the study of the language itself, but to communicate.

So with meditation, one shouldn't become so caught up in the fine points of styles—again that you miss the point—which was

- ॐ to become conscious of God and
- ॐ eternity and
- ॐ to be happy and
- ॐ aware.

Yet there are styles. And I think something can be learned from all of them.

In the beginning, when you're starting to meditate—the beginning being maybe from the first time to the first four or five years, I suppose, it depends on the intensity of a person's practice—simply what we're trying to do is settle down. Settle down. And become aware of that which lies beyond thought.

In the very beginning, we're just trying to realize that there's some possibility of awareness on other levels.

Now, theoretically, everyone's inner being knows everything. There's a part of us that's aware of all things. But that doesn't necessarily do us a whole lot of good unless we are conscious of that.

So meditation, then, is the process of becoming conscious of the part of ourselves that knows everything.

Meditation is a bridge, between the awareness that we have now, and infinite awareness.

The problem with the awareness that we have now is it's somewhat limited, in the sense that we're limited by desires, doubts, fears, frustrations, happiness, concepts of the nature of existence and ourselves.

The spectrum that most people exist in—in this world, in terms of their awareness from the time of their birth until the time of their death—is not really very exciting. It's very mundane and very unhappy. Certainly human beings are capable of experiencing great joy and happiness. But they're also capable of experiencing quite the opposite.

So meditation is the study of fields of attention, fields of awareness. Not simply to relax a little bit and overcome stress and tension, but to become conscious of our own immortality. Possibly in a religious sense, possibly not, it depends on the individual.

In the beginning what's necessary, of course, is to feel—if you're just starting the process—that there's something worthwhile to be attained. Because otherwise we won't do it. And this awareness comes to people in a lot of different ways.

Very often it comes through meeting someone who meditates, and you sense something from them that's appealing. They seem to be having a good time with their life, perhaps, they're more at ease, or whatever it may be. There's just a subtle energy sometimes that comes from them. And we feel that and part of us is in consonance with that. We resonate. We're drawn to that.

As opposed to most of the people we meet, who are just so caught up in their lives that they don't understand their lives or even see their lives before they're gone.

People who meditate, depending of course on their level of awareness and so on, seem to have a better time with their existence.

Some people are drawn to meditation without knowing why.

Their inner being just demands it. They reach a certain point where it's not up to them anymore. Their inner being realizes that they've totally fouled up their life so far, and now it's just going to drag them to the local meditation hall and make them sit there. [laughter]

It's kind of like detention. After school, I remember, in high school sometimes of course you'd get detention because you were out walking around in the halls, or doing things you weren't supposed to be doing, when you were supposed to be sitting in class being bored. [laughter]

So sometimes you'd get detention and afterwards you'd just have to sit there and contemplate your life. [laughter]

So I think for some people that's what meditation is. It works out happily.

But they've kind of burned the candle at both ends—if not a little bit in the middle—and their being finally says, "OK, you've had your chance. I tried to tell you, I tried to warn you, now it doesn't matter, I'm taking over."

And so they find themselves approaching a meditation class or a teacher, reading books on the subject. And it doesn't make much sense—it doesn't necessarily fit in with the person they've been thus far—which is exactly the point. It's time to become a new person, because this one has exhausted their resources, or just reached the point where it's gotten ridiculous to continue.

I don't really think it matters why you start to meditate, the point is that you do. And then suddenly one is barraged with ways, means and methods.

When I started to meditate about 15 years ago, there wasn't a whole lot of information about meditation in the West. You could walk into the local book store and maybe there were four, five or six books on the subject and that was about it. Today to walk into a New Age book store, there's hundreds and hundreds of books, and I wouldn't know where to start.

It was easier back then. All there was—there was Alan Watts, and there was Paramahamsa Yogananda and that was about it. And Suzuki. That was it.

So we meditate to become conscious, and in the beginning it's simply a question of realizing that if we meditate we'll change—our awareness will change—and we'll become happier, and just more aware of the moments of our lives.

And isn't that the purpose of life itself, to be aware?

To be awareness, eventually.

So we then are faced with how to meditate. Tonight I'm not going to really go into how to meditate, per se, in terms of explanation of techniques, I've already done that on tapes and books and places like that. I think we can use your time in a more valuable way, in a more experiential way.

But simply, when a person is learning to meditate, essentially what they're trying to do in the beginning is to settle down and for fifteen minutes or half an hour or forty five minutes, to sit and try and still their mind.

This is usually done through a focus, initially, of some type. The idea being that if you just sit there, thoughts will just cascade through your mind and you won't have much success. So for the beginning student it's best to have a focus, and the focus allows them to at least—even if they can't stop thought in the beginning—to direct thought. And then once one has mastered directing thought, it's easier to stop thought and move into other levels of attention.

So initially the student in some traditions is given a mantra, a particular word of power to focus on. So while the thoughts are cascading through your mind during meditation, you should be absorbed in the repetition of a mantra.

In other styles of meditation they use yantras, which are visual mantras, I suppose you might say. They're specific designs that have a great deal of power in them—as do the mantras which are words of power—these are designs of power that tap into other levels of attention. They remind us of things in other worlds.

And so we set the little yantra up in front of us on a meditation table, on a little table and we sit there and we focus on it. And instead of being fully absorbed in our thoughts, we focus on the yantra, or we repeat the mantra, or sometimes a combination of both. You might repeat a mantra for a while, then focus on a yantra. Then a time should come when you do neither.

After a while in your practice, in an individual meditation session, you might start by chanting a mantra maybe a dozen times, then focus on a yantra for ten minutes or so, or fifteen minutes, then one closes the eyes and does neither. Because to continue to focus on the mantra or the yantra throughout the period of meditation will hold us down to a very specific format. We won't go beyond it.

While it's an important way to start a meditation and to develop our ability to meditate, ultimately at least half of the meditation, and one day all of it, will be spent in silence trying to stop thought or go beyond thought.

Now, there are schools of thought—if I can underline that word—that suggest that the way to meditate is not to tamper with your thinking processes, but just to allow your thoughts to go hither and yon, wherever they will. And that what you should do is simply be detached from your thoughts.

I think this is a fine way to start meditating, but advanced meditation definitely involves the cessation of all thought. No thought, no image, no picture in the mind whatsoever.

But I personally have found that people have more success with a focal point. The other method is a little more sophisticated and doesn't work that well for most people, just letting your thoughts run all over the place.

So what I suggest normally is that a person focus on a yantra. I think mantras are more difficult to hold onto.

People who do a lot of mantra repetition, I find, don't meditate very well. Because what happens is, as they're meditating and they're repeating the mantra over and over and over, after a while the mantra doesn't mean anything.

That is to say, they just get lost in their thoughts, and the mantra's going on somewhere in the background, you see. You've got it going, and it's going in your mind, or you're saying it out loud, but at the same time, it's sort of like walking and chewing bubblegum at the same time. You can be repeating the mantra and at the same time completely absorbed in all the different thoughts that are passing through you. And this, in my estimation, is not a higher level of meditation.

Whereas I find that when you involve the visual senses, when you're focusing on a yantra, it's easier to curtail thought. I think mantras have an important place in meditation. But the idea has become somewhat prevalent in the West, and in the East to some extent, that the simple repetition of a mantra will eventually cause enlightenment to take place, and that's usually not the case. The mantra is a very preliminary exercise for the student to begin to just grasp a sense of focus.

Mantras also do have their advanced side. When they're used by persons who have reached very high levels of attention, they can open up doorways to other worlds. But for most people the repetition of those mantras would be useless, in that you have to have a requisite amount of personal power to make them work.

So essentially, I think the … I prefer the yantra method. I've just seen—after teaching meditation for quite a while—that people do better with it.

I think it's a good idea to start a meditation session by repeating a mantra, perhaps "Aum" which is the most powerful of all mantras, or you may have been given a personal mantra or something like that. And then after repeating the mantra perhaps a dozen times—nice and slowly to start your meditation session, with the eyes closed—then to focus on a yantra.

There are a number of different yantras, and each one has its own subtle qualities. It creates a slightly different type of meditation.

So then perhaps for ten or fifteen minutes, to focus on the yantra—usually starting with the dot in the center of the yantra—quite intensely for a minute or two. And then looking at the whole yantra without focusing, more just a gentle gaze. You'll notice that the yantra, this visual design, will begin to appear to move. The lines will move and stuff like that.

And not to become too absorbed in that, but just to observe it and to try and ignore thought.

That's introductory meditation, Stage One. Not to stop it, necessarily, but simply to ignore it.

And even though the radio is going on in the next room, not to be upset by it, but rather to be focusing on the yantra, which divides your consciousness in a way. It doesn't necessarily stop the thought, but it detaches us from it.

Normally we're so absorbed in our thoughts that every thought that comes through *is* a reality. That is our world. So we have to just start to detach ourselves from thought a little bit, and become aware that there are things beyond thought.

But then after focusing on the yantra for a while, to close your eyes and simply let go.

Now at this point, some people like to focus on a chakra.

Of course, there are seven primary chakras and lots of other ones, and the chakras are locations in the subtle physical body—that have corresponding locations in the physical body—that are energy centers.

And when you focus on a chakra, it's very easy to bring subtle physical energies into your consciousness.

So some people focus on the third eye, or the crown chakra, or the throat chakra, the heart chakra, the navel chakra, the chakra at the spleen or the very base of the spine.

There are also chakras in the hands. You see me use those quite frequently when I meditate. I project the *shakti* —the kundalini—through the chakras in the hands, to people I meditate with. And there are chakras in the toes, and all kinds of places. Quite a few of them in the feet actually.

Whether you focus on a chakra or not, once you've closed your eyes, and you're meditating, let's say for the second half of your individual meditation session, that's up to you. But even if you're focusing on the chakra, you don't want to do that really for the whole period of meditation, there should come a point where you *let go*.

And now we're moving into a deeper stratum of meditation.

The rest is just to kind of get us to settle down, to get off the train of thought for a while. And now we just want to look around, now that we're off the train. We've been so obsessed on this train ride that we've just seen a limited aspect of life, but now we want to finally get off the train and look around. That's meditation. It's just looking around. Being observant.

So we get off the train of thought, and we just sit.

Now, at that point, of course, a person who hasn't meditated is a little confused.

> "Well, what am I supposed to do? Am I just supposed to sit here? Isn't that going to get a little boring?"

And that's why it's important to meditate with a teacher of meditation—at least once in your life. That is to say, someone who moves into higher levels of attention.

Because what you're supposed to be doing during that period cannot be expressed in words.

When you meditate with someone who traverses the superconscious, who is a very powerful meditator, you will experience levels of awareness that cannot be described in a book, cannot be told. They can only be shown to you by a person who has entered into them.

Some people do stumble across them on their own. If your intensity is great, and if you meditate with your whole being, and if you're fairly spiritually evolved, then it is possible to move into some of the higher levels of attention without a teacher. They're available, but it takes quite a bit of willpower. Nothing else can matter, essentially.

But for most people, it's easier to meditate with someone who's enlightened or at least close. And simply to meditate with such a person, if you're at all sensitive, you will become aware that your level of attention is changing radically. You'll *feel* what it's like, which is the important thing in meditation.

Then when you sit and meditate on your own, when you reach that part of the meditation session—let's say the second half where we're not using mantras or yantras or chakras—we're just going to let go.

We're not just going to let go, what we're going to do is go back into that field of energy that we felt when we sat with the teacher.

And it's much easier to do it. It's like going swimming. It's very hard to understand it until you've been in the water. One can have a theoretical approach, but once we've been in and moved a little bit, it has a much greater meaning to us.

Now, the serious student of meditation naturally will, of course, want to meditate as frequently as possible with someone who is enlightened or in the higher fields of attention because there will be a progression in their meditation.

As you meditate from day to day and week to week, you'll progress. And the level of awareness that you are capable of receiving or feeling initially when you meditated with someone who is more advanced, you'll become successful at that.

And then when you go and meditate with them again—because you've become more receptive—you'll feel more of what they're doing, or they can take you higher or however you'd like to express it.

And at that point, when you come back again, as you progress, you'll be more conscious and then you'll have something new to focus on. So there's a hierarchy, in a sense, at least in the beginning.

Beginning Meditation, then, is a process of unhooking ourselves from thought, of being motivated to meditate. And naturally it's very exciting in the beginning, because we see the tremendous jumps we make in awareness. We find we are happier, our mind is clearer, we're inspired, our creative talents flourish.

An awful lot begins to happen in that first year, or first four or five years of meditative practice, if we stick with it.

And particularly, of course, if you meditate with someone who's a powerful meditator and learn from them. Usually the ascension is more rapid.

The second phase of meditation is very different.

It's hard to say when this takes place. It depends on the individual, but I would say around four or five years in—of serious meditation—particularly with an advanced teacher.

We could say that it begins when you can successfully stop thought for long periods of time.

At this point you begin to move beyond the awareness of this world.

Now, in the beginning, even when you start to meditate you'll begin to feel different sensations and feelings—you may see colored lights of different types—there'll be a lot of phenomena associated with the practice. For some people there's more, for some there's less.

The phenomena is not necessarily a measurement of how well you're doing. You always know you're doing well if you sit and meditate every day a couple of times a day, that's the sign.

One learns not to judge one's level of progress or assess it. It's best to leave it alone and just do it, and you'll find you'll progress very nicely then.

But when you can successfully stop thought for longer periods of time, you do move into other worlds.

This can also happen in the very beginning if a person meditates with someone who's very advanced, on the verge of enlightenment or enlightened. Because when you meditate with an enlightened person, their field of attention is so strong that you get a free ride.

When I was in college years ago, when I was an undergraduate I used to have a typical undergraduate car, at least at the time. This was back in the 1960s, and I had a Volkswagen, a little VW Bug. This was before the advent of the Super Beetle, the old little one.

And when I used to ride on the freeway with it, when you hit a hill it was a problem, to be honest. And while it was a great little car in the straightaway, it would lose it on the hill. But I learned—I used to commute a long distance sometimes to school—that if you could get behind a very large truck [laughter] the truck had a slipstream and you could get behind it and you'd actually be pulled along a little bit by it.

Now the trick of course was to be careful, 'cause the trucks tend to have very good brakes. And so you had to be a little bit wary. If he put on his brakes fast you would be in another world quickly [laughter]. If you weren't real attentive. So it involved a little risk, also saved gas. But that wasn't such a problem back in those days.

So when you meditate with someone who meditates extremely well, it's kind of like entering into a slipstream or a jetstream. You move into a level of attention that you might not have been able to attain for years and years and years—or lifetimes—which is the value of a teacher.

And it's possible to meditate with an advanced person and perhaps there'll be no thought for a half an hour. You see whereas on your own when you try it, you might be able to stop your thought for 20 or 30 seconds. And as you do that, the more you're able to do that, the faster you progress in your meditation.

But it's also important to practice on your own and develop your own ability.

Sometimes there are people who would only meditate with a teacher let's say, and they ride the teacher's energy, and they don't really learn how to meditate. They learn how to ride the energy.

So it's important to have both if both are available to you.

Intermediate Meditation then, begins when thought stops for longer periods of time, and when thought stops, of course, the world goes away. Time goes away and space goes away.

Yet there's still a sense of self. As we're sitting there and there's no thought, there's an awareness of self. It's not quite as manifest but there is a sense of being *light*.

Let's say suddenly you dissolve and you become *infinite light*. But there is this sense of being light. Even though the mind is not thinking it, one feels it, which indicates that one is still there. At least half of one is.

So at this point the study changes. And also the changes in one's personal life become accelerated. You begin to live in other levels of attention all the time, whether you're at work or driving or running on the beach or whatever it is.

You begin to be in a more meditative state all the time, and you find that it fits rather well with everything that you do. Your work improves, your life improves. Everything gets better because simply, you have the ability to be more focused, and at the same time you can stand back from things that used to drain your power and monopolize your attention.

In other words you begin to get more of a handle on life. You also become more sensitive, which is a double-edged sword in this world. But it's well worth it ultimately.

The second stage could last for the rest of one's life. One could never move beyond that—or for many lifetimes. But eventually a time does come—or it could happen in a particular lifetime, perhaps the one that you're in—where you move into the third stage which is the Advanced practice, which is *samadhi.*

Samadhi is a stateless state of awareness. There are different thoughts about how many levels of samadhi there are, Patanjali [19] classifies a certain number, you know different people have their systems. As far as I'm concerned there's really only two and the rest are so close together that it doesn't matter. One can differentiate, but I think that's about the same.

There's salvikalpa and nirvikalpa samadhi.

Salvikalpa samadhi would be absorption in eternity to the point where there's no real concept of self but there's still a karmic chain. Nirvikalpa samadhi is synonymous with nirvana, absorption in nirvana. Different words to express the same thing in my opinion.

And then this world and all worlds and the concept of worlds and self and non-self and all these things go away completely. That's enlightenment.

If a person sets out to practice meditation in this lifetime and they have a little bit of spiritual evolution behind them and they're quite dedicated, it really is not at all an impossible task to enter into salvikalpa samadhi in this particular lifetime.

Which is of course complete ecstasy, complete rapture, knowledge of God, of eternity, all the things that there are no words for.

Nirvikalpa samadhi is another matter. That's not something—I don't feel—that's really up to us. That happens at a certain time when our being has gone through countless changes and refinements. Selves have come and gone and shuffled through existence. And at that point we become—there are words for it, but I don't think they're really succinct—God-realized, enlightened, liberated. All that words do is point in a directionless direction.

---

19. *Patanjali's Yoga Sutras;* Rama's recommended translation is by Swami Prabhavananda.

So those are really the stages of meditation. Now naturally there's a lot more to it. There's thousands and thousands of aspects to the meditative practice. There are different pathways that one follows—be it Zen or Tantra, Karma Yoga, Jnana Yoga. Different ways that have been devised to do the same thing, essentially, for different types of people according to their temperament.

Some people are more emotionally inclined, some more intellectually inclined, some are work oriented. Some are mystically oriented and they are interested in the study of power. So there are many different ways to do the same thing. There are many different ways we can climb the mountain. But the result is the same.

Yet each has its own history, stories, language and culture. I don't feel one form is better than another. I myself teach nine different paths. Because I think that it's necessary not so much to be a proponent of one, but to find the pathway that works well for each individual that they'll do best at. It's not a competitive situation in my estimation—at least it shouldn't be.

So meditation then comes down—essentially—to stopping thought. Detaching one's self from thought, and eventually even going beyond stopping thought, and all such relative concepts.

The result is freedom.

Freedom not just in the sense of a happy or better life, but freedom in the sense that one is aware that you're not the body, you're not the mind, you're not even spirit.

That you're eternity itself.

You go beyond the process of rebirth, which doesn't mean that one doesn't take incarnation. But let's say that you're just no longer bound by anything. Except your love of eternity.

So it's a delightful process, it's definitely not for everyone. There are those who want to revolutionize the world with meditation, and I really don't think that that's necessary. I think the world is already revolutionized. All too much.

It's a very quiet study. It's for people who are completely out of their mind [laughter] or if they're not, they want to be. And at the same time, in my estimation, it's something that does not have to take you away from your life.

Unfortunately we've seen meditation insulted in a sense with the image of ritual. That you have to dress a certain way, act a certain way, follow a certain type of lifestyle. All that sort of thing. Very culty. And that, of course, has nothing to do with the practice whatsoever. Those are just pseudo forms that people added for their own reasons.

The practice is a very pure study. And you can do with it as you will.

There are those who feel that meditation of course is unrealistic, or takes them out of the world. And if that was your experience with meditation, you weren't meditating.

If you meditate, you'll find it's easier to blend, easier to understand people because you can *see* in them, you become psychic, easier to do just about everything. Your mind becomes sharp and efficient, you become conscious. You lose your emotions—eventually over a period of time—that are destructive. Jealousies, fears, angers, hate. Eventually all those things go away, you just never feel them.

And your higher emotional tonal range opens up dramatically, your ability to love and give and care. To be concerned with the welfare of others, becomes one's major occupation. Without any sense of self-importance that one is better because one meditates or leads a certain type of life. Real meditation engenders humility and purity. Always.

And yet I don't really think it demands any kind of lifestyle. I think the best thing to do is to meditate and see what you do. Certainly, different teachers make different recommendations that will help a person with the practice.

But ultimately you're the filter. The recommendations are only good if they make sense to you inside. You should never do what anyone says, unless it touches your heart, and you know it's true. No matter how charismatic they may be or powerful. What they say may be true, but if it doesn't have application for you, it's not necessarily something you should try to do.

A lot of people have this live-or-die attitude with meditation. It has to be all or nothing. And I don't think it should be. It's a study that you follow for the rest of your life. And it's something that you get better at, and it adds meaning and color to being. And eventually to non-being, and beyond both.

But I don't think it has to be this overwrought emotional business that people make it into. I think all they do is sidestep the actual issues. Which are leading a disciplined, clear happy life and becoming aware of others, and seeing what you can do for them, in whatever way that you choose.

At the same time it's necessary to respect, I feel, all other ways and other teachings on the subject. Because even though they may not make a lot of sense to us, they might to someone else, and it may be exactly the thing that that person needs at this stage of their development. Who are we to say?

But ultimately, I think cosmopolitan spirituality is the best. Where we go beyond, "My teacher's better than yours", or "My meditation form is better than yours", or whatever it may be. And we see that that's not the purpose of the entire thing. It's not Ford vs. Chevy exactly.

But it's rather the transition of our limited awareness into eternity.

Just to be able to smile sometimes, when things aren't going well. And maybe realize when they aren't going well, they *are*.

There's a lot to the study.

Chapter Fourteen

Tantric Mysticism

I'd like to talk to you about tantric mysticism.

Tantric mysticism is the networking of spiritual practices. Tantric mysticism, in shorthand, is living in the world and attaining enlightenment.

Of course, I don't know where else you could live and attain enlightenment.

There is a central dichotomy that seems to exist for a lot of people in spiritual practice. And that dichotomy is the spirit and the body, the world and other worlds, left and right, *yin* and *yang*, forward and backward.

The point of spiritual discovery is to show you that there is no dichotomy, that everything is one, and yet at the same time, one is diversity. People seem to have a lot of trouble with this, I've noticed.

It seems to me that most people who practice self-discovery are miserable. [laughter] They're unhappy, they lead lives that they really don't like, they don't seem to have a good time with what they do. They're always so busy trying to be good, that they don't have any fun!

So, for those individuals who have done that for a while and have decided that it's time for a change, I offer tantric mysticism.

Tantric mysticism is having fun with enlightenment.

Enlightenment is something that never happens to anyone, we all know that.

It's this carrot at the end of the rainbow [laughter] that they always tell us will occur to us. But then if we listen very carefully, of course, as they say in the *Gita* and numerous other books, they say that basically the odds of an individual attaining enlightenment in any given lifetime are so ridiculous that Nick the Greek would never, ever consider betting on the side of an individual who tries to attain enlightenment.

It really doesn't matter. That's the central theme of tantric mysticism. [laughter] But you have to understand that it really doesn't matter in a very precise way.

In other words, it really matters that it doesn't matter, quite a bit. Because if you just say, "It doesn't matter," then obviously it matters, it matters because it doesn't matter. Whereas if it doesn't matter, it really matters.

Now you're beginning to understand tantric mysticism [laughter].

Tantric mysticism is a very, very advanced form of spiritual practice and most people have a lot of trouble with it, so I don't recommend it. Because they really don't want to be happy and have a good time with what they do.

Also, it really involves a lot of sophistication. If a person still wants to follow the school of thought that there's a school of thought, it won't work. It's the pure acceptance of the ridiculousness of all life, at the same time with a sense of tremendous purpose and a want for nothing but light and purity and truth.

It's a realization that we have one side of ourselves that is immortal and luminous and perfect. And another side of ourselves that is just the opposite. And that both are equally holy and they fit together perfectly. Except that sometimes we don't think that they do, and they do anyway, but sometimes we don't think that they do.

So tantric mysticism, then, involves the use of *any* spiritual methodology. Yet it's a way in itself.

It's not simply a Unitarianism in the sense that it's a blending, and the composite end is the blend. Not at all. Tantric mysticism is a specific method of spiritual practice. Yet it can use all other methods of spiritual practice.

So for example, the student of tantric mysticism is free to practice Zen, the yoga of love, the yoga of selfless giving, the yoga of power, Buddhism, shamanism, it really doesn't matter. Any place that you find anything that will help you, regardless of what the "ism" is, it's useful. Wherever you see truth! And if you see truth at Denny's [laughter] and if you see truth in church, if you see truth out at the power spot, wherever it is, it's still truth. What's the difference?

So tantric mysticism has a lot of etiquette, but no rules. And the etiquette is not something that can be explained, per se. It's something that you learn as you go deeper into the study.

The reason it's difficult for a lot of people is because there are no rules, and people love rules and regulations, because then they have something to rebel against [laughter]. And if there's no rules and regulations to rebel against, then what are you going to do with the rest of your life? So tantric mysticism is the ultimate frustration for most people. It's the only path where they don't tell you what to do.

Lots of recommendations are made in tantric mysticism. So many in fact, that it's confusing. Because opposites will be recommended all the time. Because one thing is as good as another.

The trick with tantric mysticism is to find what works. And that will change as *you* change.

So whether we're dealing with the sophistications of the Tibetan Rebirth Process and the dissolution of the self and the assumption of caretaker personalities, if we're out at the desert moving through the luminous realities, through the vortex in the doorway, into the other worlds.

If we're at work and just being conscious and directing what we do to eternity, if we're at the movies, if we're in love, it really doesn't matter, because everything is eternal.

Yet it's not simply that realization that is tantric mysticism.

Tantric mysticism is the way of not getting stuck in any form of self-discovery, essentially. Using them all, but at the same time remaining a little bit beyond them, without a sense that one is superior to them in any way.

Tantric mysticism is fascinating because in the history of self-discovery, if we examine it, either in the West or East or anyplace else, what we find is that people like to set up oppositions. Tantric mysticism, of course, has nothing to do with oppositions. It recognizes the tension of oppositions and uses that tension, that polarity as something positive.

Tantra is the reconciliation of opposites.

The tantras, of course are the ancient sacred books of the East that outline tons and tons of ways to attain enlightenment and advanced states of spiritual consciousness. But when I use the term I mean it as "the reconciliation of opposites", seeing that opposites aren't exactly opposite. Some days they are, some days they aren't. Some days they're complements. Some days they're the same thing.

In other words, the rules change all the time. It's as if you were playing chess and suddenly they tell you that the moves that a queen can normally make can't be made anymore, because there was a rule change. And then that works fine for a while, and as soon as you learn that, they tell you, "Well it changed again."

As soon as you hold on to something, they take it away from you. And then after a while you think you can outsmart them by not holding onto anything, you see. And then they say, "Well, that doesn't work either."

Tantric mysticism gives you nothing to hold onto. There's even more in Zen, and in Zen there's nothing. [laughter]

Now, naturally, there are basic elements in tantric mysticism. The two most prominent, of course, are meditation and selfless giving. And the two primary qualities necessary for study along the way are humility and purity. It's a very traditional form of self-discovery.

But it doesn't mean that you hate yourself, it's the only thing that doesn't work, you see. The idea is that you don't need to hate yourself. Yet if you find yourself hating yourself, you use it. [laughter] There's nothing that doesn't work in tantric mysticism.

Tantric mysticism is the study not just of your own personal realization, but of life. And we feel that everything that happens to us, or that we observe, can be used for our advancement, no matter what it is.

Now, there are those in the world, of course, who think that the practice of tantric mysticism gives them license to do all the little nasty things that they've always wanted to do. There are those who think,

> "Well, God, I've always wanted to do so-and-so and such-and-such, and if I practice tantric mysticism, it means that everything is OK, and everything is taking me towards enlightenment.
>
> "So I've always had this 'urge' to go to bed with a thousand people at once. [laughter]
>
> "So now that I study tantric mysticism, of course, it's OK, because it's spiritual." [laughter]

That's not exactly tantric mysticism. No. No, it's limited to groups of a hundred and under. [Tremendous laughter from the audience, Rama joins in.]

The other side of tantric mysticism is of course mysticism. Mysticism is the study and the application of power and going through different realities and fields of attention.

Some people are under the auspices of a school of thought that suggest that all there is, is God and light and luminosity, and that there are no levels, and to be exploring other planes of reality takes you away from enlightenment. And I don't think so, because enlightenment exists in everything, in the finite and the infinite, what's the difference?

That's our koan of the night. "What's the difference?"

You can be busily at work and realize eternity. You can be meditating and do the same. It really doesn't matter.

So tantric mysticism then involves the analysis of power. How it works in your life. Where you gain it, where you lose it, how to increase it. How to move through different layers of attention, to move through different worlds, planes of existence, the bardos. While here, now. Or to see that you're not here now, that it's just an illusion. Which is very real.

So on the one hand, tantric mysticism then is the networking of various forms of spiritual discovery. And in tantric mysticism we study Zen. We study Karma Yoga. We study all the different traditional forms, and we use them. At the same time we feel that life in the shopping mall is as important as life in the meditation hall, because it's all life.

That's why this doesn't work for a lot of people. You see, people like to keep things segmented. They like their good to be good and their bad to be bad. And if the two suddenly seem to be interactive, it upsets them. So tantric mysticism doesn't work for people like that, nor should it. There are other forms that do.

Tantric mysticism is for the person who can see that there is dark and there is light, and at the same time there's something beyond both. And that we don't have to have one or the other, we have them all. That it's not bad to be physical in the world, because that's part of God. And at the same time to go beyond that is fine, too.

And then you can be beyond it and in it at the same time, or do neither. And enter into nirvana, where all such distinctions go away.

So when you practice tantric mysticism, you're always "on". You're always on stage. It's not the sense that, "Now I'm going to go sit and meditate and be spiritual. And then later on I'm going to go out and do things that are not spiritual."

There's no difference. Everything is spiritual, everything is holy.

But again, it's not simply that thought, "Well, now I know that, so everything's OK."

No. No, that's a very superficial judgment. Rather it means that you will be seeing the eternal in the finite, and the finite in the infinite.

It means that when you're with people you try and serve them without a sense of self-importance. It means that no matter what is happening, you're meditating. Not in the sense of being spaced out and not being in the world, but rather being conscious.

And that you don't mix up your realities, at least not for a while.

That when you're in the office you pay attention to office work, and you get it done *perfectly* and impeccably. And when you're meditating you do the same thing.

And you realize that there are different languages, just as we dress differently for different occasions. We may dress one way to jog, another way when we work, and it's best not to get them confused. Because it's very hot to jog in a three-piece suit, you see, and you look kind of ridiculous in your Nike shorts in the office.

So tantric mysticism is a very sophisticated study. It suggests that there's a time and place for everything and for nothing. And sometimes there's no time and place. It alters according to reality.

And you change realities constantly and depending upon the reality you're in, everything is different. So if you're in one plane of attention, there's one language to be spoken, there's one etiquette. If you move into another plane of attention—into another reality, another bardo—it all changes. As do you. You might become a different self in a different reality, or then be no self whatsoever. No doctrine, in other words.

Unless it's the reverence for life.

No preconceptions.

So the student of tantric mysticism, then, meditates, of course, and does everything that everyone else does in all the other paths. The only difference is that they have more fun.

Because in most spiritual practice—and I don't think this is necessarily the purpose of the practice, I think this is just what people do with it—people hate themselves, or they hate the study, or they hate everybody else. There's a lot of frustration.

There's this sense that in order to be a higher self or a better person or lead a better life, or whatever it might be, "I have to do this, and I can't do this." And as soon as you decide that, you go to war with yourself. And in a war, no one wins.

Because you're gonna set up polar opposites:

> "I desire, I want, I think this is good, this would be fun.
>
> "But they say in the book that I read that this isn't good. They say *this* is good. I really don't want to do it, I'm not

quite in the mood. I can *force* myself to do it.

"Yes, I'll do it. And I'll hate it every minute, and I'll get frustrated."

That does not engender spiritual progress or enlightenment, at all, that attitude.

What works is being happy. Happy not only in the relative sense of a transitory happiness, but in the sense of attaining inner peace, becoming conscious of eternity.

Becoming consciousness itself and beyond it. That's what I mean by happy.

That's what works.

You should see dramatic, tremendous changes in your self-discovery all of the time. You should be a new person constantly. The old self has dissolved, the new self, more refined self appears. That self dissolves.

That's tantric mysticism.

It's going from self to self, from form to formlessness, without ever feeling that we're really a part of anything, yet everything is our family, everything is our self.

We don't feel that we have to destroy the self to attain enlightenment, because there's no self to destroy.

So it's a very difficult way for some people. Because it means that whatever life does is right. You have to have, in other words, a complete and childlike faith in God, in eternity, whatever phrase you want to use for that miserable force that runs our destiny.

No! I mean for that wonderful force [laughter] that runs our destiny. You just have to have complete faith in it. 'Cause what choice do you have, anyway? When was the last time *you* were consulted about your destiny?

[laughter]

So you might as well go along with the program. Because otherwise you're going to be very unhappy.

In other words, eternity does everything perfectly. Did you ever try and argue with God? It's a one-way experience. [laughter]

So in tantric mysticism, we feel that rather than argue, it's better to make friends. To see that we are God, that everything is one, and everything is diverse. And to not set up rigid standards that we have to follow which we know we won't. Nor to just give in to every thought and desire that we have, because that won't make us happy either.

Rather, just to leave ourselves alone. To meditate, to do all we can for everyone else without getting stuck in that, and thinking how wonderful we are for doing that, and to just be, essentially.

To learn the various spiritual methodologies and disciplines that engender enlightenment and practice them, whatever ones appeal to us. And keep studying.

To feel that there's no end to truth, there's no end to enlightenment. There's no best way. Each way is a wonderful way, if it works at the time. And if it doesn't work for us, it may work for someone else.

To not get caught in systems, but to use them. I suppose tantric mysticism is—if I can use a computer analogy—it's spiritual systems analysis and networking.

And at the same time to just know that all there is to know is what we know at the time.

Does that make sense? I'm not sure. It's not always necessary to make sense. That's a difficult one for some people.

In other words, you don't have to understand life. You can't, it's impossible to understand life. You can become fully conscious of it, merge with it, be it, and go beyond it, but you can't understand it. That's what makes it exciting. But one should never stop trying. That's tantric mysticism.

In other words, you accept that you'll never be enlightened, because you can't possibly be enlightened. 'Cause the you you are now will never be enlightened. It will go away. Oh, something else may be enlightened, or you may be enlightenment. But that's just a word, anyway, what's the difference?

See, that *koan* comes around again. Sort of like *Alice's Restaurant*.[20]

A sense of humor is very important in the practice of tantric mysticism.

But not the sense of humor that is dependent upon the expense of others, nor the one that lacks refinement. Some people get so caught in their humor, you see, they use it as an escape. Rather, humor *is*.

Tantric mysticism is a very, very, refined spiritual pathway. It means that we've already learned how to be a very nice person, and it means that we've already done all the essentially right things, or if not, we're working at it.

It doesn't mean that we abandon ourselves to anything.

To really abandon oneself to God requires tremendous discipline and patience, and years and lifetimes of practice.

When we talk about abandonment, we don't mean the abandonment of the person who says, "Oh sure, I'll do whatever I want, that's spiritual." Well, I suppose that is. For them. But that's not tantric mysticism.

Tantric mysticism means that you already have it down, and you give it up. It means that once you've succeeded, you go beyond success.

---

20. The spoken monologue in *Alice's Restaurant,* Arlo Guthrie, 1967, repeatedly reminds the listener to wait for the chorus, when "it comes around again."

A lot of people avoid success for various reasons. And they think that by shunning success, they'll succeed in a spiritual way.

In other words, if I leave the material world, if I put it down, if I put down money, if I put down sex, if I put down my friends, all these things, somehow I'm going to be a holy person. With the thought, that all those who don't do what I do, are not holy. How ridiculous! What egotism and vanity!

Sometimes a person needs that, though. At that stage of their development, they need to say those things. Because that's the direction life is bringing them in. So there's a tremendous tolerance for all, yet at the same time, not to get stuck even in tolerance.

Tantric mysticism takes us into the superconscious. It's the only way it can really be practiced. Otherwise it's just a lot of ideas.

But when you're able to move into the superconscious awareness—in other words, deep meditation, where we go beyond the body, beyond time and beyond space—then you can begin to practice tantric mysticism on a more sophisticated level.

Because then, what will happen, is you'll do that, you'll go into a higher plane of attention, and the world goes away, time goes away, space goes away, everything goes away.

But then, you'll be here again, and it's very disconcerting at first!

> You're in the world again, and you have to fill out your tax form, and you have to arrange the meeting, and you have to talk to this person, and you have to deal with your aging body, and all the different things that are happening in the world.
>
> And five minutes ago you were meditating and you were absorbed in the superconscious, and you were perfect light, and now you're here again.

Now, for most people that's very difficult. They set up this dichotomy. One is spiritual, one is not, but you see, tantric mysticism saves you.

Because it shows you that, how wonderful, now we're here, now let's do the best we can with this particular world, and bring the awareness of the superconscious into it. Let's do everything we do as perfectly as possible, without setting up an idea of what perfection is. If you decide to will it, will it. If you don't will it and you just let it happen, let it happen. Either is fine. Trust yourself.

For about a minute a day. [laughter] That's tantric mysticism.

So see, I can't really explain what tantric mysticism is. It's more of a feeling. It's kind of like the door is shutting.

> You know there are a pair of electric doors, huge doors, right? And you want to get to the other side, what's on the other side of them.
>
> And naturally, you show up just as the doors are almost closed.
>
> So what you do is you zip through, and there is a very good possibility that you'll get crushed by these giant doors.
>
> But you just manage to slide through at the last moment!

That's tantric mysticism. It's just sliding through. Reality to reality, loka to loka, the finite and the infinite. Without a problem.

And to find that when you're frustrated, even though you were just in a very high field of attention—and there was nothing but joy and happiness and now you're frustrated, and you can't figure out why that happens—not to worry about it, to use it. To see that there's something there that can be learned.

And "Recognition," as they say in the *Tibetan Book of the Dead*, "is liberation." That's tantric mysticism. To recognize where you are.

As long as you try and cover it up and pretend it's not so, there's no growth. You're fixated.

You see, tantric mysticism has a lot to do with attraction and repulsion.

Whenever you run towards something, you're fixated. Which doesn't mean you shouldn't run towards it. You can run towards it, you just shouldn't be fixated when you run.

Whenever you run away from something, you're fixated. Well, there's some things in life it's very good to run away from. But you just shouldn't be fixated when you run away. Easy to say, difficult to do.

Tantric mysticism is the realization of eternal awareness, and to feel that every moment is of equal importance. The moment of your birth, the moment of your death. Because they're all happening at the same time constantly. You're not one finite person fixed in a body in time and space. You are!

But at the same time you pass through all levels of attention, all realities. You're a conglomerate. You're made up of countless selves.

And at the same time there is no self. It depends on the level of attention that you're in. In some levels of attention, there's no self. In others there's self. It's all the same.

Or is it? Hmmmm. In tantric mysticism, one is always suspicious. [laughter]

You can't trust anyone, particularly yourself. Which doesn't mean you shouldn't trust. You can trust without trusting. Or is it the other way around? In tantric mysticism you're never sure which way it is, except that you assume the way you're going is the way it is. And even if it's not, it might be an interesting place to go.

You're beginning to get disappointed, I can see. [audience laughs]

Use it! [Rama laughs] Hmmm.

It's a complex subject.

Most people I observe in self-discovery hate themselves. Or they try and hide themselves. The idea is, if I don't really accept what I feel, because it's not spiritual—whatever that means—if I just sort of pretend it's not there, it'll all be OK. I'll just do what it said on page 31. And it'll work out.

On the other hand, of course, the other school of thought is, "Well, don't worry about what it says on page 31, [mimics snarling] just do what you want! And that'll be wonderful." [laughter]

Now you can do either—you probably have done both at one time or another—but it didn't bring you enlightenment, did it? Ha! Got you there!

So tantric mysticism, then, is neither. You might find yourself in either, but it doesn't matter, does it. I'm not sure. I lose track. But anyway—it's in the middle.

You see, that door is closing, you just have a moment to go through it. And you've got to slide right on through. If you get stuck, what do you do then? Die. [laughter]

Well, it could be worse. There are worse things than death. Life. [laughter] You haven't lived too many lives if you don't know what I mean. But anyway. We'll let that one go by.

See, that's what you do in tantric mysticism, you see, you let it go by. It doesn't matter what it is, you let it go by.

> Somebody comes up and says, "Would you marry me?!" And they're everything you always wanted, you see. The perfect person. *Yech.* [laughter]
>
> But you know, they come up to you and they say, "Will you marry me!!??" And you say, "Uh … sure … If that's what

> you really want!" [lots of laughter]
>
> Since it really doesn't matter. Or does it?
>
> So then you go, you get the license, you get blood tests, you go through the whole thing. You get to the ceremony and you're standing there …
>
> And they say, "Will you (ahemahem) take (ahemahem) to be your lawful (ahemahem)?"
>
> And you go, "I'm not sure. It depends on what plane of attention I'm in. Which self are you asking?" [laughter throughout]
>
> At this point your perfect person will begin to eye you. "Jesus, stop it Henry, everybody's listening!"

Now you could not show up, you could just not go to the wedding at all, or you could just get all of the presents and split. [lots of laughter]

I don't know, it doesn't really matter, I don't think. It might to others though. See, that's the thing you have to consider, is the welfare of others. Otherwise it would be easy.

But in tantric mysticism we have to be more concerned with the welfare of others than with our own welfare. However, that doesn't mean that you should allow anyone to abuse you in that name.

When you try and pretend that you're something that you're not, you very cleverly keep yourself that way. To simply do everything that you want to do, won't change you either. This is what the student of Zen discovers. That,

> "Well, sure, if I do everything I want, if I fulfill all my desires then I'll still be the same. The same person. They won't necessarily go away. New ones will come. Or I'll just want to do the same things again.

"But then again, to not fulfill them won't do anything either, then I'll just be unhappy and I'll be the same.

"What do I do Zen Master?"

At which point he realizes that the Zen Master has gone. [laughter] Vacation in Barbados. [laughter] Very wise Zen Master. Leaving the student to figure it out for themselves. That's tantric mysticism.

Because in tantric mysticism no one does it for you. Because if they do then it was their experience, not yours. It's an experiential school is what I'm suggesting. You have to live your life.

There's advice along the way.

"Don't get married." [laughter]

But then there's counter advice.

"If you really want to get married you should *definitely* get married—it's the most wonderful thing you could do." [laughter]

So the poor student is perplexed and doesn't know what to do. They're making progress then.

Well then, how do you ultimately decide? Flip a coin. [laughter]

That's the way all great spiritual teachers have always made their decisions. [laughter] You flip a coin, but you flip a certain kind of coin that you get in spiritual teacher's school in another world. And of course heads are both sides. [laughter]

So if you try and pretend that you're not something, it doesn't work. Because then you lead a false life. You try and pretend that … Let's say you want to be a very reverent, spiritual person, and you have a concept of what that is.

> Sort of walking around on air, hands folded, that sort of thing. Saying to everybody in sort of a flaky, bhakti conversational mode, "Oh yes, oh, everything is so wonderful, isn't it?" [laughter]

People are dying all over the world, suffering. Everything isn't "very wonderful", necessarily. What do you mean, "It's all wonderful"? Have you lived!?

> But then again, to go to the other side, and "Everything is miserable and terrible because everybody dies."

Well, that's not so bad. Life is eternal. Everything goes on. It's just the surface that changes and when you really see, you see there is never anything to be sorry about.

The middle. That's where the extremes meet.

So, rather than trying to be your image of a spiritual seeker, or rather than taking a teacher—if you have one, a spiritual teacher—and setting them up on a pedestal and trying to make them into something that they're not, everybody should just go out to a nice restaurant and have lunch. [laughter] That's tantric mysticism.

But when you get there, you have to study the menu and assess it carefully. You have to look around, and observe the level of attention of everyone who's there. You have to learn everything you can about that moment. If you're eating a bowl of onion soup, you have to pay very, very particular attention to the onions.

And you have to decide whether it's a good soup or bad soup. You can't just say, "Well, it doesn't matter." Of course it matters, you're paying for it. [laughter] You have to pay a lot of attention to that soup.

But then at the same time, you can move into another level of attention while you're sitting there. The room will dissolve, everything will go away, you'll go into a higher plane of attention, and it really doesn't matter.

And there's no disparity between the two. Unless you get them confused. Which some people do, in which case you're confused.

Remember, you can only be confused, if you try and figure something out. [laughter, some applause]

So then, rather than try and pretend that you're something that you're not—just to be novel—why don't you just accept yourself?

And you might find out that you're many, many different things. That you do have desires, that if you follow them, will frustrate you and make you unhappy. You might have desires, that if you follow them will make you happy.

That that's karma. You have a choice, and you live with the results.

And not to be afraid of experimenting with your life. To feel that the way someone else attained enlightenment, is not necessarily the way that you did, but at the same time not to throw it all away.

To study the things that one can learn, and do your very best at all of them, all the traditional ways. Because obviously they did something for someone. Yet not to be bound by them.

To be creative in your self-discovery. And not just simply to be, if being means just being whatever you happen to want at the moment.

Because you can do that, but it's just a subway ride that goes 'round and 'round. You'll come back to the same station over and over.

No, it's necessary to engender change in your existence. But the way to do it is not by forcing yourself into some pattern.

The way to do it is to meditate and to stop your thought, and to become conscious of immortality. And then change happens by itself. It's very pleasant.

It's not torture. You don't have to hate yourself.

And to work for the welfare of others. Without feeling superior, feeling that you know more than they do, or that you're better in any way.

These things engender change in my experience. Not hating yourself. Yet if you find yourself hating yourself, to accept that as another transitory experience, another dream.

All of life is just a dream. Tantric mysticism is the study of *dreaming*. We move through different dreams. We experience each one, we accept it, we enjoy it. But then we move on to the next one.

We trust life implicitly. We simply don't bind ourselves to any dreams, and if we find ourselves being bound, we accept that and do the best we can with it.

Tantric Mysticism.

CHAPTER FIFTEEN

SEEING, DREAMING AND PLACES OF POWER

A place of power is a vortex of energy. There are really two types of places of power.

One type is a personal place of power. It's a physical locale—which is not simply physical—that has a special meaning for you. It's specific to you, in other words.

Then there's a universal place of power. That's a place where just the currents of energy are very extraordinary. Anyone who goes to one of those places of power will be affected by it. Some will be conscious of it and some will not.

A place of power, a personal place of power, is a place where you've stored something. You've had moments there that were very, very important to you. I think all of us has at least one place like that. And when we go back there, we can access those moments. We can return to them.

For example, there was a place, when I went to the university as an undergraduate, where I used to go hiking and meditating. There was a river. And it was a place that I went to many, many times and I had many experiences in other planes of reality there, where I became more conscious.

And so that's a place of power for me. It's a place that I can go back to. I don't have to go back there physically to return to it. It's a place that one can just draw power from at any time.

But most of us are concerned with universal places of power. These are inter-plane vortexes of energy. They are doorways to other worlds.

What makes a place of power what it is?

Well, no one knows precisely. We can perhaps look at it historically and say that it's a place where great warriors, spiritual teachers, seekers have been in ages past and in ages present. They have gone and spoken words, and their words had power in them, and light. They changed levels of attention there, they moved in and out of other worlds at that spot.

Why did they pick that spot—if we trace it back further?

Well, sometimes it's interesting to note that the actual mineral composition of a place of power is a little bit different. The ground usually has more metal in it. That's not always the case, but frequently that's the case.

But I don't think that's the sole determining factor. I think these are just reflections of something that's really not something that we can explain, it just is, and we perceive it and utilize it.

When you go to a place of power—no matter what shape your field of attention is in—your consciousness is affected by it. Everything is amplified.

That's why you have to be very, very careful when you go to a place of power. Because the higher thoughts and tendencies that you have—if they're dominant in your consciousness at that time—will be increased.

But if you're moving into a negative emotional state—if you're depressed or frustrated, or just you're not quite where you should be—that's amplified, too.

Both are increased at a place of power.

Power is indifferent to action.

A place of power is a place where there are not just physical things, there are mysteries there which you have to unravel when you visit them.

Some people are drawn to places of power that they've been in other lifetimes, where they've stored power.

In other words, in another incarnation—in another life, in another dream—they went to a place and magnificent things happened to them. They had experiences there of the other worlds. And either at the time of their death or just during their life, they stored power there. And returning to those places brings something out in you.

It's almost like that fellow in *Close Encounters* [21] who had this vision, and he was drawn to a place of power, and something happened there that changed his existence. That's kind of a metaphor for it.

So in the same sense, you can be drawn back to a place of power. Either something there draws you back, or something inside you draws you.

And when you return there, it will trigger something in you. Let's just say that you'll change. You'll find something that you have forgotten. Perhaps your self, or one of your selves. And you'll return a very different type of being.

To understand a place of power, you have to understand power a little bit.

Now again, we're using the language of power tonight. We could speak about the same subject in Buddhist terms, terms of Zen, terms of yoga. Each is just a language, whether we use French, or Italian or German to discuss

---

21. *Close Encounters of the Third Kind,* 1977, movie about an average man who has subliminal images and visions that lead him to an encounter with actual UFOs and extra-terrestrials.

something, it ultimately doesn't matter. Each language has it's history, it's literature, it's nuances.

So, in the language of power, of course, we deal with luminosity, which is another way of saying power.

And essentially the study is very simple. Each one of us has a certain amount of luminosity, a certain energy. Throughout the course of our life, we tend to lose that energy. We're born with quite a bit of it and we lose it as we grow older. Finally, when we lose it completely, you might say, death occurs.

Throughout the course of our life we lose energy, but we can also gain energy. We can also conduct it.

So, mysticism, or power—the study of power—is simply a sort of systems analysis in the world of power. What we're doing is analyzing the movement of power. We're learning how to store power, assess it, increase it and avoid losing it.

So a person who enters the study initially has to do some assessment. They have to try and find out where they're losing power.

When you have enough power—not power in the sense that most people would mean it, but luminosity—your field of attention changes. Your consciousness expands.

And you begin to *see* and move into other levels of reality. The structure of your being will change, and you will reach, I suppose, what we call enlightenment, eventually, that way.

And also along the way, have many adventures in the other fields of attention.

To begin with there has to be an interest in the subject. And I don't think that's something that we personally generate. It just happens. If we believe in reincarnation, then we would say that it's something to do perhaps with a past life. But then again, what's the difference? This could be the first life for that.

Something happens in our being. We're drawn to a higher level of attention. And so we become conscious of the fact that there are other layers of reality, other stratas of existence and that we're not quite who or what we thought we were.

That we're not one limited self, we're a collection of selves.

We're an aggregate of luminosity or of luminous fields of awareness and attention. That's what the human being is actually constructed of, sort of like the DNA.

So, we're drawn into the study without knowing why, and what we learn is that we have to—first of all—start generating some power. That's always the first step in the study.

Just think of it as a building. If you're in a cold place and you go into a building for shelter, the first thing you have to do is start a fire. Even if there are a lot of leaks in the building, at least you have to get something going to begin with.

Now when you have some initial heat or warmth, at that point, then you can go and be warm enough, and well enough, to begin to find where the leaks are and fill them up. And you start with the biggest ones, and then work towards the more subtle ones.

Then, of course we try and increase the heat, too.

So what one does is analyze oneself. We begin to assess ourselves. And we try to determine where it is we're losing power.

But that can only be done once we move into a level of attention that's at least high enough to understand that. So we begin then, in some way, trying to increase our level of attention. To increase our power a little bit, to at least get the flame going a little bit, and there are many ways to do that, which we'll be discussing this evening.

Then, as that increases, we begin to assess ourselves. Either by ourselves, or with the help of a teacher—someone who aids us, who has traveled that road before—and who can sometimes see us in a more impersonal way and give us a little structured advice. Or actually just imbue us with power and luminosity and increase our power tremendously. More so than we could ourselves.

Then, as we see our life changing and improving, or dissolving, or whatever happens to it, at that point, we become more conscious of the depth of the study. We begin to learn the ways of power, which involves dealing with two aspects of our lives.

One aspect, of course is the outer life, meaning the way we live, the way we talk, walk, eat, sleep, our career, the way we conduct our business affairs, our friendships. We assess every aspect of our being. Not once, but again and again, trying to bring bravery, and courage, and purity and luminosity into us. And trying to cut out those aspects of our lives which drain us, which neither make ourselves nor anyone else happy.

We reassess it constantly, because each time you move into a higher level of attention, you'll have a new vantage point to view these things from. And what you considered perfection before, will not necessarily be perfection in the next level of attention. It's kind of like going to school, and progressing, and just being more aware of a certain body or field of knowledge and its complexities, and mastering each step as we go.

So, on the one hand we have an extremely orderly, logical study. The study of power, how it's gained, how it's lost, how it's increased. And we do this internal and external systems analysis. Looking not only at the stages of our outer life, but also at our emotional body, our feelings, our thoughts, things we dwell on.

The other side of the study, of course, is stepping beyond structure completely, and order and logic, and moving into the other levels of attention. Where the world as we know it dissolves and goes away, and we become something that really can't be described in words.

We become a luminous field of energy moving through the cosmos. And we find that the cosmos is far different and far more wonderful than we had supposed. There's level on level of attention, there are worlds upon worlds in existence. And one can enter into them, visit them, become part of them, go beyond them.

And so there's another aspect of the study, which one usually does with a teacher, which involves the training of your being to move into those different levels of attention through actual exposure.

And what the teacher does, of course, is project the student into the other levels of attention, by virtue of the teacher's power, or the power that passes through them. One can become very powerful in the study, and take not only one but many people into other levels of attention.

However, while you can expose someone to another level of attention—cause them to see things that most people don't see and become aware of things, the mysteries that most people are neither aware of nor particularly interested in—while you can do that, it really relies a lot upon the student to change. To work with their life.

Because your movement into the inner worlds is very much linked to your level of togetherness in your career, in your lifestyle, in your friendships, in the way that you clean your house, in the way that you drive—everything is interrelated. And if you have a very loose life, if it's not particularly tight, then you won't do well with the study.

The study of mysticism is perhaps the most demanding of all the yogas, except perhaps for Jnana Yoga. The other yogas are much more forgiving.

Mysticism is not forgiving.

Mysticism is the study of power, and power, while it can bring you to very high levels of attention, can also do just the opposite.

The study is not for people who are interested in entities, channeling, and you know, all this sort of stuff—witchcraft, all this stuff. That's very, very, low level occultism. And such people are destroyed by what they study, eventually. Because they're dealing with planes of attention, with beings, with realities, that are very, very powerful. It's not a study for kids. It's your "serious" spiritual study.

Other pathways you can walk along and there's relatively little danger, but there's definitely some danger in the study of mysticism. The study itself is not dangerous. But let me say that when people don't approach it properly, with proper training, or if their motives are not pure, it can become quite dangerous. The study itself, when practiced correctly is not dangerous at all. But essentially, it's like driving a car. It can take you where you want to go, or you can kill yourself or somebody else with it, if you're sloppy.

So, one needs to assess one's motives in the study constantly. And if you're just learning the study so you can become more powerful, and manipulate and dominate others, get things that you might want, show off your mystical abilities to others, things like that, then you definitely shouldn't be in the study because you'll get damaged at some point.

Whereas, if you're just drawn to the study—like a moth to the flame [laughter]—and essentially you don't know why, or simply you wish to move into the other levels of attention, or whatever it may be, then if you have proper training it is not a dangerous study at all.

The big danger of course, is obsession. That's the problem with mysticism, is that people become obsessed with it—they get so into the experiential side, watching the world dissolve, moving into other levels of attention and so on—that they get too wrapped in it. And they destroy themselves, or they just lose their balance.

They don't realize that it's necessary ... Mysticism is all about balance. And it's about balancing your outer life and your other life too, and eventually, of course, seeing that there's only one.

But in the study, as in all self-discovery, you change. You make major modifications of your being. You're not the same person who started the study a year in, or two years in, or three years in. Your self dissolves.

It's not an intellectual study whereby we're going to go study History, or Philosophy or Mathematics and essentially we won't change, we'll just apprehend a body of knowledge.

In this study we actually do dissolve the finite self again and again, and become something other than human. While the body may appear to be intact—although even that shifts—nothing else remains.

I think a wonderful introduction to this study—I wouldn't say it's all inclusive at all, of course—are some of the books by Castaneda, particularly *Journey to Ixtlan* and *Tales of Power*.

The sense of humor and so on, and immensity, and poignancy that are conveyed in those books is remarkable. They're detailed books on how to do it if you have a teacher. Naturally we're dealing with the student's point of view, as opposed to a teacher's point of view. But I think he steps out of the way enough to show us something interesting—at times.

So, then, the other side, of course, is what Mr. Castaneda calls the nagual, what I call the other worlds—the other levels of attention—which you bound in and out of eventually. And places of power, and *seeing* and *dreaming* have all to do with these things.

Seeing is the art of being. When you can *see*, of course, we mean that you have the ability to shut off your thoughts. To stop all thought completely, which is *seeing*, or meditation. Synonymous words, synonyms.

When you can do that, the world changes. Reality is supported by your view. By your thoughts, by your belief systems. When thought stops, the world stops. Time stops. Life stops. Death stops.

In other words, everything that you construe as meaningful disappears. Because everything that you construe as meaningful is a field of attention that you have projected—which you have essentially created with some help from your parents, society, friends, teachers and so on—to give you some sense of meaning in life.

The universe without thought is a very different place.

The sense of order and logic, of history, of time, of value—all the things that we count on as being meaningful, that give our life a shape and a purpose—come from thought and thinking.

So when we stop that process, what we're doing is erasing the blackboard. We've taken years and years to work out all the equations. And now what we're going to do is, for a while, erase them and walk beyond them all, into something else—into something that no one ever told us about, perhaps—which is reality in its true form.

Your experiences in other levels of attention will not only change you, but they'll change your view of this world.

You'll see that everything is a dream, and that everyone is dreaming. We're all dreamers. People dream their lives. They dream their relationships, they dream their value systems. They dream their lives, and they even dream their deaths.

That everything that happens to us ultimately has to do with power. That is to say, with luminosity. With our field of energy.

Some people have very weak fields of attention, some have very strong. Some people have very strong fields of attention, but the things that they aim their field of attention at are very unusual. Simply to have a strong field of attention doesn't necessarily mean that one is advanced spiritually. You can be a very strong person and you can hurt people or you can help them. If you have a lot of physical strength.

So power itself is neither good nor bad. It depends upon its application.

The key to all self-discovery is *seeing*.

Seeing in the sense of meditating and stopping thought, but also the abilities that meditation engenders.

Which is the ability to discriminate. To look beyond what is in front of you, to see what's really in front of you.

> You can see a person, they can be smiling at you, and at the same time they can be thinking how they hate you.
>
> Now, if you rely upon your ability to perceive as you've been taught—the person's body language might be very open, they may have a big smile, they may have dressed in a way that will please you—in other words, it's possible for you to totally misunderstand their intention.

Just the opposite is true also. A person can have wonderful thoughts and feelings. And you might go right by them in life. Because they didn't fit into your "ideal role model" of what such a person is supposed to look like.

We see this in teaching constantly. That the student has an image of what the teacher is supposed to be like. They're supposed to dress a certain way, talk a certain way. Everybody has their idealized forms, which has nothing to do with reality.

So *seeing* then, aside from being something in itself—which is the stopping of thought, which brings us into other levels of attention—what comes out of that *seeing* is the ability to perceive beyond the physical. Meaning, not only to look into someone, but to look into yourself.

To look beyond the self. To perceive what's going on thousands of miles away. Millions of miles away, billions of miles away, in other dimensional planes. To become conscious that there are other dimensional planes with other beings. To see that what most people call impossible and extraordinary is actually quite ordinary.

It's possible to do things that people call miracles. They're not particularly miracles. It's just the application of power in a way which most human beings are not aware of.

These are very ancient studies.

So, *seeing*, then, is a very necessary thing—if you live in the world.

Mysticism is a very practical study. It's practical in the sense that we increase our luminosity through the study. We're able to live in the world more strongly, in a better way, in a happier way. We become free of our own thoughts, our own lack of *seeing* — be it something that was engendered by our own choices, or the choices others made as we were educated and taught about the world.

But also, we have this remarkable ability to cut through time and space and to go beyond dimension. In other words, the whole world goes away, and we go someplace else. And it's a very nice place, much nicer than many of the places that most people spend their time.

But it's a demanding study. In other words, the teacher in the study is not quite as kind. For example, I teach nine forms of self-discovery, one of which is mysticism. And when I work with my students out in the desert, when we bring them through the different levels of attention, and so on, I'm very demanding. I'm not a nice guy. I'm funny, sometimes, but I'm not nice.

Because to be nice is not to be nice at all. It's as if you're preparing someone for battle, and you say, "Well, guys, we're going to learn self defense today, but let's skip it, let's go to the beach instead." While everybody might like that initially, you're doing them no favor, because the day they're on the battlefield they may die, because you didn't teach them what they needed to know.

So the study is demanding in the sense that it's a serious study. It takes a great deal of power to move through the other levels of attention. And to not be truthful with someone is not to help them.

But that, of course, intensity is balanced by humor.

Humor is a wonderful part of the mystical study. Because it's more important than—I think—any other yoga, because what we deal with is so amazing and incredible. As you move through the other levels of attention—as you deal with the beings and forms and forces and so on—it's *so awesome* [mimics Los Angeles girl talk], that essentially, you have to balance it in some way.

And that's what the humor is for. It creates a way not simply to let off steam, but to maintain that delicate balance that you need as a perceiver.

So *seeing*, then, is the art of perception. And initially when you begin to study it, it's a way of looking at things. In other words, you have one language, you learn another language. But it's much more complicated than that. That's only the beginning.

Eventually one *sees* that one is a body of perception.

That it is not we who have perceptions,

> but we are perception itself

> and that the body of perception is endless.

At the moment these may be just words, but one day they're not. We can use that body of perception to do anything.

A place of power is something that you have to *see*.

In other words, to go to a place of power, unless you can *see*, is a useless endeavor. You wouldn't find it, to begin with, unless there were big arrows, "Place of power that way!" And when you get there, you wouldn't know what was going on. You wouldn't *see* very much.

Simply to go to a place of power is not a big deal. You have to have enough personal power. Your field of attention has to be expanded enough so that you can experience what is happening there.

And there's quite a bit happening at these places. There are more beings, and there are doorways into other worlds and things like that.

Ultimately, every place is a place of power. You can open the doorway to the other worlds anyplace when you know how.

But initially, and even later, just because it's fun, it's nice to go to these places.

We are magical beings. We are capable of doing much, much, more than you realize at this time. We live everywhere and nowhere. We are beyond the known and beyond the unknown. And yet we find ourselves—at times—in time, in between.

Life is a dream. It's something that we create, and we experience. Each moment is a dream, a lifetime in existence. They're all dreams, dreams of the self. We dream the self, but what is it that dreams the self?

Dreaming is the art of luminosity. There are different types of *dreaming*, yet they're all the same.

In *dreaming* we make a puzzle, like one of those children's puzzles, where we fit the little pieces together and make a picture.

They're just pieces, that's all the universe is. Little pieces, floating. Modules of existence in a giant ocean. There are all these little things floating, back and forth. These little pieces are out there.

We piece them together in different patterns, and we create something. A dream, a lifetime, a relationship, a feeling, an awareness, a life, a death.

We are that which glues all of those things together. We are the cement that binds the fragments of existence into something we call perception, and that which is perceivable.

When we go to sleep at night and we dream, we have an experience. We wake, it goes away.

That's your life.

At the time it engulfs you completely, there is nothing else. Then we awaken, and death is an awakening, as is life, as is *dreaming*.

There are no hallucinations. There are just different levels of attention, different ways of *seeing*.

Life is a dream and you've accepted a specific type of dream. But in the middle of the dream you can switch dreams. You can move into nicer dreams. Most people live in nightmares.

And you can have a beautiful dream, or you can go beyond the dreamer and the dreamed to nirvana. This is the power of a luminous perceiver.

Most people are bound by their own creations, they're bound by the dream. It's like having a house that you work for and you fix it up. You're paying the mortgage, and then you want to move, but you won't because you put so much into it, that you can't leave it. You're trapped by your own creation, by its perfection.

So the dream of our lives is like that. We dream a life. And then we get trapped in our own dream.

Dreaming is the art of shifting levels of attention. At a place of power we increase our power, it's easier to move into other levels of attention, we can find stored power. We can get a terrific boost.

An enlightened person *is* a place of power. They're a mobile field of attention.

Seeing is the art of perception, of becoming perception.

Dreaming is a creative art.

When we *dream*, we create different worlds. Just like dreaming at night. You can *dream* any world, anything. You're an artist with a palette and a brush, you can paint any type of picture, be it Salvador Dali, other worlds, be it a reflection of this world.

All things exist. Time exists, place, condition, and then beyond that.

So *dreaming*, then, means that we change realities. We change levels of attention. In order to do that, it's first necessary to remove ourself from the level of attention that we're in.

In other words, you're in one of those Cineplexes where they have five or ten movies going. All little theaters. You're in watching one, and you've become so absorbed in the movie that you've forgotten it's a movie and that you can stand up and walk outside and not be in the movie for a while, or go into another one. That's *dreaming*, essentially, it's a Cineplex.

So, first it's necessary to become aware that you're in a dream.

Sometimes, shock does that for a person.

> Someone dies that they love. They find out that they have some terrible disease.
>
> In other words, a tragedy, what most people would call a tragedy, occurs. [Rama claps his hands very sharply]

It wakes them up, for a moment. There's a shift. Something changes. We've been going along in life assuming that the consumer mentality really matters.

This is what Buddha used to do, he used to wake them up. He'd bring them down and see the corpse, and say, "15 days of decomposition. This is what you will look like not too long from now."

And suddenly *Flashdance* [22] doesn't matter as much. [laughter] Or it matters in a different way.

So that's one method.

Sometimes, it's simply because we realize it's time to change. Something in us wants to. It doesn't take a tragedy, it doesn't take a shock. It takes love.

Our love of God—of truth, of the Earth—impels us to move to a higher level of love, which we can't find in this world. This world not being this world, but being this world, if you know what I mean. [laughter]

In other words, many worlds exist in this world. The world that you call this world, exists in this world, for you, and maybe for someone else who shares a similar dream.

But other films are projected on the screen. You're just projecting yours. But that doesn't mean that that's all that's possible.

There are countless worlds in this world. You can walk through it and not *see* them, because your level of attention is so fixated on one particular dream, that you don't perceive it.

So *dreaming,* then, involves stepping back from our field of attention, from our current dream, viewing other possible dreams. It's sort of like seeing the trailers, and seeing what other movies are around, and we can try them on for size.

---

22. *Flashdance,* 1983, American romantic drama dance film.

And there are lots of them, reality has countless films for us to see.

Or sometimes we go beyond the dreamer and the dream to something else, which is beyond words, which we call nirvana, enlightenment, satori, the fourth level of attention. There are different names which we ascribe to something that is essentially nameless, the Tao, to that absolute perception which is beyond perception.

So, back to basics. Back to basic *dreaming*.

Well, in order to *dream*, you have to *see*. Everything always comes back to *seeing*. Because if you can't *see*, if you can't stop thought, or relinquish it to some extent, you can't get out of the movie you're in.

> You're stuck in the theater. What's sticking you?
>
> It's like there was a lot of bubble gum—it's a disgusting analogy, I know—but there was a lot of bubble gum on your seat, and oooohhh! You just can't get away from it.

And those are your thoughts. Your thoughts are so fixed, they're so formed, and you can't break out of them.

Some people have used drugs to do this. I don't recommend it. But for some people that's been a way. Because some of the power plants, they're so powerful, they just literally blast you out of your mind. But they can also do structural damage to your being. I think there are gentler ways of achieving the same result. If one has gone through that route, that's fine. What's done is done. And that was the way one was supposed to go.

But for a person beginning the path to enlightenment, I would not recommend it. There are other things that I think work even more effectively, that don't do any damage to the subtle physical body, to the luminosity.

So *dreaming* means, then, of course, that we step back, we increase our personal power by meditating, we look at the things in our life that drain our power, that make us unhappy, our attachments, problems, anxieties, limited ways of *seeing*, we gradually eliminate those things.

Another world is posited by the teacher, which is the world of luminosity and power, of being together, successful in the finite and the infinite, letting go of our lives, and yet holding on, each at the appropriate moment.

A whole other way of living. We try it on for size. If it works, if we feel better, stronger, freer, whatever it is, we continue along that pathway as long as we choose to.

And then we begin to *dream*.

Now, there's of course, the *dreaming* that we do when we sleep, meaning that it's possible when you go to sleep at night to become conscious, to wake up within a dream and to create the etheric double, and to *dream*.

So, in other words, you go to bed at night, and you wake up in your dream, and you can *see* your body there. You can travel, have experiences, sometimes you can manifest the etheric double so perfectly that it's actually, literally, a second body.

It can go have conversations with people, people can see it and so on, and all the while you were elsewhere, your physical body was elsewhere. That's harder to do.

We can go into other people's dreams with the etheric double and visit them in their *dreaming*. Go to other worlds, all kinds of possibilities for the etheric double.

That's one type of *dreaming*. But the highest type of *dreaming* is not that.

The highest type of *dreaming* of course, is not simply the creation of the etheric double—which is like having a second car—but it's moving into other fields of attention, exploring other worlds, seeing other movies.

And we have to break that fixation that we have.

The way that a fixation is broken, usually, is through a type of *gazing*. That's how we build up power.

Gazing can be done in many different ways. Essentially when we *gaze*, we're looking at something but not really seeing it. It's a type of meditation, you might say.

But it's the type of meditation that we do in the beginning with our eyes open, or partially open, and we observe something. You might sit for twenty minutes and practice *gazing*.

And, as you do, you'll disassociate yourself from your thoughts, and you'll actually enter into the essence of the thing that you're *gazing* at and then of course, beyond it. Doing this will cause you to break the fixation you have with the movie that you've been seeing. It'll just sort of go away.

And it also causes you to accrue and increase power by doing this, because you're drawing from other levels of attention.

With my own students, I have them *gaze* —at least for now, until they get to be a little bit more advanced—on yantras. These are geometric designs that have symbolic and actual value. There are many different yantras. And normally before they begin their meditation each day, I ask them to *gaze* for ten or fifteen minutes at a yantra, which is a way of changing levels of attention.

You can *gaze* on all kinds of things. Everything has an energy, a different luminosity. You can *gaze* at rocks, clouds, all kinds of things, and you can learn.

You see, mysticism is the study of the Earth. It's funny, because while in the study we go beyond the Earth, we go beyond the Earth through the Earth. One must have a tremendous reverence for life and love of this Earth.

It's not a study for people who hate the world, who hate nature. It won't work. Because it's the study of power, and we study the elementals, the essential power that exists in finite things, which are not simply finite things.

We learn about water, air, all the elements, the Earth, the power of plants, of clouds, of stars, of the Sun. You know, the kundalini exists in all these things in various degrees.

And we learn to access those things, to make friends with the fog, with the rain, and so on. Because they're not simply the fog and the rain. In this world, in your dream you defined them in one way, because that's what you were taught.

In other words, when you see the fog, you see these billowing, you know, when fog rolls in down at the ocean, you see the old fog billowing in, and the land is getting obscure.

Well, that's not what I see when I *see* the fog, at all. I can travel through the fog, and use it. It's a medium. The fog is filled with all kinds of things.

And you make friends with each one. You make friends with the fog, you make friends with the desert, with places of power, with the rain, and so on.

When you *dream,* there are some worlds you go into where there are all kinds of beings, other than physical beings. And you can make friends with those, or sometimes you have to fight them, it depends. It's like this world, it's not so different.

So then to *dream,* then, you need to break free of gravity. You see, this gravity is holding you and you need a certain amount of thrust, of energy.

So you gain that, of course, through *gazing,* through changing your life, through self-analysis, all the conventional means and methods that are adopted in the various forms of spiritual study.

But also, the teacher is a key element in this study, as in any study I think.

Because what the teacher does essentially, is inundate you with different levels and strands of luminosity and power.

> You can have a house and if you're not hooked up to the power lines, it's pretty difficult to light the lights at night. You need some candles.

So essentially, when you study with a teacher, if the teacher's any good, the teacher has moved through the luminous fields of attention and is no longer human, in the normal sense of the term.

And what they do essentially with their students—particularly with their close students—is not simply expose them to the other worlds, but they provide them with a continuous stream of luminosity. Which is something that's there to eventually aid the individual in becoming independent, in producing their own luminosity or accessing it. But for a while we lift them up into the other fields of attention. It makes it easier for them.

One of the fun parts about being a teacher of the art of mysticism is cracking the cosmic egg [23] and making an omelette.

In other words, an individual comes along. You know, when you look for students, it's a tough business, because there are all kinds of people who claim to be students.

And I always love Don Genaro's story in *Journey to Ixtlan* where he's talking about how, when he tries to go back to Ixtlan, he meets all these shadows, which were actual people, if that's what they are. I'm not sure some days.

And so, it's necessary to find a student, although it's probably like soul mates, you're better off if you don't find them. A lot of trouble.

But the fun part, anyway, is once you've found one, if they're any good at all, if they have a little spunk, what you do, is you destroy their lives completely [laughter]. This is a technical process which they teach you in

---

23. *The Crack In the Cosmic Egg,* Joseph Chilton Pierce, 1977

Spiritual Teaching School, which is in another world, of course. They teach you very definite devices and ways of completely ruining someone's existence.

And the way you do it is by causing them to be happy. Nothing will louse up a person's plans faster than happiness. It's a guaranteed way. Everybody's worked out a specific plan—each one of you has—to make yourself miserable. And you'll find that your misery will increase as you get older. Unless your plans don't work out. [laughter]

No, really, you've set yourself up for it. It's amazing how people do it.

So, what a teacher does, is they ruin your life, they ruin your plans. Because they work with you and after a while—in spite of yourself, and no matter how hard you try—if you have a little spunk, you begin to become happy. And that destroys your life completely. All your plans are shattered.

So, there are two ways of doing that when you work with someone. On the one hand, you have to appeal to their reason, to a certain extent. Because we're all reasonable beings. [laughter]

So you work with reason. In other words, you speak the language that's currently being spoken. No matter what age you find yourself in, or what planet you're on, wherever they send you.

You know, they just send you places. There's an agency. [laughter] And they just send you on assignment. So you find yourself in a certain world, and you kind of adapt. It's all the same, essentially. But you have to speak the language of the times.

So you appeal to the reason.

You say, "Well if you do this, this will happen, and this will happen." Or sometimes you impress people with miracles. Because people like that. It's sort of like HBO. So you impress, you know, do a few flashy things that aren't supposed to be possible, and they'll go "Whoa!" That's a good one.

There are different ways. In other words, you have to break through, they're in the dream, they're watching this movie, and they're so fixated that you know, it's maybe *The Texas Chain Saw Massacre*. Something horrible, people running around with chain saws, cutting each other up, terrible nightmares people are in, in their lives, their lives are nightmares.

It's what Buddha called "the nightmare of the day". They're the best kind. [Rama laughs heartily. The audience doesn't get it.] Well, anyway. [Now the audience laughs.] What do you want for five bucks, huh? [laughter] "More than this!" So …

So then you have to appeal to the reason. But at the same time, really, what you're doing, has nothing to do with the reason at all. In other words, that's what a person sees in their current level of perception. You're sitting there, you have a discussion, you present information, that sort of thing. The TM approach. Reason. [laughter] Make more money, that sort of thing.

It's great. I love the stories in *The Second Ring of Power* where they tell about how they met Don Juan and Don Genaro. Marvelous stories. How they got Pablito to be a student. You know, they promised him that they had a secret potion which if he, you know, learned how to make it, he could cause anyone to love him. You know, stuff like that. [laughter]

Great, great stories! And of course, eventually, they showed him something else instead, which was eternity.

But human beings aren't interested in eternity. They don't care. So, in mysticism, the idea is that you have to hook the apprentice. You have to—in some way—shatter their world. You have to get through to them. You know, they're, "Oh, it's so good to be asleep! Oh, no, don't wake me up, it's nice," so you have to in some way wake them up.

So you do that with reason. You say, "Did you know your house was on fire?" [laughter] That's a good one. That's what Buddha did, that was his method. "Did you know that you're dying? Have you thought about it lately?" That's one method.

And, of course another method of presentation is to show them the positive side. And that's "You could be happier, make more money, have more lovers." You know, that sort of side. Appeal to what interests people. Neither of which has anything to do with what you're actually trying to show them. But you have to get their attention somehow.

That's like advertising. You don't need a new deodorant. It's not necessary.

But they have to get your attention, so they're going to put this completely sexy person on, you know, who's just sort of walking through a field or something, and they're going to work on your responses, your system responses, and suddenly ...

You know, if they just put the deodorant on, you're going to go, "Oh, *pft!*"

So what they do, is they bring an image on which is going to catch your attention—"Ahh!"

And then you look, and once you're hooked, you'll listen to what they have to say. They'll get their message across.

Well, in spiritual teaching, it's a little bit different because the message is that you can be perfect, and enlightened and happy, and complete and luminous.

It's a very progressive message. But you still have to get somebody's attention.

Because they're so fixated in making themselves and everyone else miserable.

But what you're really doing is approaching a person on two levels at once, that's what I'm doing tonight. In other words, I'm talking to you, we're having some "reasonable discussions".

But on the other hand, of course, all the time, sort of sneaking around behind you with all these fields of luminosity and changing your attention, most of which you won't be conscious of until you get home, and you go, "My God, what happened?" [audience laughs, Rama laughs]

Except for those who are into heavy denial.

> "No, no! No, I didn't see anything, it was the lights, it was the lights! Nothing happened, no, didn't feel anything. No, no! Waste of time. Yeah!"

So, whatever. People select themselves. I'm convinced.

There's a basic law of life that you learn in self-discovery after a while, and I'll teach it to you.

This is the ultimate truth on the Earth: people do what they want to. Never forget that. You can understand people. It's the Dale Carnegie [24] quick course. [laughter]

People do ... human beings do exactly what they want to, always. And if you don't stand in their way, it works out OK. If you stand in your way, they walk all over you.

Once in a while it's possible to find a special one, who is capable of standing outside of themselves for a little while, and considering other possibilities. Even then, simply because they consider it doesn't mean they'll do it.

Once in a while you'll find one that cannot only stand outside of those possibilities, but make the requisite changes necessary to accept them, and move into them.

So on the one hand you work with the person's reason, but then on the other side, what you're doing is really working with the other levels of reality. The powers that you have at your disposal.

---

24. *How to Win Friends and Influence People,* Dale Carnegie, 1936. One of Rama's most highly recommended books.

But a person can be so stuck in their dreams. You can do the most magnificent things in front of them, and they won't even see it. Their eyes are stuck closed. They're just going to, "No, I'm not gonna look, no matter what you do, it doesn't matter, I'm gonna keep, I'm gonna close them harder, and harder, and harder."

You know, you can be standing there, you know bringing allies forth, luminous strands of existence, everything, oh God, it's unbelievable what you can do, and, "Nope, nope, nothing, nothing, nope, I'm not gonna see it."

Everybody *sees*. You just have to become conscious of what you *see*. But everybody *sees* already. But we're so stuck on our *description* of the world that we refuse to accept our own *experiences*, it's great. But I think this is good. I've come to think this now.

Because what it does, it eliminates a lot of people from the study. And that's good. That's the Tibetan way. The Tibetan Secret Doctrine approach. The idea is that the secret doctrine is not something you hide, it's simply most people won't understand it.

It's like the "sorcerer's explanation" in Castaneda. It's a magnificent piece of knowledge which people will hear, but they won't know what you're talking about. They'll just hear the words, they won't see the realities. So I don't think it's such a bad system after all.

God knows what She's doing.

But in any case, back in this world. So the other thing you do, is you approach a person on their other side. And what you do, is you just literally shoot them with luminosity, with kundalini, with energy. You have the ability to do that. One person at a time, a thousand persons at a time, you know, it depends on your own personal access, I suppose.

Now, a person isn't conscious of that, but what do we mean by "conscious"? See, that's the thing you come down to, after a while in the study. What does it mean to be conscious?

I believe everyone is conscious of everything. In other words, "Gee, I didn't know I was hurting you, Alice." Oh yes you did! Who are you trying to kid? Some part of you knew. Don't try and tell us you didn't know.

"Well, I wasn't conscious." Well, what does conscious mean? Does conscious mean just what goes on in the little mind?

It's like a very, very, very slow computer. It's got the old style chip. It just doesn't turn it very fast, that's just the mind. But that's not to be conscious.

To be conscious means a million things at once. No, we're all conscious. We're all too conscious. That's why people suffer, is because they know.

And in spite of what they know, they don't do what they should.

So you have to approach someone on two levels. You approach them through the intellect. Dazzle them, amaze them, be sensible, be funny, whatever works. But at the same time, what you're really doing, essentially, with people as a teacher, is taking all this energy and luminosity and pushing it through their beings.

And what you do is you lift them up for a moment into another world, another field of attention, which they'll forget, later, or rationalize away, if they want to, it's their business.

And they change.

The part of the teacher is fascinating. It means that you're an infant. It takes a great deal of humility to study this particular path. Mysticism. Because you have to realize that you really can't do a whole lot on your own.

That the teacher is a very important part of the study. In some studies, the teacher is not so important. It's just sort of you and God, and the teacher is just a friend who gives you a little advice from time to time.

But in the study of mysticism, the teacher is the one with the power. You might say it flows through them. They would never claim to have it, because they all say and feel that they're no one. Which is true. We are no one. We're nothing. The thin air, at best.

But yet, this power comes through that you can change people's lives with, which doesn't make you remarkable, it just is an operative fact. You're past the point where you want to be remarkable.

And so what you can do is rearrange the aggregate of a person's being.

But only if that's what they want, and even then it's hard, because one part of them wants it, and another doesn't.

In other words, what I'm suggesting, in a very round about way, here, is that in the study of mysticism you reorder the totality of yourself again and again and again.

It's as if you're one DNA structure, you're one form, you're a group of aggregate awarenesses that are linked together, and what you do is you take them and you throw them into the Sun, and they melt down and change and come back in another pattern.

In order to do that, a person has to work with you for some time and just learn how to tighten up their life, conserve their power, learn a new language—in essence—before they go into that new country. Otherwise, in the new country they'll be confounded.

But then, once they've reached that point, the art of the teacher then, of course, is to get them to that point—they have to do it themselves—but you sort of show them around a little bit, teach them the language, but they still have to memorize it and practice it.

But then you actually lead them into the other country. You take them there, and you acquaint them with it. Then one day they're alone. They don't need you anymore. But you were never anyone anyway, so what was the difference?

So that's *dreaming. Dreaming* is that process.

It's learning a new language and going to other countries. It's exploring the totality of our self.

These aren't abstractions or metaphors, they're realities. Which one can choose, or disregard, or just enjoy from a distance. Depends on your mood, of course.

CHAPTER SIXTEEN

FOR EVERY ENDING THERE'S A NEW BEGINNING

In the *I Ching*, the venerable Chinese Book of Wisdom, we are told that for every ending there is a new beginning. And if there is a watchword—a mantram—for a person who seeks eternity, it's that phrase.

Throughout the ages, human beings have sought enlightenment. We have been all of those beings throughout the ages who have sought enlightenment. Today, a few people seek enlightenment. We are those persons who seek enlightenment. In the future there will be innumerable, countless beings who seek enlightenment. We are all of those beings who have already had their so-called enlightenment.

The idea that there's a past and a future is illusory. Which does not mean that there is not a past and a future. There is a past and a future in this world, in relative time. Then, of course, there's timeless time. That realm of existence that's not defined in the superconscious.

True awareness. When we experience the ultimate reality, without words, without hidden meanings.

But between the superconscious and the conscious, there's a space—a gap—which each one of us experiences on the way towards the transcendental reality. It's the journey that we make called self-discovery.

Self-discovery comes in so many different forms and formats. The form varies according to the individual. The format is the path that you walk upon.

But for every ending there's a new beginning.

The world is filled with frustration, doubt, ignorance, hatred, fear, oppression and repression. The world is also made of pure beauty and light.

We could say that this world, this grand stage that we walk upon, that we call Earth, life—this life—is a field of action. A screen, a place to dream, many many different dreams.

All of our successive lifetimes are dreams, and yet they're real dreams.

The pathway to enlightenment is not necessarily very long, in retrospect. [audience laughs]

For one who is seeking enlightenment it seems endless, something that will never happen, it only happens to a chosen few. And it's true! Enlightenment only occurs to a chosen few. So I suppose if we could find out who's choosing and have a serious talk [laughter] with the one who's doing the choosing, it might be possible for us to become part of the chosen few.

However, I have to speak out for the unenlightened. And I think its necessary to be the defense counsel this evening, or any evening, for those who avoid enlightenment. Because I think of all actions which are noble and fruitful, this is perhaps the most ridiculous. [laughter]

But if we have a broad-based understanding of life, and if we have a heart that's big enough to accept the diversity of existence beyond the knowable—within and without reason—then some of the following may make sense. Why you shouldn't attain enlightenment.

There's really no reason to attain enlightenment, since we all know—philosophically—that we all *are* enlightened. At least that's what enlightened people say.

Yet you know that that's not true, which means all enlightened people lie! [laughter] Why would you want to become a liar? Therefore, you can be truthful and avoid enlightenment.

Being enlightened doesn't necessarily mean that you're happy all the time. This is one of the illusions of enlightenment. Therefore, if you want to be happy all the time you should not be enlightened. Enlightenment leads to intense frustration. It gives the word new character. [laughter]

Therefore, if you want to avoid frustration, you should definitely avoid enlightenment. Enlightenment, or liberation or self-realization—whatever we choose to call it—can't be very good, otherwise more people would seriously endeavor to experience it or become it.

Clearly the world is filled with persons who are wise.

We know that the more years you live in this world, the more you know. The smarter you are. We learn from our experiences, [laughter] and judging from the learned world and the knowledge that the elderly possess, we know that enlightenment can be of little value because very few elderly people are enlightened.

And even fewer young people are enlightened. So if youth has anything to teach us, it's to avoid enlightenment at all costs. [laughter] If old age has anything to teach us, it's to avoid enlightenment (in most cases) and there's nothing good about middle age, we all know that. That's the time when people raise families. As opposed to raising their kundalini.

The world has never cared much for enlightenment. If we use history as an example, and since we know that history repeats itself, we can assume that the world probably *will* never care for enlightenment. The people of the world.

The dominant themes that seem to repeat again and again historically are oppression, violence, hatred. And a tremendous, tremendous appreciation on the part of almost all—even those who oppress and hate and are violent—of beauty. Strange dichotomy.

If we consider those who are successful in the world, we will find that very often they are unenlightened. As a matter of fact—judging by worldly standards—most persons who have attained enlightenment have missed worldly success.

Therefore, if you wish to be very, very successful in life, you should not waste your time on pursuing enlightenment.

What few misfits seek enlightenment? Seriously seek enlightenment? There are many who dabble. But what few really are interested in enlightenment?

If we can do a profile, is there something that they have in common? Did they have a bad childhood? [laughter] Is there a certain socio-economic structure that they grew out of? Why should they be so dissatisfied with all the world has to offer that they seek something else?

We know *their* reasons. They say that the world is filled with suffering, frustration, that all human beings are bound by desires. That these desires lead them to experience craving. Some fleeting satisfaction followed by pain. That to live in the desiring physical consciousness is to not experience the ultimate bliss.

Crackpots if you ask me. Most of them probably couldn't even hold a job.

It might be better for the human race to eradicate these few individuals. To round them all up, and take them to the top of a mountain, and just let them sit there and meditate their little hearts out. [laughter]

And the rest of the world could just go on with life. With earning a living, procreation, the things that count! [laughter]

Now, it is possible that these few misguided souls—who have attained

FOR EVERY ENDING THERE'S A NEW BEGINNING 519

enlightenment—have had such a massive effect on certain segments of society, because they appear to have miraculous powers.

However, it's never been exactly substantiated as to whether this is true or not.

We have reports of persons walking on water, flying through the air, doing many, many things which reasonable people know are not possible.

Why should people be so preoccupied with these things? Even if they're attainable, will they bring happiness? You walk on land now. Will walking on water make you happy? [laughter]

How would the fish feel, looking up, seeing all these feet?

In short, if God wanted ... [laughter] ... human beings to fly through the air, walk on the water, She would have made it possible. But in Her wisdom, She didn't.

There are some persons who have spent time with these lunatics—the enlightened. And they claim that spending time with them has changed them. [huge laughter]

But we—as serious minded people—must ask ourselves, have these changes been for the better? [laughter]

Some have given up families, careers, noble occupations, to go and be with these persons, to spend time with them. Because they say that it has brought them a bliss and a knowledge that surpasses understanding.[25]

People who take cocaine report similar experiences. [great laughter]

As we know, the cults flourish from age to age. Be it the cult of Christianity, the cult of Judaism, whatever it may be—age after age—sometimes they become more popular, sometimes the cults become the establishment itself!

---

25. *The Bible,* New Testament, The Book of Philippians, Chapter 4, Verse 7.

And decry the rise of any new cult that threatens their supremacy.

If a cult is established, it appears to be all right. If it's in the socio-political structure. The new ones are problematic. This is history.

Now, if we really observe the enlightened, and we separate the enlightened from those who *claim* to be enlightened and who are not, we will see an interesting phenomena.

We will observe that those who claim to be enlightened very often are socially destructive. They do seem to abuse power. They develop large followings of persons who through their association are the poorer for their experience.

These are usually individuals who did not have the power of choice. They were suffering from various problems and were promised instant salvation, and gave everything for it. And their temporary euphoria seems to pass as mind control takes a grip.

You'll notice, though—historically—interestingly enough, that the persons who are actually enlightened, don't affect people in this way.

As a matter of fact, during their lifetimes, enlightened persons create practically no social change whatsoever, because they make absolutely no demands upon the individuals who come to them.

As a matter of fact, rather than trying to encourage persons to become examples or replicants of themselves—of those who claim to be or are enlightened—they do just the opposite. They suggest that everyone has to find truth in their own way, and must be themselves.

Many enlightened teachers have actually chased persons away, saying that they should not worry about enlightenment in this stage in their evolution. Rather, they should encourage themselves to live in the world and work in the world, because it is not the time yet.

So, it doesn't really seem that enlightened people are socially a threat to the world, if they're truly enlightened. Now, if they're not truly enlightened, at times they are a great threat to society, and the people who come to them. But the actual enlightened persons seem to be relatively harmless. Initially.

However, very often, after their death, they seem to wield a greater effect.

But we can discount this, perhaps, that it is just the followers of these persons interpret—to their own liking—what the enlightened person or persons said, and use it to promulgate their own ideas for social change.

But the enlightened people seem to be relatively harmless.

If we were to paraphrase what they say, we would say,

> "Be absorbed. Be absorbed in eternal consciousness.
>
> "This world is as a grain of sand unto a desert.
>
> "A desert on which many camels pass.
>
> "If you were to ride such a camel across such a desert and come to a palm tree, you might notice a crow … [laughter] … alighting on a palm tree, and a coconut falling from it.
>
> "From your vantage point on the camel's back, the camel's hoof perhaps might be resting on that very grain of sand, which is existence as we know it, past, present and future. From your vantage point on the camel, which is on existence, you might see the crow alight on the top of a palm tree and watch a coconut fall.
>
> "And you might assume that because the crow landed on the palm tree, the coconut fell. However, as it may be, the coconut could have just been falling at the time that the crow happened to stop by."

[Rama laughs, all laugh] This is the kind of nonsense that enlightened people talk about. [laughter]

That's why they're absolutely no social threat. [great laughter]

Anyone foolish to listen to this sort of nonsense certainly will not be the worse for it, nor will they probably be the better for it. It's like reading Marvel Comics.

Now, in defense of the enlightened, and in defense of the ideal of becoming enlightened—if we're going to be reasonable people, and I assume we are, and we want to examine both sides of a one-sided situation—we could say that it is observable that persons who seek enlightenment, do go through major transpositions, in terms of the personality structure and their lifestyle.

And many of them claim to be happier—more euphoric—they have a feeling of well-being which not only endures in times of adversity, but at times actually seems to increase.

While they still suffer the pains and joys of human existence, they say that in their meditation, and in their selfless giving, they come to understanding of the nature of existence.

They appear to be tranquil and relatively harmless … and while we cannot substantiate their claims … we cannot necessarily disagree, since their journeys and their sojourns are inward and cannot be quantified or measured.

But for a moment, let's enter into the world of "suppose". Let's dream along for a moment, and try and understand what the nature—from their point of view, of course—of spiritual evolution is.

Spiritual evolution is a relatively mindless process. In the sense that everything is, always has been, and will never be.

There is no time unless you're wearing a watch.

Everything is convenient, unless you happen to be frustrated. When you're feeling wonderful, the world is wonderful, if you're unhappy, the world is dark.

All heavens and hells appear to be created within the self.

Therefore, if we decide that there's no hell, and only heaven, we will experience only heaven. Reality itself seems to gain a definition through the definition that we give it. Nothing is unless we make it so.

Which does not suggest that there is not an objective world. There are crows, and there are coconuts. And there may be a causal link.

But what we must consider more deeply is the nature of truth. There are words, and there are words, and then there is silence. The art of meditation is the art of silence.

In spite of all obstacles, in spite of all frustration, one learns with patience and perseverance to quiet the mind. The mind is stimulated by many things. By the world's vibratory forces, society, past conditioning, desires.

But with patience and practice, one can still the mind.

When the mind becomes absolutely calm and quiet like a lake without ripples, one can see eternity. Eternity is neither here nor there, it's everywhere. And nowhere. Beyond definition.

Most people in this world are very, very sad. Even in their relative happiness, they're unhappy. Their happiness is fleeting. They themselves are fleeting.

Nature in its profusion brings bounty to the world. The generations come and the generations go. The worlds come and the worlds go. There seems at times to be no sense to it. And perhaps there isn't.

Yet in that stillness, in that region of light which lies just beyond the corner of awareness, there is a sense of perfection. There is perfection.

One can choose to pass through this life, going through the various experiences that one must go through, be you enlightened, unenlightened, or somewhere in the middle.

And you can go through this world with joy and belief or you can go through this world with doubt and frustration. At the end, in either case, one might say, cynically, that you will die, what was the difference?

But the difference was in the moment. Because there is no death.

Death is just another idea, another dream.

The appearance is an illusion, in the sense that what you see is incomplete.

You see yourself as an objectified being with a separate existence, with a beginning and an ending, who lives in the world. Who works in the world, who plays, who suffers, who experiences joy.

But when you meditate, when you take the time to go within yourself each day to that still point, when the mind becomes completely quiet—when nature dissolves—then we see that what we thought was reality, was partiality.

A dream. Insubstantial. While in the dream, as you know, the dream seems perfectly real. We have no sense that we're in a dream. When we meditate we gain the sense that life is a dream. When we come to that basic apprehension that life is a dream, we can then set our *dreaming* up. We can learn to *dream* different dreams, if we choose to.

Or we can go beyond the dream itself.

There are four levels of consciousness.

> The waking state,
>
> the dreaming state,
>
> the deep sleep state,

and the fourth level of ecstasy—or superconscious awareness—the stateless state. From which there is no return, because no one can go into it. It is existence in its purest form.

One form of reality is not holier than another. These are terminologies that we apply based upon relative understandings of what is and what is not.

But each person chooses in any given lifetime—at any given moment—what they wish. And what they wish is granted.

Not so much in the sense of the physical, but in the sense of consciousness.

You can choose to experience the world and play in its gardens of delight. And when the winter comes, it all goes away, as do you, the winter of our death, followed by the spring of our rebirth. The joyous cycle of existence in which the pure beauty of the cycle is enough to sustain us, to comfort us—there is a wisdom in nature, we are nature.

You can enter into the dream. The endless planes of reality, endless cycles of existence, endless worlds—coexisting, simultaneously existing, existing in a linear fashion, not existing. Existences that don't exist, and can't exist.

Beyond the mind's comprehension, we can journey. We can experience and become these realities or move through them, in the world of the dream. We can take dreaming—dreaming as in when we're asleep at night dreaming—and bring it into the daylight.

We can see that there is no difference between being awake and being asleep.

And we can consciously *dream*.

Or realize that we have been consciously *dreaming* all along. That our very self, our very nature, this very life, with all of its importances is but another dream.

But in the dream state, we only move from dream to dream. In the waking state, we move from waking to sleeping, and to waking.

The deep sleep state is—in a sense—nonexistence. There is no dream, there is no relative awareness of this world. Yet there are subtle impressions. From the seed will come the sprout, the plant, the fruit—the seed, the sprout, the plant, the fruit.

So, because one is in the deep sleep state, this does not mean that one has attained enlightenment.

Because something will come forward from it. Just as the ocean is calm, then the ocean becomes violent. So the latent impressions and tendencies from all of our past lives are stored within the individual *jiva* or self.

During the deep sleep state the ocean is calm. But these tendencies have not gone away. They're just in a state of stasis. They reawaken with wakening.

The superconscious, on the other hand, is beyond definition or experience in the sense that we must move beyond being an experiencor to know it.

The superconscious *is really* all that there is.

Except that the superconscious at times dreams itself into the dreaming state, wakes itself into the waking state, or sleeps itself into the deep sleep state.

But to one who has knowledge of the superconscious, who is it—not in theory but in reality—all the worlds, all the grains of sand, all the camels, coconuts and crows combined, are both real and unreal.

And while they appear to be in the dream, they are not. They are dreamless sleepers. They walk through this life, as in a dream, while waking. They live in a perpetual twilight or a perpetual sunrise. Not quite in one world or in the other world.

FOR EVERY ENDING THERE'S A NEW BEGINNING

We call them *jivan muktas* —liberated souls—self-realized beings.

Until the time of death, when the final liberation, for those who are liberated, occurs, and the curtain opens on a new horizon, because for every ending there is a new beginning.

Liberation does not indicate the extinction of the self. Rather, it indicates total consciousness—complete awareness—of all selves. But not in the way that the self can understand or relate to.

So, we seek the sky—that endless sky of becoming—without knowing why. We can assign reasons, but that's all we've done. Even to say it's the trend of evolution, of reincarnation, the will of God; these are all reasons assigned, seats taken in the homeroom class, waiting for the day to progress.

So, I have to come back to joy. The joy of life.

Having journeyed to the farthest reality and beyond, having seen and lived in the eternal and in the finite—ultimately I can only embrace humanity, which is eternity, and choose to be happy.

And I see pain and frustration, and ignorance or maya, as opportunities to be happier. To proclaim happiness—to fight for it—which gives it meaning and purpose, in what is otherwise a meaningless and purposeless world.

The final condition of humanity is joy.

Humanity will never *collectively* experience this joy. But yet you as an individual are a collective. You house within you all beings that have ever been or will ever be.

And when you turn your attention to the sky of eternity, whether to watch from the finite their infinite beauty or to merge with them, and go beyond the finite and become them. Two sides of a coin.

Still, there'll be joy. Even if you fight against joy and frustrate yourself and disappoint yourself, still joy will always be beckoning you. Always beckoning you.

Joy is always there.

Because it is the very nature of this transitory life.

Pain, anger, frustration, repression, oppression, hate, fear—these qualities do not in any way taint joy. Joy is joy. They're different notes in the symphony of life.

If you focus on them, you will certainly experience a great deal of misery. If you focus on joy, you will become joy.

But they can in no way stamp out the flame of joy, or belief that our life on this Earth—in this world—is *not* purposeless. That in spite of what we see in the world—which is not always pleasant, as we become mature adults and look at the nature of our planet—that this does not take away from joy.

Because these are passing shadows, dreams, phantoms in the night which in the final joy of God Consciousness—of merging with that which we really are—will dissolve.

The rain comes for several weeks and it may seem as if it's always been, but then the sun comes and the rain goes away. And then only the sun exists. This is the nature of the Earth. We experience the sun and the rain.

The superconscious is beyond the clouds. Where there is nothing but sun. All the time.

And each one of us has the capability— *is* the capability—of experiencing that endless light. We *are* that endless light, except that we forget that sometimes.

For every ending there is a new beginning.

And thank God for every beginning there's an ending.

FOR EVERY ENDING THERE'S A NEW BEGINNING

Because otherwise life would become terribly, terribly boring. We would find ourselves in the same condition, watching the same movie. I've seen *The Road Warrior* seven times. The other night I saw it for the seventh time.

But each time it was different. It was never the same.

Because I was never the same.

Whenever you see someone twice, you've lied to yourself. Because there's never been anything but now.

To change your consciousness—to raise your perceptual awareness—to bliss.

To be willing to experience the agony of the absolute ecstasy. It's worth trying! You'll never know until you do, and even then you won't be sure.

This is meditation and self-discovery. To be willing to experience so much ecstasy that you die.

And to find yourself a new self on another shore, reunited in this life, but not quite. Different yet the same. Again and again, the process. Samadhi, they call it. I call it a good time. [laughter]

Samsara is nirvana. Sally is John. [laughter]

Or as T.S. Elliott said in *Four Quartets,* "In my beginning is my end." All ways of trying to say what can't be said. But what we are continuing to say—an endless loop tape, from lifetime to lifetime.

So, don't be discouraged. And if you are, don't be discouraged that you're discouraged! You must know that you are always on the threshold of a perpetual waking.

It exists! It's there. Just as there are craters on the moon. Just as Judge Crater [26] never returned!

---

26. A famous unsolved missing-person case from 1930.

So one day you'll never return. Judge Crater, he knew something. That's what Orr was trying to tell Yossarian.[27]

There is a way out, and the way out is the way in. It is not by running away from the world, nor is it by running towards it. Rather, it's by embracing and surrendering to the world.

Nature is the guideline and the way. Observe nature. Everything comes into being, exists, and goes into nonbeing. So simple, so perfect—what software to run the universe!

IBM has a lot to learn. Think of the incredible operating system and high level language. To hold all of the worlds in manifestation. And to dissolve them. To keep track of your karmic records alone! [laughter] Endless, countless, beings. Awesome. Totally awesome.

So I can only suggest that you learn to be what my friend Theodore Roethke called "a perpetual beginner". Because if you feel that you're knowledgeable, you may be. But to be a perpetual beginner is the happy part.

Being a student is much more fun than being a teacher. So I think it's good for teachers to always be students. Because otherwise they forget and they become very poor teachers, because they forget the joy of learning.

Enlightenment is not an end product. *It's the end of the product.*

And each step is a step in that direction. If you try and run away from it, you get closer to it! If you bury yourself in oblivion, then you'll find it there too. God exists in hell, in heaven, and at Denny's. [laughter]

So, then the spiritual life—while it has many complexities which I'm not alluding to right now, certainly—is simple. It's simple in the sense that all you need to do is whatever you like. And if you do that, you're in terrible trouble.

---

27. *Catch-22.* Joseph Heller, 1961

But you have to go through that part of the cycle.

You're all willing and eager to give your will away to God, but suppose God doesn't want it? [laughter] There may be a surplus of wills. Perhaps you should wait until the economy in the inner world shifts. You may get a better price for your will.

So try and be happy. Because it doesn't matter.

And if anybody asks you why you should be happy—since nothing really matters—you could say, "Because I said so." [laughter] And they might say, "Well, that doesn't matter," and then you can say, "Well yes, but the fact that you said that, doesn't matter either. So what's the difference?"

In other words, ultimately when you probe eternity, when you meditate and obtain enlightenment and all this stuff, you see that nothing really matters, or, that everything matters.

You can look at it either way. They're both frames of reference. They are ways of seeing life. Neither of which is exactly correct, although both are definitely correct, depending on which you're using.

Beyond that is nirvana. Patent pending. For a long time! [Rama and the audience both laugh]

Now what you can make out of all this is probably whatever you'd like to. And I see nothing wrong with that.

But I will continue to declare that life is joy. Even if you're not experiencing it, that does not mean that it is not so. Someone may love you, and you may not see that, but that doesn't mean that they don't love you.

So while you go through the bardo of transitory experiences, the emotional whirlpools and hysterectomies of existence [laughter] ... and while you may get down on yourself and complain and feel crummy—you know all along that you're good!

That you're light, and that in spite of yourself ... you will succeed. And after you've succeeded it won't matter. But that doesn't matter. (Jnana Yoga.)

So try and be among the happy. It's a thriving minority. [laughter]

To be happy all you have to do is grin when it hurts. [laughter]

And it hurts sometimes. That's S&M. [laughter]

But since we have no control over anything, since *we're* not the doer ... We're the done, or done for, as some would say. And is there a difference between being baked and half-baked? I suppose, it's a matter of temperature and time. [laughter]

Try not to worry so much. All the time you worry. You worry about the present, you worry about the past, you worry about the future. All your worrying, what will it do? Give you ulcers.

If you must worry, worry about happy things. [laughter]

You might worry that you'll become really happy and it might last. [laughter]

You might worry that you'll take the energy from meditation and transform it and use it in your life with your career and personal relationships and become very successful. Which is very easy.

You might worry that you might even realize God. These are terrible things to worry about. But they're happier things to worry about.

You can worry that you're going to be audited by the IRS. [laughter] But your worries won't bring the audit closer or push it back further.

You can worry that you might attain self-realization sooner than you had expected. [laughter] Your worries won't bring it about. But it's a nicer field of attention, it's a nicer dream.

And if you must experience a nightmare, why not enjoy it? Why go to a horror movie and be horrified? Why not see it as a great comedy? You can do the same thing with life.

Humor, in my estimation, is the ultimate liberator.

Therefore, if you are an advanced spiritual seeker, you will see a great many Peter Sellers movies. [laughter] And Woody Allen movies. There's much to be learned from laughing.

Now, as you know, most people laugh at misfortune. Because it makes them feel macho. Superior to others.

And naturally, of course, the wheel of change will revolve and one day they will find themselves in the position of those they laughed at.

Knowing this in advance, it might be wise to laugh not at others but at ourselves.

Spiritual practice is never easy, and it's never hard. You may interpret it one way or the other. But it's the laughter and the humor that creates balance in our being. And even without a reason, it just is in itself a nicer dream.

You can't stop or start yourself. You're an endless reality. You are the ultimate Brahman, the Self. The one without a second cousin. [28] [laughter]

So don't try so hard. There's a natural flow of light within each of us. And if you enter into that flow of light you need not try so hard.

Meditation is spontaneous. Spiritual discovery is spontaneous. That's when it's best. Like sex, right? [audience pauses, laughs, then Rama joins in]

I was asked that recently on a panel show I didn't attend.

---

28. Rama makes a play on words. "The One without a Second" is a Buddhist and Hindu expression that God is all of reality, and that all separate beings and objects are temporary and ultimately, illusory.

"Are sex and meditation the same?" I said, "Absolutely not. You can meditate by yourself." [long laughter]

Now, I realize there is ... But I don't think that's what they asked on the panel show that I didn't attend.

So, if I were to sum this all up—I'd be in terrible trouble.

Instead I would just say ... Don't try so hard, don't be so hard on yourselves. Don't hate yourselves so much. It doesn't bring about a quicker realization.

You're here in this world to learn self-acceptance. The acceptance of your body, even though it's passing. That it is, yet that it's not. It's eternal. Because it's eternal in the moment. The moments are eternal. They never end.

We will always be, we have always been. In this condition, in this consciousness and in all consciousness. You are all of those who have ever attained enlightenment or ever will.

You are the past, the present and the future—and that which lies beyond.

Try and have more fun with your self-discovery. It doesn't have to be heavy. Find that subtle flow of light within yourself. Through experimenting. *The Year of Living Dangerously.*[29] Don't be afraid to reach and be different. Don't be afraid to be the same. Find what works. Trust yourself. If you can't trust yourself, who can you trust?

That which is not the self.

Life can be quite wonderful, and is. More people love you than you realize. You just don't want to see. Yet.

The Self veils itself in countless forms. Only to unveil them at a later date.

---

29. *The Year of Living Dangerously*, movie, 1982

So don't be frustrated. Just live. While there's life. That's really more than enough.

And if you find yourself walking my way—the way of meditation—then you'll practice stillness, self-giving. You'll enjoy humility and purity and beauty.

You'll go beyond the waking, dreaming and deep sleep states to the Turiyananda Consciousness, the consciousness of the absolute reality, and see that you were always there. That there never was a there, there never was an always, or there always is an always.

But in that stillness is perfection, and in the physical is perfection too. They're not different. They're the same.

Chapter Seventeen

Cosmic Awareness

Cosmic awareness—or cosmic consciousness as it's sometimes called—is the realization that we're light. That each one of us is light.

In the early stages of our cosmic awareness, we see ourselves as beings of light. There's still a sense of separativity. When we meditate and we're able to stop all thought, suddenly we're suffused with light. We get a sense of being outside of the body, or beyond the body. Our consciousness expands and we *see* ourselves as beings of light. And that's certainly true.

As we progress in our inundation with light, as we make friends with light, and we come to know it better, we come to know our substance and our essence, then we find that we're not really separate beings of light. That that's a dream that we're having. The dream of multiplicity.

Each one of us dreams that we're a separate individual with a history, a future, with a moment, with something to do or nothing to do.

Meditation takes us beyond the moment to eternal awareness. Cosmic consciousness. Nirvana. These states of awareness are open to everyone. It's just a question of where we focus our time and energy.

To become conscious is like swimming up from the bottom of a lake. We're down at the bottom of the lake, and we're swimming around, and everything is murky and dark. And all we have to do is swim towards the light, towards the surface. And as we go higher it will get brighter and brighter and suddenly we'll break through the surface and there'll be nothing but light. The murkiness will fade away.

In our day-to-day life, we're swimming below the surface—planning, making decisions, revisions, schedules to keep, people to meet, people to forget. [laughter]

We see ourselves changing, aging. Maybe we're conscious of it, maybe it's better that we're not. We experience pleasure, pain, freeways, which are a mixture of both, depending upon the time of day.

And people promise us enlightenment, instant satisfaction, in one form or another. But it's a very rare individual who realizes that they're not an individual. It's a very rare person who goes beyond their personality.

Now, of these there are two types—the lucky and the unlucky.

The lucky are those souls, those beings, those persons who meditate, who seek, who experience the divinity of all things, and then they go away. One day they climb on top of a mountain and they're gone. Life just takes them away. Oh, they may have died, but they couldn't have really died since they had left long before death came.

They merged with the All. They reached the end of the cycle of birth and death. The lucky. The few. The proud. [laughter]

Then there are those who follow a different path. They perhaps went to a good private school also.

They attained liberation, or liberation attained them, but they chose to—were forced to, were browbeaten by God into—working in the world with people. The unlucky. We call these people "heroes". After they've been dead for a long, long time.

During their lives we call them fools usually, put them in exile, make political prisoners out of them, assassinate them, crucify them. Emulate them occasionally. But rarely deal with who and what they are.

And even more than who and what they are—since that's actually not that important—simply what they have to say. Their expression.

The expression of an enlightened person is not what they say with words. There is nothing you can say about the superconscious. You can paint a gradual picture.

I don't know if you remember, when you were a kid, they had this thing, the Etch-a-Sketch.

It was a great device they brought out and it was this little square screen, and it had two little knobs on it, and you could draw lines with it. And these perfect lines would appear on the screen. And if you did the right one you'd get a vertical line, and the left one, a horizontal line.

And you could make intricate little mazes and designs, and if you were clever, you could do both at once, and kind of get curves.

And that's what life is like for most people. [laughter]

But for someone who's enlightened, it's not like that at all!

For someone who's enlightened, there is nothing but light. That's why we use that phrase. Nothing appears to be solid anymore, because it isn't.

They have the ability to pass through countless dreams of existence. To *see* the past, the present, the future, and beyond. They can be in thousands of places at once. Experience all tonalities of emotion.

And then go beyond the human to the superhuman. To become God, to be the awareness of truth itself.

To transmit that—to try and bring that across—it's hard to do in words.

You can do parables, analogies, exhortations, beg, plead. But the way the truth is manifested, really—by a person who's attained truth—is probably in their expression.

Maybe in the way they answer a question, not so much in what they say. Perhaps a gesture.

A way of being that's so fluid that there's no perception of being, as we know it.

Everyone likes flash. I do too. Everyone likes excitement, the brighter horizon. But there's a certain simplicity and subtlety that suggests depth which is necessary to have as a perceiver, if you follow the pathway to truth.

I can't tell you where truth lies, or what it is, because I have no words for such things. When I meditate there's nothing but that, and that's all there is now for me, is meditation.

And one day it will be the same way for you. I'm not an example of anything, I'm not a particularly virtuous person. But something has occurred to me in the process of living and dying and living and dying which has put an end to that process.

Now, I don't usually talk too much about it. Usually I lecture on meditation and self-discovery and methods, or I try and make people laugh and have a nice time. All the time meditating and suffusing them with the kundalini, the light that creates liberation, or beckons it in any case.

But from my point of view—self-realization, liberation—these big words indicate a very simplified state of being. Something that's so subtle, yet so all-encompassing that we're apt to miss it in our search for liberation and self-realization. Everybody wants to be in the program. "You're either on the bus or you're off the bus." [30] But sometimes it's nice to walk.

Going fast is just an idea that someone created who thought it would be

---

30. From *The Electric Kool-Aid Acid Test,* Tom Wolfe, 1968.

better to look at life that way. But there's no such thing as *anything* unless you think there is. As Shakespeare said it, through the voice of one of his characters, "Nothing is good nor bad, only thinking makes it so."

But if we consider that statement in its depth and all of its implications—we'll probably go stark raving mad.

Because we'll realize that nothing is the way that it appears to be. Everything is an illusion in the sense that we have constructed reality, by dreaming it into a certain form.

And that there's nothing that you can count on. Everything that appears to be real is transitory. Even your ideas about truth, and love, and self-giving. All these things are transitory. And many people become very bitter at this stage in their spiritual evolution. They reach a point where they *see* that life in a sense *is* a fabrication.

That the simplistic dreams of heaven, and good conduct, and these sort of things that we're told, aren't exactly relevant.

What's a mother to do? [laughter] Get out the soy Hamburger Helper and stretch it. [laughter] When times get tough, that's what you do. For the soy burger.

So, in the same sense you learn to stretch reality. And you can stretch reality a long way if you're talented. Take it from me.

By stretching reality I mean that to develop the despondent existential point of view—as manifested by Camus and Faulkner and others—is interesting. It's an artistic experience. But it's not a place to really live.

Walking around in that desert of the mind, with myriad strange disconnected objects appearing and disappearing without sequence. A sense of order is necessary. That's what the British brought to the world. [laughter]

People like order. It's an illusion that you can count on. [laughter]

But when the illusion of order goes away, what do you have? The illusion of disorder. If the illusion of God goes away, then what do we have? Well, the illusion that there's no God, no one cares. The mechanistic universe of the 18th Century. The big machine that no one's running. Gone out of control.

So, philosophers dealt with these ideas, I don't bother.

Because when you meditate there's nothing but light. All ideas, all notions of self, of importance, love, hate, joy, gratitude, all these things go away.

All the dreams cease. And what is, is so complete and so perfect. The radiance of the light of existence, the pure knowledge, the experience of … bliss?

There are really no words. That one experiences in samadhi, in nirvana.

When you return to that source which you are, is beyond any expression, any experience.

If you were to take all the wonderful moments that have ever been, or will ever be in any world, at any time, in any location, that you can imagine, and beyond your imagining, put them together—if you were absorbed in nirvana, you wouldn't notice. It would be a candle held up to a supernova. It would melt quickly.

So, what I'm suggesting is then, that life is far more perfect and precious than people realize.

Particularly people who seek perfection.

It seems to me that people become so caught up in the rut of spiritual seeking that they forget the moment. It's always, "I want to get to the next stage, the next plane, I want to get through this experience, because then it will all be better."

Never realizing that all they have to do at any given moment is stop all their thought, enter into sublime meditation and that's it. It won't happen mañana. It already is. There's nothing that you have to do.

Now, naturally, to *do* that, to stop all your thought—to enter into samadhi, that transcendental state of awareness, and experience truth—is difficult.

Because it means you have to accept and embrace every aspect of your self. Be it in your definition wonderful or horrible. Because everything is God.

That means that you have to accept every part of yourself as being perfect, even when you know that it's not. And even that sense of knowing that it's not—that incompletion, that question mark—has to be erased.

Gradually as you shift through the fields of attention—as you meditate—each aspect of the self dissolves. And then finally that consciousness of dissolution, that illusion that there was a self to dissolve—or there was a self or there wasn't—dissolves.

And then there's silence and stillness. And if the wind blows, who's there to hear it?

People don't like that. It's too perfect. Human beings can't stand very much reality. That's why if you wish to traverse the snowy ranges of self-realization and enlightened consciousness, you can no longer be a human being as you define human being.

You have an idea. This is a person. This is what they can do, this is what they can't do. Birds fly, people don't. People fill out tax forms, birds don't.

But in my world birds are CPAs. [audience laughs] And you see people flying around all the time! Now admittedly I live in a very strange world. I agree.

So eternal consciousness is very available, but it's necessary for a little bit of housecleaning to occur.

It's necessary to let go of your attachments. Now that's when everybody gets very nervous. Because they all know they have attachments. There are closets that have not been cleaned out. There are papers that are not in order. There are things that haven't been mailed. There are clothes that haven't been mended.

There are two approaches. One is conservative, the other is radical. The conservative approach is to go through *gradually,* through every part of the house, mending the clothing, cleaning out the closet and just to do this continually.

The other approach is to burn the house. [laughter] Collect the insurance and go some place else.

You can follow either approach. I personally like a combination. I like to clean up the house, get everything in order, make it all perfect ... then burn it. I think it makes for a better fire. [audience laughs]

Now the conservative approach involves going through every aspect of your being and perfecting it. It means gradually bringing light and love, dedication, selflessness and humility and purity into everything you do.

Not being afraid of making mistakes, realizing that through meditation and selfless giving, through time and patience, through inspiration of others, this will occur.

To find someone who has reached enlightenment, shows you—if nothing else—that if that turkey could do it so could you.

It's very inspiring when you see the people who have reached enlightenment by and large are very silly people.

And it seems to me that anyone who has their act halfway together could easily do it. I think that's why God does that. God has the silly people obtain enlightenment first, just to inspire everybody. [audience laughs]

Now the other approach of course is very radical. That's just to burn it right away. Just do it. The problem is though sometimes in our haste to burn down the house we burn ourselves.

It's riskier. That's the short path in Tibetan yoga. Very fast evolution.

But the danger is that sometimes the result is counterproductive to the very thing that we sought. We go so fast we speed ourselves up—our evolution—to such a point that we reject the entire experience. It's just too much to handle, and we leave it ... behind.

So for most persons it's best to follow the gradual path to enlightenment. The gradual path is not at all *slow.* There is no slow and there is no fast. Or if you are interested in speed, the fastest is the one that works.

So we perfect every aspect of our being. This is the gentle approach. Where we're not afraid, over a period of time—of lifetimes perhaps—to come to know ourselves, to know that we're not single, that we're not individuals. That we're not bodies of light but that we are light itself.

The actual transmission of light—to make this not theoretical but actual in your being, not have it be another nice talk that we'll listen to tonight and then we'll pass on into oblivion—if I could transmit an essence it would take two forms.

Both are meditative. Because without meditation there is really no realization.

Selfless giving in karma yoga is good as long as one meditates.

I've seen people practice selfless giving—karma yoga, working endlessly for others—who are in a *terrible* state of consciousness. Who *were* in a good state of consciousness. And then when they did too much selfless giving they were in a *lower* state of awareness.

Because they did not have the ability to maintain a high level of awareness, and remember why they were doing it, in the action.

This is the "spiritual burnout syndrome" that you see sometimes in ashrams and spiritual gathering places. They got so into helping others that they forgot to meditate. Which was only because they really didn't want to meditate at all. It was an excuse to avoid development.

"I'm gonna work so hard for others that I don't have to deal with myself." Kind of a nifty approach.

So I think that it's better always first to learn to meditate and to practice selfless giving as you are inspired to do so.

And you'll find your capacity to do more for others will increase, but never to forget the source—meditation. To always come back to stillness, to silence.

You don't have to think of what you can do. How you should change. What decision to make to make your life into what you want it to be. Because if you're still thinking about those things, the knowledge that you're gaining is coming from the *relative* mind, and it's subject to much *delusion*.

But if you meditate deeply several times a day, if that is the center of your practice, then in that meditation you will become light. You will transform and change and you will find that you don't have to inspire yourself to do what's right. Because you've already *become* what's right.

I respect self-giving and I've tried to lead my life with that as the ideal.

But real self-giving is when we take our self—our being—that which is most precious to us. Our ego, our bodies, our minds, our values, our past, our present and our futures—and we sit in meditation and we throw that all into eternity.

There's just a sense of total offering to that larger infinite self. To God. To the supreme reality. Our whole being. We just let it go. Without worrying about whether we'll come back or not or how we'll change. Because there's no trust there.

The trust must be total.

And this trust develops a little bit each time you meditate. When you see that each time you meditate, life *is* brighter. Things *are* better.

The objective world will not change! The objective world is the objective world.

You will change.

And you'll *see* that the objective world is not objective, but subjective. You can *dream* it into any form that you like, or just go simply beyond it or get into it. Whatever suits you.

So meditation then comes in two forms. One form is when you meditate by yourself. Each morning when you meditate. Each evening when you meditate.

Or at any other time of the day. You sit by yourself, to go beyond the idea that you're by yourself. There is no aloneness in meditation. There is no want for company. Your companion is eternity.

When the light is so complete, when your being is so pure and perfect that there is no separation between yourself and that effulgent ecstasy of being—who could want? Who could need? When you've become the limitless.

And this we try and do when we meditate.

On the other hand, we go to a teacher. We find someone who has merged with the limitless. Who's a reflection of the limitless in their meditation.

They'll still have a personal form. A personality of some type. A physical body.

But their consciousness is no longer human, as we know human. It's light. They broke down the barriers. The big wave came and washed everything away, and now there's nothing but ocean.

When you meditate with such a person, you change.

Because the dynamic force of eternity manifests through them in such a way, so powerfully, that it inundates all whom are present, physically.

With the power that we call the kundalini— *prana, shakti* —different names for this essential life force.

And one who is receptive to that, one who meditates, travels. Far beyond what they might have been capable of themself.

Or we could say their awareness is stretched.

And once its been stretched, it's easier for them to stretch it themself. Different terms to explain that which is an inexplicable mystery.

This is why people have gone to study with holy persons, teachers, enlightened beings, or they just travel to places of pilgrimages.

To physical locales where the vibratory energy is high and pure, because for thousands of years spirituality has been practiced there. The aura of a mountain—of a place—becomes so powerful that if one is sensitized, when you go to a place of power, it has a transformative effect on your being so that you don't leave. Someone else does. Your real self.

The problems, the delusions, the frustrations are there, but we go to the Grand Canyon, and we look into the infinite. And suddenly in that complete silence we remember something that can't be put in words.

That silence is not in that place, it's within ourselves. It is our self.

There is no death! Death is an idea in the mind of people who still have ideas.

I experience death many times a day. Every time I am fully absorbed, that's death. The same as the physical, and it's wonderful. You just return to the source.

People who fear death, it's so unfortunate. Death is never anything to fear.

It's just the emergence of your transcendental form.

So we try and combine the two, if that seems suitable to us. We find the person we feel in all this vast world—who we have access to—who knows *the least*. And we go to them to *unlearn*.

With the knowledge that what they're trying to teach us is a gesture—a way of being—not a philosophy. Philosophers teach us philosophy. From the enlightened we learn a way of being which they convey by their actions. By their conscious awareness.

There's a certain naturalness that we learn from their physical beings or their personality. But even more so, we study their awareness.

Because if we can *see* their awareness, soon we'll discover that awareness within ourselves. That's the transmission of light. That's the self-giving. That's the love. To give light to others. To *give* our very substance.

To our very substance.

So meditation for me has been that, and is that. It takes countless forms. It's like a symphony. Different movements, tonalities, instruments playing, crescendos.

It takes all the form of human personality and then goes beyond anything that we've known as human, or even our ideas of the superhuman.

Every aspect of existence is yourself. You experience them all, and then you go beyond them all into the emergence and light.

And then you find yourself back on the planet, walking out on the street, driving in your car down the freeway.

The same yet very different. Aware, watching this dream that we're in now. But you're free. In the dream you can be free. In a jail cell you can be free.

That's the freedom of a perceiver, of consciousness.

So in our journey, we shouldn't go too far. We shouldn't go farther than stillness. And stillness is something that accompanies action. It's the silence between the words that gives the words their power. Otherwise there would just be endless sound. One sound would not be distinguishable from the next.

So we don't sit simply absorbed in meditation all of the time. We meditate, and we become eternity, consciously. Then eternity changes form. And we are in the field of action. We're busy. We're laughing, we're crying, we're experiencing.

It's not necessary to kill your human nature to realize God. Because the human nature is God. There's just an addition. Of eternity. That awareness.

Gestures are important. It's the subtlety, in my estimation, that has power.

Silence has tremendous power.

And if you can give yourself enough room … to be emphatic, to be excited, to be confused, to be deluded … and then to step beyond that through that golden door to eternity, to perfection—and not see that the two are different, not even think about it or worry about it—is to lead a complete life.

Beyond life and death.

So these words that I've said, have been said for thousands of years. Millions. Billions. In different ages, in different cycles, in different places, on different planes of being. By the Self to the Self.

And I don't feel that these words can change anything, nor should they. They just are, as we all are.

But let's just say that they're a gesture. A reaching out.

Kind of like when a flower blossoms in a field, and no one will ever see it. There's an integrity to that. And then it passes away. And no one ever knew.

That makes for a happy flower.

Also by the Author

BOOKS

Surfing the Himalayas

Snowboarding to Nirvana

Lifetimes: True Accounts of Reincarnation

Total Relaxation: The Complete Program for Overcoming Stress, Tension, Worry, and Fatigue

The Bridge Is Flowing But The River Is Not

The Lakshmi Series

The Wheel of Dharma

Insights: Talks On The Nature of Existence

Rama Live! Talks and Workshops

The Last Incarnation

On The Road With Rama

Zen Tapes

Tantric Buddhism

The Enlightenment Cycle

Insights: Tantric Buddhist Reflections on Life

MUSIC

Atlantis Rising

Breathless

Canyons of Light

Cayman Blue

Ecologie

Ecstasy

Enlightenment

Light Saber

Mandala of Light

Mystery School

Occult Dancer

Retrograde Planet

Samadhi

Samurai

Surfing the Himalayas

Tantra (2 vols)

Techno Zen Master

Urban Destruction

Zen Master

Rama Live! Talks and Workshops

2023 © The Frederick P. Lenz Foundation for American Buddhism (the Foundation). All rights reserved. This product is published under exclusive license from the Foundation.

ALL RIGHTS RESERVED
No part of this publication may be reproduced, distributed, stored in a retrieval system, or transmitted in any form or by any means, including photocopying, recording, scanning, or by any information storage and retrieval system, or other electronic or mechanical methods, or otherwise, except as permitted under Section 107 or 108 of the 1976 International Copyright Act, without the prior written permission of the publisher, except in brief quotations embodied in critical articles and reviews, and certain other noncommercial uses permitted by copyright law.

Published 2023 by Living Flow
www.livingflow.com
Boulder, CO 80302 USA

Paperback ISBN 978-1-947811-41-6
Ebook . . . ISBN 978-1-947811-42-3

Publisher's Code r192-v13

Cover art & design by Meg Popovic
Interior dragon art by Janis Wilkins
Back cover photo by Greg Gorman

Made in United States
North Haven, CT
08 February 2024